M000022129

An Empowering Approach to Managing Social Service Organizations

Donna Hardina, PhD, is a professor in the department of social work education at California State University, Fresno. Her practice experience includes case advocacy, community organization, and nonprofit management. Dr. Hardina has written extensively on nonprofit management, community organization, and social welfare policy. She is the author of *Analytical Skills for Community Organization Practice.*

Jane Middleton, DSW, is a professor and chair in the department of social work education at California State University, Fresno. She is president-elect of the California chapter of the National Association of Social Workers. Dr. Middleton serves on numerous community, state, and national boards. She previously held the position of chair of the master's of social work program in the school of social administration at Temple University in Philadelphia.

Salvador Montana, MSW, PhD(c), is a lecturer in the department of social work education at California State University, Fresno, and is currently completing his doctorate at the University of Texas at Austin. He has more than 20 years of direct practice experience in public social services and more than 4 years of special projects experience related to university–community endeavors. Mr. Montana previously served as the director of children and family services in Fresno County, California.

Roger A. Simpson, PhD, is an assistant professor in the department of social work education at California State University, Fresno. Dr. Simpson has lectured and consulted on multicultural issues and culturally competent approaches to service delivery. He is a member of the National Association of Social Workers and the Council on Social Work Education.

An Empowering Approach to Managing Social Service Organizations

Donna Hardina, PhD
Jane Middleton, DSW
Salvador Montana, MSW, PhD(c)
Roger A. Simpson, PhD

SPRINGER PUBLISHING COMPANY
NEW YORK

Copyright © 2007 Springer Publishing Company, LLC

All rights reserved.

No part of this publication may be reproduced, stored in a retrieval system, or transmitted in any form or by any means, electronic, mechanical, photocopying, recording, or otherwise, without the prior permission of Springer Publishing Company, LLC

Springer Publishing Company, LLC
11 West 42nd Street
New York, NY 10036

Acquisitions Editor: Sheri W. Sussman
Managing Editor: Mary Ann McLaughlin
Production Editor: Kate Mannix
Cover design: Joanne E. Honigman
Composition: Graphic World Inc.

07 08 09 10 / 5 4 3 2 1

Library of Congress Cataloging-in-Publication Data

An empowering approach to managing social service organizations / Donna Hardina . . . [et al.].
p. cm.
Includes bibliographical references and index.
ISBN 0-8261-3815-2 (alk. paper)
1. Social work administration--United States. 2. Human services--United States--Management. I. Hardina, Donna.

HV40.E465 2006
361.2'5068--dc22

2006047587

Printed in the United States of America by Edwards Brothers.

Contents

SECTION IV: STRATEGIES FOR MANAGING THE EXTERNAL ENVIRONMENT OF THE EMPOWERING ORGANIZATION

Acknowledgments

We thank our families and friends whose support made the publication of this book possible. We especially thank Sheri W. Sussman, our editor, for her patience. We would also like to thank Kelly Kagawa, MSW, for editing the first draft of the manuscript.

Donna Hardina particularly thanks her family, Xong, Molly, and Phoua, and dedicates this book to her students, who continue to teach her about cultural competency, empowerment, and social justice.

Jane Middleton dedicates this book to her husband and friend, Raymond, now deceased, for his encouragement; to her children, Daryl, Whitney, and Kelly, whose support is always there; and to the many souls who have provided reasons to hope and the dream of a better world.

Salvador Montana dedicates this book to his family: Suzana, Leticia, Corina, and Natalie. May we know the past to understand the future. To Victor, Norma, Sylvia, and Hector for believing. To Salvador Sr. and Elena, who set into motion lives and events that are still unfolding.

Roger Simpson especially thanks his children, Andrew and Brooke: I love you infinitely. Your love sustains me.

Acknowledgments

[illegible]

Preface

Recently, a discussion of theories that should be taught about macro practice in schools of social work took place on an on-line LISTSERV for social work managers. Some of the discussants (faculty in social work programs) stated that they were unclear about what specific theories of practice are used by managers. A few of the discussants felt that knowledge of theories was essentially irrelevant, arguing that managers largely use experiential knowledge to guide their practice.

In this book, we argue that although experiential knowledge is valuable, macro practitioners need a solid framework for action. Knowledge of theories about how organizations operate (both internally and within the social environment) help managers examine various options and make informed choices about how to guide everyday organizational activities and manage unexpected crises. However, simply knowing about the theories is insufficient. Managers should also have knowledge of a variety of practice models and choose one primary approach to administer the organization, supervise staff, and deliver services to clients.

It is our belief, articulated in this book, that social work managers should use models of practice that incorporate core values of the profession. Many managers, if they use models at all, adopt models that incorporate principles often associated with for-profit businesses: cost-containment, finding low-wage alternatives to paying good salaries, and concentrating decision-making authority in a handful of top managers (Anthony & Young, 2003; Bobic & Davis, 2003). Social work textbooks on management practice either struggle with the discrepancies among these approaches or simply fail to articulate sufficient frameworks that can be applied to internal practices, such as dealing with clients and staff, and external practices, such as establishing good working relationships with neighborhood residents, local institutions, and funding sources.

This gap in the social work literature is particularly problematic because recent literature on for-profit business management identifies a number of alternatives to top-down, bureaucratic approaches to organizational management. The empowerment approach for managing private corporations incorporates principles that are consistent with good social work practice, such as granting workers the autonomy to make key decisions about their jobs, giving priority to the needs of clients and customers, ensuring that the services delivered are of good quality, and creating a work environment in which workers are actively encouraged to advocate for improvements in services (Bowen & Lawler, 1995; Shera & Page, 1995).

The basic assumption of the empowerment approach is that involvement in decision-making is believed to reduce feelings of powerlessness and alienation among organization participants and foster feelings of personal control and accomplishment (Gutierrez, Parsons, & Cox, 1998; Solomon, 1976; Zimmerman & Rappaport, 1988). Linhorst, Eckert, and Hamilton (2005) identify additional reasons social workers should engage in empowerment-oriented practice in social service organizations, such as:

- Involving clients in organizational decision-making is consistent with social work principles, including client self-determination, respect for individual dignity and worth, and social justice.
- Participation in organizational and political decision-making is a basic human right.
- The participation of clients and staff in program design and evaluation can contribute significantly to improvements in the effectiveness and quality of services.

PURPOSE OF THE TEXT

The purpose of this textbook is to develop a "how to" guide for social workers who wish to use an empowerment-oriented approach for managing social service organizations. The text contains an overview of traditional theories (such as scientific management, the human relations model, and the systems perspective) and skills used by social work managers. However, it also examines recent innovations and current theories (the feminist model, total quality management, cultural competency, and the empowerment model) and applies them to the management of social service organizations. The book incorporates recent literature on empowerment published in other disciplines (for example, business and social psychology) with skills and values associated with social work practice in order to develop an explicit model for empowerment-oriented management in the social services.

ORGANIZATION OF THE BOOK

The book is intended to give the reader some grounding in basic management principles and to highlight skills associated with 12 basic attributes shown of the empowering approach to management described in Chapter 1. Chapter 1 also contains an examination of basic concepts and theoretical assumptions associated with the empowerment model of practice. In Chapter 2, theories that focus on how organizations function and how they interact with the external environment are examined. In Chapter 3, the application of social work values and ethics to management practice is described.

Chapter 4 focuses on the structure of social service organizations, including organizations based on bureaucratic models as well as organizations designed to serve specific populations (women, ethnic communities, or persons of faith) or purposes (service delivery versus social change). In Chapter 5, skills needed by the manager to facilitate client and staff participation in organizational decision-making are examined.

Chapters 6 and 7 describe management skills needed to increase access to services for diverse clientele. Chapter 6 focuses on barriers to service delivery often experienced by members of low-income and other marginalized groups. The emphasis in this chapter is on designing social service programs that can be used to transcend these barriers. In Chapter 7, the concept of cultural competency is defined and specific management practices necessary to create a culturally competent agency are identified.

Chapters 8 through 11 focus on skills needed to empower organizational staff. In Chapter 8, management skills needed to lead organizations, set goals, guide planned change, respond to crises, and hire or retain staff are described. In Chapter 9, specific skills needed to motivate staff are discussed. In Chapter 10, the use of workplace teams to empower staff members and increase productivity is described. In Chapter 11, the responsibility of front-line workers, supervisors, and leaders to engage in advocacy to improve client services and fight for social justice is discussed.

Chapters 12 through 15 describe management strategies essential for the maintenance of organizations and the creation of an empowering environment. In Chapter 12, the management of financial resources for the organization is discussed. In Chapter 13, procedures for evaluating program outcomes, service implementation, and quality are described. In Chapter 14, skills needed by the manager to enhance the organization's power and ability to control its external environment are identified. In the last chapter, Chapter 15, a final overview of the empowerment model of management is presented. The strengths and limitations of this approach are examined.

In summary, it is our goal to articulate how this model can best be used by social work managers to improve social service delivery to clients, to make improvements in workplace conditions for the benefit of staff, and to help organizations acquire the resources and political power they need to survive in a turbulent social, political, and economic environment. We also believe that this model best promotes social work principles that require us to fight for social justice, practice nondiscrimination, and deliver culturally competent and appropriate services to the people we serve.

REFERENCES

Anthony, R., & Young, D. (2003). *Management control in nonprofit organizations.* Boston: McGraw-Hill/Irwin.

Bobic, M., & Davis, W. (2003). A kind word for Theory X: Or why so many newfangled management techniques quickly fail. *Journal of Public Administration Research and Theory, 13*(3), 239–264.

Bowen, D., & Lawler, E. (1995). Empowering service employees. *Sloan Management Review, 36*(4), 73–84.

Gutierrez, L., Parsons, R., & Cox, E. (1998). *Empowerment in social work practice: A source book*. Pacific Grove, CA: Brooks/Cole.

Linhorst, D., Eckert, A., & Hamilton, G. (2005). Promoting participation in organizational decision-making by clients with severe mental illness. *Social Work, 50*(1), 21–30.

Shera, W., & Page, J. (1995). Creating more effective human service organizations through strategies of empowerment. *Administration in Social Work, 19*(4), 1–15.

Solomon, B. (1976). *Black empowerment.* New York: Columbia University Press.

Zimmerman, M., & Rappaport, J. (1988). Citizen participation, perceived control, and psychological empowerment. *American Journal of Community Psychology, 16*(5), 725–750.

An Empowering Approach to Managing Social Service Organizations

SECTION I

Introduction to Social Service Organizations: Models, Theories, Ethical Values, and Structure

CHAPTER 1

Introduction

Empowerment in organizations has been described extensively in the literature on social work (Gutierrez, GlenMaye, & DeLois, 1995; Leslie & Holzab, 1998), social psychology (Spreitzer, 1996; Zimmerman, Israel, Schulz, & Checkoway, 1992), business (Bowen & Lawler; 1995; Forrester, 2000), and urban planning (Forester, 1999; Tauxe, 1995). Although explicit principles associated with empowerment-oriented management practices have been published in social work journals, no one has yet developed a comprehensive, empowerment-related textbook for social work managers.

These basic principles focus on increasing the political power of members of oppressed groups whose personal problems often originate from discrimination and institutional oppression (Solomon, 1976; Zimmerman & Rappaport, 1988). Often, members of these groups experience additional oppression when they apply for social services from nonprofit and public social service organizations (Iglehart & Becerra, 2000). The purpose of the empowerment approach is to ensure that low-income people and others who experience discrimination (by race, age, physical/mental ability, sex, or sexual orientation) receive access to quality services. Another basic principle associated with this management model is that the staff members who deliver empowerment-oriented services should receive supervision that encourages productivity, motivation, professional development, and the desire to advocate on behalf of clients and for improvements in services (Cohen & Austin, 1997; Latting & Blanchard, 1997). An effective approach for managing an organization that empowers its constituents should incorporate these basic principles with a skills-oriented approach for creating a social service organization that truly involves both staff members and clients. Such decision-making should involve participation in developing individual treatment plans, program design, evaluation, and membership on organizational boards of directors (Fetterman, 1996; Gutierrez, Parsons, & Cox, 1998; Hardina & Malott, 1996a). Consequently, the concept of empowerment is consistent with the social work principle of client self-determination as articulated in the National Association of Social Worker's Code of Ethics, Standard 1.02: "Social workers respect and promote the rights of clients to self-determination and assist clients in their efforts to identify and clarify their goals" (NASW Code of Ethics as cited in Reamer, 1998, p. 267).

DEFINING POWER, POWERLESSNESS, AND EMPOWERMENT

To understand empowerment, we also need to understand the concepts of "power" and "powerlessness." Mondros and Wilson (1994) define power as both a process and an outcome. The process involves actions taken to exert influence on others. Outcomes pertain to a person's ability to pressure or persuade others to do what he or she wants. Power can be *actual,* used to influence change, or *potential,* not used but available to those who possess power (Meenaghan, Washington, & Ryan, 1982). It also can be *positive,* used to persuade a decision-maker to take action, or *negative,* used to prevent someone from taking action.

Power is acquired through possession or acquisition of the following resources: authority, money, status, knowledge, professional degrees, goods, services, votes, public support, information, ability to influence the media, and relationships with powerful people (Hardina, 2002). Power also can be derived from one's authority to make decisions in organizations or by virtue of one's gender, ethnicity, social class, or personal attributes, such as appearance and charisma. People often acquire power by establishing alliances and coalitions with others to support or oppose various policies or decision-making options. As described in Chapter 2, workers in social service organizations also acquire power because they often decide whether individual clients receive services, resources, or referrals.

Powerlessness can be simply defined as the absences of power resources. However, the "Mother" of empowerment practice, Barbara Solomon (1976), defines powerlessness as a product of the interaction between individuals and the social structures that limit life opportunities for them:

> Powerlessness is defined here as the inability to manage emotions, skills, knowledge, and/or material resources in a way that effective performance of valued social roles will lead to personal gratification.

> The power deficiency so often seen among minority individuals and communities stems from a complex and dynamic interrelationship between the person and his relatively hostile social environment. (p. 16)

Individuals and groups in society who have little power are often described as "oppressed" or "marginalized." Often people with specific characteristics (age, race, social class, gender, mental or physical disabilities, or sexual orientation) are excluded from decision-making or have limited access to jobs, education, and other opportunities. This lack of choice is also called *institutional discrimination* and is reinforced by people in power who have wealth, status, or positions of authority in government or the economic sector (Davis & Bent-Goodley, 2004; Solomon, 1976). Feelings of powerlessness can also be prevalent in organizations in which individual workers and clients find that they have little ability to influence working conditions or service delivery decisions (Cohen & Austin, 1997).

The purpose of the empowerment approach is to help people overcome feelings of powerlessness by acquiring power. Mondros and Wilson (1994) differentiate power from "empowerment" by arguing that this second concept is actually a psychological state that "allows one to pursue concrete activities aimed at becoming powerful" (p. 5). The literature on empowerment in organizations focuses primarily on two distinct categories of organizational actors: program beneficiaries (clients) and staff members. Rapp, Shera, and Kisthardt (1993) define empowerment in individual clients as "confidence, control, decision authority, influence, autonomy and self-trust" (p. 733). According to Shera and Page (1995), empowerment of employees in organizations can be defined as "a process of enhancing self-efficacy among organizational members through the identification of conditions that foster powerlessness and through their removal by both formal organizational practices and informal techniques that provide efficacy information" (pp. 2–3). Empowerment in the social services can take place within the context of relationships between workers and clients, within the organization's formal decision-making structure, and within the contact between the organization and institutions or groups in its external environment (Gutierrez et al., 1998).

It should be noted that empowerment in organizations involves the redistribution of resources such as decision-making authority or goods and services. Therefore, in addition to producing specific outcomes, empowerment is a political process. Staff members may feel they will lose power and authority to make service decisions if clients are treated as equal partners in the decision-making process (Cohen, 1998). Because one of the primary assumptions of empowerment in direct social work practice is to reduce feelings of powerlessness by increasing personal self-perceptions of one's own power, the model focuses on facilitating the acquisition of leadership skills and actual political power among agency clientele. Staff members also acquire power through participation in organizational decision-making and by advocating for improvements in organizational policies and services. The organization gains political power as constituents become empowered to advocate for changes in government policies and campaign for meaningful social change (Checkoway & Zimmerman, 1992).

A BRIEF HISTORY OF EMPOWERMENT IN SOCIAL SERVICE ORGANIZATIONS

According to Burke (1983), the concept of citizen participation in government decision-making was first used in conjunction with urban renewal programs during the 1950s and in government-mandated antipoverty programs implemented in the 1960s. Although the actual term *empowerment* was not widely used, efforts to explicitly involve consumers in the management of social service organizations first appeared in the social work and urban planning literature as the concept of "citizen participation" (Arnstein, 1969; Forester, 1999). The purpose of citizen participation was viewed by a number of program planners and researchers as a mechanism for ensuring the effectiveness of service delivery and making these services more responsive to people in need (Gulati, 1982). The participation of service beneficiaries in community-based organizations was also intended to train community leaders as political activists and provide a greater sense of inclusion in mainstream society for low-income people (Gittell, 1980). Burke (1983) identified three roles for citizens in organizational decision-making:

- A source of wisdom in the development of service delivery plans
- A watchdog over citizen rights
- A constituency base for the organization (p. 115)

The participation of citizens in community planning efforts was viewed as a mechanism for social reform (Marris & Rein, 1982). The involvement of low-income people in organizational decision-making was to be used as a tool for the alleviation of poverty. Community action projects, funded by foundations and federal agencies, were operated through nonprofit organizations. Some of these organizations fulfilled government requirements for "maximum feasible participation" by placing residents of poor communities on their boards of directors.

The President's Commission on Juvenile Delinquency and the Ford Foundation initially provided funds for Mobilization for Youth (MFY), a project operated by Richard Cloward and Lloyd Ohlin, faculty members of the School of Social Work at Columbia University. The main premise of MFY was that the best way to alleviate juvenile delinquency was to create jobs for minority youth. Programs were to be operated by community-based "action" agencies that included members of the target population on organizational boards and in other decision-making roles. MFY served as the prototype for Ford Foundation– and President's Commission on Juvenile Delinquency–funded community action programs. The activities of MFY also provided a foundation for other "War on Poverty" programs that eventually were operated by the Federal Office of Economic Opportunity (OEO; Marris & Rein, 1982; Moynihan, 1969).

Marris & Rein (1982) note that OEO program planners made it clear that, in addition to low-income community residents, other constituency groups (such as religious leaders, businessmen, and mayors) were to be given prominent roles in the decision-making process. According to Moynihan (1969), the OEO's mandate of maximum feasible participation was never really intended to increase the power of minority communities but simply to ensure that members of minority groups actually received benefits from these programs. Moynihan also argues that the participation requirements actually lead to social protests and civil unrest. In fact, MFY did engage in activities intended to challenge the power structure, including school boycotts, rent strikes, and voter registration (Marris & Rein, 1982). Protest activities and scattered efforts to challenge local political elites by some of the community action agencies reduced public and governmental support for the programs. In 1967, Congress cut funds and attempted to limit the role of OEO-funded programs in job creation. In 1971 Richard Nixon terminated all OEO programs, and the "War on Poverty" was deemed a failure (Marris & Rein, 1982).

Rose (1972) came to a much different conclusion about the effectiveness of community action programs than did Moynihan. He conducted research to examine the effectiveness of community action programs in 20 U.S. cities. Rose found that program implementation did not allow for real citizen participation in program decision-making or service delivery. Few low-income people were actually involved in program development. The community action agencies often contracted with schools and nonprofit organizations for delivery of programs rather than operating these programs themselves. Most of the programs provided social services; little advocacy was conducted to change neighborhood institutions or public policies.

SOCIAL WORK AND EMPOWERMENT

References to the "empowerment approach" first started to appear in social work when Barbara Solomon published *Black Empowerment* in 1976. She defined empowerment as "a process whereby persons who belong to a stigmatized social category throughout their lives can be assisted to develop and increase skills in the exercise of interpersonal influence and the performance of valued social roles" (p. 6). The purpose of empowerment practice was to assist individuals who were members of oppressed groups in overcoming feelings of powerless and negative valuations by the dominant culture. Practice activities were intended to help individuals see themselves as having the power to resolve their own problems and to influence political change. According to Solomon (1976), one of the primary assumptions of empowerment is that all practice activities should be framed in a manner that illustrates respect for the client's culture and traditions. Appropriate social work roles included "advocate," "resource consultant," "teacher/trainer," and "sensitizer," "helping the client gain the self-knowledge necessary for him to solve his problem" (p. 348). The creation of self-help organizations by members of the client group was also expected to empower clients.

Reisch, Wenocur, and Sherman (1981) added two additional concepts to the empowerment literature by drawing from literature derived from international social work and social movements, including ideas developed by Freire in Brazil and Brun in France. From Freire (1970), they drew upon the concept of "critical consciousness" to argue that the social worker must engage the client in a trusting relationship in order to establish dialogue. The process of dialogue is used to identify problems affecting the client, reflect on the oppressive systems that have created the problem, and then take action (often involving social change) to resolve the problem. Brun's (1972, as cited in Reisch et al., 1981) concept of animation involves activities in which groups are assisted in the development of social programs to address their own needs. Group members also engage in social change activities, political mobilization, and social movements.

A direct link between the citizen participation movement of the 1960s and empowerment practice can be found in the writing of Stephen Rose (1972, 2000). Rose (1972) conducted one of the studies of community action programs in the 1960s. He also coauthored, with Bruce Black, one of the first social work textbooks on empowerment practice, *Advocacy and Empowerment,* in 1985. Rose and Black described a model of social work practice for working with individuals with mental illness. They define advocacy/empowerment practice as comprising both elements:

> With advocacy understood to be a series of problem-solving activities arising from the lives of the people we work with that cannot be successfully negotiated through direct service provision, while empowerment is meant to characterize an on-going process of direct interaction covering all contacts with all clients. (p. 17)

Rose and Black (1985) drew upon Solomon's conceptualization of the client as oppressed by the dominant society and made to feel powerless. Engagement in problem-solving activities and confrontation with oppressive institutions would help members of oppressed groups overcome internalized, negative self-perceptions. They argue that this is particularly important for people with mental illness because of their stigmatization by society and the prisonlike structures in which they are treated. Rose and Black explicitly link their work with Freire (1970), particularly the concept of critical consciousness, arguing that members of oppressed groups must educate themselves through a process of dialogue about the source of oppression and then take action against the institutions that oppress them. Consumer choice in determining treatment, access to resources, and method of service delivery is an essential component of the model.

BASIC PRINCIPLES AND PRACTICE MODELS

The empowerment literature contains an explicit mandate for practitioners to provide opportunities and resources that will assist in the acquisition of power by members of oppressed groups. Skill attainment, resource acquisition, participation in organizational decision-making, creation of self-help groups, and political activism provide vehicles that will enhance an individual's sense of personal empowerment or mastery of his or her environment (Gutierrez et al., 1998).

These empowerment-oriented activities, as identified in the citizen participation literature, can easily be used in the development of an empowerment practice model that focuses on both process and outcomes. Five change targets can be included in the model:

1. Organizational constituents, including clients, beneficiaries of social change efforts, and community members
2. Staff members
3. Organizations
4. Geographic communities or interest groups that function as communities, establishing personal relationships, informal

networks, and cultural practices that can be used to foster feelings of belonging and identification

5. Social, economic, and political systems (Gutierrez et al., 1998)

Empowerment-oriented practice that incorporates the views and preferences of service users can also be viewed as making organizations more effective in their delivery of services (Bowen & Lawler, 1995; Cox & Parsons, 2000). Logically, participatory decision-making structures in organizations should have a dual function: to empower both service users and staff members (Bartle, Couchonnal, Canda, & Staker, 2002). Staff members develop their own skills, learn to change organizational policies, and subsequently gain a sense of mastery over their own work environment. Consequently, staff members become better motivated, and productivity increases (Barnard, 1999; Paul, Niehoff, & Turnley, 2000).

Clients and community residents who participate in decision-making serve as a constituency base for the organization and provide resources to the organizations, including not just money but skills, volunteer hours, and linkages to informal networks and local institutions. Consequently, efforts to empower organizational participants also increase the power of the organization as well as the local community (institutions and residents) to acquire resources and affect changes in government policies (Checkoway & Zimmerman, 1992). The end result should be alteration of institutions in order to end discrimination and increase political power among members of historically underrepresented groups.

BASIC SKILLS FOR THE EMPOWERMENT-ORIENTED MANAGER

The literature on management in social service organizations identifies a wide spectrum of skills. Managers should have skills in the following areas: goal setting, program planning, resource and human resource management, staff training, and evaluation of services. Managers must be able to interact with various constituency groups both within the organization (clients, staff, and volunteers) and external to the organization (funding sources, government regulators, community residents, local leaders, and other agencies that deliver complementary or competing services (Edwards, Austin, & Altpeter, 1998; Kettner, 2002; Lohmann & Lohmann, 2002). In addition, managers should be able to communicate effectively (both verbally and in writing), conduct meetings, facilitate group decision-making, coordinate and direct service delivery processes, develop appropriate agency policies, manage budgets, and lobby government for funds and changes in policies that will benefit the organization and its clientele (Hoefer, 1995; McNutt, 1995).

Knowledge regarding computers and use of the Internet have contributed to the skill base associated with management practice. These new skills include the following:

- The development and maintenance of computerized management information systems
- Fundraising and volunteer recruitment using e-mail and the World Wide Web
- Web page design to inform the public about the agency and using the Internet as a vehicle for service delivery and coordination
- The use of the Internet to find information on best service practices and public policy issues
- The use of the Internet to lobby government and inform the public about social problems and policy options (Boland, Barton, & McNutt, 2002; Finn, 2000)

The ability to establish working relationships and two-way communication with organizational staff and clientele is critical to the success of the empowerment model (Gutierrez et al., 1998; Shera & Page, 1995). Facilitating the development of political power among clientele and increasing the organization's ability to influence social change are also essential skills for the empowerment-oriented manager (Rose, 2000).

AN EMPOWERING APPROACH TO SOCIAL SERVICE MANAGEMENT

The dual focus in empowerment literature—increasing the power of staff members and program beneficiaries—presents a number of dilemmas and challenges to nonprofit administrators. Appropriate organizational structures and policies are needed to foster an organizational culture that promotes participation in decision-making among all or most of its members. At least 10 attributes are associated with empowerment-oriented organizations. These attributes incorporate skills associated with traditional models of management as well as skills and basic principles associated with feminist management:

1. *Empowerment-oriented organizations create formal structures to support the participation of clients in organizational decision-making.*

   Empowerment-oriented organizations place program beneficiaries on their board of directors and may create additional structures such as advisory panels and task groups for client participation in decision-making (Beresford & Croft, 1993). This differs from traditional management practices related to board appointment; board members in formal social service organizations often are middle- or upper-income professionals who are politically connected or who can help community-based organizations raise funds (Smith & Lipsky, 1993).

2. *Empowerment-oriented organizations create partnerships with program beneficiaries in which all parties (clients, staff, and board members) are equal participants.*

   The notion that effective partnerships for service delivery and policy-making can be developed only if all parties are treated as equal participants is derived from the literature on models that focus on transformative community change and feminist theory (Chernesky & Bombyk, 1995; Freire, 1970). In *Pedagogy of the Oppressed,* Freire (1970) proposed a model of action for social change that focused on the development of partnerships between service or educational professionals and low-income community residents. Feminist theory suggests that power in traditional organizations is derived from the authority and control associated with hierarchical decision-making structures. Consequently the best way to reduce the harmful effects associated with hierarchies is to eliminate much of the social distance among staff, clients, and board members (Hyde, 1994; Morgen, 1994). Board members, administrators, front-line staff, support workers, and clients all have formal decision-making roles; most decisions are made by consensus (Gutierrez & Lewis, 1994).

3. *The purpose of client involvement in service delivery is to decrease personal feelings of powerlessness and to improve the quality of, and access to, services.*

   The participation of clients in the development of new programs helps ensure that the organization can provide services that truly are responsive to the needs of program beneficiaries (Iglehart & Becerra, 2000; Rose & Black, 1985). Traditional social service organizations often limit access to services as a method of rationing scarce resources. Sometimes these barriers are unintentional; in other instances these barriers may be associated with institutionalized discrimination. Barriers to service delivery include lengthy applications, wait time for services, the lack of public transportation to and from the agency, service fees, language differences, and indifference to the cultural norms and customs of agency clientele (Iglehart & Becerra, 2000; Smith & Lipsky, 1993). Social services can be physically inaccessible or simply fail to provide appropriate services to persons with physical and mental disabilities (Mackelprang & Salsgiver, 1999).

4. *Empowerment-oriented organizations explicitly develop policies, programs, and procedures that can be used to bridge cultural, ethnic, gender, and other demographic barriers to effective service delivery.*

   Solomon (1976) explicitly described empowerment as an approach to working with low-income populations and persons of color as a mechanism for overcoming feelings of alienation from, and oppression by, the dominant culture. Consequently, empowerment-oriented organizations use a number of strategies to ensure that services are provided in a manner that is consistent with the cultural norms and values of program beneficiaries. Methods often used to increase the cultural competency of organizational staff include ongoing dialogue with ethnic group members, ethnographic research into cultural norms and practices, providing appropriate training for organizational staff, designating seats for ethnic group members on organizational boards, and hiring staff members who are members of the ethnic group to be served (Gutierrez et al., 1998; Iglehart & Becerra, 2000).

5. *Empowerment-oriented organizations have top managers who are ideologically committed to the empowerment of both staff members and program beneficiaries.*

   Often real empowerment in organizations is a function of whether or not the chief executive officer (CEO) creates opportunities for participation by clients and staff (Hardina & Malott, 1996a). Managers should be committed to the personal and professional development of staff members (Gutierrez et al., 1995). They must be able to make sustained efforts that increase clientele access to services and increase program responsiveness (Cohen, 1998). Paul et al. (2000) identify characteristics of leaders who foster empowerment in organizations: charisma, showing a high concern for people, the ability to provide intellectual stimulation, inspirational motivation, and helping staff members achieve goals that are important to them.

6. *Empowerment-oriented organizations engage in specific strategies to increase the psychological empowerment and motivation of workers.*

   Empowerment in organizations often involves giving employees more autonomy or control over how they do their jobs and allowing them to problem-solve (Bowen & Lawler, 1995).

Strategies for increasing decision-making among workers can range from involving workers in decisions that affect their own work to allowing workers direct participation in organizational policy-making. *Psychological empowerment* is the term used to describe worker self-perceptions of their ability to perform the job as well as the ability to influence organizational decision-making (Spreitzer, 1996). Psychological empowerment is believed to be beneficial to the organization because it increases employee commitment to the job (Paul et al., 2000). It also is valued because "empowered" employees increase their own sense of personal efficacy about work-related tasks and consequently may become more productive.

7. *Empowerment-oriented organizations promote the use of team building and collaboration among staff members.*

   Some theorists (Bowen & Lawler, 1995; Spreitzer, 1995) argue that staff autonomy over service decisions is a good method for increasing staff empowerment. However, according to Cohen and Austin (1997), full autonomy to make decisions can simply create service fragmentation and conflict among workers. Instead, Cohen and Austin advocate approaches, such as teamwork, that encourage collaboration among staff members. According to Barnard (1999), the use of work teams "promotes social interaction among group members, thereby fostering commitment and developing positive attitudes" (p. 73).

8. *Empowerment-oriented organizations encourage staff to advocate for improvements in services and policies.*

   One method that empowerment-oriented organizations use to improve service effectiveness is to encourage staff members to advocate for changes in organizational policies (Bowen & Lawler, 1995; Reisch et al., 1981). According to Kaminski, Kaufman, Graubarth, and Robins (2000), staff members feel empowered when they are able to successfully advocate for other workers or clients. This, in turn, helps improve the quality of service delivery and the effectiveness of those services provided to individual clients. It also underscores the organization's commitment to social change (Gutierrez et al., 1998).

9. *Empowerment-oriented management approaches can only produce effective outcomes when a consistent funding base is available to maintain the organization.*

   Beresford and Croft (1993) argue that to effectively implement empowering approaches to social service management, organizations must have support from their primary funders. It is important that these funding sources support the organization's philosophy and mission, especially in terms of client and community participation in decision-making. Community-based organizations with little income cannot sustain formal organizational structures that encourage the empowerment of clients and low-income community residents (Hardina, 1993; Milofsky, 1988).

10. *Empowerment-oriented organizations involve clients, community constituency groups, and staff members in ongoing evaluation of services and program renewal.*

    Empowerment evaluation is the term used to describe the process for bringing clients or community residents into the program assessment process (Fetterman, 1996). Empowerment evaluation is used to conduct agency evaluations as well as assessments of projects that involve community-based collaboration. The method is believed to be preferable to the more traditional evaluation model that is often conducted by objective, professional evaluators from outside the organization because of the following factors:

    - The use of expert knowledge may sustain and even enhance traditional power imbalances between the "haves" and "have nots."
    - The information produced will be relevant to the needs of participants.
    - The findings are more likely to be used in a manner beneficial to the community.
    - Participants are "empowered" with technical skills, knowledge, and access to data.
    - Culturally competent programs and approaches to evaluation are developed (Coombe, 1999; Padilla, Lein, & Cruz, 1999; Rapp et al., 1993).

    Additional approaches to evaluation that involve client, community, and staff participation include agency "self-evaluation" and participatory action research in which community residents explicitly conduct research that will contribute to social change (Meier & Usher, 1998; Smith, 1997).

11. *Empowerment-oriented organizations act to increase their own political power as well as the political influence of program beneficiaries.*

    Leadership roles within the organization prepare people to become political activists and provide a greater sense of inclusion in mainstream society for low-income people (Checkoway & Zimmerman, 1992; Zachary, 2000). According to Reisch et al. (1981), the ultimate goal of the empowerment process is "the liberation or disalienation of those without privilege or power" (p. 115). This is to be accomplished through political action and the creation of local organizations. Activism and lobbying by members of the client group provides a powerful constituency base for the organization (Burke, 1983). Social service organizations also can acquire power by serving as mediating structures, acting to link informal networks and organizations to larger institutions and government decision-makers (Berger & Neuhaus, 1977; Cox & Parsons, 2000).

12. *Empowerment-oriented organizations acknowledge the limitations of participatory management approaches and take proactive measures to balance inclusion in decision-making with tasks associated with organizational maintenance.*

    Empowerment-oriented management is subject to a number of limitations. Forrester (2000) differentiates between psychological empowerment and actual increases in power distributed to workers. Implementation of this approach can simply consist of superficial window dressing unless real power and rewards are transferred to organizational members. A number of theorists and researchers have argued that efforts to empower community residents by giving them seats on organizational boards are simply designed to manipulate participants or result in the co-optation of opponents (Arnstein, 1969; Burke, 1983; Hardina & Malott, 1996a; Tauxe, 1995). In addition, efforts to include all organizational constituents in decision-making may impede the director's ability to respond to crises or to hire and fire organizational staff (Morgen, 1994). Consequently, the empowerment-oriented manager will need to create inclusive participatory decision-making structures but reserve the ability to respond to situations that require immediate resolution.

Empowerment-oriented social service organizations will use many of these strategies to deliver social services or to advocate for social change. The absence or presence of one or more of these characteristics may not be sufficient to include or exclude the organization from consideration as "empowerment-oriented." Later in this text, we describe strategies for assessing whether organizational staff and clients have acquired actual power or feel psychologically empowered to make decisions.

KEY CONCEPTS USED IN THE TEXT

Throughout this textbook, we use several key terms that help to describe the empowering approach to management practice described in this text:

- *Consumer of Services:* A consumer of services is an individual who receives social, health, or mental health services from an organization. Alternative terms used to describe those people who receive services include client, customer, service user, recipient, and beneficiary (Austin, 2002; Boehm & Staples, 2002). The term *client* is often criticized because it implies dependency on a social worker for provision of a service (Hardina, 1990). Some commentators also dislike *consumer* and *customer* because the terms seem to imply that the individual can choose which services to patronize and how much to pay for them. We use the terms *client, consumer,* or *client/consumer* throughout this text given the limited range of choices available to describe people who receive service.
- *Social Service Organization:* A social service organization has a permanent structure and system of governance. It provides goods, services, or counseling to clients/consumers as its primary mission. Social service organizations can be small and unstructured, or they can be large, with multiple units and a complex supervisory structure. These organizations can range from those with an all-volunteer staff to a handful of nonprofessional staff to hundreds of workers who differ in terms of task assignment, skill level, education, and authority.
- *Advocacy Organization:* An advocacy organization is one that primarily provides assistance to clients in obtaining resources or that works for social change as its primary mission. Many advocacy organizations consider themselves to be part of the social delivery system or work in partnership with social service agencies. Some organizations provide a mix of both social services and advocacy activities (Netting & O'Connor, 2003).
- *Cultural Competency:* Cultural competency is the ability to work effectively with people who are culturally different from the social worker (Lum, 1996). Culture includes values, beliefs, and lifestyle practices associated with ethnic and other marginalized groups (e.g., persons with disabilities or members of the lesbian, gay, bisexual, and transgendered community).
- *Social Justice:* Social justice involves an ethical or moral code that emphasizes "justice and fairness to individuals, a sense of collective societal responsibility for the welfare of individuals, and a sense

of altruism that accepts personal responsibility for solving problems" (Mondros & Wilson, 1994, p. 15).

- *Empowerment:* Empowerment is a state in which a person is able to change his or her personal circumstances or the environmental factors that contribute to difficulties in obtaining adequate goods, services, status, or life opportunities (Solomon, 1976). People become empowered when they gain confidence in their ability to take action on their own behalf or to influence social change.

SUMMARY

Managers of social service organizations need specific skills for setting organizational goals, planning services, hiring staff, enhancing staff development, raising funds, and evaluating service delivery. Managers committed to delivering services to historically oppressed communities should be ideologically committed to the political empowerment of organizational clients, community residents, and organizational staff. Staff and clientele in empowerment-oriented organizations should be encouraged to work in partnership with one another for the effective delivery of services. Consequently, clients can become empowered only if staff receives appropriate training and managerial support that allows them some control and decision-making authority over their work environments. This can be accomplished best through a participatory management approach that recognizes that both clients and staff bring essential resources to the organization.

CHAPTER 2

Theories for Organizational Management: Toward the Development of an Empowering Approach

In management practice, as in other fields of social work, we use theories to examine situations and guide our actions. A number of theories can be combined into specific models of practice that provide us with one overall approach that managers can use to interact with staff and design effective programs. Most theories of management practice help us examine how organizations maintain themselves, how people interact within the organization, how power and resources are distributed within organizations, and how organizations adapt to the demands of the surrounding environment. In this chapter, the differences among theories, perspectives, and models of practice are examined. We also describe the following:

- Theories about how organizations function
- The difference between formal and informal organizational structures
- Specific attributes of social service organizations
- General theories that can be used to explain the behavior of social service organizations in terms of how organizations maintain themselves, how people interact within organizations, how power and resources are distributed, and how organizations adapt to the surrounding environment
- Links among organizational theories, current management approaches, and the empowerment model of management practice

PERSPECTIVES, THEORIES, AND MODELS OF MANAGEMENT PRACTICE

In management practice, we use theory to define a specific set of actions or interventions that can be used to produce outcomes. We may also apply aspects of theories to certain situations (Hardina, 2002). However, we must differentiate among perspectives, theories, and models. A *perspective* is an approach to practice that involves basic value assumptions about best practices. Perspectives give us only general information about the outcomes produced by specific actions. Consequently, they provide only some guidelines about how or where to intervene in order to produce results. Perspectives also contain ethical principles, directives that specify how practitioners are to treat clients, constituents, or staff members (Hardina, 2002). For example, the strengths perspective tells us to look at a client or staff member's personal strengths rather than his or her deficits when planning interventions (Saleeby, 1997). The systems perspective, as applied in social work practice, is used as a justification for social workers to intervene at multiple system levels (personal, family, small group, community, and economic and/or political systems) to resolve an individual's problems. However, perspectives do not give us detailed information about the kinds of outcomes that should be produced as a consequence of following the directives associated with the perspective. Using strengths- or systems-based approaches in social work practice should make our interventions more effective, but testing a theory requires some systematic method for measuring a specific effect or change that will be produced by such an intervention (Figure 2.1).

A *theory* contains assumptions about cause-and-effect relationships that have been established as valid through empirical testing. Theories help us link specific actions or interventions with specific outcomes. Therefore, independent and dependent variables must be identified in order to test a theory. Theories must be tested using quantitative research methods. Descriptive studies (often using both qualitative and quantitative methods) are used to examine specific situations by determining links among variables that can be used later to test a theory. Alternatively, qualitative research is used to develop new theories by exploring new situations or the experiences of population groups that have not been examined by previous researchers.

In management practice, theories describe how organizations and the people within them function, how organizations maintain themselves, how power and resources are distributed in organizations, and how organizations interact with the surrounding environment. Organizational theories also describe how managers should best motivate staff members to do their jobs. Theories can be broad and abstract, pertaining to general

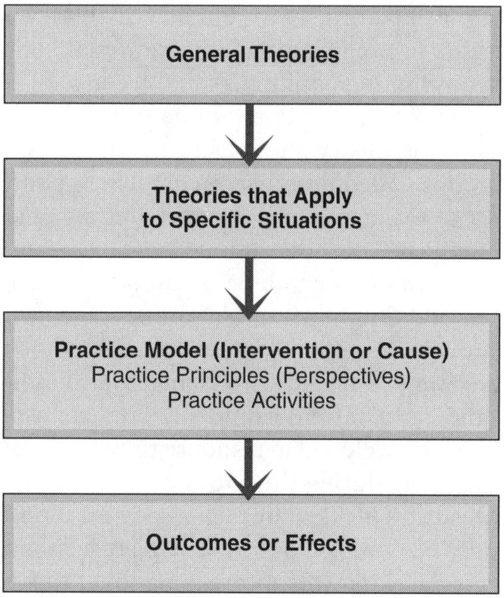

Figure 2.1 Relationship among practice perspectives, theories, and models.

patterns in society, or they can describe patterns that occur in specific situations. The "effect" aspect of cause-and-effect relationships contains outcomes, things that occur because of specific events or actions. Consequently, they suggest specific actions or skills that social workers and managers can use to produce results (Hardina, 2002).

As in other types of social work interventions, we use concrete frameworks called *practice models* to guide our interventions. These models include theories about intervention approaches, ethical principles, and probable outcomes. Models of practice are generally subjected to empirical tests to determine effectiveness, although such verification may not always be found for new or emerging models of practice. For example, there is debate in the social work literature about whether or not empowerment theory has been empirically tested (Reid, 2002). Although empirical testing of empowerment theory in social work has been somewhat limited, numerous studies conducted by social psychologists and experts in for-profit management have verified the effectiveness of the application of empowerment theory and related participatory management approaches in the workplace. Increasing the ability of organizational staff to control their own work and make policy decisions has been found to increase the employees' sense of self-mastery and personal empowerment (Kaminski, Kaufman, Graubarth, & Robins, 2000;

Lawler, Mohrman, & Ledford, 1995; Spreitzer, 1996). Involving organizational constituents in organizational decision-making and in political action also is effective in increasing personal feelings of self-efficacy and empowerment (Checkoway & Zimmerman, 1992; Itzhaky & York, 2002). Such tests of the theory allow us to develop an explicit model of management practice called *empowerment,* which contains guides for action on the part of management personnel and the outcomes expected to result as a consequence of these actions.

Models of practice often combine a number of theories into guidelines for action. In addition, most models of management practice draw heavily on previously developed models and methods. Like theory, models evolve over time in response to changes in the social, technological, economic, and political environment. For example, the feminist model of management developed in response to women entering the work force in greater numbers during the 1960s and 1970s and finding access to management positions blocked by men in powerful positions in organizations (Chernesky & Bombyk, 1995). The next sections of this chapter describe important developments in organizational theories and models of management practice. The empowerment model of management practice then is described in terms of these theoretical assumptions and management practices.

THE FUNCTIONS OF ORGANIZATIONS

An organization can be defined as "a regular and ongoing set of structured activities involving a defined group of individuals" (Austin, 2002, p. 15). Organizations can be formal or informal. According to Scott (1987), a formal organization is "one in which the social positions and the relationships among them have been explicitly specified and are defined independently of the personal characteristics of the participants occupying these positions" (p. 17). An informal organization, on the other hand, is one in which the relationships among people in the system change over time as a result of their personal characteristics and their interactions with one another. Often we think of a formal organization as one that possesses a clear mission and goals, rules that specify behavior, a plan to recruit new members, and a predetermined decision-making structure. Informal organizations are those in which people come together out of a common interest or through a process of group interaction that might occur without a specific plan for recruitment or decision-making. For example, networks of friends, relatives, and neighbors or a group of people who come together to clean a neighborhood park or collect food for the needy can constitute an informal organization (see Chapter 4).

Most organizational theory focuses on formal organizations that have clear boundaries between members and nonmembers, designated leaders, and government or other legal approval to operate. Max Weber was one of the first people to describe these large or structured organizations. His bureaucratic theory guided the research on modern organizations. Bureaucratic organizations, as developed in the later part of the 19th century, were thought to be superior to other forms of organizations because they derived authority through legal mandates, based decisions on objective or "rational" criteria, and were explicitly designed to control the performance and behavior of staff members (Hasenfeld, 1992; Scott, 1987). They were believed to eliminate management practices in which staff rewards were based on favoritism or politics. Bureaucracies also contained clearly defined decision-making structures; decision-making authority was delegated to department or unit supervisors by top management officials. According to Weber, bureaucratic organizations work best if

- The organization functions to meet a specific goal.
- Organizations are administered using a hierarchical structure. Supervisors report to their immediate superiors and are responsible for the work of subordinates in their work units.
- Power is concentrated at the top of the organizational hierarchy and often held by one chief administrator alone.
- The organization is divided into a number of work units with a clearly defined division of labor among employees.
- Clear lines of communication exist between administrators and staff and among the different work units.
- Tasks are delegated among employees and are highly standardized or are routine.
- Each employee has a clear role and responsibilities.
- Formal, written rules are established to guide administrative decision-making.
- Power and authority inherent in the supervisory structure are used to make people work.
- Employees are hired based on competency rather than favoritism (Hasenfeld, 1992; Iannello, 1992; Netting & O'Connor, 2003; Scott, 1987).

Weber assumed that organizations could be operated in a nonpolitical or rational manner. Such an approach put a limited emphasis on the values of administrators and staff, the personal aspirations or needs of employees, and the role of organizational cliques or factions in determining how or if staff members do their work and if tasks are completed.

Weber's work also discounted the role of the organization's external environment in determining how the organization functioned or how the staff performed.

Scientific management, an approach to administration practice developed by Frederick W. Taylor, also was instrumental in guiding management practice in the early part of the 20th century. This approach emphasized administrative decision-making as a purely rational undertaking. As defined by Taylor, managers were to use this approach to find the most efficient or scientific method for breaking down work into concrete tasks that could be assigned to individual workers. Efficient performance was expected to maximize work output (Scott, 1987). Often efficiency "experts" were brought into industrial plants to conduct time and motion studies to determine the best allocation of staff resources and skill assignments (Netting & O'Connor, 2003). Gardner (1999a) provides a modern critique of Taylor's scientific management approach:

> This division between thinking and doing was a natural consequence of Taylor's emphasis on specialization though simplification of industrial job tasks, the use of predetermined rules to coordinate those tasks, and the use of monitoring and performance measurements. Planning was separate from execution. Thinking was separate from, and superior to, the performance of the work itself. The consequences of this industrial model were that the organizations failed to learn from, listen to, and benefit from those who were actually doing the work. (p. 4)

SOCIAL SERVICE ORGANIZATIONS

In order to examine theories of relevance to social service managers, we must first define social service organizations. Social service organizations have formal structures and are created to deliver programs and services to individuals and families and/or to advocate for changes in social policies and legislation. Consequently, social service organizations differ in many aspects from businesses or corporations. Of primary concern is the fact that clients, or consumers of services, are one of the inputs associated with service delivery (Hasenfeld, 1992). We cannot operate our agency without a supply of willing (and sometimes unwilling, in the case of mandatory services) clients.

In addition, most of the services provided to individuals and families are free or low cost. Unlike for-profit businesses, there are no price constraints on the supply or demand for service. If we were to purchase a product from a store, we could assign a dollar value to our potential purchase based on our perceptions of product quality and product availability. We cannot perform the same process when we wish to obtain a social service.

Often, few options are available for obtaining the services we need. We must rely on the opinions of others (e.g., organizational board members, experts in the field, case managers, or former clients) to ascertain quality for us. Therefore, one of the primary problems with service delivery is the limited accountability built into social service systems. Not only do clients not know who is responsible for inadequacies in the service delivery system, often social service professionals do not know how or if the system works. This uncertainty is because of the following reasons:

- Much of what is produced in social service delivery occurs as a consequence of the interaction between staff members and clientele.
- Goals associated with service delivery often are vague.
- Some types of service outcomes are difficult to measure quantitatively.
- Organizations do not always have appropriate mechanisms for measuring whether these outcomes have actually been achieved (Ginsberg, 2001; Hasenfeld, 1992).

Another problem associated with the lack of monetary price constraints is that the demand for free services by people in need often exceeds the actual supply of service (Lipsky, 1980). The reliance by clients on social service organizations for assistance makes them dependent on the organization for future help and gives them little room to bargain for better or larger amounts of service. Therefore, power in social service organizations is concentrated in two places: (a) among administrative staff and policy-makers, and (b) among front-line social workers who make decisions about how services should be allocated (Hasenfeld, 1992; Prottas, 1979). Within social service organizations, clients are concentrated on the bottom rung of the organization's decision-making hierarchy and, consequently, are rendered powerless in most cases.

Another feature that makes social service organizations unique is their need to solicit operating funds from individuals, foundations, and government because most social service organizations do not charge a fee for their services. Many of the theories that explain how social service organizations interact with external systems focus on how organizations obtain monetary and other resources. This exchange of goods and resources among organizations takes place in the organization's task environment. Scott (1987) describes the task environment as

> Those features of the environment relevant to the organization viewed as a production system—in particular, the sources of inputs, markets for outputs, competitors, and regulators. Since no organization generates

all the resources necessary for goal attainment or survival, organizations are forced to enter into exchanges, becoming interdependent with other environmental groups, typically other organizations. (p. 181)

In the next sections of this chapter, we examine theories about how

- Organizations maintain themselves.
- People interact with one another in organizations.
- Power and resources are distributed in organizations.
- Organizations interact with other organizations in their task environment.

THEORIES ABOUT ORGANIZATIONAL MAINTENANCE

A number of theories focus on how structure guides how the organization operates and maintains itself. Two of the primary structural theories used to understand social service organizations are *systems theory* and *institutional theory.* Structural theorists believe that problems in organizations are caused by structural deficiencies and can be remedied by making changes in how the organization operates (Netting & O'Connor, 2003).

Systems Theory

One of the guiding assumptions of most organizational theory is that organizations are systems. Organizations are made of a set of interlocking parts. Programs, work units, front-line staff, clientele, boards of directors, administrators, and organizational constituents are components of organizational systems. A common understanding among participants differentiates the organization and its members from those people and structures that are not part of the organization (Norlin & Chess, 1997). A change in one part of the system produces change in the entire system. In addition, organizations are subsets of larger systems, often referred to as the organization's *suprasystem* (Hasenfeld, 1992; Norlin & Chess, 1997). For example, organizations are affected by what happens in the surrounding community or by events in social, economic, or political systems.

Through the interaction of systems within and outside the boundaries of the organization, the organization must strive to reach homeostasis, or a balance in which order and stability can be maintained (Netting & O'Connor, 2003). Some organizations are more successful than others in achieving homeostasis. Organizations with closed boundaries have relatively little communication or interaction with people, organizations, or institutions outside their own system. Such organizations are not likely to grow and develop in relation to changes in the external environment. In contrast, organizations with open but clearly defined boundaries between themselves and the surrounding environment are likely to be relatively successful in meeting challenges, addressing crises, and adapting to change.

Organizations as systems have a variety of component parts. *Inputs* are resources that are put into the system in order to accomplish the organization's goals. Inputs for social service organizations can include money, staff members, volunteers, supplies, facilities, technology, and clientele (Austin, 2002). Inputs are used to produce products or services that, in systems terminology, are called *outputs.* Most often, in social service organizations, outputs produce outcomes that are changes in individuals or their status (e.g., converting an applicant to someone who is eligible for welfare benefits). The transformation from inputs to outputs occurs within the internal structure of the organization, called *throughput* in systems terminology. Throughput consists of all the things that happen inside the organization, including interactions among staff members, interactions between staff and clients, the services provided, organizational policies and procedures, and organizational goals (Norlin & Chess, 1997). In addition to input, throughput, output, and outcomes, most organizations contain *feedback loops,* which are systems or processes that allow the organization to gather information or communicate with others about how well the organization is performing (Figure 2.2).

Parsons (1971) identified four primary functions associated with organizational systems: goal attainment, pattern maintenance, integration, and adaptation. *Goal attainment* refers to accomplishment of the organization's work. *Pattern maintenance* involves the transmission of common

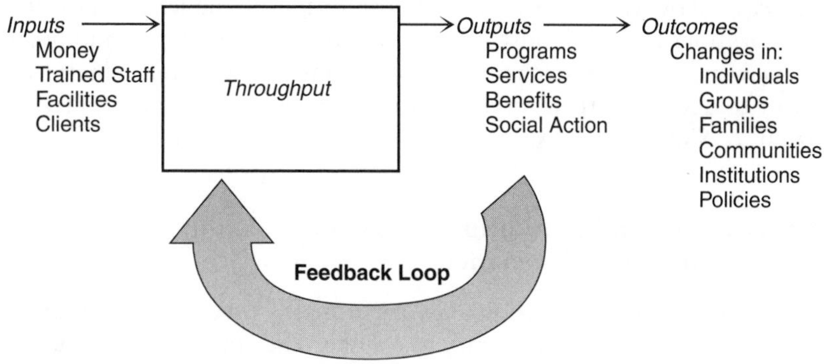

Figure 2.2 Systems model of organizations.

values and behaviors to organizational participants. *Integration* involves actual processes through which people adopt or are made to adopt common values and beliefs. *Adaptation* refers to the ability of the organization to change in relation to the demands of its external environment.

Institutional Theory

Institutional theory focuses on the rules and procedures established by organizations to maintain themselves and guide the behavior of staff and other participants. According to Scott (1995), institutions

> Consist of cognitive, normative, and regulative structures and activities that provide stability and meaning to social behavior. Institutions are transported by various carriers—cultures, structures, and routines—and they operate at multiple levels of jurisdiction. (p. 33)

Some rules are a function of the values and beliefs of organizational actors and constituency groups. Others are socially constructed, derived from the interaction among organizational participants (Scott, 1995). Rules also can derive from legislation, public opinion, or legal decisions in the courts, and they often are used to regulate the behavior of organizational staff, beneficiaries, and other people who interact with the institution (Hasenfeld, 1992). In some organizations, following the rules becomes more important than the actual delivery of services. For example, DeHoog (1984) found that government requirements for job training organizations to properly document services in order to be reimbursed created situations where staff members were more concerned about completing paperwork than in placing people in jobs.

Rules are disseminated through networks of organizations in the same industry, serving the same group of clientele or delivering similar services. Network members may choose to follow the lead of powerful organizations in their industry that develop new technologies and procedures. Using new approaches may help organizations establish their legitimacy to operate in their service sector and help them to survive (Tucker, Baum, & Singh, 1992).

Applications and Limitations of Theories About Organizational Maintenance

Systems theory and institutional theory primarily describe how organizations respond, or fail to respond, to change. They focus on the structure of the organization itself, the rules through which it operates, and patterns of communication. Systems and institutional theories are often used to develop conceptual models that can be used to analyze how organizations function and the relationships among different components of the organization. However, these theories do not examine the role of organizational actors in creating or challenging the rules (Hasenfeld, 1992). The next section examines theories about how people interact with one another in organizations.

THEORIES ABOUT HOW PEOPLE INTERACT IN ORGANIZATIONS

In addition to organizational structure, the people within an organization determine how the organization functions. The values and perspectives of these individuals can influence how programs are implemented, how the organization obtains money and other resources, who is hired by the organization, and what services the organization provides. Three types of theories for understanding how people function within organizational structures are (a) human relations theory, (b) organizational culture, and (c) social constructionism.

Human Relations Theory

The human relations theory or model describes an approach to managing staff that is quite different from Weber's and Taylor's mechanistic models, which assume that all worker behavior can be strictly controlled through administrative action. Principles associated with the human relations approach were generated by Elton Mayo, who conducted research at the Western Electric Hawthorne Works during the 1920s and 1930s. Mayo conducted experiments at this telephone manufacturing plant to test whether workers' productivity was affected by their responses to different workplace conditions. In one experiment, lighting was increased for one group of workers and decreased for another. The hypothesis was that the group in which the lighting was increased would have higher productivity than the group in which the lighting decreased. Much to the surprise of Mayo and the other researchers, productivity increased for both groups. Changing workplace conditions produced essentially the same results. Workers responded to the fact that they and their performances were being observed rather than to the experimental interventions introduced into the workplace (Hasenfeld, 1992; Kettner, 2001).

Mayo expanded on his research to develop the theory and practice principles associated with this approach. He described organizations as having a specific culture and, in some cases, several subcultures influenced by the values of participants and the tendency of individuals to form informal groups (Kettner, 2002). In some cases, informal leaders, or people without designated management positions, may influence the behavior of organizational participants. The various groups in the organization, their leaders, and the social norms shared by group members may influence workers' attitudes toward group performance. For example, group members may ostracize rather than support staff members with superior work records. Mayo argued that managers should not try to suppress these informal groups but should analyze them and use their existence to motivate workers toward better performance.

According to Mayo's theory, in order to maximize performance, staff members need autonomy over their own work and appropriate rewards. One method that can be used to motivate employees is to involve them in organizational decision-making. The organization's executive director has the primary responsibility for motivating employees and providing supportive leadership for staff members. Motivational techniques should focus both on individuals and on fostering feelings of group or team membership among staff. Individual staff members will react differently to various incentives. The workers benefit from better treatment and rewards, and the managers and the organization benefit from higher worker productivity (Netting & O'Connor, 2003).

Organizational Culture

Researchers have extensively documented differences in the culture of various organizations. Culture is generally defined as behaviors, values, perspectives, and expectations that are shared by organizational participants. Organizational culture determines how members learn about the expectations of the organization and how they subsequently behave (Schein, 1992). Organizational structure, the technology used by the organization, the organization's mission, organizational leadership (both formal and informal), and decision-making structure as well as the personalities and beliefs of organizational members are factors that can explain why some organizations develop unique "ways of doing things" (Lohmann & Lohmann, 2002, p. 102). Personality traits and the cultural values of individuals also play a role in determining organizational culture (Flynn, Chatman, & Spataro, 2001). For example, a cultural orientation that values collectivism over individualism might be expected to increase staff commitment to working as team members (Gummer, 2002).

One of the basic assumptions associated with theories about organizational culture is that organizations are most productive when most participants share an understanding or vision of the organization's mission and work to accomplish that goal (Kettner, 2002). Organizational goals and rules developed by organizational members to guide operations and establish parameters for behavior are also viewed as a reflection of organizational culture (Netting & O'Connor, 2003; Schein, 1992).

Social Constructionism

Theories about organizational culture focus on how people interpret what happens within the context of the organization's environment and the personal meaning they ascribe to certain behaviors and situations (Netting & O'Connor, 2003). Social constructionism is a framework for understanding exactly how individuals construct knowledge based on their own experiences. It assumes that existing theories are often not relevant to the lives of most individuals; instead people develop personal theories about the world and how they and the people with whom they associate function in society (Rossiter, 1996). Constructionism is associated with "postmodernism," an approach to knowledge that focuses on overcoming oppression by constructing new knowledge about the lives and experiences of members of traditionally subordinated groups (Chambon, 1999). Social constructionism also has its roots in "symbolic interactionism," the idea that people construct everyday activities with meanings associated with cultural norms, values, and use of language (Lee & Greene, 1999).

Social constructionists argue that knowledge creation varies among individuals because each person experiences a different reality and interprets that reality based on his or her own values and personal experiences (Rodwell, 1998). Existing theories are a mechanism used by the dominant culture to maintain institutional structures that oppress individuals and members of disadvantaged groups. Therefore, these theories should be discarded and new ways of understanding developed. In terms of social work practice, this perspective suggests that the work of social workers has been socially constructed as a function of society's need to regulate and control individual behavior (Hardcastle, Wenocur, & Powers, 1997; Moffat, 1999). Therefore, the meaning assigned by client groups to the intervention process may be far different from the meaning of this process to the social worker. Members of the client group may internalize the helping process, associating it with society's need to control behavior.

An additional application of social constructionism in social work practice is the work of Paulo Freire (1970). Although Freire is not explicitly a social constructionist, his work focuses on the production of new knowledge in relation to working with members of marginalized groups to bring about social change. Freire argues that the knowledge acquired by oppressed people through personal experience is valuable and, in most instances, is just as important as knowledge held by social service, education, and other professional workers. Freire advocated a method of knowledge construction through dialogue between oppressed people and experts that takes place within the context of mutual exchange. Knowledge generated through this process is used to facilitate social change and transform both individuals (through knowledge and skill acquisition) and society.

Applications and Limitations of Theories About Human Interaction in Organizations

Human relations and organizational culture are theories about how personal values and human interaction affect the operation of an organization. Social constructionism, as well as theories about organizational culture, also describes how people ascribe meaning to the actions of others and the role of personal perceptions in creating knowledge and shaping the behavior of organizations. Managers can use these theoretical frameworks to understand and guide the creation of an organizational culture that nurtures workers and motivates them toward better performance. However, although these theories can explain worker behavior as an adaptation made within the context of the organization to demands of the external environment, the influence and restraints caused by social, economic, and political systems on organizations are not examined (Gummer, 2002; Hasenfeld, 1992).

THEORIES THAT EXPLAIN THE DISTRIBUTION OF POWER AND RESOURCES IN ORGANIZATIONS

A number of theories examine how power and other resources that can be used to obtain power, such as money, authority, and professional status, are used and distributed in organizations. *Conflict theory* examines competition among organizational constituency groups and how competition between members of different social classes, ethnic groups, or demographic groups affects the degree to which organizations and individuals acquire power. *Power-dependency theory* describes how power is acquired by those who have resources and who are in a position to give those resources to others.

Conflict Theory

Conflict theory is often used to describe how members of various constituency groups obtain resources (e.g., well-paying staff positions, status, or power) in organizations. The basic assumption of conflict theory is that people form groups to protect common resources or promote common interests. These groups often engage in competition and conflict to acquire more resources or to protect what they have acquired (Hardcastle et al., 1997). Consequently, those interest groups that hold political power establish organizational policies and procedures that limit the ability of others to obtain power or resources in the organization. Specific applications of conflict theory to social service organizations include Lipsky's (1980) description of public welfare agencies and Dressel's (1992) examination of gender segregation in the assignment of social service–related staff positions.

According to Lipsky (1980), front-line workers in public welfare bureaucracies are pressured by administrators to limit service provision to most recipients. Such rationing of public benefits is possible because welfare recipients are viewed as unworthy of assistance by taxpayers and government decision-makers; much of the power in social welfare is held by front-line workers who make eligibility decisions (see Chapter 6). Dressel (1992) describes social service provision as a system in which women hold the majority of front-line staff positions (casework or clinical practice) and men occupy management positions. She attributes gender segregation to social norms (often accepted by women themselves) that women are more suitable for positions that require workers to nurture other persons than to use task-oriented work approaches that are believed to be more appropriate for men.

Conflict theory is also associated with both Marxist and feminist theories. As described by Karl Marx, capitalism is an economic system in which members of the elite constantly try to exploit, for monetary gain, the labor of the masses (Marx, 1965). This theory has been used primarily to understand the operation of large economic systems and the relationship between capitalism and class structure. Neo-Marxist theory examines how specific social, economic, and political institutions are used to sustain social inequality (Knuttila, 1992). Neo-Marxism, as applied to social service organizations, focuses on the role of social workers in mediating between members of the socioeconomic and political elites and the masses—members of the working class, the poor, and people of color. Social workers are viewed as agents of social control, applying rules that benefit the elite and keep all others powerless (Burghardt & Fabricant, 1987). Consequently, social welfare institutions are viewed by Neo-Marxists as mechanisms used by the ruling classes to maintain control and minimize political dissent. For example, Piven and Cloward (1971) have argued that political elites intentionally increase eligibility for welfare benefits in response to political unrest and reduce eligibility for services when corporations lobby for laws that force people in poverty to leave welfare for low-wage work.

Feminist theory also examines the competition for resources and status in society. Its primary assumption is that men hold most of the power in society and that they use their power to enforce institutional rules that exclude women from positions of authority (Sunstein, 1990). This exclusion contributes to the lack of gender parity in employment, income, health care, social service provision, and other sectors of society. Most feminists believe that organizations replicate the oppression of women found in society by establishing hierarchical decision-making structures in which one or a few top decision-makers control what happens in the organization. Iannello (1992) describes an organization "as a vertical and horizontal system of domination with varying degrees of centralized communication" (p. 17). According to Iannello, one of the primary problems with organizations is that workers are unable to influence workplace decisions and consequently have little status or power in the organization. The power inherent in the hierarchical structure, often implemented using sanctions or other types of negative communication, is viewed as harmful to the well-being of organizational participants, especially women.

Power-Dependency Theory

Another theory often used to describe power in organizations is the *power-dependency* or *social exchange theory.* The basic premise of power-dependency theory is that most transactions among organizations or between organizations and individuals take place within the context of social exchange (Blau, 1964). As applied to most nonprofit social service organizations, power-dependency theory holds that organizations that do not actually sell their services to individuals must depend on donors (usually government or foundations) to provide grants and contracts that can be used for service delivery. The donor consequently has the power to demand that the organization comply with the donor's wishes—these demands generally pertain to the manner in which the service must be delivered. Unless the organization can supply the donor with a good or service of equal value, the organization is obligated to do what the donor requests unless

- The organization can find an alternative source of support.
- The organization can learn to live without the donation.
- The organization can find a way to force the donor to supply support or withdraw demands for compliance.

A second application of power-dependency theory to organizations is through the examination of the relationship between people using social services (clients) and the organization. Hasenfeld (1992) argues that in order to understand organization–client relationships, the following issues must be examined:

- To what degree does the organization demand that clients comply with organizational policies and rules in return for services that almost always are free or low cost?
- How do staff members use their power to determine client eligibility and make service allocation decisions?
- What impact does the sense of obligation for free services have on the client's willingness to seek help or on his or her sense of personal identity as an individual who is forced to rely on an organization for assistance?
- What options does the client have to develop his or her own power resources in order to reduce dependency on the organization for goods and services?
- What actions are taken by the organization to minimize the power disadvantage between clients and staff members?

Applications and Limitations of Theories Related to Power

Power-related theories help us understand the competition for resources that often occurs among organizational participants. These theories also help us understand how organizations can position themselves to best advocate for social change. Conflict-related theories help us understand how social service organizations function within a political environment that uses social welfare policies to reinforce power differentials among members of different social classes. The chief limitation of these power-related models is that they offer no analysis of how people come together to create organizational cultures or the role of organizational structure in promoting or minimizing conflict. In addition, these theories give minimal information about how organizations react to the demands of their task environments (Hasenfeld, 1992).

THEORIES ABOUT HOW ORGANIZATIONS INTERACT WITH THE SURROUNDING ENVIRONMENT

Social service organizations cannot operate in a vacuum. Political, economic, and social systems are critical to the organization's survival. These organizations must recruit clients, raise funds, network with other organizations, comply with government regulations, and adopt the latest technology if they are to maintain themselves over time. Ecological and political-economy theories pertain to the organization's ability to adapt to changes in the surrounding environment and their ability to acquire power and other resources that will facilitate organizational change and survival.

Ecological Theory

Ecological theory is also known as *population ecology.* This approach has its roots in Darwin's biological determinism, "survival of the fittest." Organizations serving the same community or population actively compete for the resources needed to survive (Norlin & Chess, 1997). Money, donors, volunteers, facilities, media attention, political influence, and clients are among the resources for which organizations typically compete. This is particularly problematic in situations where a number of organizations serve the same client population or provide similar services. Because they operate in a competitive environment, organizations must adapt to circumstances by finding a specific "niche" or role in the community that allows them to acquire the power and resources they need for economic survival. Thus, organizations must find ways to make themselves unique, and they must offer specialized services or provide programs to people in the community who otherwise would not receive assistance.

Population ecologists typically look at the characteristics of organizations serving the same task environment, including population density (number of organizations serving the same population), number of organizational foundings (new organizations entering the task environment), and organizations that disband or terminate operations (Tucker et al., 1992). Also of concern are the strength and density of interorganizational networks that many organizations depend upon for survival. Most organizations exchange or share resources with one another through formal or informal processes, such as collaboration, coordination, and case management. The resources can include referrals, clients, information, and facilities.

Political-Economy Theory

Political-economy theory builds upon power-dependency theory by focusing on the organization's ability to generate funding and the organization's use of power in developing legitimacy and relationships with funders and local institutions. It examines organizational linkages with larger political and economic systems (Iglehart & Becerra, 2000). However, political-economy theory also examines the use of power and authority to achieve organizational goals (Wamsley & Zald, 1973).

Goal accomplishment is viewed not only as a function of external relationships and the ability to garner resources but also in terms of the political dynamics within the organization. The manager needs to establish various constituency groups and work units between the organization and its clients (Hasenfeld, 1992). Consequently, organizational culture and the values and norms of participants are as important in task accomplishment as is the external environment (Martin, 1980).

This approach focuses on how the organization makes strategic use of the scarce resources under its control to adapt to the demands of the external environment (Wamsley & Zald, 1973). Such resources can include clientele, service technology, grants and contracts, and cooperative relationships with other organizations (Alexander, 2000; Gronbjerg, Chen, & Stagner, 1995; Provan & Milward, 2001). Politically astute executive directors and influential board members must be able to manage the organization's external environment while dealing with internal constituency groups (e.g., clients and staff) that may have different interests and perspectives (Austin, 2002).

BOX 2.1 USING THEORIES TO MANAGE SOCIAL SERVICE ORGANIZATIONS—PART I

Pang has just been hired as the new executive director of the Northwest Women's Shelter. This organization was established 10 years ago. Much of its funding was provided by the local United Way. However, the United Way cut its annual contribution to the shelter by 60%. Therefore, one of Pang's first tasks will be to raise funds from other sources. The shelter may qualify for a large government contract that would provide most of the funds needed to operate the shelter. However, the board has expressed concerns about the impact of these funds on the shelter's autonomy. They have asked Pang to write a report about funding options and the potential impact of various types of funds on the shelter's future.

- What theories should guide Pang's recommendations about future funding options?
- Based on these theories, what kind of an impact can be expected if the organization chooses to accept government funds?

Applications and Limitations of Theories Related to Adaptation to the External Environment

These theories help us understand how organizations interact with agencies, constituency groups, and institutions in their external environment.

They also help identify strategies that organizations can use to acquire resources, enter into collaboration with other groups, and build political power. However, both theories focus on interorganizational competition and downplay the importance of the actions and beliefs of individual participants in helping the organization grow and thrive over time (Hasenfeld, 1992).

MODELS OF MANAGEMENT PRACTICE

Previous sections of this chapter described theories about organizational maintenance, the interaction of people within the organization, the distribution of power and resources in organizations, and an organization's adaptation to its external environment. Models of practice incorporate a variety of theories into a plan of action for managers. However, most models of management practice used by social workers focus exclusively on how managers should motivate their workers. Douglas McGregor described two models: Theory X and Theory Y. Theory X assumes that workers must be forced to do their jobs. The role of the manager is to control worker behavior and make it fit the organization's needs. Theory Y takes the opposite approach. Its basic assumption is that workers are intrinsically well motivated to work, but that they may become resistant to organizational demands because of workplace dynamics (Bobic & Davis, 2003). Consequently, it is the manager's responsibility to alter workplace conditions to enhance worker performance (Kettner, 2002). Management by objectives (MBO) is another commonly used model that builds upon the basic premises associated with Theory Y. MBO requires that, in addition to organization-wide goals and objectives for performance, each employee identify his or her own performance goals (Drucker, 1954). Yearly performance evaluations are based on whether employees have met these goals. William Ouchi developed Theory Z, which is based on Japanese management practices that focus on fostering loyalty to the employer, group accountability for the quality of the work, and consensus-oriented decision-making among employees (Kettner, 2002). Theories for motivating employees are described in greater detail in Chapter 9. Also, the human relations model, described earlier, is widely used. It has many components that incorporate values associated with social work practice, such as treating all workers humanely and focusing on altering management tactics to fit the needs of individual employees rather than trying to make the employee fit the needs of the organization.

BOX 2.2 USING THEORIES TO MANAGE SOCIAL SERVICE ORGANIZATIONS—PART II

Pang's second task will involve reorganizing the shelter's management structure. On her first day at the shelter, Pang held a meeting with staff members. The staff appeared to be demoralized. The previous executive director had been fired by the board and had held her position for only 8 months. No executive director has served this organization for longer than 2 years. Consequently, the workers feel directionless and unmotivated. They receive little feedback about their work. There are few clear lines of supervisory authority. Small cliques have formed among the staff, and these groups seem to have greater influence on the staff than does management.

- What theories can be used to explain the lack of direction and motivation among the staff?
- What are the potential effects of the nonexistent supervisory structure or the presence of cliques on this organization?

Recent innovations in management models include total quality management (TQM) and the feminist management approach. These approaches developed during the same time period as the empowerment model of management practice; consequently, all three share a number of characteristics.

Total Quality Management

TQM is an approach increasingly used in manufacturing to ensure greater productivity (Lawler et al., 1995). A number of authors have argued for the adoption of TQM principles in social service organizations (Gardner, 1999a; Kettner, Moroney, & Martin, 1999). This method requires that management produce an organizational culture based on product quality, consumer satisfaction, standardization of production, and employee empowerment. Staff members are required to form quality circles or work teams that focus on improving the quality of the work effort. Specific quality improvement targets are set, and data indicating whether these benchmarks have been met are constantly provided to team members. The expectation is that staff members will play a primary role in setting quality standards and altering their performance and workplace practices in order to achieve these goals. In order to motivate employees to meet these standards, managers provide incentives such as merit pay, choices in workplace benefits, and other types of recognition for good work (e.g., employee-of-the-month awards) when performance standards have been achieved (Lawler et al., 1995). In addition, TQM and the empowerment model of management place emphasis on customer service and the role of the consumer in determining whether the product or service received is actually of sufficient quality to meet his or her needs (Gardner, 1999a). This approach may be of limited effectiveness if organizational participants have difficulty defining or measuring quality and if staff involvement in organizational decision-making is insufficient in motivating them to improve performance.

Feminist Management

Feminist management emphasizes the creation of "management partnerships" among all organizational participants (board members, staff, administrators, and clients). It assumes women manage differently than do men, focusing on forging good interpersonal relationships among staff members to motivate them rather than using traditional, hierarchical approaches that require using power and authority to make people work (Chernesky & Bombyk, 1995). Decision-making takes place within the context of collaboration and consensus rather than by executive order or majority rule–related procedures common in traditional male-dominated organizations (Hyde, 1994). Ideally, authority in such consensus-oriented organizations is believed to rest with the members of the organization as a whole, and rules or division of labor is minimal (Iannello, 1992). These organizations rely on informal relations among organizational staff, board members, and clients to maintain control and recruit new members. However, as Hyde (1994) and Morgen (1994) have noted, actually retaining motivated staff and improving the quality of work may be difficult because of the lack of performance incentives, assumptions that people will work because they are committed to the cause, and the fact that many decisions are based on friendship ties rather than objective criteria.

BUILDING AN EMPOWERMENT MODEL OF PRACTICE

In social work practice, the empowerment model is a multisystems approach that recognizes that social problems have their origins in interconnected systems. Hence, effective intervention must often occur at multiple levels—individual, group, family, organization, and community systems. Social work practitioners often must assume multiple roles, such as therapist, broker, advocate, enabler, mediator, and conferee, in order to intervene at these multiple levels (Lee, 2001). The empowerment model (Gutierrez, 1990; Rose & Black, 1985; Solomon, 1976) is used to intervene at three levels: intrapersonal, interpersonal, and community and/or political. It explicitly focuses on low-income people, communities of color, and members of other oppressed groups. It requires use of the problem-solving model as well as assessment, intervention, and evaluation strategies that require the direct participation of clients. Inherent in the empowerment model are social work approaches that incorporate the principles of social justice and a commitment to culturally competent practice (Gutierrez, Parsons, & Cox, 1998).

Reid (2002) identifies the empowerment model as one of three practice models (in addition to generalist and ecosystems approaches) associated with multilevel or multisystems practice. According to Reid, multilevel approaches are "particularly applicable to vulnerable populations, such as the poor, whose problems have strong environmental components" (p. 14). The rationale for adoption of this approach by social workers is that many of the people who receive services experience multiple problems (e.g., poverty, unemployment, and teen pregnancy), which can be addressed only through interventions at multiple systems levels by social workers who are competent in cross-cultural practice and who have the political skills necessary for facilitating social justice. Empowerment-oriented multisystems practice has been described in the social work and psychological literature as appropriate for interventions with persons of color who often experience hardships associated with oppression and multiple barriers to service delivery (Gopaul-McNichol, 1997; Solomon, 1976).

Many of the theories about organizations discussed in this chapter have been incorporated into the empowerment model of management (Gutierrez, GlenMaye, & DeLois, 1995; Shera & Page, 1995). Relevant perspectives and theories include the following:

- *Systems and Ecological Theories*—Systems theory helps us understand how organizations function within communities and larger social, political, and economic systems. Such an understanding provides us with the basic assumption associated with the systems approach to social work and empowerment-related practice. Intervention to change individuals, groups, families, organizations, and communities must occur at multiple levels—intrapersonal, interpersonal, and political. In order to resolve individual problems, intervention in larger systems—organizations, communities, and social institutions—is often necessary.
- *Conflict Theory*—Various social groups in society and within the organization compete for resources. Allocation of services is often

determined by perceptions of in-group versus out-group status of recipients. The best way to influence social change is through the acquisition of power by marginalized groups.

- *Human Relations Model and Theories About Organizational Culture*—Staff should be involved in organizational decision-making. To empower workers, managers must provide opportunities, training, and incentives to help workers obtain a sense of competence and psychological empowerment. Management approaches must respond to the needs of individuals in the organization. Therefore, the manager must provide appropriate incentives to motivate individual employees.
- *Feminist Management*—All organizational constituents, including board members, clients, staff members, and managers, are to be included in the decision-making process. Decision-making requires that constituents engage in dialogue about management issues and make important decisions through consensus as a collective group. Feminist organizations actively reject the power and control approach to motivating staff members and making decisions in a manner associated with traditional hierarchical organizations.
- *Social Constructionism*—Service consumers should be equal partners with staff in the decision-making process. Consumers reduce their feelings of oppression and low self-esteem by engaging with the organization in social action.
- *Power-Dependency Theory*—Clients are dependent on social service organizations to meet their needs. Consequently, they may become obligated to the organization for assistance and feel powerless unless they can offer the organization a good or service of equal value. Inclusion of clients in organizational decision-making and inclusion of clients in volunteer work are two mechanisms that reduce feelings of powerlessness.
- *Political-Economy Theory*—Organizations can best be understood in terms of the multiple constituency groups within the organization that often compete for resources and the social, economic, and political forces that require the organization to adapt to changes in the surrounding environment. Managers must adopt strategic approaches to help organizational participants respond to multiple demands. Building a strong constituency base for the organization is one method for increasing the power of the organization to influence social change.
- *Total Quality Management*—Employees are organized into teams and are required to closely monitor their work and to find ways to improve the quality of their work. The emphasis is placed on

using teams both to support workers and to increase their productivity. In the social service industry, TQM also focuses on improving quality of life for underserved or marginalized populations (Gardner, 1999a).

As in TQM, the empowerment approach focuses on increasing the quality of services in order to increase the benefit they provide to clients. The empowerment model also draws upon feminist management principles as well as concepts associated with the citizens participation movement in the 1960s to encourage the involvement of organizational clientele in organizational decision-making.

BOX 2.3 CHOOSING A MODEL OF MANAGEMENT PRACTICE

Pang has worked to identify and apply for new sources of funds for the Northwest Women's Shelter. She has set up weekly supervisory meetings with the staff as a "stop gap" measure to provide leadership to her workers. However, during several meetings with organization clients, she has received feedback that the shelter's services are perceived as being of poor quality. Clients feel that their needs have not been considered in service planning or evaluation. Community-based organizations that refer clients to the shelter have made similar complaints.

Given this feedback, Pang realizes that she will need to focus on both external relations and internal problems in order to keep the shelter running. She also needs to find a way to improve client and community perceptions of the shelter's services. Therefore, Pang will need to choose an overall management model or philosophy to guide her work. The model should also provide a framework for creating a new staff supervision process and an internal decision-making structure for the organization.

- What model do you think Pang should choose?
- Is there one overall model that is appropriate to address the problems in the Northwest Women's Shelter?
- Could Pang choose to adopt specific components of several models? What criteria should she use to make her choice?

SUMMARY

Theories about how organizations operate, gain power, and adapt to changing conditions help managers develop strategies to acquire funds, lobby for legislation, and interact with other organizations. Theories about interpersonal interactions help managers adopt techniques to motivate staff and stimulate better work performance. Models of management practice are mechanisms used to help managers combine ethical values, workplace philosophy, and actions into integrated approaches that are used primarily to guide managerial interactions with staff members. Some models also provide guidance for serving the consumers of services as well as interactions with the organization's external environment. The empowerment model includes all three of these components: staff motivation, involving consumers in organizational decision-making, and increasing the organization's ability to acquire resources and influence social change. The next few chapters discuss the basic components of the empowerment model, including ethical practices, the structure and function of social service organizations, and the skills needed to create decision-making partnerships between staff members and consumers of service.

QUESTIONS FOR CLASS DISCUSSION

1. As an employee, what type of management model would be more likely to motivate you and increase your work productivity?
2. Do all the organizations in which you participate conform to the hierarchical model of organizations described by Weber? In what ways do they differ?
3. In the organizations in which you participate, do all members agree on organizational goals? Can you think of reasons why constituency group members (managers, staff, clients, board members, etc.) may have different goals and expectations about what the organization should do?
4. What type of characteristics can be associated with organizations that are classified as closed systems? What characteristics are associated with open systems?
5. What are the advantages and disadvantages of creating organizations in which staff members and clientele have a high degree of input into important management decisions?
6. Political-economy theory focuses on strategies that organizations can use to adapt to both external demands and the preferences and values of internal constituency groups. What types of strategies do you think can be used by organizations to acquire grants and contracts given the great deal of competition among organizations for funding?

SAMPLE ASSIGNMENTS

1. Interview the top CEOs in the organization in which you are employed or in which you are completing a field internship. Conduct a short interview with them to determine any management models, theoretical frameworks, or perspectives they may use to guide decision-making in the organization. Conduct additional research on models of practice. Write a four- to five-page paper describing how these models affect (or do not affect) how services are managed in this organization.
2. Identify a problem in your agency. Find a theory that can be used to describe the problem, its causes, and possible solutions. Using the theory as a guide, propose a tentative strategy that could be used to resolve this problem.
3. Interview several staff members in your field agency or place of employment and spend some time observing staff behavior. Write a two- to three-page paper describing aspects of the organizational culture that you feel are unique.
4. Conduct a brief assessment of your organization using Weber's rational–legal model of organizations. How does the organization compare or differ with Weber's model? How does Weber's model compare and contrast with the empowerment model? Does your organization contain any of the components described by the empowerment model?

CHAPTER 3

Values and Ethics for Management Practice

Values and ethics frequently are the subject of great debate. These concepts often appear to have different definitions depending on who is addressing these critical notions. Frequently, values and ethics are used to polarize people around the varying perceptions held in relation to a particular issue or position. Both values and ethics appear to be interpreted based on situation and circumstance rather than shared meaning. In this chapter, we discuss

- The concepts of social justice, values, and ethics as contributors to the synergy of an empowerment-focused organization.
- Social welfare management as a special instance of social administration.
- The National Association of Social Workers (NASW) *Code of Ethics*.

BACKGROUND: SOCIAL JUSTICE

The social fabric of a society is composed of many different variables. Its structure is dependent upon a sense of what is right and what is wrong. And yet, in the broader societal structure, we agree upon increasingly fewer things. Issues related to values and ethics are rooted in the very nature of human interaction. They are associated with issues of empowerment and social justice, as well as issues concerned with professional behavior. Issues related to professional behavior are discussed later in this chapter. The concept of social justice sets the context for the development of standards and establishes parameters by which we engage in human social interaction. What is the source of our concern with respect to social justice? For many, it is rooted in the early histories of human beings.

From the beginning of recorded history, human societies have struggled with issues associated with how to care for persons among them who were unable to provide for themselves. The activities associated with attempts to address these issues have led to the establishment of social welfare—a collective response to the question "what should we do?" According to Phyllis Day (2003):

> Social welfare in any society has two major purposes: social treatment (helping) and social control. We easily agree with the helping purpose but are generally almost unaware of the social control function of social welfare because it is hidden in the ideas about equality and what we consider our "right" to change our clients. Society needs certain social controls, for some behaviors must be regulated so that interdependent people can live and work together. However, not all such control is positive, and social welfare controls aim at our most vulnerable citizens. Because our clients need our help, they must meet our (and society's) demands. (p. 2)

It is clear that a power differential exists among social institutions that are intended to help persons in need and those who require services from these institutions in order to survive. This situation creates the concern about social justice. According to Rawls (1971), "justice is the first virtue of social institutions" (p. 3).

Social justice becomes an important consideration in management practice and is a critical component in issues related to values and ethics. Social justice is the foundation upon which much of social interaction is based. Rawls (1971) describes the concept of social justice in the following manner:

> Let us assume to fix ideas, that a society is a more or less self sufficient association of persons who in their relations to one another recognize certain rules of conduct as binding and who for the most part act in accordance with them. Suppose further that these rules specify a system of cooperation designed to advance the good of those taking part in it. Then, although a society is a cooperative venture for mutual advantage, it is typically marked by conflicts as well as by an identity of interests. There is an identity of interests since social cooperation makes possible a better life for all than any would have if each were to live solely by his own efforts. There is a conflict of interests since persons are not indifferent as to how the greater benefits produced by their collaboration are distributed, for in order to pursue their ends they each prefer a larger to a lesser share. (p. 4)

The concept of the social contract suggests that those who govern and those who are governed have a tacit agreement, a contract. The agreement comprises the principles of justice for the basic structure of society and defines the fundamental terms of their association (Rawls, 1971). If one assumes that there is a "social contract" inherently manifested in human interactions, that people will seek to maximize their own interests, and that those who are disenfranchised are most vulnerable in these interactions, then the mechanisms by which some sense of equity is established are essential:

> A society is well-ordered when it is not only designed to advance the good of its members but when it is also effectively regulated by a public conception of justice. That is, it is a society in which (1) everyone accepts and knows that others accept the same principles of justice, and (2) the basic social institutions generally satisfy and are generally known to satisfy these principles. (Rawls, 1971, p. 5)

As a society, some would suggest that we are well beyond the point of having a significant agreement with respect to a shared meaning of justice. Further, we are remiss in our understanding of the inherent role justice plays in shaping the social arrangements in which all persons share, to a greater or lesser degree, the benefits of the society.

Principles of social justice inform the values and ethics within the social arrangements established by a society. These principles not only are manifested in the opportunities made available to its members; they are reflected in how the social well-being of those unable to take advantage of such opportunities are addressed. To the extent that a society is perceived to be just, the greater is the agreement between those who serve and those who are served.

VALUES

Social institutions are human creations. Day (2003) defines them as "a set of interrelated and interlocking concepts, structures, and activities enduring over time that carry out the necessary functions of a society, such as socialization, childrearing, education, and commerce" (p. 27). These social institutions are subject to dominant social values. According to Miringoff and Opdycke (1986), values

> Are always in a state of change; sometimes they merge to form coherent systems, sometimes they have vague relationships, often they are in conflict . . . [They] may be influenced by occupation, race, age, class position, or by external factors such as changing economic conditions and new norms of social behavior. (p. 2)

Given the variability of values, it is important to note that several values are identified as unique to the United States. According to Day (2003), many values affect social well-being. She further suggests that we rarely question these values because they tend to be positive in their orientation even while they are contradictory to each other. Day identifies eight basic American values:

1. *Judeo-Christian Charity Values:* These values, based on Judaic teachings, view social justice as an ethical consideration in human interaction; however, in practice there is often reliance upon individualistic values.
2. *Democratic Egalitarianism and Individualism:* This value suggests that all citizens are equal before the law and that no privileges are based on other factors.
3. *The Protestant Work Ethic and Capitalism:* These values form the moral basis for American capitalism. They are linked inextricably to each other and affirm the notions of individualism, personal achievement, and wealth. Conversely, it is inferred that the lack of resources is representative of unworthiness.
4. *Social Darwinism:* A biological theory applied to social and economic issues. It supports the notion of worthiness and unworthiness in the context of social provisions.
5. *The New Puritanism:* Puritanism promotes a strict sense of personal values and morality. This ideology introduces a more activist religious orientation to the political arena.
6. *Patriarchy:* These ideas focus on power and authority being vested in men.
7. *Marriage and the Nuclear Family:* These values are positive attributes; nevertheless they can evoke negative perceptions of those who do not fit this specific concept of family.
8. *The "American" Ideal:* This value relates to the preference of white people as the ideal and is promoted through media in all forms. This value places significant importance on personal appearance and is important because of its potential influence in relation to diversity and culture (Day, 2003, pp. 8–12).

Although many other values may be strongly held within the society, these eight basic values can be found at every level of our social structure. The synergy of these values helps to create the unique American psyche. Their presence in the culture is often masked and ill defined, but is manifested in our social institutions and influences the manner in which social services are managed. The management of social institutions involves making ethical decisions and resolving ethical dilemmas.

Just as societal values influence how social services are delivered, they also define those areas in which issues of discrimination are identified. These areas go beyond individual prejudices; they reflect institutionalized strategies and behaviors for addressing specific issues or populations. These are important considerations because, not unlike values, their influence is significant. The literature is replete with discussion on issues related to discriminatory practices. For example, Day (2003) identifies the following:

- Classism
- Poverty
- Institutional racism
- Institutional sexism
- Institutional ageism
- Homophobia

Upon a closer look, however, we can speculate that these issues hold a special place in how society responds to persons in need. Day (2003) says:

> Our complex value systems legitimate social welfare as a helping process, but also sets up expectations that can be negative and controlling. These negative and controlling expectations dominate economic life and social welfare services, creating classism/poverty and institutional discrimination in the United States. (p. 12)

The hidden nature of societal values and issues of discrimination creates the sense that all members of the society have equal opportunities. Consider that social service organizations are created to fill the gap between what is believed to exist and what actually is available. To be certain of those individuals to whom discrimination "rules" apply, we create stringent criteria assuring that persons in need fit within specific categories of need. We protect the public good with policies that determine who gets what and how. Social service organizations are sanctioned to provide that service on behalf of the general public. It is in this arena that values, ethics, and discrimination converge. The synergy of values, discrimination, and ethics creates an extremely powerful force guiding actions that sometimes are unjust. The force is such that no one acculturated in the society can escape or avoid its influence. Thus, ethics becomes something to be considered, as we are not free of our values, and our level objectivity is lost to self-interest.

ETHICS

Just as values reflect the perception of what is and what ought to be, ethics are concerned with what is right and what is wrong. In essence, values represent a framework for ethical considerations and behaviors. Attempts to align both values and ethics pose a significant dilemma at every level of the society. Who determines what societal values are important, and who makes the determination of what is right or wrong? A dominant value in American society is individualism. As a consequence of individualism, a pattern of individual behavior has emerged such that each person does what is right in his or her own eyes. In so doing, there is the tendency to immerse ourselves in personally held values and attempt to ascribe our personal values to others who, in fact, might not share them. This behavior leads to deep divisions within the culture. As we become more diverse as a nation, we must develop mechanisms for interaction that can incorporate a multiplicity of values and beliefs. The notion of the social contract found in the writings of Locke, Rousseau, and Kant (Rawls, 1971), for example, suggests the need for some agreement among people about what is the purview of those who govern by those who are governed. The social contract is dependent upon the "good will" and "trust" among members of the society that the "best interest" of all members will be considered. The concern about ethics is immersed in the private, as well as the political, structure and reflects the competing interests of diverse groups.

> The breakdown of consensus concerning societal goals, the increasing scarcity of resources that are available for social welfare, and the use of new technologies not only have also intensified traditional ethical dilemmas but have also given rise to what may well be a new generation of ethical issues in social work practice. (Lowenberg & Dolgoff, 1996, p. 8)

When the concepts of right and wrong are introduced as a part of the discourse, it inevitably leads to consideration of morality. There is little open discussion about morality, and yet at the core of discourse is a sense of what is right or wrong. *Morality* is a term often avoided because it appears to represent a response that is judgmental regarding the behavior of others. Those who hold moral views that differ from those of the majority can experience fear. The fear centers around imposing values on others. When assertions about behavior are made within specified realms of social interaction, these assertions have the potential to be generalized to those areas not necessarily intended. In some instances those interactions can intrude into areas normally considered to be within the sphere of private or personal matters.

> One might hope that morality consists of a set of general rules that apply to everyone in society. These rules are neither enacted nor revoked by a legislature, but are accepted and changed by general consensus. They define the relationship between the members of the society. As Goldstein (as cited in Lowenberg & Dolgoff, 1996, p. 22) observed, "A moral sense . . . involves not only individual thoughts and actions but relationships with others."

Moving away from the notion of right and wrong to the notion of what is right and good as the basis for ethical considerations suggests that we have the capacity to know both (Lohmann & Lohmann, 2002). Broadly defined, we could consider the good to be that which serves the benefit of the majority. However, the rights of those in the minority also must be embraced at some level if there is to be a sense of fairness and equity within the society and its institutions. Social service organizations must find ways to address the built-in inequities when an oppressive majority wields its power over those who are disenfranchised. It then is incumbent upon social service organizations to establish mechanisms to assure that those most vulnerable receive fair and equitable treatment.

Values and ethics no doubt will continue to be a source of dissonance among individuals as well as within the broader structures of society. Nevertheless, those in organizations serving persons who are marginalized must act in the best interest of those who require services. This is best accomplished through social service organizations that hold empowerment practice as a core value.

SOCIAL WELFARE MANAGEMENT PRACTICE

Social service agencies are entities established to perform activities that respond to the social welfare needs of the society. They exist within the context of social and societal norms. The dominant values of the society are reflected in what types of entities are established, which social issues are addressed, and the range of service options made available to recipients. The manager of a social services agency must work within the context of competing societal interests. He or she must recognize and address some of the disempowering aspects of the society with respect to classism, racism, poverty, and ageism as well as issues associated with cultural diversity. In other words, social service organizations find themselves located within the triad of values, ethics, and discrimination. It is within this contextual environment that the manager must operate. The manager of an agency dedicated to the provision of social welfare services must find ways to bridge the gap between satisfying the demands inherent in managing the agency and optimizing the organization's response to the consumers of services.

There is considerable discussion in the literature with respect to the generalizable and transferable nature of knowledge and skills in organizational management (Gummer, 1997; Rapp & Poertner, 1992; Rimer, 1987). In general, the literature suggests that "business administration is the dominant paradigm against which all others are compared" (Patti, 2000, p. 7). The position taken here is that "social welfare management is a distinctive variant of general management," and "effective management in social welfare requires a theory and praxis tailored to the distinctive needs and characteristics of the organization" (p. 7). Although a variety of techniques and approaches can be universally applied across disciplines, an understanding of the dynamics associated with the direct interaction and input of those who are disenfranchised is often missing. Success based on strictly statistical data can, in fact, mask the actual experiences of persons who use personal social services. Patti sets forth propositions that are illustrative of what social welfare managers must address in order to produce good organizational outcomes:

1. Social welfare managers are routinely confronted with moral dilemmas that require ethically defensible decisions.
2. Management practice in the social services requires attention to mediating, reconciling, and influencing the preferences and expectations of external constituencies.
3. Social welfare managers advocate for stigmatized, devalued groups to mobilize public sentiment and resources.
4. Social welfare managers collaborate with other agencies to mobilize and focus resources on a common clientele to achieve the benefits of an enlarged pool of specialists and of improved cooperation.
5. Social welfare managers articulate values and goals that inspire the moral commitment of supporters, staff, and volunteers.
6. Social welfare managers seek measures of organizational performance that are responsive to standards of accountability imposed by funding and policy bodies while attempting to reconcile these with available resources, the unpredictable efficacy of service technologies, and the preferences of service providers and consumers.
7. Social welfare managers seek to develop supportive and empowering processes in the agency to build commitment and ownership and to maintain a climate conducive to psychological and physical health.

8. Social welfare managers must maintain some control of their programs even while they cannot be in control of them.
9. Because consumers of social services are active participants in the service experience and are largely responsible for the changes that are sought, social welfare managers must attend to how they can be directly engaged in the choice of means and outcomes of service delivery (Patti, 2000, pp. 8–15).

Even with some direction provided by the propositions previously noted, issues that further complicate the situation exist within the context of social welfare management. Because of the nature of the work, social service organizations must be responsive to the consumer of services, to the professional who delivers the services, as well as to the funding source. Often the interests of the stakeholders differ not only with regard to "what" services are offered but to "how" the services are delivered as well. The social welfare administrator must identify ways to provide leadership not only as it relates to social work professionals but also to the community.

> The problem of administrative ethics is . . . complicated. Social workers engaged in social administration practice, unlike other organizational actors, must be concerned not only with the propriety of their own conduct but with their duty to uphold the interest of the organization. (Lohmann & Lohmann, 2002, p. 469)

The pattern of interconnectedness within social service organizations requires guidelines that can serve as a framework for social administration practice. These guidelines for social work can be found in its professional code of ethics. At best, professional codes are intended to serve as guidelines for the professional behavior of those who identify themselves as members of a specific discipline or profession.

BOX 3.1 COMPETING VALUES

The Mission Street Anti-Poverty Organization (MSAPO) provides emergency food, emergency shelter, and a small substance abuse counseling program. In addition, the organization has a youth group that focuses on community development issues. Currently, the youth group is campaigning against local liquor stores that sell alcoholic beverages to teenagers. The prevalence of liquor stores in this community is perceived by residents to contribute to crime and the presence of many homeless people with substance abuse problems.

Because of the level of need in the Mission Street community, the organization is chronically short of funds. A new donor, the Harrison Family Wine Distillery, has stepped forward. This company produces cheap wine that is heavily marketed in low-income communities. Because of the low price, many homeless people purchase the Harrison Family's products. Larry Littlefeather, the executive director, must decide whether or not to accept these funds. Some members of the board believe that acceptance of this money conflicts with the organization's mission to reduce poverty, substance abuse, and homelessness. The board has requested that Larry make a written recommendation that will be reviewed at the next meeting.

- What factors should be considered in Larry's recommendation?
- What social work-related values should influence the decision-making process?
- Are specific criteria included in the NASW *Code of Ethics* that Larry can use to help him make a decision?
- What recommendation would you make to the board in this situation?

THE NATIONAL ASSOCIATION OF SOCIAL WORKERS *CODE OF ETHICS* AND MANAGEMENT PRACTICE

The National Association of Social Workers (NASW)*Code of Ethics* embodies the values of the profession. Its purpose is to help professionals identify ethical issues in practice, provide guidance in decision-making, and determine appropriate and inappropriate behaviors of members of the profession. Although social work identifies with basic societal values, differences can result in ethical problems (Lowenberg & Dolgoff, 1996). According to Lohmann and Lohmann (2002):

> Social administration is concerned not only with rights, wrongs, and the pursuit of good by an individual professional but also explicitly with how that individual may command, lead, direct, and in other ways elicit, ethical conduct from others as well. (p. 469)

The NASW *Code of Ethics* sets forth standards for professional practice and behavior. Although some standards can be described as prescriptive, others represent things to which the profession ascribes—always evolving toward a higher state of being. The profession acknowledges its commitment to the individual and the primacy of relationships within the helping process. Further, the NASW *Code of Ethics* recognizes the importance of social justice and empowerment as important domains in which value conflicts and ethical dilemmas arise. Although the Code focuses on the behavior of the individual social worker, a review of the Code suggests a broader application. Because management is perceived as providing leadership, consideration of key elements of the Code is appropriate.

Management is associated with leadership and goes beyond the effectiveness and efficiencies of organizational outcomes. Robert Dworkin (1978) indicates that the first principle of a just society is that everyone is entitled to equal concern and respect. Also included is a sense of morality, a sense of what is right and what is wrong. The question then is posed as follows: Who sanctions any entity to provide the moral compass for participants within an organization? What needs to take place within the context of personal, societal, and professional values?

Earlier in this chapter, we discussed the potential for value and ethical conflicts. We presume, sometimes based on historical documents such as the Declaration of Independence and the Constitution (1776), that the ideals espoused in those documents regarding who we are with respect to others is somehow embedded in our universal consciousness. We fail to see the fulfillment of the promise, for despite the power of the words in each of these historical documents, the promise for many is yet to be realized. The hope is that the perception of these documents as "living" will encourage each person to find himself or herself as the focus of the document's intent. In the Declaration of Independence, for example, we find the following:

> We hold these truths to be self-evident, that all men are created equal, that they are endowed by their creator with certain unalienable rights, that among these are life, liberty, and the pursuit of happiness. (*The Constitution of the United States with the Declaration of Independence,* 1973, p. 1)

The Constitution has similar idealized constructs regarding the nature of this country and its ethos and promise.

> We, the people of the United States, in order to form a more perfect union, establish justice, insure domestic tranquilly, provide for the common defense, promote the general welfare, and secure the blessings of liberty to ourselves and our posterity, do ordain and establish this Constitution for the United States of America. (*The Constitution of the United States with the Declaration of Independence* 1973, p. 11)

However, when we review those documents in light of the day-to-day interactions of its citizens, we find that we have not truly realized the dream—the ideal of what we can be.

If at the broader levels of the society there is no resolution with respect to what is right and good for all, then it would seem likely that the responsibility would fall elsewhere. It would seem to be a viable "solution" for those institutions, which are sanctioned to provide for the general well-being of members of society, to attempt addressing those issues within their sphere of influence.

We use the NASW *Code of Ethics* as an example of how larger societal ideals can be manifested in social service organizations as well as in professionals. The Preamble of the Code establishes a set of core values and parameters for the profession:

> Social workers are sensitive to cultural and ethnic diversity and strive to end discrimination, oppression, poverty, and other forms of social injustice. These activities may be in the form of direct practice, community organizing, supervision, consultation, administration, advocacy, social and political action, policy development and implementation, education, and research and evaluation. Social workers seek to enhance the capacity of people to address their own needs. Social workers also seek to promote the responsiveness of organizations, communities, and other social institutions to individuals' needs and social problems. (Reamer, 1998, p. 263)

The Preamble of the Code identifies, in addition to social justice, a set of core values for the profession that include service, integrity, competence, respecting the dignity and worth of the person, and the importance of human relationships.

We see reflected in the Preamble ideals similar to the historical documents referenced earlier. The *Code of Ethics* brings greater specificity to those areas spoken of in generalities. The intent is to provide "guidelines" that can be beneficial in the resolution or amelioration of issues related to values and ethics. The Code is essential for an organization that seeks to operate from an empowerment perspective. The six broad areas of ethical responsibility articulated in the NASW *Code of Ethics* are as follows (Reamer, 1998):

- Ethical responsibilities to clients
- Ethical responsibilities to colleagues
- Ethical responsibilities in practice settings
- Ethical responsibilities as professionals
- Ethical responsibilities to the social work profession
- Ethical responsibilities to the broader society

Each area of the Code has several standards associated with the ethical principle.

Ethical Responsibilities to Clients (Standard 1)

Ethical responsibilities to clients are concerned with social workers' relationships with individual clients, couples, families, and small groups. They focus on the nature of social workers' commitment to clients, client self-determination, informed consent, and client access to records. Additional ethical provisions in the Code pertain to the competency of social workers to work with clients and require social workers to acquire cultural competency in working with diverse groups. The Code mandates that the social worker interact with others to advocate for social diversity. Other ethical imperatives focus on social worker conflicts of interest and the protection of client privacy and confidentiality.

The Code strictly prohibits sexual relationships between social workers and clients (current and former) and clients' relatives or other individuals with whom clients maintain a close personal relationship. It also prohibits physical contact between social workers and clients, sexual harassment of clients by social workers, and social workers' use of derogatory language. The Code requires specific actions be taken by social workers with regard to client payment for services, the provision of service to clients who lack decision-making capacity, the interruption of services, and termination of services (Reamer, 1998).

Ethical principles associated with clients are perhaps the most fully developed in the NASW *Code of Ethics*. This section contains significant details that reflect the manner in which social workers relate to consumers of services. The standard includes areas such as commitment to clients, self-determination, informed consent, and competence of the professional (this list is not exhaustive; see the NASW *Code of Ethics* for full text). Ethical responsibility related to consumers is an important aspect of an empowerment-focused organization. This principle addresses a core function of what much of social work practice is about. Consideration of the consumer is essential in any empowerment-focused organization (Pearlmutter, 2002). Social service organizations should make provisions to address all of these issues within their organizational policies. As an example, consider Standard 1.12: Derogatory Language. The standard states the following:

> Social workers should not use derogatory language in their written or verbal communications to or about clients. Social workers should use accurate and respectful language in all communications to and about clients. (Reamer, 1998, p. 92)

Words leave lasting impressions on those who are identified in terms that may be described as derogatory. Terms not intended to adversely describe an individual may have unintended negative consequences. For example, terms used in the 1960s may take on different meanings in 2004. Consider the way groups describe themselves—Black, African American, Afro-American; Chicano, Hispanic, or Mexican American—the variations within groups, and the way positive terms become negative over time. Is this a serious issue? It depends upon to whom we address the question. One approach might be to elicit from respondents how they identify themselves.

Social workers are required to maintain client/consumer records. In addition to the factual aspects of an encounter with the consumer, highly subjective observations are often made by social workers. Value-laden words can be used that suggest or ascribe some behavior or trait to the consumer that can be considered derogatory. Describing someone as "hostile," for example, rather than describing the behavior that is considered hostile feeds the assumptions of those who read the record. The record sets the tone and ascribes certain attributes to an individual that may or may not be true.

It is the responsibility of the organization to set the standard. The standard should be consistent with the ethical principle. For example, the use of open-ended intake forms that do not force people into specific ethnic or racial categories might be helpful. The organization also sets the standard for process notes. Supervisors should include, as a part of the supervisory process, some review of records or case notes. The content of client records is subject to review by others, particularly quality assurance teams. The content of the record speaks volumes in relation to what the organization does, but it also provides insight into how the organization views the people it serves.

Ethical Responsibilities to Colleagues (Standard 2)

The principle on ethical responsibilities to colleagues is concerned with social workers' relationships with professional colleagues, particularly other social workers. They are concerned with treating colleagues with respect, handling shared confidential information, interdisciplinary collaboration, disputes involving colleagues, consultations, referrals for services, sexual relationships with and sexual harassment of colleagues, impairment and incompetence of colleagues, and unethical conduct of colleagues (Reamer, 1998).

Social work as a profession, in general, requires collaboration among colleagues. This works not only to benefit the consumer but the organization and individual practitioners as well. Collaboration is often difficult. Social workers come to the profession with a passion for helping others, making a difference, and even changing the world. At the same time, ideology and philosophical orientations may be in conflict with those of other colleagues. The conflict derives from a sense of how to address an issue and the choice of strategies or interventions that are most appropriate. It becomes a "means" and "ends" scenario. The ideologies are steeped in values that can be difficult to resolve. Conversely, there is an expectation that professionals will behave in a manner befitting their positions. Social work professionals are expected to take the high road in their interactions with each other.

An organization that focuses on empowerment practice will attempt to ensure that interactions among colleagues remain civil. Such an organization will attend to interpersonal interactions that are disruptive, create inefficiencies, and impact service quality. The organizational environment needs to be supportive and respectful of all members of the organization. Not only do social workers need to protect consumers from derogatory language, they also should refrain from unwarranted, negative criticism of colleagues. Standard 2.01(b) defines unwarranted criticism as "demeaning comments that refer to colleagues' level of competence or to individuals' attributes such as race, ethnicity, national origin, color, sex, sexual orientation, age, marital status, political belief, religion, and mental or physical disability" (Reamer, 1998, p. 113).

From a management perspective, it is difficult to know some of the day-to-day interactions of personnel. These interactions can have a significant influence on the operation of the organization. Criticism can create discord among personnel and create an environment with little trust or collaboration. The organization, through its management structure, must develop mechanisms for handling interpersonal conflicts resulting from criticism in order to prevent low morale among employees. When employee morale is an issue, the consequences impact consumers of services.

Another area under ethical responsibilities to colleagues of concern to management practice is that of unethical behaviors. Standard 2.11(b) states that social workers should be familiar with the policies established by their employers for handling situations related to the unethical behavior of colleagues. They also should be familiar with the regulations and complaint procedures established by state licensing boards as well as the complaint processes established by NASW and other professional organizations.

The organization must make known to all of its employees and consumers of services what is deemed to be unethical behavior. Violations should have consequences. This particular aspect of the Code is extremely difficult especially because it reflects values that sometimes are not universally held by workers. In-service training on the organization's position on standards of behavior should be required of all employees on a regularly scheduled basis. It is important that management participate in these activities.

Ethical Responsibilities in Practice Settings (Standard 3)

Ethical responsibilities in practice settings are concerned with social workers' relationships in social services agencies and other work settings. They concern issues related to supervision and consultation, education and training, performance evaluation, client records, billing, client transfer, administration, continuing education and staff development, commitments to employers, and labor–management disputes (Reamer, 1998).

Ethical responsibilities in practice settings go to the core of organizational functioning. It addresses the management aspects of the Code. To be an empowerment-focused organization, management must attend to the nuts and bolts of ethical requirements in the organization. It is hard to imagine an aspect of organizational functioning that does not raise issues for those who may be inside and those outside the agency. According to Reamer (2000), "Administrators face ethical dilemmas involving program design, administrative policy, organizational design, management decisions, and program development" (p. 73). The social work profession, for example, widely uses supervision and consultation. It is a practice that is intended to benefit the organization at every level. This aspect of the profession encourages dialogue among workers that is intended to enhance employee functioning and improve the provision of consumer services. This practice also creates a transparency within the organization regarding its overall mission and goals. In sharing information via supervision and consultation, the organization is able to maintain openness and a sense of a commonly held organizational focus. Although this certainly does not address all the ethical dilemmas faced by managers, at minimum it is a means of keeping lines of communication open.

> Some of the most common ethical dilemmas emanate from hierarchical relationships that produce a clash between administrative routines and professional, personal, or democratic values. Day-to-day decisions highlight the fact that even apparently routine decisions about budgeting and financial issues, personnel procedures, marketing strategies, supervisory styles, and reporting functions involve ethical issue and consequences. (Reamer, 2000, p. 73)

Without adequate resources, even the most empowerment-oriented organization can lose its focus. Standard 3.07(a) states: "Social work administrators should advocate within and outside their agencies for adequate resources to meet clients' needs" (Reamer, 1998, p. 174).

There is little doubt that a manager must address the adequacy of resources within the organization in order to fulfill the organization's mission. Although this is an expectation of the role of management, it nevertheless can create the potential for ethical conflict. As the expectation to find additional resources is posed, management's attention is diverted from organizational operations to external sources that may be available to provide fiscal support. In times of fiscal conservatism, this generally means competition among organizations for scarce resources. Making the case for a particular population to the exclusion of another is an ethical dilemma of significance. The advocacy function, on the other hand, is a viable strategy in making the case for one's organization. Having clearly defined and agreed upon eligibility criteria is helpful when dealing with resource allocation. The manager must consider the source of external funds and determine whether the acceptance of such funds will compromise the program's mission and goals.

An organization with a commitment to empowerment must consider how it carries out its mission. Sometimes there is organizational shift. If this shift occurs, employees may find that they are in conflict with the organization in which they are employed. Standard 3.09(a) states: "Social workers generally should adhere to commitments made to employers and employing organizations" (Reamer, 1998, p. 183).

Organizations want loyalty from their employees. There is an expectation that an employee will not undermine the agency's functioning. The reputation of the organization is important to those who are employed by it and to those who are served by it. Also of note is the damage done to the social work profession when employees malign the organization. The reputation of many is impugned by such actions. Conversely, the organization must fulfill its mandate to serve in the capacity designated. When the actions of the organization are harmful to recipients of services, it is the duty of the social worker to uphold the ethical standards of the profession. An organization that understands the potential to drift from its mission and goals will build into its policies and procedures mechanisms that will help the organization stay focused.

Ethical Responsibilities as Professionals (Standard 4)

The section on ethical responsibilities as professionals is concerned with social workers' professional competence, discrimination, private conduct, dishonesty, fraud, deception, and impairment; misrepresentation and solicitation of clients; and acknowledgement of work done by social workers and others (Reamer, 1998). These ethical issues can be associated with "truth in lending" requirements used in business, law, and medicine. In other words, what is presented to consumers relative to their expectations and the qualifications of the service provider? Standard 4.01(a) states: "Social workers should accept responsibility or employment only on the basis of existing competence or the intention to acquire the necessary competence" (Reamer, 1998, p. 201).

Many organizations represent social work as a job classification and not a professional discipline. In such situations, the organization undermines the profession and represents those who are performing functions associated with social work practice as social workers. Even though employers may have a difficult time finding a full complement of graduates from accredited schools of social work to fill vacancies within their organizations, it is their responsibility to honestly represent who is providing services. The practice of classifying persons with non–social work degrees as social workers sets poor precedence and, in fact, is an ethical issue. Consumers of services have a right to know who is providing the services they need. The ethical issue extends beyond the consumer of services. The practice has resulted in the social work profession's inability to define what it is. The profession is acknowledged as being valuable in the delivery of services to persons in need, but its image is tarnished by the actions of those for whom social work is merely a job description. The empowerment-focused organization accurately presents its workers to consumers, to the profession of social work, and to the broader community.

In essence, many organizations are in violation of the NASW *Code of Ethics* with respect to the aforementioned practices. Standard 4.06(c) states: "Social workers should claim only those relevant professional credentials they actually possess and take steps to correct any inaccuracies or misrepresentations of their credentials by others" (Reamer, 1998, p. 215).

The Code speaks to the actions and behaviors of social workers. Should the Code be applicable to those who present themselves as social workers? It would seem that if one were identified by title as a member of a professional group, the standards applied should be equivalent. The organization is ethically and perhaps legally responsible for how it presents itself and its staff. An empowerment-focused organization presents itself honestly to all members of the community.

Ethical Responsibilities to the Social Work Profession (Standard 5)

Ethical responsibilities to the profession are concerned with issues related to the integrity of the social work profession and of social work evaluation and research (Reamer, 1998). The integrity of the profession of social work is the responsibility of social workers and those who value the role social work plays in the broader society. Organizations that focus on the empowerment of its stakeholders complement social work values and ethics. Social service organizations have the potential to promote change. The professionals and others employed by them represent a wealth of knowledge and understanding relative to the needs of persons served and those in need of services. Management can benefit from the actions of those who engage in activities that promote the social work profession, including "teaching, research, consultation, service, legislative testimony, presentations in the community, and participation in their professional organizations" (Reamer, 1998, pp. 225–226).

The empowerment-focused organization connects with its community. Its involvement via its staff promotes the interest of the social work profession as well as its own concerns. Outreach efforts move the organization beyond its walls to the larger community. It fosters relationships and encourages involvement. This involvement is especially important to the organization's image and the perception of its responsiveness to its constituencies.

Ethical Responsibilities to the Broader Society (Standard 6)

Ethical responsibilities to the broader society are concerned with issues related to the general welfare of society, promoting public participation in shaping social policies and institutions, social workers' involvement in public emergencies, and social workers' involvement in social and political action (Reamer, 1998).With a focus on social welfare, our discussion comes full circle. The social work perspective on problems is holistic, is based in an environmental context, acknowledges strengths, and embraces the primacy of relationships with the belief that people have the capacity to grow, learn, and change. Standard 6.01 states:

> Social workers should advocate for living conditions conducive to the fulfillment of basic human needs and should promote social, economic, political, and cultural values and institutions that are compatible with the realization of social justice. (Reamer, 1998, p. 247)

What is perhaps social work's greatest strength and its greatest weakness is its holistic perspective of the people served by the profession. Because social workers are educated to take the broad view, limiting the scope of practice is difficult. Rather than compartmentalizing people into categories that fit the service sector's or organization's focus, social work views the person within his or her environment.

Social service organizations are created to serve and address specific populations or issues. Service organizations cannot be everything to everyone. On the other hand, management can facilitate the empowerment of its workers and recipients of services by allowing problem identification to find the locus of concern within the broadest context possible. In identifying the similarities in the problems shared by individuals across a range of differences, we promote the common good. We limit the isolation and stigmatization of persons in need of services. We honor and affirm a commitment to social justice, which is foundational to empowerment.

The NASW *Code of Ethics* is intended to serve as guidelines for social work practice. Although administration and management practice are not discussed within each of the standards of the Code, the applicability of each standard can be applied to management practice. Consideration of the constructs of values, ethics, and social justice is critical to management practice. Organizations that seek to function within an empowerment perspective must be rooted in principles that are meaningful and are shared by all members.

BOX 3.2 INTERPRETING THE NASW *CODE OF ETHICS:* WHEN PRINCIPLES CONFLICT

In order to address problems associated with service quality in the Northwest Women's Shelter, Pang has met with a group of current and former clients. Members of this group have complained that the shelter manager rigidly enforces shelter rules, such as imposing a curfew on residents, limiting outside phone calls and visitors, and imposing sanctions on adult residents who refuse kitchen duties or who do not properly control their children. The clients have suggested that they would be more likely to comply with these rules if they have a role in developing them. Megan, the shelter manager, tells Pang that she will not work with clients to develop new rules. She believes that the current rules are adequate. Megan feels that some of the rules, such as the curfew and restrictions on phone calls and visitors, are necessary to protect the safety and confidentiality of the clients—women and children who have experienced domestic violence. She also views these policies as necessary for protecting staff members who may be at risk if batterers are able to gain access to the shelter. Pang tells Megan that despite her objections, she must assume responsibility for convening a task force of current and former clients, shelter staff, and a few board members to review and possibly revise the rules. Megan feels torn between her responsibilities to staff, her responsibilities for client safety, and her loyalty to the shelter.

- What ethical principles in the *Code of Ethics* apply to this situation?
- Under these circumstances, what should Megan do? What are the benefits and risks of the following options?

  1. Resign from the shelter.
  2. Put off convening the task force. Megan should continue to advocate for her position.
  3. Comply with Pang's request. Establish the task force and find a way to reconcile the client demands with safety and confidentiality concerns.
  4. Refuse to comply. Accept the consequences of noncompliance.

- Are there any additional alternative steps that Megan can take to address this problem?

SUMMARY

In this chapter, we attempted to show the relationship among social justice, values, and ethics in management practice within social service organizations. We discussed the influence of societal values on the management of social service organizations. The NASW *Code of Ethics* was presented as guidelines that inform management practice and the uniqueness of social welfare management. In Chapters 4 and 5, we examine how values and ethics are operationalized in the development of organization structure and through the inclusion of organization clients and staff members in organization decision-making.

QUESTIONS FOR CLASS DISCUSSION

1. What do you view as the single most important ethical issue facing the social work profession today?
2. Should we be concerned with social justice as an issue? If yes, why? If no, why not?
3. Which social work skills would you use to address issues of social injustice?
4. Select three of the dominant values identified in the chapter and discuss how are they reflected in your agency's policies and service delivery.
5. Describe a situation in which you were faced with an ethical dilemma (you can use your role as student, worker, client, or volunteer).

SAMPLE ASSIGNMENTS

1. Conduct a participant observation. Sit in the waiting room of a service-providing organization. Observe who the clients are. How are they addressed? Are differential engagement strategies used? Describe the setting. Can you or should you draw conclusions regarding ethical/values issues based on your observations? Discuss your observations.
2. Using poverty as an example of a social problem, identify some of its causes. What role do values play in how the problem is defined and in society's response to the issue?

CHAPTER 4

The Structure of Social Service Organizations: Where and How Do People Find Help?

When people need help with personal or family problems, assistance is provided either through the context of an interpersonal relationship with another individual or group or within a larger structure called an *organization*. As described in Chapter 2, an organization is an entity that contains clear boundaries that delineate organization members from nonmembers. Organizations also contain mechanisms that allow individuals to work collaboratively to produce a good or service. Formal social service organizations operate within the context of a set of rules called *policies and procedures* that standardize the way in which assistance is provided to qualified applicants. In this chapter, we examine

- The context of help giving, including the provision of goods by friends, relatives, and neighbors and the provision of assistance by formal organizations.
- Three types of formal social service organizations: public, nonprofit, and for-profit.
- Decision-making structures in hierarchical, social movement, feminist, ethnic, and faith-based organizations.

These various organizational structures may enhance or impede the empowerment of organization participants, program beneficiaries, and community residents.

INFORMAL HELP AMONG FRIENDS, RELATIVES, AND NEIGHBORS

The provision of social services often involves interaction between individuals or groups who need material goods or emotional support and someone who can provide goods or services (Gilligan, 1988). The service provider can be another individual, a small group of people, or an organization. Much of what we think of as social services or support is provided outside the context of formal organizations. Studies of how people obtain assistance in low-income communities indicate that low-income individuals and families provide a great deal of help to relatives, friends, and neighbors. Day care, emotional support, emergency shelter, car repairs, and food are types of help typically given to others (Neighbors & Taylor, 1985; Stack, 1974). Many of these helping relationships are reciprocal, involving an exchange of resources and a group or network of people with close personal or familial ties (Delgado, 1996). For example, a household might exchange baby-sitting help with one neighbor in exchange for transportation to a health clinic from one neighbor and baby clothes from another. According to Figueira-McDonough (2001), "exchange can be measured by the patterns of visiting, frequency, and spread of telephoning among residents of the locality, congregation in public places, membership in local informal groups, and the level of sociability among neighbors" (p. 18). In some ethnic communities, helpers include traditional folk healers and shamans who may provide emotional support and health or mental health care to individuals and families (Patterson & Marsiglia, 2000). It should be noted, however, that although informal helping often occurs in middle- and upper-income households, low-income or traditional ethnic communities often rely on informal help because it can take place without the use of monetary resources and reaches people who may be reluctant to approach, or are unfamiliar with, formal social service organizations (Iglehart & Becerra, 2000; Oliker, 1998).

Informal help often occurs within the context of interpersonal networks, groups of people who interact with one another to exchange assistance. These informal networks also provide emotional or social support to members by helping people to form strong bonds with one another. According to Miley, O'Melia, and DuBois (2004), "support occurs when relationships are based on reciprocity, mutuality, and shared power in an atmosphere where people can offer what they have to offer and receive the resources they seek" (p. 352). Wellman and Wortley (1990) argue that these informal networks are critical for creating strong links between individuals and their communities. Informal networks

> Provide social support that transcends narrow reciprocity. They make up much of the social capital people use to deal with daily life, seize opportunities, and reduce uncertainties. They underpin the informal arrangements crucial for a household's survival, expansion, and reproduction. (p. 559)

INFORMAL ORGANIZATIONS

As described in Chapter 2, organizations are often characterized as either informal or formal. The strength of informal networks and individual attachment to community can also be measured by examining participation in informal organizations (such as block clubs or sports teams), volunteerism, and participation in elections and other forms of public life (Figueira-McDonough, 2001; Putnam, 2000). Informal organizations can be defined as groups that form spontaneously and that work toward a goal without a formal structure or governance process (Venkatesh, 1997). An informal helping network becomes an organization when members come together on a regular basis to address a common problem and set up some type of mechanism to address it. Regular meeting times, designation of a meeting place (such as a home, local park, or church basement), and an interested group of potential members may be all that is needed to convert an informal network to an organization. Informal organizations have small budgets and mostly volunteer staff. Boundaries between service providers and recipients may not be distinct. Therefore relationships among members often can be characterized as partnerships based on reciprocity rather than as power-dependency relationships (Milofsky, 1988). In most informal organizations, there may be a designated leader but no formal decision-making structure.

The term often used to describe organizations based on mutual exchange is *self-help groups*. Self-help groups can be defined as "actions and activities undertaken by collectives and/or other groups that result in the creation and organization of a service delivery entity (a service, a program, or an agency) that provides direct services" (Iglehart & Becerra, 2000, p. 7). According to Johnson and Johnson (2003), people join these groups because they face a common problem. Generally, there is no monetary cost associated with membership. However, members are expected to help one another.

Whereas some local self-help groups are affiliated with national self-help organizations (such as Alcoholics Anonymous), many self-help groups come together spontaneously to address common problems. For example, local residents may come together to start a neighborhood watch to prevent gang violence, or parents of autistic children may collaboratively explore options for obtaining group home and other support services as their children move to adulthood.

Many of these organizations will retain their informal structure indefinitely. However, some groups will wish to raise funds and hire staff (Milofsky, 1988; Perlmutter, 1990), and to do so they will have to satisfy numerous Federal and state requirements. For example, to raise funds the group must apply to the Federal government for tax-exempt status and obtain a tax identification number so that payroll taxes for each employee can be paid. Incorporation as a nonprofit requires that the organization establish a formal board of directors. Hiring staff mandates the maintenance of adequate payroll records and the monitoring of expenditures by the board. Taking these steps changes the nature of the organization from an informal arrangement among friends and acquaintances to a formal, structured entity with appointed or elected decision-makers. The placement of policy decision-making in the hands of the board both legitimizes the organization and makes the board accountable to the public for the organization's work. However, this action also imposes significant interpersonal changes on organization participants. Relationships among participants are less likely to be friendships. Only a small group of people in the organization (members of the board or the board president) are involved in decision-making. Consequently, some members who had helped make decisions or had delivered services may actually lose their voice in organization decision-making and have less power when the group is restructured as a formal organization.

The establishment of the board and the process of hiring staff members who will be accountable to the board impose a hierarchical structure on the organization. The creation of a standardize set of policies needed for staff supervision and service delivery mandates the imposition of some degree of bureaucracy on the organization. In addition, the acceptance of funds from outside sources (individual donors, government bodies, or private foundations) will remove from the hands of the membership some of the decisions regarding the organization and the people it helps (Smith & Lipsky, 1993).

FORMAL ORGANIZATIONS

Some self-help groups retain their original identity, structure, and purpose, but others eventually become established, formal organizations (Iglehart & Becerra, 2000). For example, many social service organizations are established as nonprofit corporations under the U.S. tax code. Formal, nonprofit organizations have boards of directors, a designated administrator (executive director), and nonprofit registration with the state and/or Internal Revenue Service. Organizational participants have designated roles and responsibilities. Distinct boundaries exist between service providers and recipients. Venkatesh (1997) defines a formal organization as an entity that has an established structure, and the delivery of its services are "expected (i.e., both recurrent and predicted) and falls under some set of understood—legal or agreed on—guidelines" (p. 78). Other characteristics of formal organizations include a written statement of purpose or mission and a structured governance process with designated leaders (Norlin & Chess, 1997). The three basic types of formal organizations are public, nonprofit, and for-profit. Each has a distinct type of governing structure and resource attainment process.

PUBLIC ORGANIZATIONS

Public social service organizations are government agencies. They can be branches of Federal, state, county, or local governments. Except in small jurisdictions, government agencies almost always conform to Weber's definition of bureaucracy, with multiple layers of supervisory staff responsible for overseeing front-line workers. They compose part of the executive branch of government. Under the leadership of a chief executive (president, governor, county executive officer, or mayor), these agencies implement legislation passed by Congress, state legislatures, county boards, or city or towns. Consequently, legislatures or members of oversight boards are responsible for monitoring the operation of these public agencies. Staff must be accountable to the public as well as to elected officials. Much of the government's focus in recent years has been to limit expenditures by government agencies and to minimize benefits provided to individuals and groups who may be perceived as unworthy of assistance. Consequently, funding for services to low-income people often is reduced during periods of fiscal uncertainty or weak public support for social welfare expenditures (Jansson, 1999).

NONPROFIT ORGANIZATIONS

Many of the agencies that provide assistance to people in need are nonprofit organizations. Nonprofit organizations are groups that are privately incorporated under the Federal tax code and state laws. All revenues generated by these organizations can be used only to maintain the organization and provide services or engage in activities that will benefit the public. No board member or staff person can legally receive a portion of the organization's profits. Nonprofit organizations are also referred to as voluntary organizations, nongovernmental organizations (NGOs), and community-based organizations (CBOs).

Nonprofits are commonly believed to be more trustworthy and able to deliver better quality services than can government agencies simply because nonprofits must verify that their mission is to enhance the public good in order to qualify for tax-exempt status (Ferris, 1993). These organizations are also perceived to be more flexible, more likely to introduce new and innovative services, and better able to alter the delivery of services to meet individual needs (Smith & Lipsky, 1993).

Nonprofit organizations are governed by independent boards of directors (generally business, professional, or religious leaders and neighborhood residents) who have an interest in ensuring that services are provided to particular communities or population groups. Board members are legally required to be accountable to state and federal governments for how organization funds are used; they also are expected to make sure that the organization is accountable to the community (see Chapter 5). In some nonprofit organizations, the board is elected by dues-paying members and is expected to represent the interest of these members or to provide direct benefits to them.

Nonprofit organizations are formed when interested people come together as a group and take action to meet a goal, setting up a formal governance structure to do so. As described earlier, any informal organization may evolve into a formal, nonprofit organization. Perlmutter (1990) identifies three stages of a typical organization's life cycle:

1. *Self-Interest:* The organization is formed to address the interests and problems of members. Emphasis is placed on providing help to as many of the people identified in the organization's mission as possible.
2. *Professionalism:* Factors in the organization's external environment (e.g., pressure to obtain government or foundation funds) contribute to an emphasis on improving service quality and hiring organization staff. Policies and procedures become standardized, and staff members make more of the decisions. The role of the board is reduced.
3. *Social Interest:* The organization broadens its mission in terms of clients served and social problems addressed. The board is actively involved in setting policy for the organization; an emphasis is placed on offering more service and retaining the organization's ability to offer quality programs.

There has been much debate in the literature on nonprofits about why these private organizations are needed to deliver services. For example, do these organizations represent a failure on the part of the government or the economic market place to deliver services to people in need? Should nonprofit groups be the primary provider of services (Salamon, 1995)? Often the answer to this question is dependent upon political philosophy. For some people, private provision of services is preferable to "big government" that taxes the public for "Cadillac" services; others maintain that providing a safety net for the poor should be a primary role of the government (Gibelman & Demone, 2003; Hefetz & Warner, 2004).

As described in Chapter 2, most nonprofit organizations that provide services to people in need do not charge money for their services. Consequently, nonprofits must secure their funding from government agencies, foundation grants, corporate donors, or individuals. The Independent Sector, an organization that conducts research on nonprofit organizations, estimates that 31% of the funding for all nonprofit charitable, social welfare, and faith-based organizations comes from government (Independent Sector, 2001). It should be noted that not all nonprofit organizations provide services to the less fortunate. Some nonprofits advocate on behalf of others or campaign for social change. Nonprofits can include churches, private hospitals, schools, museums, and other groups that promote arts or culture.

FOR-PROFIT ORGANIZATIONS

Formal, for-profit organizations are businesses that operate to make money. The primary decision-maker is the owner(s) or the corporate board of directors. Profits may be distributed to shareholders or retained by the owner. In the social services, for-profit providers can include day care centers, group homes, residential substance abuse or mental health facilities, hospitals, nursing homes, and job training programs (Gronbjerg, Chen, & Stagner, 1995). In contrast to nonprofit organizations, the owner or owners of a for-profit corporation are not required to be accountable to the community, although they must pay federal, state, and local taxes on any revenues and follow government regulations when they conduct business. Because the purpose of for-profit organizations is to make money, they must only convince potential customers that their service is of good quality, is at a low price, and is preferable to similar services. Without government constraints to provide services to benefit public welfare, for-profit organizations have greater incentives than do nonprofits and public agencies to keep the cost of service low (Smith & Lipsky, 1993).

For-profits can sell their services to middle- and upper-income individuals who can pay out of pocket or use insurance to pay for some types of services (e.g., health or mental health care). In addition, government may reimburse the costs of care for low-income individuals. Medicaid and Medicare are examples of two Federal programs that are used to reimburse private physicians, hospitals, and nursing homes for individual services. Because of government efforts to limit costs and efforts made by for-profit providers to submit low bids for contracts, the amount of service offered by for-profits may be low or conform to protocols that limit the amount of services provided to individuals. For example, state and Federal governments contract with private health maintenance organizations (HMOs) to deliver health and mental health services for some of the people who receive Medicaid and Medicare. HMOs use managed care plans to reduce costs by limiting and standardizing the care available to individuals who may have different problems and needs (Mordock, 1996; Shera, 1996).

THE MANAGEMENT STRUCTURE OF TRADITIONAL NONPROFIT SOCIAL SERVICE ORGANIZATIONS: HIERARCHICAL LEADERSHIP

Although nonprofit organizations often are not as large as public agencies, the nonprofits often are structured to resemble bureaucracies. One leader or a small group of administrators and/or board members make most of the decisions for the organization. The leader or leaders delegate authority to one or more layers of administrative staff who are then responsible for managing the work of the people below them in the organizational hierarchy. However, these administrators are accountable to the leaders above them in the hierarchy for the behavior and productivity of the people they supervise. Information, power, and decision-making authority originate with the leader or director and then are disseminated to people at lower levels in the organizational structure.

Except in very small organizations, administrators have very little direct contact with clientele. Interaction with clients, assessment of client problems, and delivery of services are activities usually delegated to front-line workers in social service organizations. Because most low-income clients receive free services and consequently are dependent on workers for the things they wish to obtain from the organization, their status in the organization is very low. Consequently, a hierarchy of status and power in organizations can be constructed. The group with the greatest degree of power is the administrative staff, followed by front-line workers. Clients in traditional organizations have the least amount of power in traditional social service organizations. Often clients, by virtue of their position in the organization hierarchy, have limited contact with the

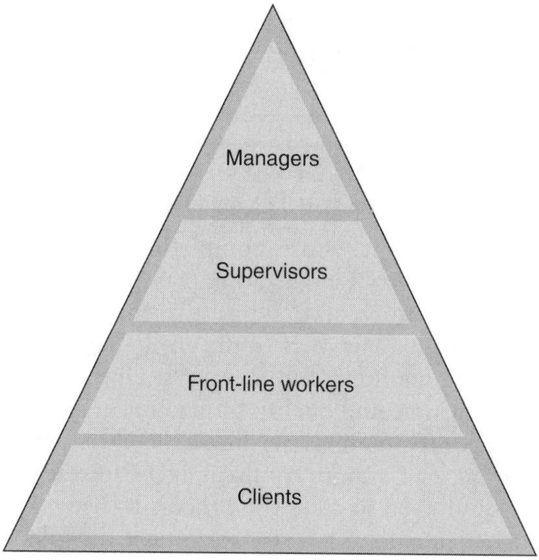

Figure 4.1 Staff composition and the concentration of power in a hierarchy.

administrative staff or other organization decision-makers (such as board members) who are responsible for designing and evaluating client services. Limited access to these decision-makers makes it less likely that clients will receive services that actually meet their needs (Figure 4.1).

Another characteristic of traditional social service organizations is related to their mission or purpose. Traditional organizations are fairly conservative in terms of their purpose and who they serve. As noted by Netting and O'Connor (2003), traditional organizations "deliver socially acceptable programs to socially acceptable clients in need" (p. 12). Funding sources and the agency mission may be products of both long-standing patterns of operation as well as public opinion and the preferences of those groups permitted to have input into how services are designed and allocated. Board members, administrators, and individual donors in such organizations typically are prominent business people, professionals, or philanthropists (society). Traditional organizations generally have long life spans and receive funding from government and foundation sources that is both adequate and stable. Because of the dominance of powerful board members and external funders, the clients who most need services are not consulted about how and when the services should be offered. Often these clients are those less likely to receive services or to benefit from programs that meet their needs. Consequently, the demand for service from groups excluded from the service delivery system will stimulate the development of new or alternative organizations to meet their needs.

BOX 4.1 ORGANIZATION DEVELOPMENT: CONVERTING AN INFORMAL GROUP TO A FORMAL ORGANIZATION

Keisha is an MSW student who is completing an internship with the Mission Street Anti-Poverty Organization (MSAPO). One of her responsibilities involves providing staff support to the organization's young mother's self-help group. Members of the group have informally started a baby-sitting exchange for group members. One of the members has reported that the group could qualify for a grant to provide information and referral services for families needing child care. Although MSAPO has agreed to serve as a temporary fiscal agent for the group, the new organization would need to start the process to become a tax-exempt nonprofit. Current members of group support this plan in principle. However, there is concern about the impact of creating a formal organization and the responsibilities it would place on members.

Keisha has been asked to conduct research on the impact of incorporation.

- What should she tell the members about the benefits and risks associated with changing the organization from an informal self-help group to a formal organization?
- How would conversion from an informal group to a formal organization change relationships among members?
- What new responsibilities would new members need to assume?

ALTERNATIVE MANAGEMENT STRUCTURES: SOCIAL MOVEMENT, FEMINIST, ETHNIC, AND FAITH-BASED ORGANIZATIONS

Often communities and population groups that are excluded as clients or decision-makers from participation in social service systems will come together to develop their own alternative social service agencies (Netting & O'Connor, 2003). Organizational structure and responsibility for decision-making are quite different in traditional versus alternative organizations (Table 4.1). For example, one of the purposes of alternative organizations is to increase the power of their members, especially those people who may be excluded from decision-making or from receiving benefits from traditional social service organizations. The emergence of

Table 4.1 Comparison of Traditional and Alternative Organizations

Characteristic	Traditional Organizations	Alternative Organizations
Clients	Deliver socially acceptable programs to socially acceptable clients	Formed to advocate for or deliver services to groups whose needs are not met elsewhere
Leadership	Have designated administrators within a defined structure	May be inspired by a charismatic leader or social movement with the ability to mobilize volunteers and staff
Service delivery	Have established service structure and protocols	Must establish service delivery approaches with input from clients
Size	Medium to large	Small
Staff	Staff salaries are roughly equal to those of other agencies	Heavily dependent on volunteers and staff who are paid low wages
Values	Those of the dominant culture	Values are different from those of the dominant culture

Source: Netting, F. E., & O'Connor, M. K. (2003). *Organization practice.* Boston: Pearson Education.

organizations that are not part of the traditional service delivery system requires that the organizations obtain resources, often from untapped or innovative sources, to support them. Members of excluded communities often draw on their own strengths, histories, and cultural traditions to develop new models of organization governance (Chow, 1999; Yoshihama & Carr, 2002).

Pearlmutter (1988) identifies four characteristics commonly associated with alternative agencies:

1. A group of people committed to starting a new organization
2. A clear mission for the new organization
3. A value framework inherent in the organization mission and in its delivery of services that is substantially different from values espoused by traditional agencies
4. A charismatic leader who can recruit volunteers and solicit support for the new organization

These organizations often struggle to survive in resource-poor environments and, during the start up phase, may have difficulty attracting monetary and other resources needed for operation (Netting & O'Connor, 2003). They may rely heavily on volunteer and nonprofessional staff. Alternative agencies can take on a variety of purposes and structures. However, four primary types of alternative organizations with distinct structures are social movement organizations, feminist organizations, ethnic social service organizations, and faith-based social service providers.

Social Movement Organizations

Social movement organizations are groups formed explicitly to advocate for social change or to address common problems that affect specific groups of individuals. Social movements are "coalitions of loosely connected groups that attempt to change a social target" (Swank & Clapp, 1999, p. 50). There are at least three types of social movements: collections of organizations that work to increase the civil, social, and economic rights of historically disadvantaged groups; groups that are oriented toward improving the quality of life for others (e.g., children's advocacy groups; environmental and animal rights groups); and organizations that support a return to traditional or conservative values (Hyde, 1994; Rothman, 1996). Service-oriented self-help groups that develop in response to public perceptions of need that establish linkages among one another (e.g., substance abuse treatment groups, acquired immunodeficiency syndrome [AIDS] treatment programs, and homeless shelters) also can be defined as organizations formed in response to social movements (Milofsky, 1988). Alternatively, some self-help organizations focus on changing communities, legislation, social policies, or institutions rather than service delivery. Consequently, social action–oriented social movement organizations may range from community organizations to local groups that represent the interests of disadvantaged populations to statewide and national groups that lobby state government and Congress. Many of these groups are affiliates or local chapters of national advocacy organizations or are members of broad-based coalitions that fight for social change (Mizrahi & Rosenthal, 1993).

The dichotomy between organizations that are initiated to support movements fighting for change and self-help organizations that respond to social movements promoting resolution of individual problems is often described in terms of cause advocacy versus service provision. Rights-oriented organizations devote most of their energy to advocacy, whereas service organizations use most of their resources to meet individual needs rather than to address social problems. Often the service-driven organizations have greater success in obtaining government, foundation, and other private sources of funds to meet their goals.

Advocacy-oriented organizations may threaten the political status quo and consequently may not be able to obtain government funds.

According to McCarthy and Walker (2004), membership recruitment and retention pose special changes to organizations that advocate for low-income people. When social change–oriented groups become formal organizations, one of their primary tasks is to constantly identify and solicit new members. Monetary, volunteer, and staff resources are needed to engage in one-on-one outreach activities, print flyers, advertise in the media, and hold workshops or engage in protests. Consequently, social movement organizations may devote a high percentage of their budgets to these and other activities that help attract members. Little money may be left over to hire staff; many of these organizations rely on leaders who are not paid and on volunteer staff. Charismatic leaders, slogans and other symbols that solicit empathy for the cause, and committed and idealistic volunteers can often compensate for limited access to a stable funding source. Wealthy or celebrity donors, media coverage, public support of the cause, and successful accomplishment of advocacy goals also help social movement organizations recruit new members and attain financial stability (Hardina, 2002; Jasper & Paulsen, 1995; Wolfson, 1995).

Another important characteristic of cause-related social movement organizations is that, unlike most service-oriented self-help groups, members retain some control over the organization after it takes on a formal structure. Members are not limited to a dues-paying role. They also elect board members and officers, are often consulted on policy matters, are involved in social action-related activities undertaken by the organization, and are prepared or trained to assume future leadership roles in the organization (McCarthy & Walker, 2004). However, social movement organizations that recruit many members or obtain large donations from government or other external sources also are at risk of limiting the role of supporters in decision-making. Larger memberships may make consulting with all participants about important decisions more difficult and time-consuming. External funding sources may take on an important role in determining organization priorities, thereby limiting the amount of input grassroots supporters have in the organization (Guo, 2004).

Feminist Organizations

Feminist organizations are explicitly created to address inequities that women experience in obtaining adequate services to meet their needs (Hyde, 1994). Feminist organizations can include organizations formed solely to advocate for the rights of women, forums for raising the consciousness about the problems women face in a male-dominated society, and social service agencies that provide nontraditional services to a client population consisting primarily of women (Hyde, 1989). For example, a feminist social service organization could help women find employment in jobs typically held by men, such as construction-related work or management positions in large corporations.

As described in Chapter 2, one of the basic assumptions of feminist management is that hierarchical decision-making in organizations is based on male-oriented norms that value structures that use sanctions and authority to make people work (Iannello, 1992). Feminists believe that these practices promote conflict and are often used to exclude women from full participation in decision-making. From a feminist perspective, organizations should ideally operate on a partnership model, establishing equalitarian relationships among all organization participants. Therefore most organization decisions should be made through consensus and cooperation.

Feminist organizations generally have difficulty raising adequate funds from government and private sources. Consequently, they often operate with small numbers of paid staff and volunteer labor. Often they must rely on ideology and politics rather than large paychecks or other tangible benefits to motivate staff and volunteers. These organizations emphasize the importance of interpersonal relationships and feelings of solidarity with other members to influence worker performance (Gilligan, 1988). Because social change is often one of the primary goals of these organizations, management can use feelings that workers are at the forefront of a social movement and are engaged in essential altruistic activities to sustain experienced staff over long periods (Hyde, 1994).

Despite the importance of these organizations in improving services for women, feminist organizations have several disadvantages. Staff and volunteers can become demoralized and experience burnout if other rewards other than pay are not sufficient to motivate staff. Some members may have a greater role in decision-making because of their professional status, social class, ethnicity, or sexual orientation. Such divisions may create an ongoing conflict that makes consensus and cooperation difficult to achieve. Research on feminist organizations suggests that these power struggles are most evident in the relationships among staff members and clientele precisely because they take place within the context of power and dependency (Vaughn & Stamp, 2003). Workers who hold professional degrees can choose to allocate goods and services to female clients who must depend on them for assistance.

Ethnic Organizations

According to Iglehart and Becerra (2000), ethnic communities form their own agencies in instances in which organizations established to serve the general public do not address the needs of the ethnic community or where members of a specific ethnic group are explicitly denied access to these services. Ethnic group members may be denied services because they are regarded as unworthy of assistance because of social stigma associated with minority group status. For example, Hein (2000) conducted qualitative interviews with Hmong immigrants in Wisconsin. Respondents were asked to describe personal encounters with non-Asian residents. Hein found that the Hmong men and women he interviewed experienced five different forms of interpersonal discrimination in their daily lives, including verbal harassment, rejection, physical harassment, avoidance, and police mistreatment.

Strongly held negative perceptions of members of oppressed groups often can carry over to encounters between social workers or other public officials and people needing assistance, resulting in denial of services (Lipsky, 1980).

Social service organizations that target services to the general public may be reluctant to provide forms and applications in languages other than English, to hire ethnic group members to deliver services, or to incorporate culturally appropriate practices in their programs (Iglehart & Becerra, 2000). Inability to communicate with social service staff as well as fear of discrimination often keeps members of ethnic communities from seeking services from agencies and individual providers outside their own ethnic or cultural group (Yamashiro & Matsuoka, 1997).

All the factors described can discourage the use of traditional social service agencies by minority populations. Consequently, many ethnic groups may establish their organizations to provide services to members of their own culture. Iglehart and Becerra (2000) identify the following characteristics associated with "ideal" ethnic social service agencies:

- The organization primarily serves clients from one ethnic group.
- Most of the organization's staff is of the same ethnicity as the clients.
- The organization has a majority of ethnic group members on its board of directors.
- The organization has support and derives its legitimacy from the ethnic community it serves.
- The organization integrates ethnic appropriate content and cultural norms into service interventions and programs.
- The organization promotes ethnic identity and participation in the organization and in the ethnic community it serves.

A number of benefits are associated with the use of ethnic social service agencies to deliver programs to designated ethnic groups (Iglehart &

Becerra, 2000). Potential clients may be more comfortable receiving the service from members of their own culture and consequently will be more likely to use the service. Clients are also less likely to feel stigmatized or unworthy of receiving assistance if it is obtained from someone belonging to their own ethnic community. The services provided by ethnic agencies are more likely to be effective than those obtained from organizations outside the ethnic community because the staff incorporate cultural understanding into assessments, interventions, and identification of outcomes, making service delivery more effective. In addition, staff and clients speak the same "language" or use the same terminology to describe needs and services, increasing the likelihood that the client will receive services that are wanted or needed.

A number of disadvantages are associated with the delivery of services by ethnic organizations (Iglehart & Becerra, 2000). They often serve ethnic communities with small populations, and potential clients may be afraid that community members will know about their problems. Ethnic communities may vary by social class, income, or other demographic characteristics that differentiate people with power and status from people who are excluded from the life of the community. For example, in traditional Southeast Asian communities, women may be excluded from decision-making or find it difficult to obtain staff positions. Consequently, they may find it difficult to obtain services to meet their needs (Yoshihama & Carr, 2002).

Ethnic organizations face obstacles to becoming formal service delivery agents. They may find it difficult to obtain funding for services; funds may be available only for services not wanted or needed by the ethnic group. Other resources also may be hard to obtain. For example, as the organization moves from an informal to a formal organization, professional staff may be required (because of the complexity of needs or because of funder requirements). Few members of the ethnic group may have professional degrees and wish to work for ethnic organizations.

Faith-Based Organizations

Beginning in colonial America, churches and formal organizations affiliated with religious denominations (e.g., Catholic Charities, Lutheran Social Services, or the Jewish Federation) have played an important role in the delivery of social services to the poor (Netting & O'Connor, 2003). Faith-based organizations (FBOs) can include Muslim, Buddhist, and other religious groups. In 1996, Congress included language in welfare reform legislation (the Personal Responsibility Act [PRA]) that gave preference to FBOs in contracting out for the delivery of welfare services

(Cnaan, 1999). This clause in the legislation was given the term *charitable choice*. The legislation specified that local welfare offices were to involve both religious and other nonprofit groups in the delivery of services to help people leave the welfare system.

Faith- or religious-based social service organizations can be defined as "purposive organizations that draw staff, volunteers, and board members from a certain religious group and are based upon a particular religious ideology that is reflected in the agency's mission and operation" (Cnaan, 1999, p. 26). Sider and Unruh (2004) argue that the degree to which faith is incorporated into an organization's mission and service delivery can be conceptualized as a continuum with four categories:

1. Completely secular (nonreligious) organizations that contain no religious content.
2. Partnerships between religious and secular organizations in which administration is strictly secular. However, the organization relies on religious partners for volunteers and other resources.
3. Faith-background organizations that are almost entirely secular in nature but have originated within the context of a faith tradition. In some situations, these organizations are found within religious institutions, and some staff may be members of the religion but are not selected on that basis. Faith-centered organizations are founded explicitly for a religious purpose, and most staff members and decision-makers are affiliated with the faith. Clients and other participants may decline to participate in religious activities.
4. Faith-permeated organizations have an explicit connection with a religious group. This affiliation is evident in the organization's governance function and service delivery. Staff members and decision-makers are members of the religion.

One of the rationales for specially including FBOs as nonprofit sector providers of services was the idea that the voluntary sector rather than government should be the primary source of assistance for low-income people (Center for Faith-based and Community Initiatives, 2001; Salamon, 1995). Advocates of faith-based services also argue that programs that provided emotional support, assistance with housing and food, or substance abuse treatment were more effective if they involved a spiritual component that helped people solve personal problems and became moral citizens (Rosenthal, 2003). An additional argument on behalf of faith-based delivery is that the use of volunteer, nonprofessional staff would substantially lower the cost of provision, making FBO delivery more preferable to government assistance (Gibelman & Gelman, 2002).

The rationale for mandating faith-based provision of job training and other services in the PRA was that many churches or religion-affiliated organizations had declined government funding because of cumbersome regulations. For example, federal Affirmative Action and fair employment laws require that people not be excluded for consideration of employment because of their religion (Center for Faith-based and Community Initiatives, 2001; Cnaan, 1999). Many church-based organizations prefer to hire only members of their denomination. In addition, service delivery may be intended to help only members of the religious group providing the service or to be used as a mechanism to recruit new members for the church. Another barrier to church-based delivery is that many small churches are not formally incorporated as nonprofit organizations and consequently cannot accept government grants and contracts (Netting & O'Connor, 2003). The PRA removed many of these restrictions on church-based delivery. For example, the PRA loosened restrictions that prevented FBOs from hiring only members of their own faith. However, prohibitions on the use of service delivery to proselytize are still strictly enforced.

In the early 2000s, the administration of George W. Bush issued two executive orders setting up the White House Office of Faith-Based and Community Services and removing some additional regulations that were viewed as limiting the participation of churches and religious organizations in the delivery of services (Center for Faith-Based and Community Initiatives, 2001). Whether these initiatives actually increase the effectiveness of social services is not clear; few systematic evaluation studies have been conducted (Rosenthal, 2003). Gibelman and Gelman (2002) argue that there is no evidence that FBOs are any more accountable to clients or to the public for the use of funds than are government agencies.

BOX 4.2 CHOOSING AN ORGANIZATION TYPE

The young mother's group affiliated with the Mission Street Anti-Poverty Organization has decided to incorporate as a nonprofit organization. However, members do not agree about the type of organization they want to establish. Several strong churchgoers in the group prefer a faith-based organization that would be affiliated with their congregation. Two of the members identify themselves as advocates for women and would like to create an organization structured around feminist principles. Another member of the group prefers that the organization focus on advocating for more government funding for service delivery rather than trying to deliver services itself. A few of the members also feel that the new organization should incorporate service delivery practices that are culturally relevant to the primarily African American community that it would serve. Given these strong feelings, the group has not been able to come to a decision about incorporation.

Keisha has been asked to describe the benefits and limitations of each of these organization types.

- What should she tell group members about their options?
- Is it possible for an organization to combine some of the features described (faith-based and advocacy orientation; feminist principles, and culturally competent services)?
- If so, how should the new organization structure itself?

SUMMARY

People in need can obtain help from many types of individuals, groups, and organizations. Help can be obtained from one's own circle of friends, relatives, and neighbors, exchanged with others within the context of a community's informal helping networks, or obtained from an informal self-help group. Consequently, few boundaries may distinguish the people who give help from those who receive help. However, for groups to maximize the help they provide, they must be able to raise funds and develop a formal structure for the organization.

Formal organizations have hierarchical structures in which one or several people make decisions for other participants. Traditional social service organizations use hierarchical decision-making structures and provide services and other assistance to members of society who are deemed worthy of assistance. These organizations may be public, nonprofit, or for-profit. Alternative organizations, on the other hand, often are nonprofit organizations, created by a committed group of volunteers in order to provide services to people who cannot obtain those services elsewhere. Alternative organizations can include social movement, feminist, ethnic, and faith-based organizations. Each of these types of organizations can expand access to services for people in need. Responsibility for setting organizational goals and policy and monitoring the work of agency staff often lies with the organization's board of directors. The role of organization boards is examined in Chapter 5. The use of organization policies in expanding or limiting client access to services is described in Chapter 6.

QUESTIONS FOR CLASS DISCUSSION

1. Who do you think should be the primary provider of goods and services to people in need: informal helping networks, government agencies, for-profit groups, or nonprofit organizations? Why?
2. What are some of the benefits and limitations of government provision of services?
3. To what groups are nonprofit and government organizations accountable?
4. How extensive is your own helping network? Who are the people in your personal life who help you obtain the things, including emotional support that you need?
5. Are there reasons why people would prefer help from friends, relatives, and neighbors rather than from public or nonprofit organizations? What are they?
6. What are some of the specific cultural norms that you would expect to see reflected in the programs and policies of ethnic social service organizations?
7. From what type of organization would you prefer to receive help?

SAMPLE ASSIGNMENTS

1. Determine the type of organization in which you are completing your field placement. Create an organizational chart that displays the different levels of decision-making in this organization.
2. Select two teams for a formal debate in your classroom and prepare either a "for" or "against" argument for the following statement:

    - Faith-based delivery of social services to the poor is preferable and superior to government provision of assistance.

3. Conduct community-based research using resource directories and interviews to identify all the service providers that provide services in a particular field of service, in a neighborhood, or that address a particular social problem (e.g., child welfare, aging, mental health, homelessness, hunger, etc.). Within that geographic location and field of service, identify public agencies, nonprofits, for-profit providers, as well as informal organizations that address the problem or issue in question. Also document the provider's target client population, eligibility service, and any monetary fees charged for services. Based on your research, indicate whether you think that everyone who needs the service

can actually obtain it, and describe obvious obstacles to service receipt.

4. Conduct an interview with two agency directors. One director should be affiliated with a traditional organization and the other with one of the four types of alternative organizations described in this chapter. The interviews should examine the purpose and mission of the organization, the client population, eligibility requirements, leadership structure, and funding sources. Using data from your interviews, compare and contrast the two types of agencies.

SECTION II

Management Skills for Creating an Empowering Organization: Increasing Consumer Access to Services

CHAPTER 5

Creating Decision-Making Partnerships With Staff and Clientele: The Role of Boards and Committees

Almost all organizations establish formal structures to facilitate group decision-making and to set policy. One primary assumption of empowerment practice is that social service organizations should make special efforts to ensure that the constituents who are often rendered powerless in social service organizations, the clients, play a prominent role in organizational decision-making and program planning (Rose & Black, 1985). Consequently, empowerment-oriented social service organizations also use formal decision-making structures, such as boards and committees, to solicit input from clients and other program beneficiaries.

The purpose of client participation is to increase the client's feelings of self-competency and control; consequently, such involvement is a component of empowerment-oriented interventions that are intended to foster change in individuals. Another primary assumption of empowerment practice is that all potential participants should be treated as equal partners in organizational decision-making and that decisions should be made in the context of dialogue and mutual learning (Freire, 1970; Gutierrez et al., 1998). Empowerment is accomplished through the acquisition of leadership and decision-making skills. Public and nonprofit organizations typically empower citizens by giving them formal roles in decisions that affect their lives (Forester, 1999). In addition, membership on an advisory council, formation of a constituency group for parents of school children, knocking on doors to organize a block club for neighborhood residents, giving testimony at a public hearing, and confronting public officials at a community forum are all avenues for empowerment-oriented skill attainment. Transmission of advocacy and leadership skills empowers both the users of the information as well as the practitioners who transmit these skills, increasing the effectiveness of social change efforts (Hardina, 1997).

In formal organization structures, boards, advisory groups, and committees are most often used to provide a mechanism for these discussions. This chapter examines

- The function of boards in social service organizations and the roles and responsibilities of board members.
- The relationship between the organization board and the executive director.
- Methods used to increase board member diversity, including board recruitment and training.
- The role of advisory boards and organizational committees.
- Barriers to full participation of clients and other constituents in organizational decision-making and methods used to overcome these barriers.

THE FUNCTION OF BOARDS IN SOCIAL SERVICE ORGANIZATIONS

In formal organizations, the board of directors make most policy decisions. In nonprofit organizations, an appointed or elected board makes policy decisions, supervises the executive director, and provides oversight to ensure that funds are used appropriately. It is board's responsibility to ensure that the nonprofit organization serves the public interest. Boards of directors of for-profit corporations perform similar tasks, ensuring that the interests of shareholders are advanced. Federal, state, and local governments also use a variety of boards and committees to carry out specific functions. Members of these public boards (e.g., school boards or local land use planning committees) are elected by the public or are selected to serve by elected officials. It may be the responsibility of staff members or administrators in government agencies to serve as liaisons to these boards, providing them with the information and technical expertise needed to make appropriate decisions. Chief operating officers (COOs) or chief executive officers (CEOs) in corporations or nonprofit organizations are also responsible for communicating staff performance and goal achievement to board members. In instances of poor organizational performance, generally the CEO is held accountable by the board.

According to Lohmann and Lohmann (2002), there are at least three types of public, corporate, and nonprofit boards:

- *Boards That Govern.* Governing boards are accountable to the public and various organization constituency groups for how the organization operates and how the organization spends its money. Governing boards in most nonprofits are responsible for setting policy and for hiring and firing the executive director.
- *Boards That Regulate Government and Private Activities.* Regulatory boards may be either public or nonprofit entities that monitor how tasks are carried out or that establish standards for organization or individual behavior. For example, federal regulatory boards set standards for media ownership, protection of the environment, and utility costs. State regulatory boards establish licensing standards for professionals such as doctors and social workers.
- *Boards That Give Advice.* Advisory boards provide consultation on program design and service delivery. However, members do not have decision-making authority in the organization. They can only make recommendations to the board of directors, program administrators, or government officials.

Legislative mandate or government authority most often establishes public governing, regulatory, and advisory boards. This chapter focuses primarily on nonprofit governing boards and advisory groups. However, most of the skills identified in this chapter can be used by administrators and staff members working with all three types of boards.

GOVERNING BOARDS

Much of the literature on governing boards focuses on the roles of these decision-making structures in nonprofit organizations. Most nonprofit boards are "self-constituting," that is, they are formed when interested people come together as a group to develop a formal organization in order to achieve a specific goal (Lohmann & Lohmann, 2002). Self-constituting groups can establish any goals or decision-making procedures they want. These groups are most often established when informal groups or collectives of people decide to raise funds and take action on a variety of issues. As described in Chapter 4, boundaries among decision-makers, staff members, and service beneficiaries are unclear or nonexistent in informal organizations. All participants may be involved in making important decisions. However, decision-making processes often change substantially over time as these groups take on many of the characteristics of formal organizations.

A number of factors contribute to the development of formal organization structures. The primary factor is fundraising. Money allows the organization to hire staff or provide ongoing support for volunteers. According to federal law, organizations with annual incomes of $25,000 or more must incorporate and report income and expenditures to the Internal Revenue Service (IRS; Englund, 2003). In addition, most foundations and government agencies will not provide grants or contracts to organizations unless a formal structure is in place to account for how the organizations' funds will be used. Consequently, to raise money, new organizations must either (a) contract with a nonprofit that already is incorporated under the Internal Revenue Code as a 501 (c) (3) organization for accounting services and fiscal oversight (Hummel, 1996), with the 501 (c) (3) organization then becoming the "fiscal agent" for the new organization; or (b) undertake federal incorporation under section 501 (c) (3) or 501 (c) (4) of the tax code. Section 501 (c) (3) organizations are tax exempt, and donations made to them are tax deductible for the donor. Section 501 (c) (4) organizations also are tax exempt, but donations are not tax deductible. Both types of organizations receive tax exemption because their activities are expected to promote the public good. The difference in the tax treatment of the two types of organizations is determined by the types of activities to be undertaken. For example, organizations operating under section 501 (c) (3) of the tax code may devote only a small proportion of their expenditures to lobbying activities; 501 (c) (4) organizations have no restrictions on lobbying (Arons, 1999). Both types of nonprofit organization are required to submit annual reports on expenditures and revenues to the IRS. All funds collected by incorporated nonprofits are to be spent on organizational activities and must not benefit members of their board of directors. Laws in most states require that nonprofit organizations file articles of incorporation with the secretary of states office and register as a charitable organization that will raise funds in that state (Englund, 2003).

An incorporated organization is required to have a formal board of directors and a set of rules, called *by-laws,* to guide decision-making in organizations. By-laws typically describe the purpose of the organization, membership rights, how people are selected or elected to be board members, board officer positions, responsibilities of officers, terms of service for board members, board committees, number and scheduling of meetings, voting procedures, and methods for amending the by-laws (Hummel, 1996). Some by-laws include statements about how access to funds is to be controlled as well as language limiting the legal liability of board members.

BOX 5.1 BYLAWS OF THE *FAMILY ADVOCACY NETWORK*

ARTICLE I—NAME AND PURPOSES

Section 1.01 Name. The name of the organization is the Family Advocacy Network.

Section 1.02 Purpose. The Corporation is organized for the charitable and educational purposes of providing information, advocacy, and referral services to low-income families.

ARTICLE II—AUTHORITY AND DUTIES OF DIRECTORS

Section 2.01 Authority of Directors. The Board of Directors is the policy-making body and may exercise all the powers and authority granted to the Corporation by law.

Section 2.02 Number. The Board shall consist of at least 10 and a maximum of 12 directors.

Section 2.03 Tenure. Each director shall hold office for a term of two years. However, in order to establish a process of board member rotation, 50% of the initial board members will be appointed to one-year terms and 50% will be appointed to two-year terms. Each director shall be limited to serving two continuous terms on the Board of Directors.

Section 2.04 Selection. At least 25% of all board members will be individuals with incomes below the poverty line. Vacancies existing by reason of resignation, death, incapacity, or removal before the expiration of his/her term shall be appointed by the nominating committee. A director selected to fill a vacancy shall be appointed for the unexpired term of that director's predecessor in office.

Section 2.05 Resignation. Resignations are effective upon receipt by the Secretary of the Corporation of written notification.

Section 2.06 Regular Meetings. The Board of Directors shall hold at least 6 and a maximum of 12 regular meetings per calendar year. Meetings shall be at such dates, times, and places as the Board shall determine.

Section 2.07 Special Meetings. Meetings shall be at such dates, times, and places as the Board shall determine.

Section 2.08 Notice. Meetings may be called by the Chairperson or at the request of any two (2) directors by notice e-mailed, mailed, telephoned, or telegraphed to each member of the Board not less than forty-eight hours before such meeting.

Section 2.09 Quorum. A quorum shall consist of a majority of the Board attending in person or through teleconferencing. If less than a majority of the directors is present at said meeting, a majority of the directors present may adjourn the meeting on occasion without further notice.

Section 2.10 Voting. *Decisions to be made* by majority vote of those present at a meeting at which a quorum is present.

Section 2.11 Committees. The Board of Directors may, by resolution adopted by a majority of the Directors in office, establish committees of the Board composed of at least two (2) persons which, except for an Executive Committee, may include non-Board members. The Board may make such provisions for appointment of the chair of such committees, establish such procedures to govern their activities, and delegate thereto such authority as may be necessary or desirable for the efficient management of the property, affairs, business, and activities of the Corporation.

Section 2.12 Nominating Committee. There shall be a Nominating Committee, appointed by the Board. The Nominating Committee shall consist of one Board member and two individuals who do not hold seats on the Board. Each member of the committee shall have one (1) vote and decision shall be made by the majority. Nominating committee members will be charged with selecting board members representative of the community and its interests. Twenty-five percent of board members shall have incomes below the poverty line. Other demographic characteristics to be considered in the selection of board members include age, ethnicity, gender, disability status, and sexual orientation.

ARTICLE III—AUTHORITY AND DUTIES OF OFFICERS

Section 3.01 Officers. The officers of the Corporation shall be a President, a Vice-President, a Secretary, and a Treasurer, and such other officers as the Board of Directors may designate.

Section 3.02 Appointment of Officers; Terms of Office. The officers of the Corporation shall be elected by the Board of Directors at regular meetings of the Board, or, in the case of vacancies, as soon thereafter as convenient. Terms of office may be shall not exceed two (2) years. Officers shall hold office until a successor is duly elected and qualified. Officers shall be eligible for reappointment to a second consecutive term.

Section 3.03 Resignation. Resignations are effective upon receipt by the Secretary of the Board of a written notification.

Section 3.04 Removal. An officer may be removed by the Board of Directors at a meeting, or by action in writing pursuant to Section 2.08, whenever in the Board's judgment the best interests of the Corporation will be served thereby. Any such removal shall be without prejudice to the contract rights, if any, of the person so removed.

Section 3.05 President. The President shall be a director of the Corporation and will preside at all meetings of the Board of Directors. The President shall perform all duties attendant to that office, subject, however, to the control of the Board of Directors, and shall perform such other duties as on occasion shall be assigned by the Board of Directors.

Section 3.06 Vice-President. The Vice-President shall be a director of the Corporation and will preside at meetings of the Board of Directors in the absence of or request of the President. The Vice-President shall perform other duties as requested and assigned by the President, subject to the control of the Board of Directors.

Section 3.07 Secretary. The Secretary shall be a director of the Corporation and shall keep the minutes of all meetings of the Board of Directors in the books proper for that purpose.

Section 3.08 Treasurer. The Treasurer shall also report to the Board of Directors at each regular meeting on the status of the Council's finances. The Treasurer shall work closely with any paid executive staff of the Corporation to ascertain that appropriate procedures are being followed in the financial affairs of the Corporation, and shall perform such other duties as occasionally may be assigned by the Board of Directors.

Section 3.09 Paid Staff. The Board of Directors may hire such paid staff as they deem proper and necessary for the operations of the Corporation. The powers and duties of the paid staff shall be as assigned or as delegated to be assigned by the Board.

ARTICLE IV—ADVISORY BOARDS AND COMMITTEES

Section 4.01 Establishment. The Board of Directors may establish one or more Advisory Boards or Committees.

Section 4.02 Size, Duration, and Responsibilities. The size, duration, and responsibilities of such boards and committees shall be established by a majority vote of the Board of Directors.

ARTICLE V—FINANCIAL ADMINISTRATION

Section 5.01 Fiscal Year. The fiscal year of the Corporation shall be January 1–December 31 but may be changed by resolution of the Board of Directors.

Section 5.02 Checks, Drafts, Etc. All checks, orders for the payment of money, bills of lading, warehouse receipts, obligations, bills of exchange, and insurance certificates shall be signed or endorsed by such officer or officers or agent or agents of the Corporation and in such manner as shall from time to time be determined by resolution of the Board of Directors or of any committee to which such authority has been delegated by the Board.

ARTICLE VI—AMENDMENT OF BYLAWS

These Bylaws may be amended by a majority vote of the Board of Directors, provided prior notice is given of the proposed amendment in the notice of the meeting at which such action is taken, or provided all members of the Board waive such notice, or by unanimous consent in writing without a meeting pursuant to Section 2.07.

Although new nonprofit organizations have a variety of options for structuring decision-making, boards often share some characteristics, such as size, board officers, and rule-making procedures. Most boards consist of between 10 and 15 members (Community Tool Box, 2004). Smaller boards are generally preferred to larger boards because large numbers of people involved in decision-making makes the process longer and more complex. The exception to this rule is instances where boards are intended to be representative of a variety of interests of the community sectors. A larger board allows for a greater degree of inclusion than does a smaller board.

The person who chairs board meetings serves as the president of the organization and is the primary liaison with the executive director. Other officers generally include a vice-president, secretary, and treasurer. The vice-president chairs board meetings in the president's absence. The secretary is responsible for taking meeting minutes and sending notices to board members. The treasurer's role is to report organizational expenditures and revenues to the board. In most formal organizations, this means the treasurer relies on information provided by staff rather than actually maintaining the books and depositing checks. However, the treasurer has an important role in ensuring that organizational funds are spent properly and reporting this information to the board.

Other possible board officers include a president-elect or immediate past-president, positions that allow for smooth transitions to new leadership (Community Tool Box, 2004). Some organizations also select or elect a sergeant-at-arms to maintain order at meetings and enforce decision-making rules. Another variation on board structure and officer positions involves situations where the board president also functions as a paid staff member. Preference for this type of structure usually is found in organizations where one person is regarded as the organization's "founder" and holds a seat on the board as well as a paid administrative position (Block & Rosenberg, 2002). This model is also used in advocacy organizations where the elected board president has substantial responsibilities for interacting with the public and with government decision-makers.

Many boards specify decision-making procedures in their by-laws. Often these rules are based on the book, *Robert's Rules of Order.* The procedures in *Robert's Rules of Order* are predicated on the premise that the organization is a hierarchical organization (Figure 5.1). The board president is responsible for chairing the meeting and enforcing the rules. Decision options are to be presented to the board as formal motions that

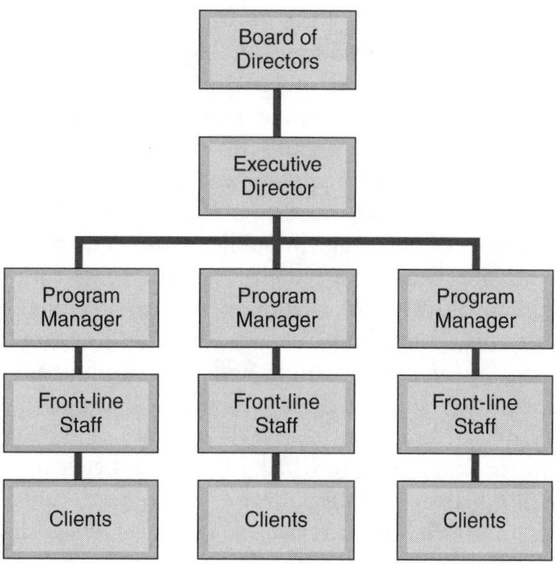

Figure 5.1 Traditional pattern of a board's position in the organizational hierarchy.

must be seconded by another board member; for a motion to pass it must be approved by a majority of board members *(majority rule)*. There are specific rules in terms of how discussions are to be conducted and the number of board members needed to hold a meeting *(quorum)*. However, it should be noted that many nonprofit boards use some, but not all, of the procedures outlined in *Robert's Rules of Order* (Lohmann & Lohmann, 2002). Variations in decision-making practices (such as consensus style decision-making) may be attributed to the preferences of the board president, ideology, the organization's culture, or decision-making styles associated with certain demographic or cultural groups. For example, as discussed in previous chapters, feminist organizations and some ethnic groups (Asian and Native Americans) prefer consensus-oriented decision-making to majority rule or hierarchical decision-making structures.

THE ROLE OF BOARD MEMBERS

Board members can play a variety of roles. The governance function is often defined differently depending on the type of organization, its history, and the degree of power held by individual board members. In most nonprofit organizations, board members establish the organization's mission, set policy, and are responsible for hiring and firing the executive director (Inglis, Alexander, & Weaver, 1999). As specified by IRS and state regulations, board members are responsible for ensuring that funds are used properly, and board members may be held legally liable for misuse of funds or other inappropriate or criminal acts on the part of the organization, the board, and the staff (Englund, 2003). In some organizations, board members are expected to raise funds for the organization. This activity can range from selling raffle tickets to negotiating for contracts and grants to lobbying government for funds (Community Tool Box, 2004; Miller-Millesen, 2003).

Board members often engage in public relations work: writing letters to the editor, giving media interviews, attending press conferences, and otherwise publicizing the work of the organization (Holland, 1998). In some organizations, board members are expected to participate as volunteers in many of the organization's activities: stuffing envelopes, providing transportation, editing the organization's newsletter, organizing special events, and/or lobbying.

One of the primary areas in which board members can be engaged is to serve as a link between the organization and its external environment (Miller-Millesen, 2003). Often board members serve simultaneously on the boards of other organizations or professional associations. Interlocking boards of directors are effective tools for establishing informal and formal networks among organizations that work to achieve similar goals (Hardina, 2002). These networks can be used to initiate coalitions, task groups, and service-related partnerships. They also can be used to recruit new board members and used as a source of power and influence to lobby for legislation and promote social change.

Ideally, boards also serve as a link between the organization and the community. They help communicate to the board about community needs and serve to articulate the interests of the organization to community residents and institutions. The board can help ensure that the services delivered by the organization "fit" the needs of the community (Abzug & Galaskiewicz, 2001; Inglis et al., 1999). Such a role is important because an organization's funding sources can have a large influence on how the organization delivers services. The presence on the board of directors of community residents and leaders who are community advocates can serve as a counterbalance to funder demands (Hardina, 1993; Tourginy & Miller, 1981).

The remaining responsibilities of the board are to plan and evaluate. It is the board's responsibility to develop organizational plans for future growth and development and to determine whether current programs have produced desired outcomes. The board also is responsible for conducting regular evaluations of the performance of the executive director that determine whether the CEO is retained or terminated from this position. Experts on nonprofit management also recommend that the board evaluate its own performance on a variety of factors, including board member recruitment and retention, decision-making processes, goal setting, and task accomplishment (Holland, 1998). Many self-evaluation instruments and tool kits are available on the Internet or are published by professional organizations and accreditation groups (Association of Community College Trustees, 2004; Jackson & Holland, 1998; McNamara, 2004). Such an evaluation should assist the board in the development of procedures that will increase the effectiveness of the board in meeting its goals. Holland (1998) identifies six competency areas for board members:

- *Contextual.* The board understands the norms and values that influence the organization's culture and uses this understanding to guide its actions.
- *Educational.* The board ensures that all members are informed about organizational operations and their own roles in decision-making.
- *Interpersonal.* The board members engage in activities that help them develop a sense of group cohesion.
- *Analytical.* Board members adequately gain an understanding of the issues they address and take into account a variety of perspectives on these issues.

- *Political.* The board develops and maintains good relationships with constituency groups within and outside the organization.
- *Strategic.* The board is actively involved in making decisions that pertain to the organization's future direction.

For organizations with staff, these activities are carried out within the context of a relationship with a chief administrator or executive director. However, the nature of the relationship between the board and the staff person it appoints to manage the organization on a day-to-day basis varies substantially across organizations.

THE ROLE OF AN EXECUTIVE DIRECTOR VIS-À-VIS THE BOARD

Executive directors in nonprofit organizations and, in many circumstances, administrators who are directly responsible for providing staff support to public boards are theoretically subordinate to the boards. In most nonprofit organizations and public boards, the executive director is hired or fired by the board. However, the executive director has a vast amount of power within the context of that relationship (Kramer, 1985). The executive director has a greater degree of knowledge about program operation and the activities of the staff than does the board. The executive director is often the person most familiar with organizational expenditures and the status of grants and contracts. He or she can set the agenda for board meetings and provide or withhold information from board members (Block & Rosenberg, 2002).

In many instances, the executive director can (and in many circumstances should) lobby individual board members to take action on specific issues or to vote a certain way (Tropman, 1997). By virtue of the executive director's status and technical knowledge, board members will seek out the executive director's opinion and sometimes base their decisions on his or her recommendations. Because many of the board's decisions may require technical knowledge or complex issues, the knowledge and skills of the director help ensure that decisions are made in a timely manner.

The nature of the relationship may variety substantially among organizations. Murray, Bradshaw, and Wolpin (1992) identify five distinct types of board member–executive director relationships:

- *An executive director–dominated board.* Board members are unlikely to participate in the development of plans and policies but simply approve the CEO's recommendations.

- *A board president–dominated board.* The president is able to influence the votes of the other members or may have the power to select allies for open seats on the board.
- *A fragmented board.* In this board, cliques or factions engage in a decision-making process characterized by conflict. Such divisiveness may be due to ideological differences or the personalities of board members. Ongoing conflict prevents the board from reaching its goals.
- *A power-sharing board.* In this type of board, members are committed to the full participation of all members in decision-making. Rules are enforced to ensure that no members exert undue influence over others. Decisions are made by consensus.
- *A powerless board.* In this type of board, members are not clear about their roles. Few people attend meetings, and little is accomplished.

Some experts on board development believe that because board members and executive directors hold a variety of different power resources within organizations, the hierarchical relationship inherent in the traditional structure of nonprofit boards is somewhat outdated. Holland (1998) argues that the relationship between board members and the executive director should be a partnership between two entities with equal status. Carver (1990), on the other hand, suggests that the executive director has the knowledge and expertise to make most of the organization's decisions. He recommends that the board's role be limited to policy-making and providing a strategic vision for the organization.

Regardless of philosophies about whether the board or the executive director should have the most control, managers of nonprofit organizations or public employees responsible for liaison with public boards should have the following skills:

- Choosing and packaging information to be presented to the board
- Helping board members establish and apply a set of ground rules for decision-making
- Selecting items to be placed on the agenda
- Building working partnerships with board members
- Facilitating consensus and establishing trusting relationships among board members
- Using effective verbal and written communication of recommendations for policies and procedures
- The ability to work with a variety of people who may differ with regard to gender, sexual orientation, ethnicity, age, social class, and professional status and/or authority.

- The ability to communicate the experiences and perspectives of clients and staff to the board and to advocate for these constituency groups.
- The ability to communicate with board members about strategies that should be used for interactions with people and institutions in the organization's external environment, including funding sources, government decision-makers, accreditation agencies, the media, and the public at large.
- The ability to work with the board and other key constituency groups to develop operational and strategic (long-term) plans for the organization (Hardina & Malott, 1996a; Holland, 1998; Murray et al., 1992; Tropman, 1997).

CREATING A DIVERSE BOARD

One primary assumption of much of the recent literature on boards is that boards should be diverse in terms of gender, ethnicity, and social class. Inclusion of people with diverse interests in organizational decision-making is believed to improve the quality of services, stimulate innovation, and help the organization balance the demands of funders with the needs of the community (Parker & Betz, 1996). The term *diversity* as it pertains to organizational boards generally refers to member skills and experience as well as demographic characteristics, such as age, gender, ethnicity, physical or mental disabilities, sexual orientation, and social class (Daley, 2002). Empowerment practice often focuses on placing members of low-income and other underrepresented groups on organizational boards. According to Zimmerman and Rappaport (1988), the inclusion of low-income people on boards increases their power and helps build leadership skills and increases the participants' perceptions of their own self-efficacy.

Research on board membership indicates that many nonprofit boards consist of members who are overwhelmingly male and Caucasian (Bradshaw, Murray, & Wolpin, 1996). Often such board members are not representative of the clients or of the interest groups actually served by the organization. Board members are often middle-income professionals or members of social and economic elites who are politically connected or who can help community-based organizations raise funds (Abzug & Galaskiewicz, 2001; Smith & Lipsky, 1993). Persons of color or low-income people seldom are seated on the boards of traditional community-based organizations unless the organizations were founded by, or are intended to serve, ethnic and other underrepresented communities (Iglehart & Becerra, 2000; Widmer, 1987).

An empowerment-oriented manager should be actively involved in helping the board set appropriate parameters for selecting new members, ensuring an appropriate range of skills and interests. The executive director should ensure that this framework includes policies that lead to diversity by gender, ethnicity, and social class. The board should be representative of the geographic community, client population, and identity communities served (e.g., cultural groups; persons with disabilities; or lesbian, gay, bisexual, and transgendered [LGBT] individuals). It may not simply be enough, however, for the board to set these parameters. The executive director will need to use a variety of mechanisms (role modeling, relationship building, board training) to ensure that individuals who are members of traditionally marginalized groups (such as clients or persons with incomes below the poverty line) are treated in the same manner and are accorded the same degree of power as other board members (Hardina & Malott, 1996a; Zachary, 2000). Two chief mechanisms for ensuring a cohesive, well-functioning board that stimulates participation by all its members are board recruitment and board training.

BOARD RECRUITMENT AND TRAINING

In order to maintain a board of directors that can accomplish tasks, take responsibility for governing the organization, and function with a minimum of conflict, many organizations develop written recruitment plans and make an effort to provide leadership training to board members (Holland, 1998). Recruitment helps to ensure an appropriate mix of people on the board who bring creativity and vision to the organization (Daley, 2002). An established board orientation and training process helps members run effective meetings, set goals, and work well with organizational staff and constituency group members.

Board Recruitment

Board members are, at least in theory, chosen by the board or elected by the organization's membership. Most organizations specify in their bylaws procedures for appointing new board members. The vehicle for recruiting new people to the board is a standing "nominating committee." The nominating committee screens potential board members and is responsible for putting together a slate of candidates. In membership organizations, a ballot that lists candidates for each open seat and any vacant officer positions is mailed to all eligible members. In organizations that do not have members, persons selected by the nominating committee may simply be appointed to the board with the approval of sitting board members.

Recruitment of new board members can take place in a variety of ways. Members of the nominating committee, sitting board members, and in some cases, the executive director can recommend people with whom they have personal, professional, or business relationships. However, many boards have explicit nepotism rules that prohibit the use of family ties in hiring relatives of board members or, conversely, appointing relatives of staff members to the board (Community Tool Box, 2004). Many boards look for people who fit specific demographic profiles or who have skills that may be useful to the organization. Some boards develop detailed recruitment plans or write board job descriptions that can be used to help them find people that will help the organization achieve specific goals related to community representation or task accomplishment (Brown, 2002).

The organization's philosophy often determines the demographic profile of people who serve on the board. When filling vacant positions, boards often look for people with special expertise in the organization's field of service. For example, an organization that serves people with mental illness might try to recruit psychiatrists, psychologists, and social workers for board membership (Abzug & Galaskiewicz, 2001). Some organizations fill board positions with people with managerial and other professional experience that can be useful to the organization, such as accountants, business people, and lawyers. People with expertise in fundraising or planning special events also are valuable board assets. Many organizations try to include politicians or relatives of politicians to their board of directors, believing that such people can "pull strings" for the organization. Organizations also recruit prominent community leaders and celebrities for their boards, believing that these people help to establish the organization's legitimacy with the community. The presence of celebrities on an organization's board or at fundraising events can be used to help raise funds and bring recognition to the organization (Hardina, 2002).

In any case, most organizations want to have a mix of people on their boards. Some organizations that operate as closed systems allow founding members to have unlimited terms on the board or to continue recruiting new members from a handful of social or organizational networks. Such organizations are not believed to be effective; new board members are believed to help motivate the board for better performance (Brown, 2002; Community Tool Box, 2004).

Many boards actively commit themselves to ensuring that they reflect the demographic diversity of the community served in terms of gender, ethnicity, socioeconomic status, and age. Other demographic characteristics, such as health status, disability, and sexual orientation, also may be taken into account, particularly if the organization serves people with those characteristics or has been established to explicitly meet the needs of marginalized groups (Cox, Rouff, Svendsen, Markowitz, & Abrams, 1998; Silvestre, Faber, Shankle, & Kopelman, 2002). Another philosophical issue for boards is the idea that former or current clients should be elected or selected for board membership. The presence of clients on boards is believed to help ensure that services are accessible and responsive to the people who need them, are culturally appropriate, and are effective (Hardina, 1993; Iglehart & Becerra, 2000). In some organizations, it is important to ensure geographic representation of community residents, especially in organizations that serve diverse populations with different interests in various locations in the community. Often boards of directors make explicit efforts to ensure board representation by demographic group or geographic area by including representation requirements in their by-laws (Parker & Betz, 1996). For example, an organization could specify that one board member should be elected for each of the eight neighborhoods served by the organization or that 25% of all board members should have incomes below the poverty line.

Some organizations resist diversifying their membership (Brown, 2002). Board members are concerned that diversity will make agreement upon organizational goals more difficult (Daley, 2002). One rationale for an organization's failure to recruit new members is that prospective board members cannot be recruited outside established organizational networks. However, Parker and Betz (1996) identify a number of effective methods for recruiting members of diverse groups for membership on boards:

- Ask community leaders to identify prospective board members.
- Extend face-to-face invitations to potential recruits.
- Use established community groups as recruiting pools for participants.
- Identify and recruit informal community leaders.
- Hold board or planning meetings at times when prospective members can easily attend them.
- Plan special events or activities that can be used to introduce the organization to new people.

Board Training

Most boards provide to new board members some sort of orientation that introduces them to the organization, its programs, and staff members.

Orientations also are used to help new members become acquainted with other board members, pending issues, and decision-making procedures. Organizations may provide instruction on leadership skills to new members or provide training to inform members about technical issues that may come before the board. Board orientations and ongoing training may be used to establish group cohesion and develop consensus about goals. Holland (1998) recommends that boards periodically plan retreats to assess their own effectiveness and decision-making procedures and to develop new methods for working effectively. Often resources for performing this work are available through paid consultants and nonprofit organizations that specialize in board development. Information on board development or improvement also can be found on the Internet.

Whereas information about how to improve board effectiveness is plentiful, less information is available on how to bring together the diverse people and interests that may be represented on the board. Procedures that can be used to reach consensus and produce a common vision for the organization are crucial in circumstances where the board has chosen to include many different types of people from the community or clients of the organization in decision-making. Parker and Betz (1996) identify a number of strategies associated with empowerment-oriented boards:

- The provision of translation and signing services
- The establishment of appropriate ground rules that encourage people to participate
- A committee structure that provides adequate resources for task completion
- A mechanism that can be used for conflict resolution
- A process for mentoring new members
- Regular board and meeting self-evaluations

One of the key factors in establishing guidelines for empowerment-oriented boards and committees is power sharing. If all the decisions are made by one or two people or if active participation in decisions is confined to members of the dominant culture, the board or committee will be an ineffective vehicle for promoting inclusion. According to Zachary (2000), group processes that emphasize shared power rather than authoritarian-style decision-making should be used especially when recruiting informal community leaders for participation on boards. He argues that a traditional hierarchical approach in which one leader directs other members simply replicates power inequities inherent in the dominant culture. Zachary's approach to training board members includes three primary elements:

1. Power and meaning are located in the group, not the individual leader.
2. Leadership is considered a largely functional position that does not confer special privileges and status.
3. Mutual dialogue between the group's leaders and its members is used to set the agenda (p. 75).

BOX 5.2 BOARD DEVELOPMENT AT THE NORTHWEST WOMEN'S SHELTER

After 6 months as Executive Director at the Northwest Women's Shelter, Pang feels that she does not receive sufficient support from her board of directors. Of the 15 board members, only 5 consistently come to the monthly board meetings. A group of three people on the board, the President, the fundraising committee chair, and the board secretary make most of the decisions. Consequently, all board members outside of the small clique are largely uninformed about what is happening in the program. Pang's recommendations for restructuring the organization and for fundraising are often ignored or voted down by the board.

Pang is also concerned about the composition of the board. Most of the members have served on the board for the entire 10-year period in which the organization has been in existence. Many of these individuals are female, heterosexual, white, middle-income professionals. No clients or former clients serve on the board. Clientele of the Northwest Women's Shelter are primarily low-income women of color, primarily Latino and African American. A recent needs assessment indicates that about 20% of the clients are bisexual or lesbian victims of domestic partner violence. Many of the changes in services that Pang would like to make would improve the quality of services to members of these population groups; however, there is currently no support for changes in service delivery among current board members.

- Keeping in mind that the board can fire Pang at any time, what things can she do to improve her relationship with the board?
- Currently, the board's nominating committee recommends new members for seats on the board. What role should Pang take in recruiting new members for the board?
- What strategies can Pang use to increase the likelihood that her recommendations will be approved by the board?

COMMITTEES

Many of the decisions needed to conduct organizational business often are made by committees rather than boards. Committees are small groups constituted within an organization to perform specific tasks. These committees often are appointed to perform activities that are better performed by a small number of people rather than all members of a board or a department (*Robert's Rules of Order,* 1982). These small groups often are asked to make recommendations to the full board for actions that can be approved, rejected, or modified by the board or by the organization's administrator.

The three primary types of committees in social service organizations are

1. Committees of the board
2. Internal working committees, often consisting of staff members but sometimes including other constituents such as clients, board members, and key community leaders
3. Committees organized around a task area that consists of organizational staff and representatives from other institutions and groups in the community

Social service organizational staff, board members, and clients may all be members or serve as chairpersons of these committees. Staff members may also be called upon to provide information, technical expertise, and other resources to these committees.

Board Committees

Committees of the board generally consist only of board members or board appointees. Usually, a member of the board acts as the chairperson of the committee. The executive director or another staff member provides information and other support to committee members. Most organizations with boards have a number of committees. An "executive" committee consists of board officers (president, vice-president, secretary, and treasurer) who usually are charged with setting agendas for the board members or with making decisions in circumstances where consulting with all members of the board is difficult. Many organizations also have fundraising committees, which are charged with soliciting contributions from individuals, planning special events, or helping to negotiate grants and contracts. Other committees may be constructed around specific program areas addressed by the organization. Committees may be "standing" committees in that they derive their purpose and mandate from the organization's by-laws and meet on an ongoing basis. The board may choose to authorize "ad hoc" committees that are initiated to address new issues or situations encountered by the board. Most ad hoc committees cease to operate after they accomplish the intended goal.

Internal Working Committees

Social service organizations can establish internal working committees, composed primarily of staff, to complete designated tasks, develop programs or policy recommendations, and improve workplace conditions or morale. Establishing internal structures that can be used to give staff members a decision-making role in the organization and the ability to problem-solve is an important component of empowerment-oriented practice (Bowen & Lawler, 1995). In addition, proponents of empowerment-oriented practice advocate for use of internal committees that include clients, staff, administrators, and members of the board to design programs and evaluate service delivery (Fetterman, 1996). Consequently, using this type of committee requires that organizational staff assigned to leadership or support roles have the interpersonal skills needed to incorporate a variety of perspectives in the decision-making process and work to facilitate a consensus.

Task Forces

A third type of committee structure, the task force, generally consists of staff members or other representatives of organizations who serve the same community or target population. These groups may include community leaders and representatives of constituency groups. Task forces or groups are intended to be time limited and are established to address unmet needs or urgent problems. One advantage of this type of decision-making vehicle is that it permits an organization to engage in problem-solving on one new issue without losing its ability to focus on its primary goals (Community Tool Box, 2004). It also allows for the participation of a variety of groups that may not have a previous history of engagement. Often, task forces begin as informal groups and transition into formal coalitions or collaborative partnerships in which organizations establish formal decision-making structures to lobby government for funds or legislation or engage in the joint delivery of services (Hardcastle, Wenocur, & Powers, 1997).

Leadership Roles and Staff Support

Most committees or task groups elect a chairperson, although administrators may appoint internal committee chairs. Committee leaders are responsible for chairing meetings, helping the group to set goals and decision-making rules, resolving conflicts among members, and identifying tasks to be completed by the group (Tropman, 1997). In most cases, the chair sets the agenda and schedules meetings, although some of these responsibilities may be delegated to staff members (Hardcastle et al., 1997). The chair is responsible for ensuring that the agenda is followed during meetings and for following up with group members to ensure their assignments have been completed. This activity is particularly critical for the chair. Committee members may not contribute to the group unless they feel that they are involved in decision-making and that they have participated in the group's success. Consequently, the group facilitator must be able to effectively engage with members (Tropman, 1997). Chairpersons should ensure that the group has an opportunity to evaluate its own decision-making processes and goal achievement. Many committees in social service organizations also receive support from a designated staff person. Staff responsibilities can include the following:

- Establishing a good working relationship with the chair
- Helping the chair set the agenda
- Providing information about what decisions should be made and when
- Preparing written agendas and meeting minutes
- Researching issues to be addressed by the committee
- Sending out meeting reminder notices to members
- Providing technical expertise
- Preparing reports and other written products in consultation with community members (Tropman, 1997)

Many of these activities are similar to those used by executive directors when working with the full board and can be used for providing staff support to advisory committees.

ADVISORY BOARDS

Advisory boards are generally of two types: expert knowledge and service user. In the first type of advisory committee, people perceived to be experts in the delivery of the service provided by the organization or community leaders are recruited for membership on the advisory committee. In some cases, federal and state funding to social service organizations for program operation and planning is contingent upon the establishment of consumer advisory councils (Poindexter & Lane, 2003).

For example, the Ryan White Act requires the establishment of community advisory boards by community-based agencies that provide services to people with human immunodeficiency virus (HIV). In many cases, advisory board members have input into the design and evaluation of programs (Silvestre et al., 2002). The establishment of a "blue ribbon" advisory committee is used as a mechanism to increase the organization's legitimacy and public recognition (National Respite Network and Resource Center, 1993). Often a list of "expert" advisory board members is prominently displayed on the organization's letterhead or Web site.

Advisory committees can be of great benefit to organizations that want to ensure that services are delivered in a culturally competent manner, particularly in situations where staff members have little knowledge about some of the cultural or marginalized communities they serve (Lohmann & Lohmann, 2002; Poindexter & Lane, 2003). In such cases, advisory boards serve as a source of expert knowledge about how program beneficiaries perceive the organization and how programs can be improved to meet their needs. For example, Cox et al. (1998) describe the use of citizen advisory boards to develop appropriate procedures for clinical trials of treatments for people with AIDS and the procedures for recruiting people for these studies. Other roles often assigned to advisory boards include public relations, creating direction and support for staff in the delivery of services, and raising funds. In some instances, advisory board members are simply called upon to make financial donations or to use their business, political, or professional contacts to help the organization (National Respite Network and Resource Center, 1993).

It should be noted, however, that advisory committees are often just that—they have little or no power and authority to set policies or procedures for the organization. Administrators and members of the organization's board of directors are free to ignore issues, concerns, and policy directives developed by the advisory committee. Often service user and expert advisory boards lack clear mandates, and members are given limited guidance regarding their roles (Cox et al., 1998). In many instances, they may be reliant on administrative staff members to establish a direction or specific task for the advisory board.

Advisory boards in which members have no direct influence on decision-making are often not effective in increasing feelings of empowerment among members. Julian, Reischl, Carrick, and Katrenich (1997) conducted an experimental study of citizen participation in the planning process of a local United Way affiliate. Community volunteers were assigned to one of three advisory groups established to set program priorities for the distribution of funds. Each of the three groups was given different amounts of information to set priorities and varying amounts of access to the actual decision-makers. The researchers found no differences among members of the high-, medium-, and low-access groups in terms of their perception of the amount of influence they could assert in the planning process.

In contrast, an effective advisory board is one in which communication takes place within the context of mutual exchange and partnership between the organization's decision-makers and its committee members (Lohmann & Lohmann, 2002). Silvestre et al. (2002) describe an organizational structure established to enhance participation of young people in developing HIV prevention strategies. Round tables were established that were representative of members of at-risk populations. Each of these round tables elected members to a larger planning council. All members were encouraged to participate in the decision-making process. Consequently, the members were able to design interventions that were effective in reaching members of these at-risk populations.

BARRIERS TO FULL PARTICIPATION IN ORGANIZATIONAL DECISION-MAKING

Whereas organizational boards, committees, and advisory councils are the primary mechanisms used to include consumers in service delivery, many social service organizations either do not include clients in decision-making or fail to take action to maximize client participation (Cnaan, 1991). Barriers to full participation can include organizational structure and power differentials between clients and other low-income constituents and more privileged board members. In addition, organizational staff may have difficulty in establishing working partnerships with clients who serve on boards and committees.

Organizational Structure

According to Milofsky (1988), community-based organizations become much less representative of community residents (and consequently fail to represent community needs) as the community-based organizations develop from relatively informal organizations and take on formal roles, structures, and responsibilities. Milofsky argued that this is a consequence of the organization's need to respond to its external environment, especially funders who require that the organization develop a hierarchical structure and appoint one or two designated leaders or spokespersons. Often the structures established by nonprofit organizations or public advisory councils result in decision-making by groups of people who are not representative of community interests. For example, few boards in neighborhood organizations actually are elected through a vote of the membership (Cnaan, 1991). As described earlier in this chapter, selected boards may have nominating committees that simply reappoint sitting members to the board or rely on a handful of community social or business networks to recruit people to the board. Consequently, such boards are not open to new members, are not responsive to demographic shifts in the neighborhood or client population, and are not responsive to changes in the organization's task environment that may require new leadership or new decision-making approaches.

The intent of the organizational structure established to enhance community or client involvement in decision-making often is problematic. If a nonprofit or public agency actually wanted to cede full control to clients, consumer interests would dominate the board or decision-making body. However, because members of social, economic, and political elites dominate both nonprofit and public citizen participation processes, it is difficult for members of marginalized groups to gain control of the decision-making process (Hardina & Malott, 1996a). Arnstein (1969) identified eight levels of citizen participation in public decision-making that are relevant to understand how recruitment of new board members from among client populations is often used by organizations to maintain the status quo. These eight levels constitute what Arnstein calls a *ladder of citizen participation,* ranging from very high levels of consumer involvement to minimal participation:

- *Citizen control.* Program beneficiaries have full control of the organization.
- *Delegated power.* Seats on the board are designated or power is delegated to members of marginalized groups for them to develop their own service systems outside of existing service networks.
- *Partnership.* Participants share decision-making power.
- *Placation.* Seats for members of marginalized groups on decision-making boards are allocated, but a situation is created in which members of the elite can easily outvote them or permit the actual decision-makers to discount the views of participants.
- *Consultation.* People are asked to state their views, but no mechanism is in place to ensure that the perspectives of constituents are incorporated into the final decision.
- *Informing.* Constituents are simply given information about decisions that are already made.
- *Therapy.* The planning process is used to change the behavior of members of marginalized groups so that they will adopt the values and perspectives of the dominant group.
- *Manipulation.* Participants are "educated" so that they will adopt decisions made by others.

Arnstein (1969) argues that most types of public and nonprofit decision-making structures are oriented to processes located at the lower level of the citizen participation continuum: consultation, informing, manipulation, and therapy. Instead of citizens having real input into decisions that are often made by members of economic and social elites, board membership can be used simply to limit dissent, to "co-opt" opponents, to legitimize decision-making as a public relations ploy, or to convince members of marginalized groups to accept decisions made for them by members of the dominant culture.

One specific type of advisory process that is particularly problematic is the use of citizen boards and committees in public or quasi-public organizations (nonprofits that receive funding to carry out government activities) to allocate government funds to organizations and communities. Hardina and Malott (1996b) conducted a review of research on citizen planning and funding allocation boards in the United States and Canada between 1970 and 1990. They found that these boards often lacked a clear definition of their roles and were often used as a vehicle for government to authorize service planning or ration resources. When members of these panels requested that additional funds be allocated for health and social services, government often acted to terminate these boards or to limit their role in planning. Although government mandated consumer participation, few consumers were actually seated on these boards. Silverman (2003) examined the ability of elected citizen advisory boards to influence community development and planning. He found that although members of the board often acted as advocates for residents and as liaisons with developers, their power to improve the quality of life in the community was limited because the city failed to fund the boards adequately or to give them sufficient autonomy to perform their work.

Interpersonal Relationships Among Participants

As noted by Cnaan (1991), board members often are not members of the constituency groups expected to benefit from the organization's activities. Decision-making can be dominated by administrators or by a small number of board members. Staff members and middle- or upper-income board members usually have professional degrees that increase their power advantage vis-à-vis representatives of low-income or other underrepresented groups. Consequently, when members of these low-income or other underrepresented groups are appointed or elected to boards, they may find themselves marginalized, with little ability to voice concerns or raise issues at board meetings (Hardina & Malott, 1996a).

In addition, clients and other members of oppressed groups have few power resources (money, contacts with politicians, and social status) with which to bargain with professional staff and government officials (Winkle, 1991). Often former clients and other board members must rely on staff members for information on how the agency is operated and for technical details on how services are delivered. The technical language used by professional staff is a formidable obstacle to the inclusion of non-experts in the decision-making process (Hardina & Malott, 1996a).

Other factors that may put clients at a power disadvantage vis-à-vis staff include hardships associated with the client's marginalized status, including stigma, money, and time for travel to and from meetings, and problems with daily living associated with the client's status or situation. For example, barriers to the involvement of mentally ill clients in organizational decision-making can include homelessness, social isolation, and the impact of psychiatric disabilities (Manning, 1999). Power differentials between consumers and staff members also are problematic. Vaughn and Stamp (2003) conducted qualitative interviews that focused on the nature of interaction of staff members in shelters for battered women with their clients. Despite the fact that the mission of these organizations is to empower women who have been victimized, staff members described themselves as "different from" clients because they had not experienced domestic violence and were better off financially. They also described themselves as "having power over" clients in that the workers "educated clients" about domestic violence, controlled resources allocated to clients (such as job referrals, length of stay in the shelter, and food), and enforced household rules.

TECHNIQUES FOR PROMOTING EQUITABLE PARTICIPATION ON BOARDS

Even in situations where power brokers make well-intentioned efforts to include underrepresented groups in the planning process, all potential participants may find that their perspectives on the issue are ignored (Tauxe, 1995). Participation in organizational decision-making should increase the power of low-income people and members of other marginalized groups vis-à-vis the organization. However, program administrators and board members cannot assume a paternalistic role and "empower" individuals and groups. According to Segal and Silverman (1993):

> If empowerment in the social service environment is a process that can be initiated and sustained only by those who seek power and self-determination, then it cannot be conferred by others who can define

> the parameters of such power. Thus, mere consumer participation allowed in professionally run services must be seen as distinct from true consumer control. (p. 710)

True consumer control originates in organizations developed and controlled by the consumers of service (Arnstein, 1969). One of the premises of empowerment practice is that the act of creating self-help organizations provides consumers with the opportunity to develop advocacy and organizational development skills, increases their problem solving-capabilities, and helps them develop feelings of self-competency and empowerment (Gutierrez, et al., 1998). Therefore, empowerment-oriented organizations interested in facilitating consumer empowerment can provide staff members and other resources that assist clients in the creation of self-help groups. Clients can use these groups to identify common problems, develop strategies for problem resolution, and advocate for the resources needed to address the problem (Staples, 1999). The organization can further assist new self-help groups "spin off" from the larger organization to create their own programs and services.

In addition to supporting the development of self-help groups, social workers must take a lead role in social service organizations to establish institutional structures (boards, committees, advisory groups) that place community residents, low-income consumers, and members of culturally oppressed groups in decision-making roles. Beresford and Croft (1993) identify the following attributes of an inclusive decision-making process:

- Organizational structures that enhance involvement
- Information about the problem to be addressed by the group, the resources that can be used to address it, and possible solutions
- Resources (places to meet, clerical support, publicity, and money to cover travel expenses to and from meetings)
- Equal access to services and opportunities to participate
- Training in participatory processes
- Use of language and terminology (including appropriate translation services) that can be understood by all participants

O'Neill (1992) argues that representatives of low-income and other marginalized groups are more effective on boards when they represent powerful community constituency groups. Such groups obtain power through their membership (strength in numbers), their ability to influence the media, and their linkages with community institutions.

O'Neill identifies four characteristics of successful constituency group leaders:

1. A source of adequate and accurate information
2. Support from other constituency group members
3. The personality to stand up to administrators and other decision-makers
4. Established mechanisms for feedback from constituency groups

There are a number of additional components of effective consumer empowerment initiatives. According to Hardina and Malott (1996a), consumers are more likely to be empowered in instances where all organizational constituency groups support consumer inclusion; a high degree of agreement exists with regard to organizational goals; the board is representative of the community in terms of race, income, and gender; and training on technical language and decision-making is provided.

Silvestre et al. (2002) recommend a number of actions/conditions to ensure participation: decision-making bodies are representative of the population in need, participants to a decision-making body are elected by members of smaller deliberative groups, voting rights are granted to all members, all participants are given an equal amount of respect, and efforts are made to ensure that all aspects of the process are culturally appropriate. Performing these activities, however, requires sufficient monetary resources to support the decision-making process. As Silverman (2003) notes, seldom are deliberative bodies, established to represent the interest of marginalized groups, given sufficient resources to support participation. Consequently, the empowerment of service consumers on organization boards and public decision-making bodies requires not only the commitment of organization boards and executive directors but also support from foundation and government funders and sufficient autonomy to engage in decision-making to support community needs (Beresford & Croft, 1993).

BOX 5.3 INVOLVING CLIENT/CONSUMERS IN ORGANIZATION DECISION-MAKING

No clients or former clients serve on the board of the Northwest Women's Shelter. Many of the changes in services that Pang would like to make would improve the quality of services to members who primarily are African American or Latino and bisexual or lesbian clients.

Pang would also like to strengthen the shelter's services to children, who are often housed in the shelter with their mothers. Despite the fact that clients have recommended some of these improvements, there is currently no support for changes in service delivery among current board members.

- If board members agree that client/consumers should be seated on the board, what types of things should Pang do to ensure that consumers actually have input into board decision-making?
- In addition to client/consumers, what other types of people should be recruited to make the Northwest Women's Shelter board inclusive of the needs of the community?
- What additional organization structures should Pang establish to include client/consumers and community residents in program planning and evaluation?

Many of these elements suggest that a continuum of client/consumer participation can be developed to assess the degree of participation in social service organizations. Full consumer control would be at the highest level of participation in an empowerment-oriented organization (Staples, 1999). At the second level of the continuum are organizations in which constituency groups that represent clients or members of other underrepresented groups actually elect a number of members to the organization's board. Organizations at the midrange of the continuum have designated seats for consumers on their board or allow only token representation by consumers. Also in the middle of the continuum are organizations in which consumer participation is confined to membership of some consumers on internal committees that plan or evaluate programs. At the bottom of the participation continuum are organizations in which consumers are simply consulted about their needs or are informed about organizational activities, organizations in which participation is confined to client dialogue with staff members about their service needs, and organizations that allow no consumer participation in organizational decision-making (Figure 5.2). It should be noted, however, that empowerment-oriented organizations should use multiple techniques for involving consumers in decision-making: board membership, inclusion in program planning and evaluation, and ongoing dialogue and collaboration with social workers and other staff to assess client problems and choose interventions.

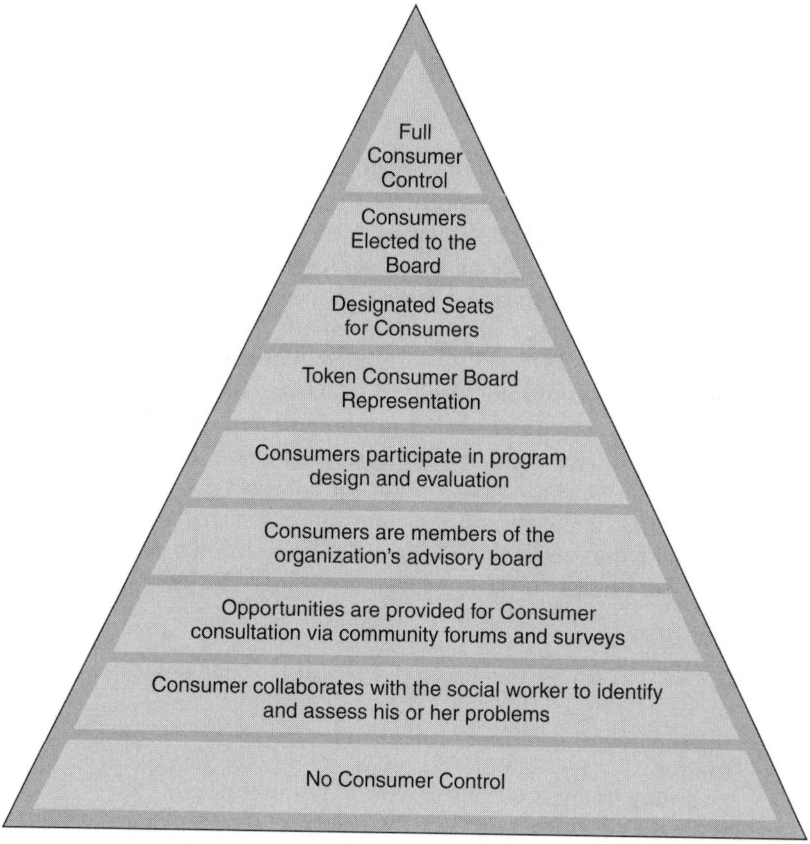

Figure 5.2 Continuum of client/consumer involvement in empowerment-oriented organizations.

MEASURING THE SUCCESS OF PARTICIPATORY DECISION-MAKING

In addition to increased service effectiveness, participatory processes should have a number of other outcomes that will benefit both participants and the organization. According to Parker and Betz (1996), a successful empowerment structure in social service organizations will

- Increase the degree of participation of various groups in the community.
- Help participants feel a greater sense of belonging to the organization or the surrounding community.

- Increase the degree to which program beneficiaries have access to the resources they need to meet their needs.
- Increase the leadership skills of clients, board members, staff, and other constituents.

Inclusion should increase the organization's ability to develop new programs and adopt new technologies that will make programs more effective (Brown, 2002). If implemented properly, empowerment-oriented practices can be assessed using a board self-evaluation tool that incorporates many of the techniques and principles identified in this chapter. For example, an empowerment-oriented board will recruit diverse members, support participation by service consumers, encourage active participation by all members, and rotate leadership. These boards will engage in a wide variety of activities, including policy-making and planning, fundraising, fiscal oversight, and public relations. Part of the role of board members is to serve as a conduit for communication between the organization and its constituency groups. Such a board will maintain a partnership with the executive director and evaluate its own performance as well as the performance of the organization on a regular basis (Table 5.1).

Table 5.1 Self-Evaluation Tool for Empowerment-Oriented Boards

		Yes	No
	Diversity		
1	Are board members committed to the inclusion of diverse people and clients/consumers on the board?		
2	Does the board have a written, diversity-oriented recruitment plan for new members?		
3	Is the board diverse on a variety of dimensions, including gender, ethnicity, age, social class, disability, and sexual orientation?		
4	Are mechanisms in place (such as a written recruitment plan or designated seats on the board) to ensure inclusion?		
5	Is terminology understood by all members used at meetings?		
6	Are translation or signing services offered for those members who need them?		
	Structure and Goals		
7	Are new board members chosen in one of the three following ways: elected by the organization's membership, selected by a nominating committee, or elected by members of one of the organization's key constituency groups?		
8	Are participant roles in decision-making clearly specified?		

(*Continued*)

Table 5.1 Self-Evaluation Tool for Empowerment-Oriented Boards (Cont.)

		Yes	No
9	Do board members agree on immediate and long-range goals?		
10	Are there ground rules that govern decision-making that are understood by all members?		
11	Is a board orientation provided for new members?		
12	Is regular training provided to board members on leadership skills, decision-making processes, and technical language or knowledge?		
	Decision-Making		
13	Are all participants encouraged to speak during meetings?		
14	Are decisions made on important agenda items at most meetings?		
15	Does each board member feel involved in the work of the board?		
16	Are efforts made to make decisions by consensus rather than majority rule?		
17	Are board members able to function as a cohesive team?		
18	Is responsibility for leadership rotated among members and the various interest groups on the board?		
	Board Activities		
19	Are board members actively involved in developing policies and plans for the organization?		
20	Do board members provide fiscal oversight for the organization?		
21	Do board members serve as a communication link between program beneficiaries or community residents and the board?		
22	Do board members engage in public relations activities to promote the organization's interests?		
23	Do board members raise funds for the organization?		
24	Has the board established a working partnership with the executive director?		
	Evaluation		
25	Does the board evaluate the performance of the executive director on a regular basis?		
26	Does the board engage in self-evaluation on a regular basis?		
27	Does the board assess its own ability to achieve its goals?		
28	Does the board monitor the overall performance of the organization?		

SUMMARY

Organizations have a variety of options for establishing decision-making structures that provide constituents and community leaders with a voice in the work of the organization. One of these vehicles, a board of directors, is a legal requirement. Boards bring a wide variety of skills and perspectives to organizational decision-making. However, in some organizations board members forfeit their governance role or are rendered powerless because of limited information about pending issues, conflict among different factions on the board, or failure of board leaders and administrators to consult with others. An empowerment-oriented administrator will seek opportunities to work in partnership with board members to make policy and other decisions for the organization. Such an administrator will be proactive in using other decision-making vehicles, such as internal and external committees, task forces, and advisory groups, to ensure that clients and other constituency groups can participate in policy-making, program design, and evaluation. The involvement of clients in program planning and assessment improves the effectiveness of service delivery and helps to ensure that programs actually meet their needs. Techniques used to design effective and accessible programs are described in Chapter 6.

QUESTIONS FOR CLASS DISCUSSION

1. What problems or issues would you expect when clients are seated on boards that are composed primarily of middle-income professionals?
2. What social work skills could you use to establish a cohesive board composed of diverse members?
3. As an executive director, in what situations would you establish an advisory committee? What should be the purpose of such a committee?
4. Ethically, how much power should an executive director have to set the board's agenda, provide or withhold information, or select board members? Are there provisions of the National Association of Social Workers (NASW) *Code of Ethics* that address executive director–board relations?
5. What options do members of governing boards or advisory committees have if their decisions are overruled by parent organizations or government agencies?

SAMPLE ASSIGNMENTS

1. Conduct an analysis of a board meeting. What is the demographic composition of the board? How does it differ from the demographic profile of the people who actually attended the meeting, the organization's staff, and the clients? What sources of power and influence do these board members have? How were decisions made during the meeting? Does the group appear to operate by consensus or by conflict? Who were the people who appeared most able to influence these decisions?
2. Create two organization charts for the organization in which you are interning or are employed. One of these charts should focus on the organization hierarchy. The other chart should portray the position of various decision-making structures (boards, committees, and task groups) in the organization. After you finishing constructing these charts, answer the following questions: Are these charts adequate to identify how decisions are made in the organization? Does each of these entities really have power to influence decision-making? If not, is power concentrated at certain levels of the organization to the exclusion of others?
3. Facilitate a committee meeting in an organization in which you are a member. Develop an agenda and set a goal for task completion prior to the meeting. Write a three-page paper that analyzes the decision-making process. Who participated? Were there obvious disagreements among members? What decision-making rules were used? How easy or difficult was it to move the agenda? Did you achieve your goal? If not, what were the barriers to goal attainment? What could you have done to improve the outcome or to make decision-making more efficient?
4. Analyze decision-making in your field agency or place of employment using the client empowerment continuum presented in this chapter. Do clients actually have a role in decision-making? What structures are used to encourage their participation or to limit it?
5. Team up with four or five students in your class to "form" an organization. Develop a statement of purpose or mission, elect a chairperson, and draft a set of by-laws for the organization.

CHAPTER 6

Program Design: Increasing Service Quality and Access

In addition to decision-making structures, social service organizations must establish appropriate internal systems to select clients and provide services. Most social service organizations create formal structures that require clients to apply for services. Applications are screened to determine eligibility for service. Clients enter the service delivery process, are turned away, or are referred elsewhere. In addition, the organization must determine what services are suitable for the client, the intensity of such services, and their duration. Consequently, organizational decision-makers are required to establish a standardized, formal system of care that requires successive actions and tasks be carried out by both clients and staff. The actual structure of this service delivery system will determine whether clients actually receive services and the quality of the services provided. In this chapter, the following attributes of social service organizations are described:

- Service delivery structures
- Mechanisms (such as policies and procedures) that are used to define the service system
- Procedures for ensuring program quality
- The concept of client access to services
- Organizational barriers that may or may not block access to services for clients
- The impact of government regulations and social worker discretion on program quality and client access to service
- Conducting needs assessments

The steps that must be taken by administrators, front-line staff, and organizational planners to plan, develop goals and objectives, monitor program implementation, and collect management information about how the program is working also are described.

THE STRUCTURE OF SERVICE DELIVERY SYSTEM

One of the common fallacies about social service organizations is that anyone can go to an organization for help and automatically receive services. Most organizations do not have sufficient resources for them to provide services to everyone who applies. Rein (1983) has argued that in any social service organization, tensions exist between efforts to get clients to adjust to organizational rules and the principle of client self-determination. Client "adjustment" or compliance with organizational policies is often used as a mechanism to help the organization standardize services and keep their costs to a minimum. Organizations that try to make services "fit" client needs or individualize them will encounter the higher costs associated with maximizing benefits. The process of standardization also takes place in situations where social service organizations must verify that services are provided in an equitable manner to all eligible people who apply for them (Smith & Lipsky, 1993). This is particularly the case with public agencies that are accountable to taxpayers for the manner in which they spend public funds. In addition to equitable treatment, such agencies must make efforts to minimize the amount and costs associated with service delivery while providing services in an equitable manner.

Public and nonprofit social service organizations may not intend to exclude clients, but they must preserve their own resources in order to keep the organization intact. Staff members must be paid. The organization must send a check for monthly payroll taxes to the Internal Revenue Service. Vendors must be reimbursed for office supplies, utilities, cleaning services, and photocopying costs. Most organizations pay monthly rent or make mortgage payments. If any of these actions do not take place on a regular basis, the organization will cease to exist. Consequently, most organizations find ways to limit or ration the distribution of organizational resources (Lipsky, 1980).

If the organization cannot meet the demands for service, they must turn people away or refer them elsewhere. In order to limit demand, some organizations establish intake processes that may actually discourage people from applying for services. For example, the organization may require prospective clients to wait 30 days between when they apply for service and the first day of service or require that applicants have a referral letter from a case manager. Organizations may try to limit demand by establishing narrow eligibility requirements that restrict service to specific population groups or people for whom the service is likely to produce successful outcomes.

In addition, some organizations may attempt to limit service delivery using criteria derived from societal perceptions of specific demographic groups (Iglehart & Becerra, 2000). Members of traditionally oppressed groups, such as people of color or individuals living in poverty, may have some difficulty in obtaining services. In addition, people such as substance abusers or unemployed, single adults may be viewed negatively by society as unworthy of assistance (Lipsky, 1980). These views are often shared by organizational decision-makers and front-line workers (Sandfort, Kalil, & Gottschalk, 1999). Making service decisions based on moral worth is a tradition in U.S. poverty policy and can be traced back to English Poor Laws. Although such viewpoints often are abhorrent to social workers and violate the National Association of Social Workers (NASW) *Code of Ethics,* we need to be aware that such viewpoints often are incorporated into service delivery allocation decisions.

Some nonprofit organizations are also guided by the principle of *particularism,* the notion that the organization should serve only people who share some characteristics with organizational decision-makers. For example, the provision of charity may be limited to members of one religion, a particular geographic community, or an ethnic group. Smith and Lipsky (1993) argue that although such selectivity runs counter to values such as equity and equality that are often paramount in government agencies, nonprofit organizations are more likely to be responsive to individual needs and to dispense with procedures that require prospective clients to verify that they actually need the service.

TOOLS FOR DEFINING THE PARAMETERS OF SOCIAL SERVICE ORGANIZATIONS

Because of the need to preserve resources while maximizing services, organizations must place some parameters on the structure of their social service delivery systems. Consequently, in developing a service delivery structure, organizations must specify the following elements:

- Mission statement
- Organizational goals
- Programmatic goals and objectives
- Protocols/policies for establishing eligibility for service
- Protocols/policies for actually delivering services
- Policies for hiring/firing staff and staff behavior (Kettner, 2002)

The organization's mission statement is the primary source document that sets a direction for the organization to follow. The organization's mission statement should include the following elements:

- A definition of the problem to be addressed by the organization
- A statement of the need or social problem to be addressed
- One or more goals that pertain to the problem
- Information about how the problem will be addressed
- The identification of core values that the organization will follow
- A description of a target population or intended beneficiaries (Hummel, 1996)

For example, a mission statement for an organization providing health services may set a goal of providing affordable, accessible, and high-quality health care services for undocumented immigrant families. This goal is designed to address the problem that such families lack access to health care services. Furthermore, the mission statement delineates the geographic area in which these services will be provided and limits services to residents of this neighborhood. By identifying these elements in the mission statement, the organization has narrowly defined the group of people who will receive services, thereby maximizing the benefits that can be provided with limited resources. The mission statement is used to guide future activities and set additional goals (Dropkin & LaTouche, 1998). The organization can use the mission statement to inform the public about what it intends to do and how it intends to recruit clients and solicit funds.

BOX 6.1 ORGANIZATION MISSION STATEMENT

Needs Statement:

People with incomes under the poverty line need *affordable, accessible, and high-quality* health care.

Problem Statement:

Many low-income people, especially those who are undocumented residents, have difficulty finding *affordable, accessible, and high-quality* health care services.

Client Population:

Undocumented individuals and families living in the Mission District.

Goal:

To provide *affordable, accessible, and high quality* health care services to undocumented individuals and families.

Table 6.1 Documents Needed for Organization and Program Development

Organization	Program Development
Mission statement	Goals and objectives
By-laws	Timelines
Annual budget	Evaluation plan
Organization policy manual	Eligibility criteria
Personnel policies	Rules and procedures
Strategic plan	Management information systems

Policies and procedures can pertain to the entire organization or to specific organizational components called *programs* (Table 6.1). A program can be defined as "a major ongoing agency activity or service with its own set of goals, objectives, policies, and budgets that produces a defined product or service" (Martin, 2001, p. 11). In order to operate these programs effectively, the organization must develop policies and procedures that determine who is served by the organization, how the service is delivered, and how staff are to function in specific circumstances. Weinbach (1998) differentiates among policies, rules, and procedures. *Policies* are general statements used to guide decisions and shape behavior, and their interpretation may be left to the discretion of administrators and front-line workers who are responsible for implementing them. On the other hand, organizations use *rules* to standardize behavior and decisions. *Procedures* are rules that must be implemented in chronological order in order to ensure compliance.

SERVICE QUALITY

No nonprofit or public organization intends to offer services that are not of high quality. However, resource restrictions, interpersonal dynamics within the organization, and the sociopolitical environment in which the organization operates may limit program quality. *Service quality* can be defined as those factors that are important to the organization's clients while they are receiving services (Kettner, 2002). As discussed in Chapter 2, the total quality management (TQM) approach involves workers in defining quality service and working to achieve quality as an organizational goal (Lawler, Mohrman, & Ledford, 1995).

In for-profit organizations, program quality is determined by customers or the people who actually pay for the service. Conceivably consumers will not obtain the product unless they believe it is the best they can purchase for a specific price. As noted in Chapter 2, most nonprofit organizations do not sell their products or set a price. Often clients have few alternative sources from which they can obtain the service. Unlike products distributed by manufacturers, the quality of service delivery is difficult for consumers to evaluate and often cannot be determined before the service is delivered (Gardner, 1999a). Usually it is assessed in terms of both outcome of the service delivery process and the interaction between front-line staff members and the client/customer.

Because of these measurement problems, a number of constituency groups associated with the organization, such as clients, organizational staff, board members, funding sources, and knowledgeable experts in a particular service field, can play a role in establishing standards of quality (Kettner, Moroney, & Martin, 1999). The accreditation or licensing processes required for many nonprofit organizations, such as day care centers, foster care agencies, and nursing homes, also examine program quality, looking at predetermined factors such as programmatic resources, staff qualifications, facilities, fiscal stability, and service delivery plans (Ginsberg, 2001).

Regardless of whether they must report to accreditation agencies, many organizations establish internal indicators of standards to determine if quality services are provided. For example, Zeithmal (as cited in Gardner, 1999a) asks questions to identify five types of quality criteria:

- Are staff members empathic to client concerns?
- Are staff members knowledgeable and courteous?
- Are staff members responsive to client needs and provide services promptly?
- Can the organization be relied upon to provide the service accurately?
- Does the appearance of staff members, physical facilities, and equipment convey that the service is of high quality?

Examples of quality-related standards can include whether staff members in a mental health center are licensed clinical social workers, whether the nutritional content of snacks provided by day care facilities meets predetermined standards, whether a specified number of counseling sessions were provided by a family service agency, or if a homeless shelter met predetermined standards for cleanliness. Organizations that are committed to maintaining quality services develop internal systems to continually monitor whether these standards are met (Hawkins & Gunther, 1998).

Consumer satisfaction surveys are also used to measure service quality. These surveys, distributed to current and former clients, ask participants if they liked the services and if they received the services they needed. Clients may be asked to report on the nature of the interaction between themselves and their workers. Although many organizations use these surveys, most experts believe they are at best imperfect as a measure of program quality. Consumers' perception that their confidentiality may not be protected may lead to the attainment of very high satisfaction ratings. In addition, it may simply be difficult to try to measure a concept such as satisfaction, which is difficult to define (Hardina, 2002).

CLIENT ACCESS TO SERVICES

Access to services can be defined as the ability of program applicants or clients to obtain the services they need. The establishment of narrow eligibility criteria is the most common method for limiting the flow of clients into organizations. The term *client* actually is controversial because it implies that the client is dependent upon, and controlled by, the organization or the staff member who determines eligibility (Hardina, 1988, 1990). Consequently, the eligibility process may have the effect of placing the applicant in a subordinate and therefore powerless role in the organization (Cohen, 1998; Hasenfeld, 1992).

In addition to narrow eligibility criteria, organizations can control the number of people they assist by creating organizational structures, policies, and procedures to determine the degree to which people can seek help. For example, people who are asked to fill out lengthy applications or who are told they must meet work requirements in return for assistance can become discouraged and consequently discontinue the application process. Some programs require that applicants be subjected to an income test to determine eligibility. Income testing is often a difficult process. Applicants are required to prove that they have no disposable income. This requires that applicants disclose a great deal of personal information and provide documentation of financial status, including pay stubs, living expenses (such as rent and utilities), and tax forms. In many cases, applicants also must provide extensive documentation of personal identity that includes birth certificates and social security numbers for all family members. The process of collecting this information can involve substantial financial costs for impoverished families; they may be required to pay fees to obtain public documents and often must make photocopies of any documents submitted to organizations during the application process.

Prottas (1981) calls such procedural requirements "the cost" of applying for service. When people face numerous procedural barriers to help-seeking, the cost (psychological, time related, or monetary) often outweighs the perceived benefit of receiving the service. Some organizations impose these costs deliberately, making their services unobtainable to all but the most persistent applicant. In other organizations, procedural barriers can originate in the client's attitude about the help-seeking process or the social stigma often associated with the process of seeking help. For example, clients may feel that it is socially inappropriate to apply for government programs or free services from nonprofit organizations. They may believe that they will be regarded as bad or immoral if they become a service recipient.

BOX 6.2 BECOMING A CLIENT

Rosa is a single mother with two children, ages 4 and 16 years. She has been laid off from her job as a bookkeeper for a small business. She has exhausted her unemployment benefits during her job search. However, she has managed to find a part-time retail position without health benefits. Her youngest child has asthma, and she believes her oldest child has been abusing drugs. Her aunt has announced that she can no longer take care of the younger child while Rosa works. Rosa decides to apply for welfare benefits and has also decided to obtain family counseling from a local nonprofit organization.

Rosa goes to the local welfare office to apply for welfare benefits, food stamps, day care assistance, and Medicaid. The intake clerk provides her with lengthy forms to fill out. The office is crowded and somewhat dirty. Rosa must communicate with the clerk through a plate glass window. After a 6-hour wait, her name is called and she is interviewed by an intake worker. Rosa is told that it will take several weeks to process her application and that she may not qualify for assistance because of her income. She also is told that she must provide the welfare office with birth certificates and social security numbers for each child, proof of residence, and proof of income in order to qualify for benefits. The worker informs Rosa that if she does not have birth certificates, she must pay a fee to obtain them from the county in which the child was born. Rosa is advised to photocopy all of the required documents rather than submit the originals to the welfare department because of the high risk that these documents might be lost. Rosa's visit to the welfare office leaves her depressed and demoralized.

She has somewhat better luck at the family service agency. The waiting area is clean and inviting. Rosa is greeted warmly by the receptionist and given a two-page application to fill out. She waits only 30 minutes to see a social worker. Although Rosa is treated with respect by the social worker, she requests a great deal of information about Rosa's current situation and family history. She is told that the agency can provide her with job training assistance in addition to family counseling services. However, she is told that there will be a small fee for these services unless she qualifies for welfare. Consequently, she will need to wait to obtain services from this agency until after her eligibility for welfare is established.

In some cases, just the fear of social ostracism associated with welfare receipt can cause potential applicants to experience psychological distress or to think twice about enrolling in a program (Goodban, 1985). For example, Fix and Passel (1999) performed a study of welfare recipients in Los Angles County and reported that enrollment of immigrant families in the Medicaid program dropped substantially after an anti-immigration legislative proposition was passed by voters but never implemented in California. Some potential recipients feared they could be deported if they applied for benefits. Studies of welfare caseworker attitudes toward clients have documented that workers sometimes ascribe moral worth to uncooperative clients, viewing them as hostile, capable of manipulating program requirements for their own benefit, or inappropriately demanding of their rights (Hasenfeld & Weaver, 1996; Sandfort et al., 1999).

Other types of access barriers can include program elements such as inaccessibility of physical facilities to wheelchair users or to other people with disabilities, the lack of translation services for deaf individuals and non-English speakers, geographic locations of organizations without access to public transportation or public parking, and hours of program operation (e.g., 9 to 5) that make it difficult for working people to obtain services. Organizations that do not attempt to make their services or written material language or culturally appropriate also exclude some groups of clients (Iglehart & Becerra, 2000).

BOX 6.3 COMMON TYPES OF ACCESS BARRIERS

- Hours of agency operation may make obtaining the service difficult.
- Wait time for service is long.
- Applications are lengthy, complex, and difficult to complete.
- Eligibility is income tested. Applicants may need to "spend down" to a specific level in order to qualify for services.
- Applicants may be required to provide a number of documents, such as birth certificates, social security cards, and employment stubs, in order to establish eligibility.
- Applicants may face substantial monetary costs in order to obtain or copy documents.

- Service is associated with monetary fees.
- Hours of operation, for example, 9 to 5, make it difficult for working people to obtain service.
- Geographic location of the agency is difficult to reach or is dangerous.
- Public transportation and/or parking may make travel to the agency difficult.
- The agency is not responsive to the language or cultural needs of clientele. For example, does the organization have printed documents, translation services, or bilingual staff in the appropriate languages?
- Child care services are not available at the agency.
- Clients are discriminated against or stigmatized when they apply for a service.
- Physical access to the agency for disabled clients is limited.
- Appropriate services, such as Braille documents for the blind or interpreters for deaf clients, are not provided by the agency.
- Federal or state regulations may prohibit undocumented residents from obtaining the services.
- Service coordination, case management, and other gatekeeping processes limit the supply or availability of services.
- Substantial monetary or personal costs may be associated with foregoing another opportunity (e.g., a job interview) in order to obtain the service.

Some barriers occur because of special attributes of a subgroup among the target population. For example, Stromwall (2002) has described the difficulties faced by the mentally ill in complying with job training and placement requirements in the Temporary Assistance for Needy Families (TANF) program. Psychologically disabled recipients not only experienced more difficulty in finding appropriate job placements, but recipients previously diagnosed with mental illnesses experienced increases in emotional distress when they participated in TANF jobs programs.

It should be noted that many of the criteria used to determine service quality also pertain to client access to services. For example, many government agencies require that the nonprofit services that they fund be made physically accessible to people with disabilities or linguistically accessible to deaf or non–English-speaking clients (Gardner, 1999b). Standards that focus on the quality of interaction between clients and staff members and the importance of customer service should provide safeguards against the use of negative social stereotypes that exclude some groups of clients from the service system.

THE ROLE OF GOVERNMENT REGULATIONS IN DETERMINING CLIENT ACCESS AND PROGRAM QUALITY

Although organizations often try to ration services in order to preserve their own resources, rules established by government agencies, foundation, and corporate donors also determine the degree to which services are accessible to clients. In Chapter 2, we used power-dependency theory (Blau, 1964) to explain why organizations become dependent upon funders and consequently may be forced to comply with donor demands. Such demands may make services more or less accessible for clientele. For example, a foundation may require that an organization serving homeless people actually reserve seats on their boards of directors for low-income or homeless individuals. Funds obtained through a federal grant could be conditional on an organization's hiring staff members with specific qualifications or maintaining facilities that meet government standards.

Government agencies that provide funds to nonprofits require that these organizations comply with certain standards. In government-funded public and nonprofit programs, regulations determine who is eligible for the service, how the service is delivered, and how outcomes will be reported. *Regulations* are administrative rules established to ensure that government programs are carried out in a proscribed, standardized manner across all jurisdictions (Jansson, 1999). Haynes and Mickelson (2005) describe the regulatory process as "the power to guide the behavior of others and the opportunity to make decisions about the basic allocation of services" (p. 99).

Government agencies develop regulations in order to implement laws. When government bodies such as Congress or state legislatures pass legislation, it often is broad and ambiguous because decision-makers find reaching a compromise that will satisfy a majority of the individuals involved in the legislative process easier (Lindblom, 1959). Consequently, some pieces of legislation lack specific details about how laws actually should be implemented. Federal, state, and local government agencies are responsible for writing rules and regulations that will be used to implement new laws and policies. All jurisdictions provide the opportunity for public comments on the rules either in writing or at public hearings. However, these agencies are not required to incorporate public comments into the final version of published regulations (Haynes & Mickelson, 2005).

Examples of regulations include state child welfare codes, Medicaid reimbursement requirements, Affirmative Action and fair employment laws, school attendance policies, and state social work licensing laws. Although individual social workers must develop personal strategies for working within the confines of regulations, it is the responsibility of the organization's administrator to implement regulations and develop internal organizational policies for doing so. However, administrators must be aware that regulations implemented in the manner intended by government may have both positive and negative impacts on the organizations. Regulations can affect

- Whether services are actually accessible to the people who need them.
- Whether the organization actually "sticks with" its primary mission and target population.
- The degree to which the eligibility process incorporates popular perceptions of morality and social stigma into eligibility determinations.
- The degree to which the organization can meet the unique needs of their target client population and the community it serves.
- Whether the organization is realistically able to achieve the quality measures specified by government with available resources (Smith & Lipsky, 1993).

Although continuation of funding is contingent upon compliance with regulations, organizations have a certain degree of latitude in actually implementing them. Some of this latitude can be attributed to differences among organizations in the actual implementation of regulatory standards and the degree to which government agencies monitor compliance in different jurisdictions and individual organizations. In addition, front-line workers who must interpret policies often have a degree of autonomy in the decision-making process. The ability to interpret laws and policies as they pertain to individual clients or specific situations is called *discretion* (Lipsky, 1980).

THE ROLE OF WORKER DISCRETION IN SELECTING CLIENTS, ALLOCATING SERVICES, AND MAINTAINING QUALITY

Social workers act as gatekeepers in many social service organizations. Simply put, they determine who gets what services. Social workers who conduct intakes determine if clients are eligible to receive services from the organization. Social workers who perform assessments determine the type and quantity of services that clients will receive. Although some of these decisions are restricted by organizational policies or government regulations, the social worker often has the final say in determining eligibility for service. How the assessments are conducted, whether the worker engages in advocacy to expand client access to services, and the nature or quality of the interaction between client and worker are largely up to the worker.

When policies are broad and ambiguous, complex, or inconsistent, workers often have latitude in the way the policies are applied. The interpretation of policies by social workers and other staff members is called *discretion.* Lipsky (1980) has written extensively about the power possessed by "street-level bureaucrats," social service workers who apply government and organizational policies on a day-to-day basis. Handler (1992) contrasts the power of organizational staff and the average social services client:

> Workers are members of organizations, and it is the organizations that determine how their resources are to be allocated. If the clients want these resources, then they must yield at least some control over their fate. In addition, workers have other sources of power: expertise, persuasion, legitimacy, specialized knowledge, and interpersonal skills. (p. 281)

Power-dependency theory can be used to describe the client–social worker relationship in many social service organizations (Blau, 1964). In the context of social service delivery, power-dependency theory can be applied to both the relationship between the funding source and the organization (as represented by staff members) and between the organization and the client. The organization is obligated to comply with the demands of the funder in order to protect its budget The client is often dependent on social workers for free services. Consequently the client is obligated to act in an appropriate manner in order to continue to receive services. In many cases, the organization must require clients to comply with funder-imposed demands (such as verification of income eligibility) in order to survive (Figure 6.1).

Although regulatory demands may seem to be quite explicit, these policies often provide opportunities for workers to make discretionary choices regarding to whom and how services are allocated and delivered (Handler, 1992). Especially in government agencies, the policies that guide service allocation decisions are complex, contradictory, and confusing. In addition, organizational managers and unit supervisors often urge staff members to limit the amount of services provided to clients. In some cases,

Figure 6.1 Power-dependency in social service organizations.

workers may be subject to explicit or even implicit sanctions if they advocate for increased access to services for individual clients. As described at the beginning of this chapter, because of the complexity and ambiguity in program policies, it may be easier for workers to apply social norms and values about the moral worth of various applicants in making eligibility decisions (Lipsky, 1980). These morals and values may reflect stigma directed toward vulnerable or marginalized groups outside the dominant culture. Because stigma is often directed toward new immigrants, people in poverty, persons of color, people with disabilities, or sexual minorities, members of these groups receive fewer services or are more likely to have benefits terminated than are other recipients (Iglehart & Becerra, 2000).

Social workers value the ability to practice autonomously, using professional knowledge, values, and skills to make good client-related decisions. Many times, guided by the NASW *Code of Ethics,* social workers interpret policies in a manner that incorporates the best interest of the client or engages in advocacy so that the rules are changed for the client's benefit. Lipsky (1980) argues that the organization's need to limit demand for service and negative social stereotypes about people who apply for service can result in the use of discretion to limit client access to services or to render clients powerless. It is important to note, however, that the profession of social work has an ethical code (as described in the NASW *Code of Ethics*) that strictly prohibits the use of discretion to harm clients or limit their access to resources.

Problematic for social workers and managers is that the TQM model actually is designed to eliminate discretion, focusing on the process of standardization of worker tasks, outcomes, and quality control measures (Kettner et al., 1999). Although the empowerment model does not contain explicit references to discretion, much of the literature on this topic does focus on the need to give workers more autonomy to make decisions. It also encourages advocacy by workers to improve customer service (Spreitzer, 1996). Consequently, social work managers will need to adopt personnel management strategies that balance the need for standardization of service delivery with mechanisms that encourage worker autonomy and discretion.

THE ROLE OF MANAGERS AND FRONT-LINE WORKERS IN IMPROVING CLIENT ACCESS AND ENHANCING QUALITY SERVICES

The first step necessary in the creation of a service delivery system that provides quality service and is accessible to clients is simply to reject the concept of "clienthood." Handler (1992) has argued that beneficiaries of service should not be the recipients of a one-way exchange of resources from the organization. Instead, the concepts of mutuality and reciprocity should be incorporated into the service delivery process. Each service recipient brings unique resources to the exchange of services and should be looked upon as a potential volunteer or decision-maker (Gamble & Weil, 1992; Hardina, 1990).

An empowerment-oriented organization should be managed to ensure maximum accessibility and program quality. Managers may use deliberate problem-solving approaches to managing staff or resources to shape how services are delivered. Such overall approaches are called *strategies* (Lohmann & Lohmann, 2002). Gilbert, Specht, and Terrell (1993) identify strategies used by social service organizations to control client access and participation in decision-making: advocacy, citizen participation, hiring former clients to deliver services, coordination with other organizations, and income testing (Table 6.2). Each of these strategies contains at least two discrete service delivery options that can be used to enhance or impede client/consumer control in the organization. For example, an organization can choose to use income testing to determine an applicant's eligibility for service or can choose to use other criteria depending on regulatory restraints. As previously described in this chapter, income testing requires that applicants prove they have no income through the submission of pay stubs and verification of expenses, a process that often is time consuming and demeaning. Similarly, the organization can choose whether to involve program participants in decision-making. The organization can try to make services more responsive to

Table 6.2 Professional and Consumer-Oriented Strategies to Control Access to Services

Strategies	Professional	Consumer
Advocacy	Case advocacy	Self-help advocacy and/or political participation of constituents
Citizen participation	Give decision-making authority only to board members and experts	Give decision-making authority to consumers
Coordination	Coordinate efforts with other agencies	Limited communication and resource sharing with other agencies
Eligibility requirements	Income testing	No income testing
Staffing	Hire only professionals	Hire consumers of service

the needs of clientele by hiring paraprofessional staff from the target community served rather than hiring exclusively professional staff that may be of a different social class and often culturally different than their clients (Iglehart & Becerra, 2000).

Gilbert et al. (1993) argue that using an income test, choosing not to hire former clients, and refusing to include clientele in organizational decision-making are strategies that enhance the power and control of professional staff in organizations. In addition, their use excludes clients from participation in the service delivery system. The strategies of advocacy and coordination also have implications for enhancing or limiting the power of service users. According to Hardina (1988, 1990), case advocacy, conducted only by organizational staff, enhances the power of professionals to secure resources from clients and thereby keep them dependent on the worker for continued support. Self-advocacy, on the other hand, empowers the service user. The client learns to acquire the good or service for himself or herself and consequently acquires power (Gutierrez, Parsons, & Cox, 1998; Rose & Black, 1985).

Service coordination, which often is used to reduce duplication of service and to allow a client to submit one application for multiple programs, also increases the power of professionals in service-related decisions. Most coordinated service delivery systems require that a designated case manager or gatekeeper screens clients for eligibility for service before the clients are allowed to approach a second organization for help (Gilbert et al., 1993; Hasenfeld, 1992). Although the availability of referrals or services at one site makes it easier for clients to use service coordination, in some instances it may actually limit the client's ability to select the service that best meets his or her needs. In addition, coordination generally focuses on eliminating duplication of services and consequently the client's ability to obtain as much service as needed from multiple sources.

Organizations interested in maximizing access to services and empowering clientele will choose strategies that enhance client/consumer control of the organization and decline to use the professional control strategies. However, organizations may not apply these strategies consistently (Hardina, 1990). Another reason that consumer control strategies are not always adopted is that service professionals are not likely to cede power to clients (Cohen, 1998). However, one of the basic assumptions of empowerment practice is that to empower clients, agency staff members must feel empowered (Gutierrez, GlenMaye, & DeLois, 1995). Techniques for empowering staff members are described in Chapter 9.

Design Options for Empowerment-Oriented Services

In addition to access structures, specific types of programs or approaches to the actual provision of service can be used to reduce the power differential between clients and workers. One of the basic premises of empowerment practice is that clients should be equal partners with staff in problem assessment and intervention planning (Gutierrez et al., 1998). Consequently, empowerment-oriented organizations need to incorporate the values of mutual learning and partnership into the design of service delivery programs. Studies by Boehm and Staples (2002) and Bartle, Couchonnal, Canda, and Staker (2002) indicate that the quality of the relationship between clients and workers or the actual process used to foster mutual decision-making is the key to achieving empowerment-oriented service outcomes.

Linhorst and Eckert (2003) have identified a number of strategies that can be used to incorporate empowerment principles into the development of social service programs:

- The provision of training in leadership and decision-making to clientele
- The provision of organizational resources, such as advocates who can serve as liaisons between clients and staff
- The provision of logistical support, such as meals, transportation, and child care, to clients involved in organizational decision-making
- The provision of incentives to both staff members and clients to work together cooperatively to make decisions
- The provision of information to clients that allows them to choose among available service options

Another strategy that can be used to empower program beneficiaries in organizations, as noted in previous chapters, is the inclusion of agency clientele in conducting needs assessments and program planning.

NEEDS ASSESSMENT: THE IMPORTANCE OF CLIENT AND WORKER PARTICIPATION IN THE IDENTIFICATION AND REMEDIATION OF SERVICE DELIVERY PROBLEMS

Needs assessment is the process through which social service organizations and community groups systematically identify common client problems that can be addressed through service delivery or advocacy

(Chambers, Wedel, & Rodwell, 1992). Ideally, needs assessments take place before new organizations are started or prior to the development of new programs or services by existing organizations. Task forces and advisory committees may be established to involve a variety of program stakeholders, ranging from clients to front-line staff, program administrators, community residents, leaders of local organizations, knowledgeable professionals, and other interested parties in the needs assessment process (Burch, 1996; Durst, MacDonald, & Parsons, 1999).

There are a variety of approaches to needs assessment. Common types of needs assessments include community surveys and interviews with clients, community residents, staff members, and other key informants (Hardina, 2002). The purpose of these approaches is to develop a priority ranking of needs to be addressed by new programs or to determine if services are provided to all those who need them (Royse & Thyer, 1996). Needs assessments are also conducted to determine whether serious gaps exist in service delivery or whether existing services are accessible to people in need. Interviews and document analyses are undertaken to determine what services are available, who is served by these programs, and whether any obvious demographic groups are not receiving services from already established organizations (Marti-Costa & Serrano-Garcia, 1995).

Information for needs assessment can be generated using group techniques. One common method for obtaining information about community preferences for services is focus group interviewing. In a focus group, five to ten key informants (clients, residents, staff members, representatives from community institutions) are asked six to eight open-ended questions about community needs, the structure of service delivery systems, potential improvements in programs, or perceived gaps in services (Chambers et al., 1992). Participants are generally not selected at random but are picked to provide a cross-section of key informants. The facilitator encourages participants to elaborate on previous responses from other group members. In this manner, a consensus on client needs and solutions to problems is generated (Berg, 1998).

Organizations may hold community forums to gather information about what their constituents want and need (Hardcastle, Wenocur, & Powers, 1997). Given the potential for gathering a great variety of different viewpoints about the issue, structured decision-making techniques are generally used to try to arrive at a consensus about common problems. The most commonly used method is called *nominal group technique* (Chambers et al., 1992). This method requires that each participant provide the facilitator with a short list of problems or issues to be addressed. This information is posted on a blackboard or written on butcher block paper for all members to see. It soon becomes evident that some participants have identified the same problem. A short list of priority problems is identified, and participants are asked to rank which of these problems is most important to them. The problem or issue ranked the highest by most of the participants is chosen by the organization, and a program to address this problem is planned (Hardina, 2002).

Data for needs assessments can be obtained through analysis of agency records and data on people who have applied for or who have used the service. In addition, standardized data collected by state and federal agencies on social problems or program use can be used to assess need. Many government agencies post this information on their Web sites, and the information can easily be downloaded for inclusion in needs assessment reports (Royse & Thyer, 1996). Obtainable data can include welfare participation, public health records, hospital utilization, traffic accident information, and crime reports. The most commonly used source of data for needs assessment is the United States Census (Hardina, 2002). Census information includes information about the number of people by block, census tract, neighborhood, city, or county. Types of information available include gender, age, income, housing conditions, ethnic group membership, single-parent households, and occupations of residents. It should be noted, however, that although the Census represents a good source of data, collected in a standardized way, that can be used to make comparisons across geographic jurisdictions, it also has important limitations. It is conducted only once every 10 years, and many people, usually those who are low income or undocumented, are uncounted. There is controversy about how some of the indicators used are constructed, especially those that measure race and ethnicity and whether household income is under the federal poverty line (Hardina, 2002).

Needs assessment is generally considered "applied" research. There are few standardized measurement instruments; it may be difficult to obtain a random sample of respondents because of the size of the population studied or because of difficulty in obtaining lists of potential respondents. Different groups of key informants (e.g., clients and staff members) may view needs very differently, so the program planner may experience difficulty in setting priorities using these data. Often surveys and measuring instruments are constructed to fit a specific situation or to provide hard data to verify what the program planner already knows: that a need exists for a specific program or service. In order to enhance the reliability and validity of needs assessment findings, program planners generally use a number of techniques to verify need (Royse & Thyer, 1996).

DESIGNING ACCESSIBLE AND QUALITY PROGRAMS: STRATEGIC AND OPERATIONAL PLANNING

Another basic assumption of empowerment practice is that agency clientele along with other key constituents (such as staff, board members, community residents, and key informants) should be involved in planning and designing programs (Rose & Black, 1985). The inclusion of clientele in the design of services ensures that the programs actually fit the needs of the client, are culturally appropriate, and are more likely to be used by clients. Often organizations establish task groups explicitly to involve constituency groups in the development of new programs (Chambers et al., 1992). However, time and money constraints may limit the planning process to a small group of organizational administrators or grant writers. Three primary types of plans can be developed: strategic, long-term, and program or operational plans (Kettner, 2002).

Strategic planning is an approach explicitly used to help an organization respond to changes in its external environment by using scarce resources in a manner that best contributes to the long-term health of the organization (Eadie, 1998). The strategic planning process requires that an organization bring together key constituency groups in one or a series of meetings to examine the organization's mission statement and future direction.

In new organizations, a mission statement that will guide future operations is developed. In already established organizations, the mission statement may be revised, or constituents may "recommit" themselves to the original mission statement and the values inherent in that mission. A facilitator then guides participants through an analysis of the organization's operations, its external environment, and the organization's strengths and weaknesses (Kettner, 2002). Participants will try to anticipate future trends (including client needs and the implications of new technology for service delivery), challenges or difficulties, and opportunities to expand markets and services (Eadie, 1998). At the conclusion of the process, recommendations for program and policy modifications and new programs are made. These changes usually are to be undertaken over a 5-year period. The end result is that the organization has prepared a "new vision" that contains goals for the future and values that will characterize how these goals are obtained (Lohmann & Lohmann, 2002). Eadie (1998) differentiates between values and vision:

> Values are the most cherished principles—the "golden rules"—that guide an organization's planning and management activities. A vision is a word picture of an organization's desired impact on or contribution to its community or service area and of the organization's role in the community. (pp. 455–456)

Long-terms plans are used to put the organization's vision into practice during the 5-year strategic planning period. Organizational planners, sometimes working alone and sometimes working with a representative task group of key organizational constituents, conduct an assessment of the information and resources needed to put the strategic plan into operation (Kettner, 2002). What monetary, staff, and operational resources will be needed to achieve these goals? The implications of adding or dropping programs and targeting new constituency groups are analyzed. Alternative plans and their potential consequences for the organization are examined (Lohmann & Lohmann, 2002). At the conclusion of the process, appropriate constituency groups are presented with these alternative scenarios, and decisions about program planning and resource allocation are made.

Program plans are used to develop new programs and services in response to newly identified needs and client demands. In some situations, new programs are developed simply in response to the fact that a government or other funder has made money available for that purpose. Generally, the first place in which the outline of a new program is described is in a funding proposal. Funders require that applicants submit proposals that contain a number of elements, including a statement of the problem, a needs assessment, goals and objectives, a budget, and a plan for program evaluation (see Chapter 13).

GOALS AND OBJECTIVES

Goals and objectives are used to put the organization's mission into action. *Goals* are broad, ambiguous, and pertain to an ideal we want to reach, such as "end homelessness" or "improve the quality of life in the community." *Objectives* are steps to reaching the goal and must be related to a specific task or process, must be time limited (accomplished within a specific time frame), and must be measurable. By measurable, we mean that objectives can be quantified or otherwise subjected to some type of assessment to determine whether the objective has been accomplished. It is advisable that some type of evaluation tool be specified, often in addition to simply counting whether some quantity has been achieved (Hardina, 2002; Kettner et al., 1999).

Goals and objectives can focus on either a task or a process. *Task objectives* focus on completing a specific activity or delivering a specific number of services. An example of a task objective is as follows:

Objective: **Providing 20 new beds in a homeless shelter per month.**

Process objectives are a means used to complete a task-related activity. Process objectives are most often related to recruiting new participants, leadership development, increasing public awareness, providing skill training, or strengthening the organization (Mondros & Wilson, 1994). An example, of a process objective is as follows:

> *Objective:* **Enhancing the leadership skills of 30 community volunteers by providing leadership training seminars twice per year.**

Once goals and objectives are in place, the organization must develop a program structure, set up a process for selecting clients, and develop specific policies for delivering the service.

The construction of goals and objectives should be congruent with a specific theory that relates cause and effect. In program planning, *cause* refers to specific actions that are taken to achieve a goal. *Effect* is the goal or outcome of the program. Theories that relate a set of actions or interventions to programmatic outcomes are called *theories of action* (Patton, 1997). Theories of action can be found in the theoretical literature, in reports, and in other documentation about the organization's "best practices," or they can be derived from the experiences of program planners and participants. Regardless of how these theories are generated, it is the program planner's responsibility to make explicit the rationale for the program, the intended goal or outcome of the program, and the steps the organization will take to reach the goal. In some cases, program goals and objectives can be categorized in terms of timelines needed for their achievement. For example, a program may need to achieve short-term and intermediate objectives in order to meet its ultimate goal.

For example, Itzhaky and York (2002) describe a theory of action and goals for the Community Empowerment Program that was developed to improve a community's self-image by using an empowerment approach (Figure 6.2). Community activists are to be recruited to identify community needs and carry out social action campaigns that address community problems. The primary theoretical assumptions are that participation in community projects fosters a sense of personal self-efficacy and empowerment among volunteer activities, and that these feelings most often arise when people assume some degree of control over community problems. These assumptions are derived from the work of Solomon (1976) and Zimmerman (1995).

The immediate objectives for the program is to recruit participants, carry out a needs assessment, and create task groups to address community problems. The intermediate objectives are to complete community projects, increase the number of people in the community who are political

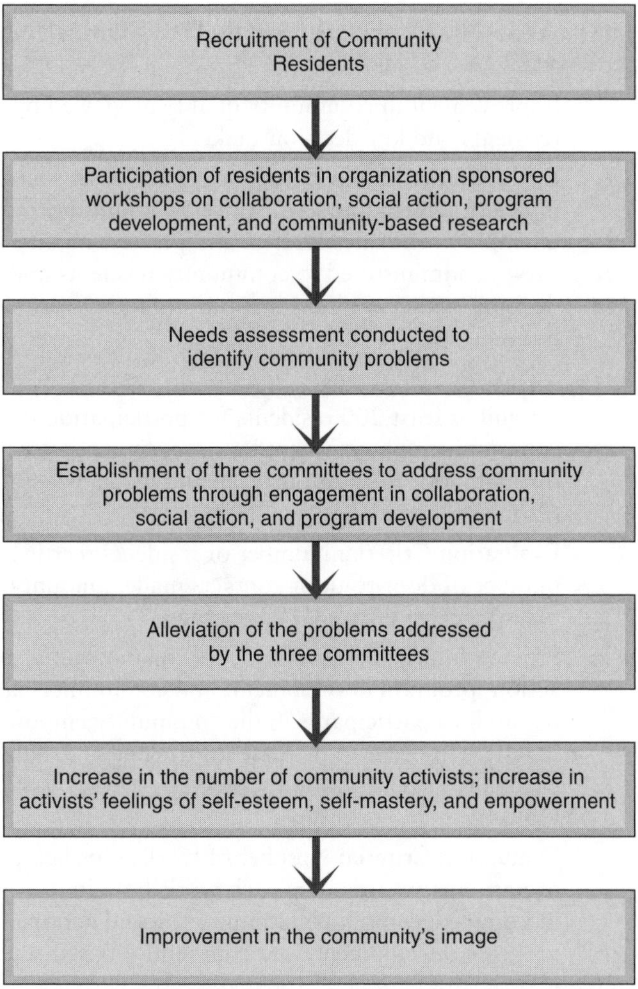

Figure 6.2 Theory of action for the Community Empowerment Program. [Adapted from Itzhaky, H., & York, A. (2002). Showing results in community organization. *Social Work, 47*(2), 125–131.]

activists, and improve the self-esteem, self-efficacy, and sense of personal empowerment among those participating in community activism. The ultimate goal of improving the perception of the community cannot be achieved unless the immediate and intermediate objectives have been accomplished.

BOX 6.4 GOALS AND OBJECTIVES FOR THE COMMUNITY EMPOWERMENT PROGRAM

Ultimate Goal: Improvement in community quality as viewed by residents and key decision-makers.

Evaluation criteria: Changes in a number of social indicators, including crime poverty, infant mortality, and unemployment rates; Pretest and posttest quality-of-life surveys administered to community residents and key decision-makers in local institutions and government bodies.

Immediate Objectives

Objective 1: Recruit at least 200 residents for participation in the community empowerment initiative by April 30, 2005 through door-to-door outreach and media coverage. (Process Objective)

Evaluation Criteria: Number of residents recruited; number of door-to-door contacts made; amount of newspaper, radio, and TV coverage.

Objective 2: Provide four training sessions on collaboration, social action, program development, and community-based research to participants in the community empowerment initiative in order to increase knowledge and skills needed for social action by June 30, 2005. (Process Objective)

Evaluation Criteria: Number of workshops held; number of participants attending each workshop; improvements in knowledge about collaboration, social action, program development, and community-based research.

Objective 3: In partnership with community residents, conduct a needs assessment of community problems by September 30, 2005. (Task Objective)

Objective 4: Create a minimum of three citizen committees by October 31, 2005 to resolve the top three community problems identified by the needs assessment. (Process Objective)

Evaluation Criteria: Number of meetings held, number of participants attending; creation of intervention plans by each group.

Intermediate Objectives (Cont.)

Objective 5: Complete work on three community projects to address problems identified in the needs assessment by October 31, 2006. (Task Objective)

Evaluation Criteria: Successful completion of community projects.

Objective 6: Increase the number of people who regularly participate in community-based social action activities from 10 in 2000 to 100 in 2000 by December 31, 2006. (Task Objective)

Evaluation Criteria: Number of people who are still participating in the community empowerment initiative; number of people who participate in other community activities more than twice per year as measured using sign-in sheets for community meetings and membership lists for local organizations.

Objective 7: Increase activists' sense of self-mastery, self-esteem, and personal and political empowerment by December 31, 2006. (Task Objective)

Evaluation Criteria: Pretest and posttest surveys of community empowerment initiative participants.

Adapted from Itzhaky, H., & York, A. (2002). Showing results in community organization. *Social Work, 47*(2), 125–131.

Additional components of the program planning process include specifying activities that must be carried out in order to meet objectives and a specific time frame for each activity. The purpose is to structure these actions in sequential order, starting with those tasks that are necessary in order for succeeding steps to be taken. This specification of actions and timelines usually is contained in a matrix called a *Gannt chart* (Figure 6.3).

The entire process of planning a program can be broken into multiple stages that correspond to the problem-solving model (Meier & Usher, 1998). In addition, intervention planning should take place subsequent to the process of choosing program goals (Table 6.3). This phase should include the adoption of a specific intervention approach for problem resolution, the development of program policies and procedures, and a process for monitoring the implementation of the intervention plan. The last phase of program development is program evaluation. Evaluations can focus on program quality, implementation, processes, effectiveness,

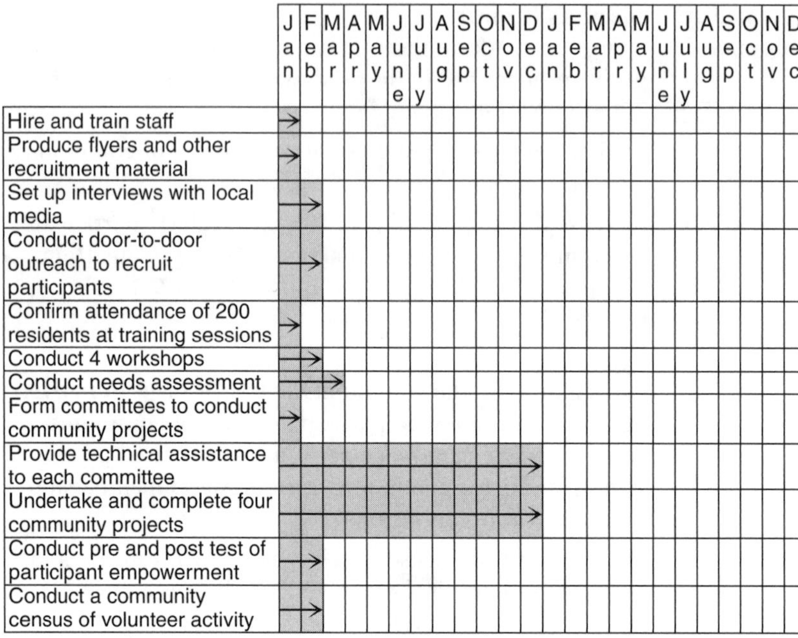

Figure 6.3 Gannt chart for the Community Empowerment Program.

and efficiency (see Chapter 13). Most foundations and government agencies that provide funding for social services expect that applicant organizations will specify program goals and objectives and will submit a detailed evaluation plan in their grant proposals (see Chapter 12).

For each individual objective specified in the program plan, some type of evaluation should be conducted to establish if that particular objective has been achieved. These evaluative indicators can include measures that indicate simply if the task has been accomplished to the degree specified in the objective, whether outcomes have been achieved in the manner intended (e.g., self-esteem as measured by a standardized instrument), and assessments of program processes or quality. For example, if the objective specified that 100 people will receive services within 24 hours of initial application, the evaluation will focus on if or in what percentage clients received services within that time frame (Kettner et al., 1999). If program quality is measured in terms of client satisfaction, a satisfaction survey can be used as the evaluative tool.

Table 6.3 Using the Problem-Solving Model to Design Programs

Problem-Solving Process	Program Design Activities
Problem identification	Specify the client or community problem to be addressed. Identify ways in which this problem is related to the organization's mission. Identify intended beneficiaries and other stakeholders who may be affected by problem resolution.
Assessment	Conduct a needs assessment to determine the scope of the problem. Review the theoretical, best practice, and empirical literature to determine: A. Factors that could cause the problem. B. Methods to address the problem. C. Effectiveness of previous interventions.
Goal setting and intervention planning	Identify the program's primary goal. Identify several intervention models that can be used to address the problem and the expected outcomes. Establish criteria that can be used to choose the best intervention model. Choose the intervention. Establish objectives. Set timelines for accomplishing objectives. Develop a plan for monitoring program implementation and outcomes.
Implementation	Hire and train staff. Develop program policies, rules, and procedures. Collect data to monitor program implementation.
Evaluation	Conduct an outcome evaluation to assess effectiveness. Use evaluation data to make modifications in the program.

Adapted from Meier, A., & Usher, C. (1998). New approaches to program evaluation. In R. Edwards, J. Yankey, & A. Altpeter (Eds.), *Skills for effective management of nonprofit organizations* (pp. 371–405). Washington, DC: National Association of Social Workers.

Program planners need to determine program inputs and outputs. As mentioned previously, *inputs* are the resources needed to carry out the program. Inputs can include, but are not limited to, money, staff members, office space, supplies, volunteers, and media coverage. Procedures for acquiring resources and planning for their use (budgeting) are discussed in Chapter 12. Program *outputs* are the units of service; people served, recruited, or trained; and other tasks accomplished as specified in a list of immediate and intermediate objectives (Kettner et al., 1999). Outputs differ from outcomes in that outcomes are the long-term effects associated with changing people, organizations, and communities (Hardina, 2002). For example, in the Community Empowerment Program described above, the outputs are the activists recruited, the needs assessment conducted, the completion of successful community projects, and the changes in feelings of self-mastery and personal empowerment. Accomplishing these tasks was assumed by program planners to lead to improvements in the ultimate outcome for the study—improvement in the overall quality of life in the target community (Figure 6.4).

PROGRAM MONITORING: GATHERING INFORMATION ON HOW THE PROGRAM IS WORKING

One easy method for determining if a program is meeting the needs of clients is through a review of information gathered from clients to determine eligibility for services. This process is called *program monitoring* (Chambers et al., 1992). Organizations generally gather basic demographic information about applicants, such as gender, age, income, and family size. Information is retained about whether the applicant was found to be eligible for service and the disposition of the application. If not eligible for service, was the applicant referred elsewhere, placed on a waiting list, or turned away?

This case record data allows organizations to look at factors such as demand for service and the incidence and prevalence of social problems. Demand is an indicator of all those people who actually try to obtain a service (Burch, 1996). Consequently, demand includes the number of people who apply for and obtain a service, the number of people who are referred elsewhere, and the number of people who are turned away without receiving the service. Incidence and prevalence are data used to describe the number of people who experience a particular problem. *Prevalence* is an indicator of the number of people in a particular population group who actually have the problem, whereas *incidence*

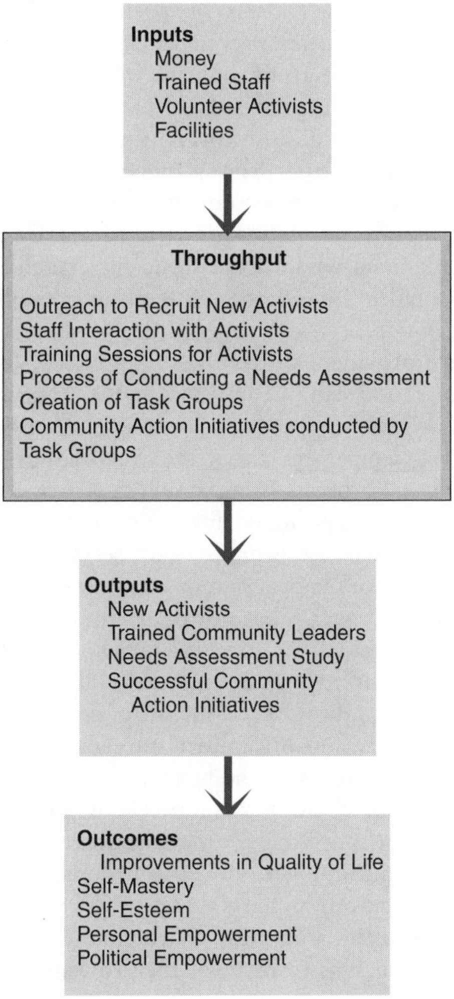

Figure 6.4 "Throughput" model for the Community Empowerment Program.

refers to the number of new cases within a specific time period (Hardina, 2002).

In some agencies, spatial analysis is used to examine the data. Geographic information systems (GIS) software can be used to pinpoint the location of clients (home address) or specific social problems (Weir & Robertson, 1998). Incidence and prevalence of clients with common problems can be plotted on a map to indicate whether people with similar problems are located within specific neighborhoods and geographic areas. Such an analysis allows organizations to target specialized services to areas in which incidence or prevalence is highest. For example, if a map of the incidence of teen pregnancies indicates that a cluster of 12 teenage girls had pregnancies in the last year in a rural, heavily Latino neighborhood, program planners would have sufficient evidence to support the development of a culturally competent teenage prevention program in that community. In addition, GIS analysis allows planners to examine the location of service providers vis-à-vis people in need. Identification of a high-need neighborhood without sufficient service capacity can provide a rationale for developing new programs that serve isolated communities.

Information is kept on file about the outcomes associated with the actual service delivery process. Was the service provided successful? Did the client complete the program, or did he or she drop out? Is the client's case still pending? Were referrals or advocacy services provided? The failure of clients to complete the program or unsuccessful case outcomes can be indicators that the program has not been implemented in the manner intended (Chambers et al., 1992). As Hawkins and Gunther (1998) note, it is important that organizations not focus exclusively on outcome measures but incorporate quality control measures into program monitoring and evaluation processes. Quality control standards are often some of the few measures available to assess the process of service delivery or what goes on in the "black box" of the program (Hawkins & Gunther, 1998). Common methods for monitoring program quality include flowcharts that trace communication, client movement or paper processing in the organization, cause-and-effect charts that describe why problems happen and how they can be fixed, and "run" charts that describe trends in organizational activities, such as referrals or the provision of certain types of services (Figure 6.5).

Program planners look at data on current and former clients to determine if the organization provides services to all intended beneficiaries. The program conceivably can serve only a portion of the eligible population, exclude some eligible clients, or provide services to people who do not fit the eligibility criteria. Components of the organization's access or decision-making structure could work to exclude certain demographic groups who otherwise would be deemed eligible for the service. *Program coverage* is the term used to describe whether members of the program's target population actually receive the service (Rossi & Freeman, 1982). *Program bias* refers to whether the people served by the program are demographically representative of the target population.

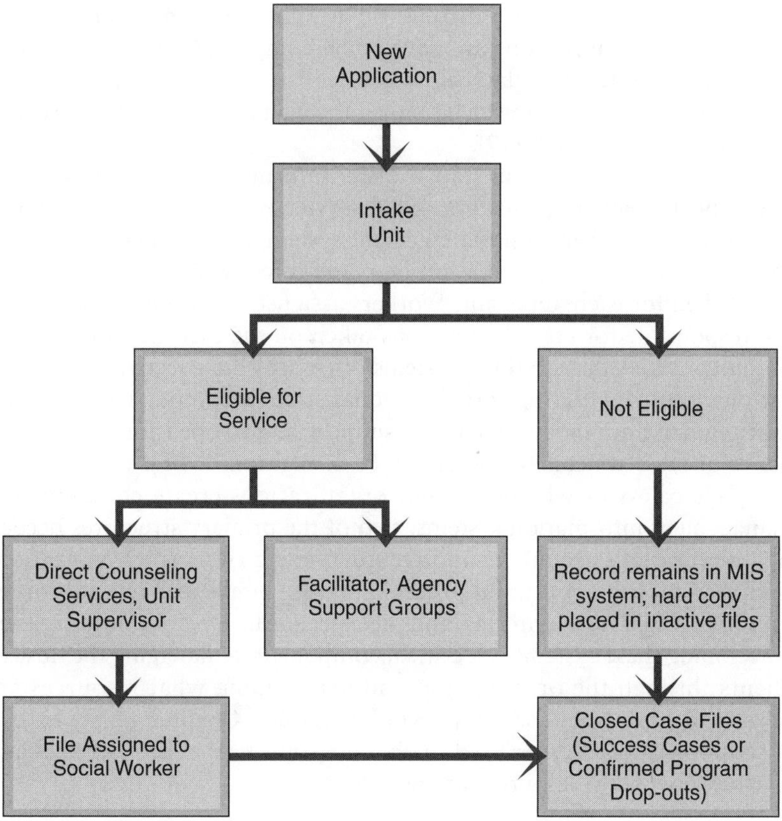

Figure 6.5 Flowchart for organizational case record-keeping process.

When such problems are discovered, program planners, evaluators, and other decision-makers develop new programs or make plans for programmatic reforms. In some instances, program monitoring also requires that decision-makers examine whether program resources or inputs are used appropriately and whether outputs are being produced in the expected quality or quantity.

MANAGEMENT INFORMATION SYSTEMS

All case record information can be consolidated and summarized for all of the organization's applicants and clients. More funders are requiring that detailed statistical information be gathered about the organization's outcomes and program processes. However, going through individual case files to obtain this information is time consuming and costly. Increasingly, organizations are developing computer-based management information systems. A data file is created for each new applicant, and information is added as the client moves through the organization's service system (Kettner et al., 1999).

In some cases, clerical staff transfer information from applications and reports kept by front-line social service workers into a computer spreadsheet or other data management system. Some organizations are requiring that client information be typed directly into a computer file established for each applicant. Workers assigned to the client's case then are responsible for recording actions taken on the case and information on outcomes. Although these systems often are cost effective for organizations, they require that organizational staff be computer literate and that regular training and technical support be provided for the maintenance of these systems (Zimmerman & Broughton, 1998).

Regardless of whether or not organizations create computerized management information systems, two of the primary structures needed by organizations are intake and record-keeping systems. Organizations need to establish application processes, create intake and referral forms, establish eligibility criteria, and keep records on continuing cases. Developing these systems is a critical component in managing the flow of clients through the organization and determining what resources are needed or have been used in providing services. Chapter 12 provides a description of procedures used to obtain resources to deliver services and to track how fiscal resources are used.

SUMMARY

This chapter discussed the basic components of program design. Organization mission statements, polices, procedures, and service plans are important documents that can be used to examine how an organization operates and how successful it is in meeting its goals. In addition to goal accomplishment, the two criteria that can be used to assess service delivery are client access to services and program quality. Access pertains to the manner in which clients are able to obtain services or are restricted from applying for benefits or limited in what they are permitted to achieve. Service quality can be described in terms of predetermined service delivery standards established by the organization and/or external licensing or accreditation that pertain to how the service is provided or how the resources are used to deliver the source. Quality can be measured in terms of the degree of consumer satisfaction with the service. Both quality and access to services can be limited or enhanced by government regulations, internal agency policies, or worker discretion.

Social service organizations typically monitor programs in order to determine if client need is being addressed and if programs are accessible or meet quality standards. An additional criterion used by many social service organizations to measure both access and quality is cultural competency. Well-performing social service organizations ensure that staff members are responsive to the needs of a broad range of clients, including people from a variety of backgrounds and experiences. Chapter 7 describes the adoption of policies and procedures that facilitate the development of cultural competency among organizations and their staff.

QUESTIONS FOR CLASS DISCUSSION

1. Do you think some client groups are more deserving of services than are other groups? Why? What attributes make someone a "worthy" client?
2. Are the concepts of individualization, particularism, and standardization consistent with the NASW *Code of Ethics*?
3. Should organizations try to serve everyone who applies? What practices should be adopted if an organization cannot meet the demand for services?
4. What attributes should characterize a consumer-inclusive organization?
5. What are the risks and benefits associated with including clients and other program stakeholders in conducting needs assessments, designing programs, and evaluating services?
6. Where should social workers and managers find information about the theoretical assumptions that are used to develop programs? Are all programs explicitly tied to theories?
7. What are the benefits and limitations of computerized management information systems?

SAMPLE ASSIGNMENTS

1. Conduct an accessibility assessment for the organization in which you are employed or for which are completing your field internship. Examine at least five of the components of access described in this chapter. Use a combination of observation, document analysis, and interviews to collect information. How easy or difficult is it for clients to receive services? Why?

2. Develop a set of quality control standards for one program operated by your organization. Are these standards currently met by the organization? Describe mechanisms in place to monitor service quality. Are these mechanisms ineffective or nonexistent? Why? How feasible would it be to enforce quality control standards? What resources are needed?
3. Identify the goals and objectives for the program in which you work or in which you are completing a field internship. Assess through a combination of observation, interviews, and document analysis whether the organization really works toward the identified goals and objectives. Are there other implicit program goals? How does the organization monitor goal achievement or conduct program evaluations?
4. Write a set of goals and objectives with evaluation criteria for a new program for your organization. Develop a Gannt chart for identifying tasks needed to implement and operate the program and a timeline. What should be the primary goal of such a program? What logical steps (objectives) will help the organization achieve this goal?
5. Examine the information management system in place in your organization. Does this system allow data to be easily examined by workers and transmitted to funders? What data are collected? Are these data sufficient to monitor program quality, outcomes, and client access? Why? What additional steps should be taken to ensure that sufficient, reliable data can be obtained?

CHAPTER 7

The Culturally Competent Organization

As described in Chapter 6, social service organizations that fail to recognize or respond to the cultural backgrounds of their clientele cannot adequately provide services to people in need. The term *cultural competence,* in its broad use across disciplines, represents varied attempts to conceptualize and contend with the reality of changing demographics, cultural dynamics, and the painfully slow empowerment of groups that, historically, have had little or no access to power. The present state of any discipline or attendant field of practice reflects a culmination of both scholarly discussions and practical applications. In social work, conversations about cultural diversity, multiculturalism, cultural pluralism, and cultural competence act to refine our professional language while fostering the transmission of values that promote effective social work practice. It is important, however, that the application of this concept not be limited to the client–therapist context but to the entire organizational domain. That is, social service organization management and administration must be just as adept in its practice of cultural competence with regard to hiring practices, employee relations, and community partnerships as it expects its front-line staff, counselors, and other professionals to be in service provision. This notion is becoming more widely accepted even in disciplines that traditionally have not been culturally responsive (Lopez & Guarnaccia, 2000).

This chapter offers a practical definition of cultural competence and presents key elements required to achieve cultural competence in social service organizations. The chapter puts forward a view of organizational administration and service delivery that moves beyond a simple acknowledgment of culture to an organizational milieu that incites practitioners and agencies to make changes in personal perspectives and professional processes. The chapter delineates the major components and assumptions of an ethnoconscious approach and offers it as a response to demographic trends. These shifts highlight the need for increasing recognition of people of color and cultural variables as these factors relate to social services. Therefore, the skill sets of social workers must rise to meet the attendant challenges and needs of misrepresented or maligned groups. This will ascertain a greater understanding of both the cultural and the racist social contexts that are the bases of experience for people of color. The framework also represents a prototype for application to other non-dominant, diversity groups in our society.

This chapter also examines

- A number of models of social work practice that includes an understanding of culture and skills for working with people who are not members of the dominant culture
- Practice activities associated with culturally competent service provision
- Characteristics of culturally competent organizations
- The importance of attracting and retaining staff that reflect the larger community and the necessity of drawing on the knowledge, expertise, and commitment of current staff to strengthen the organization's level of commitment to diversity
- Methods for measuring cultural competency in social work practice and within service organizations
- The importance of the inclusion of consumers in creating the culturally competent organization

DEFINING CULTURAL COMPETENCY

The search for a consensual definition of cultural competence is elusive at best. The lack of a "grand definition" should not, however, impair our efforts to equip social service agencies and their personnel with key values and principles associated with the term. Nor should it hinder us from continuing to struggle with developing a relevant and useful definition. Several years ago, an article focusing on child protective service training noted that the challenges of preparing workers to be ethnically sensitive fall into three areas—a lack of skills, a lack of knowledge, and attitudinal biases (Stevenson, Cheung, & Leung 1992). A functional definition of cultural competence must at least address these issues. In the same year, Orlandi (1992) reinforced this notion by defining cultural competence as an academic and interpersonal skill set that sensitizes the individual to cultural experiences outside of his or her own.

Later, McPhatter (1997) asserted that such knowledge and personal awareness must be fused with "health and/or psychosocial interventions that support and sustain healthy client-system functioning" (p. 261).

In 2001, the Board of Directors of the National Association of Social Workers (NASW) ratified a set of 10 standards for cultural competence in social work practice. These standards require that social workers examine how the needs of diverse clients may conflict or be compatible with professional standards, and that social workers develop self-awareness of their own cultural beliefs as a means of understanding the values of others. Social workers should develop cross-cultural knowledge and skills for working with members of diverse groups. In addition, the standards require that social workers be able to make appropriate service referrals for diverse clients, examine the impact of programs and policies on members of diverse groups, and advocate for changes in policies to better serve these populations. Social workers are required to advocate for organizational policies that help build a diverse workforce and for the provision of language appropriate services to their clientele. They must participate in professional training workshops on cultural competency and take leadership roles in disseminating cross-cultural knowledge and skills to members of other professions.

These standards, in tandem with the NASW *Code of Ethics,* reflect the profession's allegiance to the core values of diversity, empowerment, and social justice, all sought in the context of strengths-based service provision. Similarly, the Council on Social Work Education (CSWE) continues to address the issues of cultural competence in educational programs designed to prepare professionals for effective service delivery. The Education Policy and Accreditation Standards (EPAS) developed by the CSWE in 2001 provide a blueprint for the academic domain of social work to handle the preparation of culturally competent practitioners. EPAS requires not only that social work curriculum content must include cultural diversity content but that students must have experiences that help them garner skills for working with diverse populations (Galambos, 2003).

Lum (1999) defines cultural competency as "the set of knowledge and skills that a social worker must develop in order to be effective with multicultural clients" (p. 3). To be sure, cultural competence is a concept that must be continually refined as professionals come to know themselves as well as those with whom they interact, whether colleagues or clients. Overall, cultural competence can be conceptualized best when viewed as an ongoing educative and experiential process reflecting ever increasing levels of effectiveness with diverse populations. Cultural competence might be defined as the professional's "ability to combine identified cultural styles as well as cultural and personal strengths of people with a compatible, culture-affirming set of knowledge, skills, values and methods enabling the development of effective working relationships" (Simpson, 2003).

Cultural competency within this context does not simply apply to work with members of specific ethnic groups. It also pertains to work with individuals and groups outside the dominant culture. Lum (1996) defines culture as the "lifestyle practices of particular groups of people who are influenced by a learned pattern of values, beliefs, and cultural modalities" (p. 72). Culture involves patterns of viewing and interpreting reality that provide people with a guideline or design for living and is a template that group members can use to respond to each other and to their environment. The primary forum for transmission of culture and socialization is the family, and it is in this context that most individuals learn how to "be human": and how to survive. Personal empowerment and its converse, disenfranchisement, also are conveyed in this context but also are collectively experienced in the context of community (Simpson, 1990). Consequently, the term *culture* as we use it in this chapter refers to any group that engages in behaviors or practices that make them distinct from the dominant culture.

Although this definition of culture is fairly broad, in social work practice we primarily focus modifying practice methods in relation to our clients' membership in the following groups: women, persons of color, immigrants, older individuals, persons with disabilities, and gay, lesbian, bisexual, and transgendered (GLBT) individuals (Council on Social Work Education, 2002). Religion and income level are other factors that should be taken into account when assessing the cultural orientation or values of the people we serve. The notion of defining cultural groups in relation to their subordinate position vis-à-vis the dominant culture also requires that social workers understand how social, economic, and political oppression have contributed to the experiences and needs of members of these various cultural groups. Because most social work practitioners work within the context of cultural competency in organizations, this situation then implicates at least two, if not more, sets of people, social systems, and the attendant skills, practices, attitudes, policies, and statutes that guide interaction within a social and organizational context.

BENEFITS OF DIVERSITY AND CULTURAL COMPETENCY IN SOCIAL SERVICE ORGANIZATIONS

The U.S. workforce is increasingly becoming more diverse; almost 85% of all employees are women, immigrants, or people of color (Gutierrez, Kruzich, Jones, & Coronado, 2000). Corporations are not becoming more benevolent but only more cognizant of the importance of managing diversity in efforts to ensure their own survival in a heterogeneous consumer marketplace (Billings-Harris, 1998). Social service agencies possibly were the conceptual forerunners in this movement because of the values guiding the disciplines that inform social work, counseling, and other helping professions. Organizational diversity in social service organization asserts its relevance both to the staff in their contact with the community and to the administrators who must model the values they are espousing. Therefore, the foundation for diversity must be an integral part of the philosophical mission of the organization itself.

Many for-profit, public, and nonprofit organizations commit themselves to diversity and the adoption of policies and practices to promote cultural competency for a number of reasons. For some organizations, the adoption of antidiscriminatory employment practices is simply viewed as a method for avoiding government sanctions for violating federal or state regulations about hiring or lawsuits for civil rights violations or sexual harassment (see Chapter 8). Other rationales for the adoption of ethnic-sensitive, cultural diversity–oriented, or culturally competent practices can include increasing productivity and improving client–customer relations (Bendick, Egan, & Lofhjelm, 2001; Combs, 2002; Hyde, 2003).

As described in Chapter 6, the lack of appropriate cultural or linguistic services in social service organizations creates substantial barriers to service delivery for people who are members of marginalized groups (Iglehart & Becerra, 2000). The incorporation of social stigma into decisions about program eligibility and the provision of service also make it harder for communities of color and/or cultural groups outside the social mainstream to obtain service (Lipsky, 1980). Organizations that wish to expand their programs to historically underserved populations or to improve program quality often seek to become more sensitive to the needs of various cultural communities or to become culturally competent (Hyde, 2003). Social service organizations may decide to become culturally competent in compliance with accreditation standards or professional guidelines (Van Den Bergh & Crisp, 2004). Ethical principles, especially those articulated by the organization's leadership, can bring about changes in practice interventions or organizational polices (Walker & Staton, 2000). Advocacy on the part of organizational staff, clients, or community members can lead to the adoption of culturally competent practice by social service organizations (Almeleh, Soifer, Gottlieb, & Gutierrez, 1993; Baines, 2000).

MODELS OF SOCIAL WORK PRACTICE THAT INCLUDE CULTURAL AWARENESS AND SKILLS

Foundational theories at the base of practice in social service organizations do not reflect an awareness of, or appreciation for, difference. For example, community mental health centers have used psychoanalytic theory and therapy, with its focus on the individual and intrapsychic processes that have been engaged as a result of developmental experiences. Historically, these methods have been critiqued for their lack of inclusion of the voices of women, for example, and for having effectively disregarded the implication of culture in these processes (Schriver, 2003). From research and practice that descend from European philosophy and that have been structured relative to a Euro-American frame of reference, the theory assumes that family of origin interactions, transitional crises in the developmental stages, and subconscious conflicts are virtually universal or, at the least, that their fundamental dynamics are interculturally indistinct. Over time, this theory, and others with as many deficits, have benefited from critical analysis and an examination of how the cultural background of the individual, family, or community affects the process and outcome of human development. As a result of such critique, practitioners have become equipped with a stronger interventive knowledge base.

Whatever the theoretical base or practice modality of the practitioner, the client–worker relationship may be impeded, at least in part, by cultural and racial differences (Simpson, 1990). In either case, they are aggravated by institutionally supported barriers to service delivery. Barriers such as discrepancies in client–therapist power, mistrust, denial of access, and premature termination all lead to an interventive process that threatens rapport and is ineffective for, if not harmful to, people of color (Stevenson et al., 1992). The emergent challenge for social service administrators is to promote reformed policy and practice that systematically and effectively integrates culturally relevant information.

Nagda, Harding, and Holley (1999) identify three methods used by organizations to incorporate culture into social service delivery: ethnocentric practice, ethnic-sensitive practice, and ethnoconscious practice. In this context, *ethnocentric practice* refers to traditional patterns of service delivery historically used by organizations that represent the interest of the dominant culture. It should be noted, however, that organizations that offer services to a specific ethnic or cultural group and use practice methods that incorporate cultural norms and values that are appropriate for this population can also be viewed as ethnocentric (see discussion of ethnic social service organizations in Chapter 4). Practice methods used by traditional organizations that are ethnocentric and exclusively incorporate the values and beliefs of the dominant culture into service delivery often are oriented toward the assimilation of people of color and other marginalized groups. In some cases, agency activities involve *decculturation,* the process of repression of culturally appropriate values, beliefs, and language (Cross, 2001).

Ethnic-sensitive practice as developed in the 1960s and 1970s involved intervention techniques that attempted to correct deficiencies inherent in the ethnocentric approach; practitioners were to display respect and tolerance for cultural beliefs, values, and needs of communities of color (Devore & Schlesinger, 1981). Nagda et al. (1999) argue that the ethnic-sensitive approach is insufficient because it does not examine the role of social structure in the oppression of marginalized groups or mandate social worker participation in activities to address social injustice. They call for the adoption of an approach that combines ethnic-sensitive and empowerment practice. This approach often is referred to as *multicultural social work* or *ethnoconscious practice.*

Multicultural social work broadens culturally appropriate practice by including within its parameters members of other nondominant groups, for example, women, persons with disabilities, immigrants, people in poverty, older people, and GLBT individuals (Van Den Bergh & Crisp, 2004). *Ethnoconscious practice* requires that social workers recognize the strengths of members of these various marginalized groups and engage in social action to address client problems rooted in social inequities and oppression (Simpson, 1990). Nagda et al. (1999) use the term *ethnoconscious practice* to encompass practice methods that focus exclusively on the cultural values and beliefs of one ethnic group (e.g., an ethnic agency that specifically designs services for members of that group) or multicultural practice in which social workers who are culturally different from clientele adopt a variety of practice methods that can be used successfully to address the needs of a diverse group of clients. Hyde (2003) differentiates between these two types of approaches, stating that the "ethnoconscious approach has considerable merit in improving service delivery to disenfranchised populations, but it does not embrace the broader goals of diversity, valuing differences, and cross-culturalism" (p. 43).

Nagda et al. (1999) argue that organizations that adopt either the multicultural approach or ethnoconscious practice can work effectively with multiple cultural groups. "Multicultural organization development (MCOD), an organization transformation approach that embraces social diversity and social justice goals, helps formulate the potential for social service organizations from empowerment and social justice" (p. 284). According to Lum (1999), "culturally competent practitioners in multiculturally focused organizations help the consumer bring together values and beliefs from the consumer's own culture and those of the dominant culture" (p. 3). Gutierrez, Lewis, Nagda, Wernick, and Shore (2005) state that multicultural practice is oriented "toward the empowerment and economic development of disenfranchised groups while creating mechanisms for greater inter-group interaction and change toward greater inclusion in the society generally" (p. 344).

Cross and Friesen (2005) identify five attributes of multicultural organizations that engage in culturally competent practice. These organizations should

- Value diversity and embrace culture as a resource.
- Be capable of cultural self-assessment.
- Be conscious of the dynamics, risks, and potential conflicts inherent when different cultures intersect.
- Have institutionalized knowledge about various cultures and cultural issues.
- Have services that can be adapted to fit the culture of the community served (p. 445).

Ethnoconscious or multicultural organizations should operate on two distinct levels. First, culturally competent workers should engage in appropriate practice activities. Second, the organization should be culturally competent. In the organizational context, competency includes actions such as hiring diverse staff; adopting policies and procedures that support worker efforts to deliver services to culturally diverse clients; and engaging with community residents to design, implement, and evaluate the effectiveness of these services (Hyde, 2003, 2004).

CULTURALLY COMPETENT SOCIAL WORK PRACTICE

Solomon (1976) explicitly describes empowerment as an approach to working with persons of color as a mechanism for overcoming feelings of alienation from, and oppression by, the dominant culture. In order to assist clientele, staff members must become culturally competent, tailoring activities to fit the values and practices of program beneficiaries. The literature on cultural competency in social work identifies the following practice activities that are associated with culturally competent practice in social work:

- Conducting research to gain knowledge about other cultures
- Acknowledging one's own biases and beliefs
- Acquiring the ability to communicate cross-culturally
- Participating in cultural events and the daily life of a community
- Respecting cultural values and traditional leaders
- Recognizing barriers to community participation that originate in institutional racism (Lum, 1999; Rivera & Erlich, 1999)

In addition, the culturally competent practitioner should possess self-awareness and be able to assess what resources he or she will need to deliver appropriate interventions. For example, the practitioner should be

- Aware of his or her cultural heritage and values.
- Aware of how his or her biases affect cultural perceptions.
- Comfortable with cultural difference.
- Sensitive to circumstances that may require the social worker to seek a cultural guide.
- Demonstrate a good understanding of social power structure and how nondominant cultural groups are treated (Gutierrez & Alvarez, 2000).

Lum (1999) classifies cultural competency in social workers in terms of four specific dimensions: cultural awareness, knowledge acquisition, skill development, and inductive learning, or the ability to conduct ongoing research to expand social work knowledge about culturally competent practice. Practice techniques should focus on decreasing feelings of powerlessness and building on client strengths. In addition to conducting strength-based assessments, Lum (1996) advocates incorporating the following outcomes associated with the empowerment approach into multicultural practice in communities of color:

- The client's feelings of self-efficacy or the ability to take action are increased.
- Group consciousness is developed about how social structure or the individual's lack of political power contributes to personal problems.
- The client's feelings of self-blame about problems he or she cannot control are reduced.
- The client takes personal responsibility for changing his or her problems.

Two methods for increasing the knowledge and skills of social workers for culturally competent practice include the use of ethnographic interviewing techniques and linkages between individual social workers and community guides.

Ethnographic Interviews

Ethnographic interviewing is one of the primary tools used by social workers to obtain information about a client's background. According to Lum (1999), social workers should use the ethnographic approach to

> Learn about clients both as individuals and as members of their culture or ethnic community, they should investigate the relevance of culture

> to the client's lives, and then they should build on this knowledge and incorporate it into the helping process. (p. 73)

Although interviewing and engagement skills are important for all social workers practicing at all systems levels, Okayama, Furuto, and Edmondson (2001) identify three general practice skills needed to conduct culturally competent interviews and to apply interventions: relationship skills (effective listening and body language), an awareness of different cultural communication styles in verbal and nonverbal interactions, and the use and interpretation of time and space by members of different cultural groups. All of these skills are essential for conducting an ethnographic interview.

Questions used in an ethnographic interview usually are global in nature; they focus on understanding the client's perception of the problem within his or her cultural context. Although some research on the client's cultural background and likely problems can be completed prior to the interview, preparing questions in advance sometimes is difficult. Questions often flow based on responses to previous questions or information provided by the client (Green, 1999; Lum, 1999). Green identifies four primary types of information that a social worker should collect in an ethnographic interview:

1. Determine the client's definition of and understanding of a problem.
2. Determine how the client uses language to categorize or describe the problem.
3. Determine how the client's cultural community generally engages in help-seeking to address this specific problem. Keep in mind that help-seeking can include assistance from informal helpers, religious leaders, community decision-makers, and faith healers.
4. Determine how the client's own cultural community generally resolves the problem and the outcomes that usually are associated with problem resolution.

In addition to ethnographic interviews, Lum (1999) recommends that social workers engage in ongoing research in collaboration with community groups to gain in-depth knowledge about the culture of the people they serve, as well, to develop new, culturally appropriate interventions and to evaluate the effectiveness of these approaches.

Community Guides

Another mechanism used to increase cultural knowledge among organizational staff requires the use of cultural guides (Green, 1999). According to

Ungar, Manuel, Mealy, Thomas, and Campbell (2004), a community guide is a nonprofessional, community resident or "member of the group being served, whose skills and relationship with the community is valued because of his or her social position" (p. 551). In Chapters 4 and 14, we refer to natural or informal helpers, people who are leaders in their own communities and who provide information and other assistance to friends, relatives, and neighbors. Much of the help provided by these leaders takes place within the context of multiple exchanges among members of informal networks. In an organizational context, a community guide is an informal helper who has an informal or formal relationship with a social service organization and who provides the organization with information and insight about local customs, practices, and beliefs. These guides can potentially educate social work professionals about the community they serve while providing a linkage between people in need and the organization.

EXPLORING COMPONENTS OF CULTURAL COMPETENCY IN SOCIAL SERVICE ORGANIZATIONS

Social service organizations cannot simply be classified as either cultural competent or culturally incompetent (Bendick et al., 2001). Cross (2001) describes cultural competency as a developmental process that can be conceptualized on a continuum. The lowest rung on the continuum is *cultural destructiveness,* the ongoing use of policies and practices oriented toward destroying entire culture or individuals within those cultures (e.g., genocide or the suppression of culturally related beliefs and behaviors or language). The second rung on the continuum is *cultural incapacity,* in which organization members assume that they are racially superior to others and consequently discriminate against people who are not part of the dominant culture. Such organizations proactively exclude culturally different clients and staff and fail to deliver adequate or appropriate services to members of nondominant groups. At the midpoint of the cultural competency continuum is a category that Cross classifies as *cultural blindness,* organizations that operate out of a commitment to treat all clients in the same manner. He argues that the services delivered by these agencies tend to be ethnocentric in that the services reflect only the values of the dominant culture, encouraging assimilation and ignoring cultural strengths in the delivery of services.

Somewhat higher on the scale is the category *cultural pre-competence.* Organizations in this category recognize that services must be adapted to respect cultural norms and values. According to Cross (2001), the "culturally competent agency works to hire unbiased employees, seeks advice and consultation from the minority communities, and actively decides what it is and is not capable of providing to minority clients" (p. 2). *Advanced cultural competency* is the highest rung on the scale. In this type of organization, staff members are proactive in the development of culturally appropriate services, conduct research to find the best practice approaches, and disseminate this knowledge to others. Advanced cultural competency also requires a commitment to hiring culturally competent staff and advocating for the development of culturally competent services and public policies.

According to Cross and Friesen (2005), culturally competent organizations are consumer oriented, focus on the strengths of clients and their families, and encourage participation of clientele at all levels of the organization (intervention planning, organizational decision-making, political advocacy). The literature on culturally competent organizations identifies a number of actions that should be taken by culturally competent organizations:

- Develop written cultural competency plans.
- Establish advisory boards with diverse members.
- Provide applications and other materials in different languages and Braille; pretest material to ensure it is usable.
- Provide translation services (including sign language).
- Provide culturally acceptable treatments.
- Provide cultural competency training.
- Provide staff from a variety of cultural groups.
- Hire staff members who are competent in a variety of languages.
- Provide applications and forms in appropriate languages.
- Ensure service providers have specialized assessment and treatment skills needed to treat diverse clients (in terms of ethnicity, sexual orientation, ability, age, social class, and gender).
- Engage in intervention on multiple systems levels (e.g., with individuals, families, groups, communities, and the political system).
- Display and disseminate agency materials (e.g., brochures, artwork, toys, and games) that portray members of a variety of ethnic groups. These materials should not be racist, sexist, or heterosexist (British Columbia Ministry for Children and Families, 2005; Gutierrez et al., 2005; Miley, O'Melia, & Dubois, 2004; National Technical Assistance Center for State Mental Health Planning [NTAC], 2004).

Cultural competency should be inherent in the organization's structure, mission statement, policies, and service plans (Cross & Friesen, 2005). According to Kahn (1991), organizations become culturally competent with the development of formal organizational structures that foster equity in resource sharing, administration, and leadership. Such organizations provide ongoing education about race and cultural issues to both staff and constituents. Cultural and social activities designed to maintain the organization and sustain participation should be both culturally appropriate and inclusive of the various cultural groups that participate in the organization.

Small changes in the process of service delivery are not sufficient to create culturally competent organizations. Cornelius and Ortiz (2004) identify a number of structural and policy changes that organizations should implement in order to sustain cultural competency efforts:

- Staff members should include a mix of racial and ethnic groups.
- Minimum standards are set for culturally competent care.
- Data are collected on service provision and outcomes for specific ethnic and racial groups. Programs are modified in response to identification of inequities in the provision of services.

Methods used by social service organization to increase the cultural competency of organizational staff include providing appropriate training for organizational staff, designating seats for ethnic group members on organizational boards, and hiring staff who are members of the ethnic group served (Gutierrez et al., 2000; Iglehart & Becerra, 2000). In Chapter 5, we discussed steps for developing a diverse board. Hiring practices for creating a diverse workforce are described in Chapter 8. Training for cultural competency requires a commitment of the organization's time, skills, money, and staffing resources for organizational staff.

According to Hyde (2003), there are two primary approaches for implementing multicultural principles in organizations in which the staff are culturally different than the majority of clientele:

1. *Managing Diversity.* Administrators focus on creating a culturally diverse workforce, adopting nondiscriminatory hiring, recruitment, and retention policies.
2. *Cultural Competency.* The organization helps staff develop culturally appropriate knowledge and skills to serve diverse clientele. Appropriate training is provided to staff.

According to Hyde (2003), either approach may be insufficient to address issues of power and status inside the organization, issues that create glass ceilings or other forms of discrimination that limit the advancement within organizations of women and people of color and perpetuate stereotyping and discrimination. She stresses the importance of creating strategic plans to guide MCOD activities, monitoring the implementation process, and evaluating outcomes. The philosophy and commitment of leaders at all levels of the organization (executive director, board members, staff, and clientele) to the pursuit of cultural competency and equity are critical for the success of these efforts. A lack of real commitment on the part of organizational decision-makers will produce few real changes in the organization. Fong and Gibbs (1995) offer as an example organizations that express a commitment to cultural diversity and competency but that offer only one or two training sessions on multicultural practice per year. Organizations may need to undergo a more complex process of transformation, changing core values of the organization, offering new services, or creating a new decision-making structure (Hyde, 2003, 2004).

MAINTAINING DIVERSITY: RETAINING AND TRAINING A CULTURALLY DIVERSE STAFF

The government regulations that prohibit discrimination in hiring and the organizational policies and procedures that are required to implement these regulations are described in Chapter 8. The retention of diverse staff members is likely to be more problematic for many organizations than the hiring process itself. According to Baines (2000), affirmative action–related hiring practices often focus on low-paying positions that require few skills or professional credentials. Fong and Gibbs (1995) point out that in many social service organizations, diversity goals are achieved when indigenous paraprofessional workers (such as the community guides described earlier in this chapter) are hired to help professional staff communicate appropriately with communities of color or link the organization with the surrounding community.

Consequently, hiring policies may simply serve to perpetuate racial and gender differences in social service organizations, restricting people of color, especially women, to low-wage work. A commitment to maintaining a culturally diverse workforce may therefore require that the organization adopt personnel practices that provide assistance to staff members who wish to acquire professional degrees and seek positions with more responsibility and status (practitioner, supervisory, or management) in the organization. Other types of problems often encountered by persons of color and other culturally different people in organizations include pressure placed on new, culturally diverse staff: new hires may have limited status and power in the organization, they may be viewed as outsiders, and they may have limited access to information. They may be resented for bringing change to the organization or viewed as having preference in the hiring process (Fong & Gibbs, 1995). In addition, staff members of color who may be present in an organization in small numbers may feel compelled to advocate for clients or community residents from the same cultural group if their needs are not met by the organization. Organizational decision-makers may not necessarily be responsive to requests for service modifications, or they may deliberately sanction workers for taking on the advocacy role (Gant, 1996). In order to keep culturally diverse staff, organizations must establish a set of structures to support new staff (retention) and to train all employees to function appropriately in a culturally diverse environment.

Staff Retention

Organizations that are successful in retaining cultural diverse staff members must be able to take action on a number of levels to provide support to staff consisting of people of color or members of other diverse groups. For example, Gant (1996) identifies a number of characteristics of social service organizations that are successful in providing support to staff members of color:

- Organizational policies support cultural diversity, cultural knowledge acquisition, and referrals to culturally appropriate resources in the community.
- The organization provides nondiscriminatory services.
- The organization provides in-service trainings to increase staff awareness of diversity issues.
- The organization encourages staff to collaborate with culturally oriented resources in the community.
- The organization establishes cooperative relationships with culturally oriented organizations in the community.

Gant (1996) conducted research to determine if these indicators of the degree of cultural sophistication in social service organizations were associated with the amount of stress experienced by persons of color in social service organizations. He found that positive responses on these cultural sophistication items were found to be moderately associated with decreased job-related stress among separate samples of African-American and Latino NASW members (Gant, 1996; Gant & Gutierrez, 1996). Hyde (2003, 2004) examined staff retention as a component of MCOD. She interviewed organizational staff members and consultants. She found that few of these organizations made an effort to retain diverse staff beyond recruitment or efforts to link new staff members with mentors.

Mentorship is one of several supportive techniques (such as the formation of support groups or encouragement of professional networking opportunities) that are used to facilitate the retention of professional staff members, especially women and persons of color. It is believed that mentors can help orient these new staff members to organizational culture and expectations and can advise them on promotions and other career development opportunities (Kelly, 2001). However, mentorship in itself may be sufficient to help some employees (women, people of color, and members of other marginalized groups) to break the "glass ceiling," barriers (such as overt discrimination or performance standards that are not applied uniformly) that prevent career advancement. Ragins, Townsend, and Mattis (1998) conducted a survey of more than 1,000 women executives in *Fortune 1,000* companies. Respondents identified four strategies for obtaining top management positions: having an influential mentor, exceeding performance expectations, developing a management style that male supervisors and peers found acceptable, and seeking out challenging work assignments. Ragins et al. emphasize that advancement and retention will occur only when organizational leaders make explicit efforts to treat all employees equally.

Fong and Gibbs (1995) state that the barriers to long-term retention of culturally diverse staff members are formidable. They recommend that multicultural organizations not limit themselves to simply hiring diverse staff members; rather, multicultural organization should take the following actions:

1. Define concrete outcomes associated with hiring multicultural staff.
2. Adopt an organizational development model that will help the organization achieve these outcomes.
3. Ensure that cultural competency or language expectations for various staff positions are well defined and that multicultural staff members are not limited to positions that require them to be translators or cultural guides.
4. Establish linkages with leaders in the organization's target community and with other organizations. These resources can be used to subcontract for culturally appropriate services or to hire consultants to deliver cultural competency training for staff.
5. Place the focus of diversity hiring on the organization as a whole rather than confining the focus to specific job classifications. All staff members should have access to professional development opportunities, should be encouraged to develop cultural competency-related skills, and should participate in organizational decision-making.

Training to Enhance Organizational Diversity

For some social service organizations, their commitment to diversity simply extends to hiring a diverse staff. In other organizations, cultural competency in service delivery is their primary long-term goal. In either case, the organization must find a way to ensure that staff members respect one another and that they are able to work together cooperatively. Consequently, one type of training in social service organizations may simply be oriented toward promoting nondiscriminatory behavior. According to Combs (2002), simply offering training content on cultural values and beliefs and techniques and practice principles for working with culturally different groups is insufficient for putting these principles in action or ameliorating conflicts among staff members or between workers and clientele. She argues that upper and middle managers must role model specific skills for working cross-culturally and empower staff members to acquire the knowledge and ability they need to successfully apply these skills in the workplace:

> The . . . focus on managing diversity operates from a time bound emphasis on what actions are inappropriate and what workers are not to do. This time bound leadership continually misses opportunities to stress the correct skills and to develop in employees the level of confidence needed to direct their diversity response. Employees must feel confident in their capabilities to engage in the risky business of prompting and initiating change in their own responses and the responses of others toward a more pluralistic work environment. If diversity training is to improve its perception of effectiveness, individuals in the workplace must be able to successfully apply behaviors learned in diversity training to their work settings. (pp. 12–13)

Bendick et al. (2001) also argue that training in itself is insufficient to change employee behavior. A more comprehensive approach for changing organizational culture is required. In order to identify effective diversity-enhancing approaches, the authors surveyed for-profit training providers as well as nonprofit organizations (universities, professional associations, and antidiscrimination advocacy groups) that provided diversity training. Diversity training services were provided to a variety of for-profit and nonprofit organizations in a variety of industries. The content of training included material on the cultures of different ethnic groups, discrimination, stereotyping, and the benefits of maintaining a diverse workplace. Based on the findings of the survey and observation of 14 training programs, Bendick et al. identify nine characteristics of comprehensive organizational development approaches to diversity training:

1. The organization's management strongly supports staff training on diversity issues.

2. A training approach has been developed to best fit the needs of the organization.
3. The content of the training is explicitly linked to organizational goals.
4. The trainers have experience in organizational development or have worked as managers. Bendick et al. suggest that experiential knowledge possessed by members of cultural communities often is not sufficient to provide effective training to employees.
5. All organizational employees participate in training.
6. The training focuses on discrimination as a general process rather than on the discrimination experienced by one or two groups. Bendick et al. note that discussing discrimination solely in terms of abuse to women or people of color can reinforce conflicts among staff members and can offend some trainees.
7. The training focuses on changing behavior rather than attitudes.
8. The organization changes policies related to hiring and retention that may restrict the organization's ability to maintain staff diversity.
9. The entire culture of the workplace is changed to support diversity. These changes can include comprehensive policy reforms, values, and beliefs, and staff appointments that reflect diversity goals.

TRAINING FOR CULTURAL COMPETENCY

Hyde (2003) posits that practitioners in social service agencies believe that an agency's multicultural perspective can emerge as a result of a confluence of values, goals, and activities. When staff represent the community served by the agency, the agency may be more likely to be viewed as an empowering ally rather than an alienating aggressor. Yet whether staff are technically representative of their surrounding communities is, perhaps, less consequential than if staff are not prepared for cross-cultural intervention. Training for cultural competency often involves presentations on cultural values and beliefs of specific demographic groups and appropriate assessment or intervention techniques. In some cases, training includes role plays and specific applications of skills (Gutierrez et al., 2000).

Although some schools of social work teach culturally competent practice to their students (Garcia & Van Soest, 1997; Gutierrez, Fredricksen, & Soifer, 1999), a social service organization cannot assume that staff members come prepared for culturally competent practice. In fact, the organization must cultivate in its staff an understanding of the essentiality of this practice through regularly planned workshops, seminars, and other organizational pedagogies. As important, however, is the need for organizations to identify, acknowledge, and dismantle the hindrances to diversity in the workplace that are fostered by their own institutional practices, whether formal or informal. To this end we offer the following tool to engage practitioners in proactive discovery of basic principles and applications of culturally competent practice.

Using the Ethnoconscious Model

Concurrent with the move of social work toward discussing and struggling with issues of culture has been its attempts to relinquish a medical model and to view the person-in-environment. In order to increase effectiveness with clients of color, social workers must view the problems of living in a cultural context as well as an environmental one. The ethnoconscious perspective reflects the systematic consideration of cultural processes and ethnic and family history and the recognition of the impact of societal structures on individuals, families, groups, and communities (Simpson, 1990). Consequently, the foundation of this approach includes a mixture of cultural, historical, and social structural variables. By considering these elements, practice, research design, and even theory building can be culturally sensitive as well as consciousness-raising and empowering. We live in a society in which people struggle to respond to a wide range of oppressions from ableism and ageism to sexism and racism. Ethnoconsciousness assumes that issues of culture and oppression are integral parts of the experiences of diversity groups in our society.

Components of the Ethnoconscious Model

The ethnoconscious approach comprises five components. Each is presented as one facet of an approach that encourages, in fact, demands, that the administrator, practitioner, theorist, or researcher be proactive on the journey toward cultural competence.

1. *Cultural Salience.* The basic premise of *cultural salience* is that individual, group, family, or community theory and practice cannot be adequate if they do not consider the impact of culture in their theoretical, methodological, and interventive paradigms. In relation to social work intervention, Pinderhughes (1989) points out that culture is implicated in a problem's exhibition, consequence, interpretation, and choice of treatment modalities. In short, social work values regarding empowerment practice are

impotent if they are implemented without regard for the cultural context.

2. *Ethnohistory.* Ethnohistory refers to the historical experiences of an ethnic or racial group as they influence cultural, family, and individual development. The significance of history as a promoter of cultural understanding cannot be overstated, whether in the context of individual, family, or community intervention. It also may serve to provide a testimony of the strengths of a people. Hence, an *ethnohistorical* analysis provides a forum for viewing social and economic triumphs and obstacles that have an impact on institutions such as marriage and the family.
3. *Culture-Coping Bond.* A view of culture as the common assumptions, behaviors, and beliefs that enable a group in society to respond to each other and to their environment underlies the *culture-coping* concept. Insofar as individual and family therapies are concerned with the functioning and coping capabilities of clients, culture is immediately relevant and may provide a set of empowering coping mechanisms. Upon assessing a group's *ethnohistory,* pertinent information concerning the structural variables that have shaped its culture is revealed. Furthermore, a number of values and behaviors that represent survival techniques and tools used in the struggle against various oppressive social and psychological conditions become evident. In the African-American family, a number of cultural practices illustrate the cultural-coping bond, including the following:

   - *Extended Kin–Friend Networks.* African-American families are generally well integrated into larger kin–friend networks in which there is economic cooperation, sharing of responsibilities, socialization, and social control. Practitioners should consider strengthening the role of extended family systems in the treatment of African-American individuals, families, and communities.
   - *Adaptability of Family Roles.* The development of flexibility in family role definition, responsibility, and performance among African Americans is due, in part, to socioeconomic pressures imposed by a racist social structure. The African-American household is likely to contain at least two wage-earners who finance family needs. Socialization and child care is often assisted by older siblings and sex role expectations may be less stereotypic with regard to some tasks.
   - *Bicultural Socialization.* African-American families and communities may be seen as holding a variety of bicultural

characteristics. Because the larger society does not fully recognize the rights and dignities of its citizens of color, the African-American family becomes a training ground for maneuvering and surviving in the dominant society while honing the skills to thrive in the nondominant culture. Biculturalism represents a duality wherein African-American family members maintain a public self and private self, alternating between or combining cultures when appropriate. This duality increases the chances for survival.

4. *Personal/Family Ecology.* Upon gaining an awareness of the importance of culture, of the social, political, and economic experiences of a cultural group, and of the keys to its survival, the temptation is to treat as one all individuals who fall into a social category. The *personal/family* component merely expresses the need to consider an individual's or family's unique identity. However, distinctions occur within races as well as between them. African-American families may be compared not only cross-culturally but, at times, intraculturally. This argues for the need to consider the social milieu and to include ecological variables in the interventive process. The *personal/family* component encourages this process by its use of certain interventive tools (e.g., a genogram or ecomap) that provide the practitioner with an opportunity to assess the client system itself in relation to its environment.
5. *Self-Culture Awareness.* The ethnoconscious perspective is a tool for analysis of the client system, used to enhance practice and to sensitize practitioners to the crucial tests that confront people of color. Rather than simply increasing awareness, this model is a tool for self-analysis and education. The therapist's examination of the place of culture in his or her own life is crucial to the effective implementation of any ethnically sensitive practice method. The previously discussed components of the ethnoconscious approach provide a useful framework. For example, the therapist must consider his or her own culture as a distinct contributor to his or her own personal development. In addition, it is necessary for the therapist to know what institutions, systems, and relationships form his or her own world and how these factors affect lifestyle and practice.

Other Applications of the Ethnoconscious Approach

This ethnoconscious approach, which incorporates values, practices, and beliefs into social work assessment and intervention planning, can easily be adopted for use with other cultural groups. For example, Van Den Bergh and Crisp (2004) identify a similar set of principles for culturally competent social work practice with sexual minorities (GLBT individuals). Using Lum's cultural competency framework as a guide (Lum, 1999), they have constructed a number of attitude, knowledge, and skills-related criteria for appropriate practice in the GLBT community (see Framework for Cultural Competency with Sexual Minorities in Box 7.1).

BOX 7.1 FRAMEWORK FOR CULTURAL COMPETENCY WITH SEXUAL MINORITIES

Attitudes

1. Self-reflect on the development of one's own sexual orientation.
2. Examine one's own previous personal and professional interaction with GLBT individuals.
3. Evaluate one's own positive and negative reactions to GLBT individuals.
4. Self-evaluate the cognitive, affective, and behavioral components of one's responses o GLBT individuals in order to become aware of one's own potential heterosexism or homophobia.
5. Participate in activities that foster a greater understanding of GLBT individuals and culture.

Knowledge
Acquire knowledge in the following areas:

1. Terminology used by GLBT individuals to describe themselves and identify-affirming language
2. Demographic representation of GLBT individuals in the general population; diversity within the GLBT community
3. Cultural traditions and history
4. Experiences associated with oppression
5. Influence of social programs, government policies, and recent legal decisions (i.e., court rulings and public referenda on gay marriage)
6. Culturally sensitive practice models and theories
7. Community resources

Skills

1. Create an agency environment in which GLBT individuals will feel safe.

2. Conduct an assessment to determine a client's sexual orientation; do not make assumptions related to homosexuality or heterosexuality.
3. Examine the client's problem within the context of his or her life as a GLBT individual.
4. Support clients who struggle with sexual orientation.
5. Determine how "out" each GLBT client is and whether he or she receives support from friends, family, or coworkers.
6. Include family and significant others in the intervention process, using a flexible definition of family that can include both birth family members and the individual's "family of choice."

Adapted from Van Den Bergh, N., & Crisp, C. (2004). Defining culturally competent practice with sexual minorities: Implications for social work education and practice. *Journal of Social Work Education, 40,* 221–238.

MEASURING CULTURAL COMPETENCY IN SOCIAL SERVICE ORGANIZATIONS

If diversity or cultural competency training is to be offered in social service organizations, its effectiveness should be measured. In some cases, the effectiveness of training is simply measured in terms of knowledge acquisition or skill building during the training (Gutierrez et al., 2000). Lum (1999) recommends that social workers engage in regular self-assessments of their practice, examining their competency in each of the four areas identified in his cultural competency framework: cultural awareness, knowledge acquisition, skill development, and inductive learning. Cross and Friesen (2005) recommend that social service agencies conduct regular assessments of the cultural competency of staff members as well as of organizational procedures and policies. However, as Combs (2002) states, the real test of knowledge and skills acquisition as a consequence of training is whether employees transfer this knowledge to the workplace. In addition, involvement of consumers in the evaluation of the cultural competency of staff members and the organization as a whole is essential. Only consumers can determine if the program incorporates values and practices that are congruent with their worldview or that are sensitive to their needs (Gilbert & Franklin, 2001). Gutierrez et al. (2000) argue that program evaluation in organizations that have undergone cultural competency training or used the MCOD for comprehensive change should take a more comprehensive approach. Outcome assessment should focus on whether cultural competency efforts have improved service delivery to clients.

A number of self-assessment tools are available for use by practitioners and organizations, including the *Social Work Cultural Competencies Self-Assessment* by Lum (1999) and the *Cultural Competency Assessment Tool* developed by the British Columbia Ministry for Children and Families (2005). Most of these tools measure concrete behaviors on the part of organizational staff members or staff perceptions about whether workers have knowledge about appropriate practice methods for engagement with culturally different clients or have exhibited certain types of behaviors (e.g., showing respect for the consumer's cultural values or displaying pictures of diverse people in the organization's brochures).

Recently, efforts have been made to develop concrete, operational definitions of cultural competency and to empirically test standardized instruments designed to assess cultural competency in social service organizations. Green, Kiernan-Stern, Bailey, Chambers, Claridge, Jones, Kitson et al. (2005) conducted an empirical test using a sample of practicing social workers of the *Multicultural Counseling Inventory,* a scale designed to assess practitioners' self-assessments of their competency in terms of four dimensions: multicultural counseling skills, knowledge, awareness, and quality of the counseling relationship. Although the scale was found to have a high degree of internal consistency (reliability), only two of the subscales measuring each of the four dimensions of competency (multicultural counseling skills and the counseling relationship) were found to be empirically valid.

Cornelius, Booker, Arthur, Reeves, and Morgan (2004) worked with a community-based research team in the state of Maryland to develop a consumer-based measure of cultural competency in the delivery of public mental health services. The 52-item scale was found to have a high degree of reliability and validity when tested empirically using a sample of mental health consumers. The NTAC (2004) also developed a standardized measure to examine the cultural competency of state mental health agencies. This scale focuses on the behaviors of senior-level management, staff competencies (such as linguistic abilities of staff), and whether the agencies have developed appropriate policies and procedures to ensure services are delivered in a culturally competent manner.

THE IMPORTANCE OF CLIENT INVOLVEMENT IN DESIGNING A CULTURALLY COMPETENT ORGANIZATION

The primary purpose of attaining cultural competency in social service organizations is to improve client services and to make organizations more responsive to the needs of the people who use them (Hyde, 2003;

Nagda et al., 1999). Access to resources is fundamental to community empowerment. The diverse organization is a conduit for resources necessary to sustain community subsystems. The foundational charter and mission statements of the organization must assure access to culturally competent services provided by the diverse organization. On the other hand, this assurance must be represented in all contacts between the agency and the community, that is, it cannot be artificial, pretentious, or inconsistent. Policies must evolve into practice and words into deeds. The communication expressed by intake workers upon a potential consumer's initial contact must be consistent with that of the chief administrator's communication in addressing the media or funding organizations. All employees have their place in forming the agency's persona, which is vital to the acceptance of the organization by the community it serves. Community members must be made aware not only that programs exist but also that they are not at risk of extending their frustrations by obtaining those services. Those who need and would use services often are thwarted by agency stipulations that are culturally insensitive. One example of this practice is the use of cultural identifiers such as "Hispanic" or "Latino/Latina," which in light of the political connotations behind these terms may not be readily accepted by all in the focal community (Bernal & Enchautegui-de-Jesus, 1994).

As in other forms of empowerment-oriented practice, it is critical that the consumers of service have a central role in designing and evaluating social service programs. Chapter 6 pointed out the necessity of viewing the process of service provision as reciprocal. Staff increase their own knowledge and practice wisdom in the context of their experience working with consumers. Consultation with clients/consumers should take place at all levels of the organization. The organization should take explicit steps to conduct outreach and market its services to cultural groups (Lum, 1996). This requires that efforts be made to find the most effective cultural and linguistic means to reach these communities. Workers must be able to engage clients in ongoing dialogue about the clients' needs, how they view the origins of their problems, and the most effective way to address these problems (Barrera & Corso, 2002; Green, 1999). Clients and other key informants from cultural communities should be invited to sit on boards of directors, advisory committees, and task groups charged with developing new programs and evaluating their effectiveness.

BOX 7.2 STARTING A CULTURALLY COMPETENT ORGANIZATION

The young mothers group at the Mission Street Anti-Poverty Organization has agreed to form a Child Care Resource and Advocacy Center. The group has decided that the type of organization the members want to form should be a feminist organization that incorporates African-American culture and values. They have asked Keisha, an MSW intern, to review the management literature and to identify an appropriate organizational structure and service delivery practices that are consistent with feminist and African-American values.

- What are some of the reasons why the participants in the young mothers group would wish to start an organization based on feminist and African-American principles? What are possible sources of information that Keisha should use in researching this issue?
- What are some of the feminist principles, previously identified in this book, that should be used to guide the development of the organization's structure?
- What are the components of ethnoconscious organizations that should be considered in the development of the Child Care Resource and Advocacy Center?
- Keisha conducts research on the incorporation of African-American values in service delivery. She finds that Graham (1999) describes Afrocentered services as those that recognize the collective identity of individuals, the value of interdependent relationships, and the connection between the body, mind, and spirit. How would you design services that incorporate these principles?
- As described in this chapter, what other characteristics of African-American families should be considered when developing culturally competent services?
- If this organization successfully adopts Afrocentered principles and incorporates them into its service delivery system, will this be sufficient to ensure that the organization is culturally competent? Why? Are there situations in which the organization may need to review its practices in order to remain culturally competent?
- The young mothers group would like to hire a part-time staff member to serve as the director of this organization. Are they limited to hiring an African-American woman for this position? If not, how should they assess the cultural competency of prospective staff members?

It is critical that social service organizations actively network with local cultural resources and consult extensively with community residents and clientele in the development of appropriate curriculum and training material for use by new social workers (Hyde, 2003, 2004). Voss, White Hat, Bates, Lunderman, and Lunderman (2005) suggest that, in addition to traditional methods for consultation, Internet technology can be used to stimulate dialogue between educational institutions, social service organizations, and cultural groups, with methods that include distance education, chat groups, faculty exchanges, and collaborative research projects. Developing a community–agency collaborative is a logical and necessary extension of grass-roots community coalition building. Furthermore, the organization that sees itself as part of the community, rather than as a benign attachment, will have a better chance at social change and community empowerment than organizations that are less entrenched. Research indicates that the concept of empowerment is more striking at the individual, community, and organizational levels. Attempts to expand or apply it beyond this, for example, in setting federal programs and policies, diffuses its meaning (Perkins, 1995). The alliance between community and agency, then, is a heart-line that can bolster both systems.

SUMMARY

Community empowerment can be fully realized only when consumers from the community are valued and are integrated in the developmental process of establishing a diverse organization. Effective service delivery to consumers is dependent upon the cultural competency of organizational staff, the organizational policies and procedures that promote both diversity and cultural competency, the leadership of organizational decision-makers (administrators and board members), and advocacy on the part of both clients and staff members. MCOD entails a number of activities directed at the recruitment and retention of a diverse staff, the provision of training to eliminate discrimination and conflict among staff members, and professional development activities oriented toward preparing staff members to deliver culturally competent services to clients across a variety of culturally diverse groups. Empowerment-oriented managers within the organization are essential for the creation of multicultural organizations. Chapter 8 describes the types of leadership skills needed by social service managers to sustain empowerment in organizations.

QUESTIONS FOR CLASS DISCUSSION

1. How would you define cultural competency?
2. How does your field agency or the organization in which you are employed put cultural competency into action?

3. Other than the ethical implications, why is cultural competency important?
4. Are there any risks or problems associated with implementing cultural competency plans in social service organizations?
5. What are the responsibilities of a social worker in situations where the social service organization's procedures and policies are harmful or unresponsive to diverse client groups?

SAMPLE ASSIGNMENTS

1. Conduct an assessment of the organization in which you are completing your field placement or in which you are employed. Determine if the organization is engaging in any of the cultural competency–related activities identified in this chapter. Assess how well these activities have been implemented. Determine where the organization "fits" on Cross's (2001) continuum of cultural competency using the evidence that you have collected.
2. Identify a cultural competency deficit in your organization. Describe how this deficit affects the organization's clientele or the community it serves. Write a cultural competency plan that will address this problem.
3. Conduct a group interview with people from one or more cultural groups who receive services from social service organizations. Develop an interview guide that includes questions about how the clients perceive the organizations that serve them in terms of cultural competency and the responsiveness of the services to their needs. Participants also should be asked to identify ways in which these services could be improved.

SECTION III

Empowering Staff Members

CHAPTER 8

Administrative Leadership

Implementation of empowerment-oriented management approaches requires that organizational leaders, including board members, recognize and guide the empowerment process in organizations. One of the dilemmas of empowerment-oriented management practice is that although empowerment approaches focus on creating opportunities for participatory decision-making throughout the organization, a "top-down approach" is critical to creating a structure that supports staff members, clients, and volunteers in the change process. In this chapter, we describe

- The role of administration staff in creating an empowering organization.
- The traditional approach to organizational management compared with empowerment-oriented and participatory methods.
- The role of organizational administrators in recruiting and hiring a diverse, well-trained, and competent workforce.
- Empowerment-related methods for supervising, training, and evaluating the performance of staff.
- The process of recruiting and using volunteers to supplement an organization's workforce.
- The dilemmas of managing a diverse organization consisting of volunteers, professional staff, nonprofessional workers, clients, and board members while responding to turbulence in the organization's external environment.

TRADITIONAL APPROACHES TO LEADERSHIP

Weinbach (1998) defines leadership in organizations as "the manager's conscious efforts to influence other people within the organization to engage willingly in those behaviors that contribute to the attainment of organizational goals" (p. 257). Kettner (2002) identifies five characteristics of effective leaders:

1. Creating a vision that focuses on the organization's future goals
2. Understanding how an organization should function
3. Using interpersonal skills to motivate staff
4. Using analytical skills to collect and interpret data that can be used to improve the organization's performance
5. Possessing personal qualities that include values and ethics (such as honesty and integrity) and the ability to inspire staff and other organizational constituents

Most of what we believe to be appropriate traits and behaviors among effective organizational managers are derived from McGregor's (1969) conceptualization of Theory X and Theory Y. As described in Chapter 2, Theory X describes a management model that relies on the use of power and authority derived from hierarchical decision-making structure (Kaiser, 1997). Managers on the top rung of the hierarchy delegate staff management tasks to supervisors in units lower on the organizational ladder. Management is largely a function of the use of sanctions and rewards to control staff behavior and enforce work requirements. The purpose of management is to alter worker behavior in order to enhance the organization's performance. Theory Y, on the other hand, focuses on using management approaches to meet the needs of the workers. Consequently, the Theory Y manager will attempt to alter the workplace environment to enhance the performance of workers. Given that individual personalities, organizational culture, and the task environment contribute to a wide range of worker expectations, values, behaviors, and needs, the leadership challenge for the social service manager is to foster a consensus about the organization's goals and future direction and a sense of loyalty and commitment among the various constituency groups (Kettner, 2002).

Facilitating this type of organizational atmosphere requires that managers structure the decision-making process in organizations to support worker autonomy and feelings of personal empowerment. According to Pine, Warsh, and Maluccio (1998), two of the primary vehicles for empowering workers involve employee involvement in workplace decision-making and flattening organizational hierarchies by moving responsibility for managing production areas from supervisors to groups or teams of employees (see Chapters 9 and 10).

LEADERSHIP FOR THE EMPOWERING ORGANIZATION

Shera and Page (1995) define an empowered organization as one in which "leadership and responsibility are shared, communication and interaction patterns are based on principles of empowerment, and organization changes are possible from below as well as from the upper levels of the organization" (p. 3). Spreitzer (1996) identifies three dimensions of psychological empowerment among employees:

- The degree to which individuals have a choice in determining what they do or how they behave in the workplace
- The degree to which employees feel that they can do the job well (self-efficacy)
- The degree to which employees care about their jobs

Organizations cannot simply decide they want to empower workers. According to Kaminski, Kaufman, Graubarth, and Robins (2000), empowerment is

> A developmental process that promotes an active approach to problem-solving, increased political understanding, and an increased ability to exercise control in the environment. As people develop through the stages of empowerment, they become more able to analyze issues in context and apply their skills to successfully revolve them. (p. 1357)

The process of empowerment does not simply occur because a manager or board of directors has decided to adopt a new approach to operating the organization. The empowered workplace requires the active leadership of the organization's top managers in identifying core values and principles for the organization and putting these principles into action.

Leadership Models for Empowerment-Oriented Organizations

The social work literature offers little in the way of concrete management models or approaches (Gellis, 2001). Most models of management practice are derived from the for-profit business literature. However, the social work literature suggests that leaders who want to promote empowerment in the workplace should be able create a vision for the organization and help staff "transform" themselves and the workplace in order to provide better quality services (Gutierrez, GlenMaye, & Delois, 1995; Shera & Page, 1995).

Smith, Montagno, and Kuzmenko (2004) identify four management models described in the current literature on for-profit management. Each of these models "fit" with the definitions of good leaders described in the social work literature:

- Charismatic leadership
- Transactional leadership
- Servant leadership
- Transformative leadership

Gellis (2001) defines *charismatic leaders* as those who have the "ability to arouse devotion and articulate a vision through personal dynamics such as self-confidence and emotional appeal, for subordinates to identify with and develop higher order goals, and instill respect and loyalty for the leader" (p. 18). As described in Max Weber's writing on leadership in bureaucracies, charismatic leaders are those who acquire power by virtue of their personal attributes (such as attractiveness or interpersonal skills) and because their followers believe in them (Smith et al., 2004). As described by Bass and Avolio (as cited in Gellis, 2001), other attributes of charismatic leaders include the ability to motivate workers to take action and inspire belief in a cause (inspirational motivation). In addition, the charismatic leader should be able to understand and resolve workplace problems in an innovative manner (inspirational motivation). The leader should be able to treat each worker with care (individual consideration). A limitation of this approach is simply that not all leaders have the personal attributes necessary to attract followers (such as personality or appearance). Situational concerns that are not predictable (such as crises or resource availability) may impede or enhance the charisma of the leader. For example, it is easier to inspire others to take action if individuals, communities, or organizations perceive themselves as threatened or at risk. An abundance of resources (such as money, meeting space, flyers, and media coverage) can be used to attract people to a cause, whereas the absence of funds can make change more difficult to achieve.

Most leadership analysts agree that the ability to inspire others and create a vision for the organization is an essential component for successful use of transactional, servant, and transformative leadership approaches. *Transactional leadership* involves the application of social exchange theory. The leader enhances good worker performance through provision of a system of rewards and punishments (Bryant, 2003). Transactional leaders work closely with team members to develop goals. They also respond to the needs and self-interests of the workers if such response increases the chances that the work will be completed as intended. Gellis (2001) distinguishes between positive and negative applications of transactional leadership. This model will have a positive impact on workers if the manager takes action to reward workers for accomplishing the agreed upon goals. Conversely, the transactional approach can backfire if the manager takes action or passively contributes to a supervisory system that focuses on mistakes or delays, taking action when crises occur. Bryant identifies another limitation of this model: transactional leaders tend to focus almost exclusively on goal accomplishment and existing policies and procedures; they often fail to reward creativity and innovation. As with charismatic leadership, this model emphasizes the role of the manager rather than focusing on the role of followers/workers in guiding the organization toward planned change (Farling, Stone, & Winston, 1999).

A third management model, *servant leadership,* emphasizes the role of employees in the organization. The servant leader perceives his or her role to be that of a "servant" to the workers. According to Smith et al. (2004), servant leadership

> Views a leader as a servant of his/her followers. It places the interest of followers before the self-interest of a leader, emphasizes personal development and empowerment of followers. The servant leader is a facilitator for followers to achieve a shared vision. (p. 80)

In this approach, the leader is regarded as someone who is recruited or urged to accept a management position by the organization's members rather than an individual who has taken action to acquire the position (Farling et al., 1999; Smith et al., 2004). The servant leader works for the good of the organization and the people it employs or serves. This model of leadership emphasizes personal as well as organizational development. The leader is not the ultimate authority, but shares power with members. Servant leadership also emphasizes the perception of the organization as a community in which members have common values and goals; the role of the leader in such an organization should be to work for the common good.

Characteristics associated with servant leadership emphasize the leader's interaction with other members of the organization and include attributes such as "listening, empathy, healing, awareness, [and] persuasion" (Sendjaya & Sarros, 2002, p. 58). According to Farling et al. (1999), a commitment to becoming a servant leader emerges from the individual's personal philosophy and values. Principles often associated with servant leadership include social justice and equity. Servant leaders focus on assisting people who may be marginalized by the organization or larger systems external to the organization (Sendjaya & Sarros, 2002).

Although this model seems to correspond well with social work values and ethics, it might be difficult to implement in social service organizations. Funding sources, government regulatory bodies, and the general public want accountability from the organization and often expect leaders to sanction staff for poor performance or behavior. An effective servant leader would need to find a way to inspire both an appropriate vision for the organization as well as good behavior among staff members. In addition, such a leader would struggle with some of the same issues as those of staff charged with empowering clients: can power or the use of authority easily be given to others? Smith et al. (2004) argue that the chief limitation of this model is that it is oriented toward maintaining organizational stability and the status quo. Consequently, the servant leader may have difficulty responding to changes in the organization's external environment or fostering an atmosphere that leads to innovation. Another concern about this model is that it is a philosophy about how organizations should work rather than a theory that has been tested empirically (Farling et al., 1999; Sendjaya & Sarros, 2002).

The leadership model most often associated with both total quality management (TQM) and empowerment practice is the *transformational model* (Gutierrez et al., 1995; Rago, 1996). This approach to management incorporates many elements of the charismatic, transactional, and servant leadership model. Pearlmutter (1998) defines transformational leaders as those that

> Recognize the need to obtain and use power in positive ways to assure support and resources to bring about change. They are politically astute, viewing others in the organization as allies in producing change. They are willing to take risks to challenge existing beliefs and conventional wisdom. They communicate conviction and commitment and are persistent in their efforts, sharing their beliefs in the viability of change. (p. 29)

According to Hacker and Roberts (2004), transformational leaders help employees think creatively and produce results. Transformational leaders facilitate employees to achieve self-fulfillment and professional growth (Schmid, 1992). The transformational leader works effectively to build a sense of community among organizational participants and helps members build a common vision, establish goals for the future, and identify shared values (Lewis, Lewis, Packard, & Souflée, 2001).

Charisma and working for the good of the organization and its members is an important component of this approach:

> Transformational leadership occurs when a leader inspires followers to share a vision, empowering them to achieve the vision, and provides the resources necessary for developing their personal potential. Transformational leaders serve as role models, support optimism and mobilize commitment, as well as focus on the followers' need for growth. (Smith et al., 2004, p. 80)

This model is viewed as involving both power sharing and exchanges among the leader and organizational participants. The leader does not only "work for" the organization's members, he or she engages in positive interactions to guide or stimulate better performance among employees (Lewis et al., 2001). As noted by Rago (1996), the purpose of adopting a transformative or empowerment-oriented approach is to change or "transform" the behavior of the leader and employees. This change is intended to increase service quality, transfer at least some degree of power and authority to staff, and improve the quality of services provided to consumers. Explicitly in empowerment-oriented social service organizations, the adoption of a transformative approach is intended to transform clients, facilitate their acquisition of skills, leadership ability, political power, and other resources they need to improve their quality of life.

The transformative leader is responsive to the organization's external environment and acts to create an organization that can adapt to situational demands (Smith et al., 2004). Stimulation of staff creativity and innovation, encouragement of advocacy on the part of workers and clients, and acquisition of political power by the organization and its constituency group members are methods that transformative leaders can use effectively to guide the organization through the change process.

The Role of Transformational Leaders in the Empowerment-Oriented Organization

Most of what we know about the effectiveness of transformative management models can be found in the for-profit business literature (Lawler, Mohrman, & Ledford, 1995; Spreitzer, 1996). However, Gellis (2001) conducted a study of perceptions of leadership effectiveness among clinical social workers employed in hospitals. He found that workers' perceptions of leader effectiveness and managerial behaviors associated with the transformative model (communicating a sense of purpose, acts on behalf of the group rather than self-interest, inspirational motivation, intellectual stimulation, and giving consideration to the needs of individuals) were positively associated with increased work effort and feelings of job satisfaction on the part of employees.

Pine et al. (1998) argue that the success of participatory management approaches depends on the leadership of top executives. The leader should be able to communicate a vision of the organization in the future, introduce the participatory approach as a means to cope with change demanded by a turbulent external environment, and articulate a sense that participation in decision-making will improve the organization and the services it provides. Leaders should be skilled in group facilitation and team building and be able to communicate the administration's commitment to participatory decision-making. According to Gallagher (1997), leaders in empowerment-oriented organizations

> Need to be willing to confront their own continuing resistances to empowerment e.g., their own desire to hold onto control, to manage all the details, impatience, the need to shift from a "psychological contract" of dependency to one of "autonomy in relationship," or interdependence. (p. 1)

Rago (1996) describes barriers associated with implementing an empowerment-oriented TQM approach in a large government agency using a top-down management approach. These barriers included lack of trust that others would make the right decisions, management problems establishing the agency's purpose and communicating this vision to the staff, the time required for staff to learn to work together collaboratively, the lack of preparedness among staff to take responsibility for decision-making, and difficulty providing the necessary information to decision-makers.

Gutierrez et al. (1995) conducted qualitative interviews with staff members and administrators in six nonprofit organizations to examine how organizational structure and policies supported or discouraged empowerment practice. Barriers to empowerment identified by staff members included problems measuring positive outcomes over time, competition with other agencies, difficult-to-serve clients (such as those with physical or mental disabilities who may have difficulty following through with services), and worker reluctance to allow clients to make their own choices in terms of services and outcomes.

Workers identified a number of supportive factors, including the provision of appropriate training opportunities, encouragement of staff initiatives to develop new programs, provision of rewards for good performance, and flexible work hours so that workers could attend to personal business. Respondents also viewed administrative leadership as important.

Good leaders articulated a vision for the organization and served as role models for staff engaged in empowerment practice. According to Gutierrez et al. (1995):

> Having an administrator on your side as an advocate for consumers and staff is seen by many participants as a critical support for maintaining an atmosphere of empowerment. For instance, one participant stated, "To know that someone's at your back. Somebody is going to look out for you, [the executive director] you know. She may yell at me later, but she is not going to let nobody else dog me out, you know." (p. 255)

A leader who supports staff efforts is not the only essential ingredient for transforming organizations, staff, and clients using the empowerment approach. The organization must also have employees who are committed to the organization, loyal to the employer, and supportive of efforts to empower clients and other program beneficiaries. However, program administrators must be able to recruit, hire, train, and supervise a diverse workforce capable of providing quality services. Administrators must be able to evaluate staff performance and identify areas in which staff skills and knowledge should be strengthened.

STAFF RECRUITMENT AND HIRING

The process of hiring, training, retaining, or terminating staff is one of the most difficult task areas for organizational managers. Managers must be prepared to make ongoing assessments of staffing needs. They must be able to develop a strategic or long-term plan that allows the organization to anticipate what staffing resources will be needed during the next few years. Often organizational managers will need to develop an explicit outreach and recruitment plan to find new staff members with the wide variety of skills and experience needed to support the organization's function and goals (Kettner, 2002). As described in Chapter 7, social service organizations function best when they are able to hire a culturally and demographically diverse staff. Diversity should include not only people of different ethnic or cultural backgrounds, but older adults, gay, lesbian, bisexual, and transgendered individuals, and persons with disabilities. Social service mangers should be aware of federal and state laws that govern the hiring, retention, and termination of staff, the manner in which these laws are enforced, and steps that employers should take to minimize legal liability in the event these laws are violated by managers and staff. In addition, social service managers who are committed to the development of a diverse workforce must take proactive steps to recruit, train, and maintain staff members who enhance the capability of the organization to deliver services to its clientele.

Federal and State Regulations Related to Employment and Retention of Staff

Employers must develop internal policies and procedures in order to comply with federal regulations that must be used to hire employees in nonprofit, public, and for-profit organizations that receive federal grants and contracts (Pecora, 1998). The following laws and regulations govern the hiring, treatment, and termination of staff:

- Federal and state Affirmative Action laws prohibit discrimination by gender and race during the hiring process.
- The Equal Pay Act requires equal pay for equal work.
- The Americans with Disabilities Act (ADA) prohibits some types of employment discrimination based on mental or physical disability.
- The Civil Rights Act outlaws discrimination in hiring based on sex, religion, race, or national origin.
- The Age Discrimination Act provides employment protection to workers between the ages of 40 and 70 years.
- The Vietnam-Era Veterans Readjustment Act requires that employers give preference in hiring to veterans who fought in the Vietnam War.
- Equal Employment Opportunity Commission guidelines explicitly prohibit sexual harassment (Kettner, 2002; Perlmutter, Bailey, & Netting, 2001; Shank, 1994; Weinbach, 1998).

In addition to these laws, employers must be knowledgeable about state legislation on fair employment practices, as well as local and state laws that explicitly focus on specific types of discrimination. Some states and local government have implemented laws that prohibit discrimination based on sexual orientation (Perlmutter et al., 2001). There are also some exceptions by state in terms of the enforcement of Affirmative Action laws. For example, the states of California and Washington have adopted laws (via ballot referendums) that prohibit the use of gender and race in making decisions about hiring state employees (Kranz, 2002). State and federal courts currently are in the process of clarifying if or how federal law preempts state anti-Affirmative Action measures for organizations that are federal contractors.

The term *Affirmative Action* refers to federal regulations that pertain to the hiring process. These regulations prohibit employment practices that can result in discrimination. For example, organizations in which a diverse group of participants apply for a specific type of position but only people from one demographic group are routinely hired may be found to violate these guidelines if the organizations cannot demonstrate compliance with Affirmation Action guidelines. The federal Equal Employment Opportunity Commission (EEOC) is the agency responsibility for developing Affirmative Action and other regulations prohibiting discrimination in the workplace. For example, the EEOC prohibits employers from asking about disability status, race, gender, marital status, children, or child care arrangements during a job interview (Pearlmutter et al., 2001). Failure to comply with these requirements may result in heavy fines imposed by the EEOC or a significant degree of legal liability exposure if employees sue the organization for employment discrimination or harassment.

There are some misconceptions about Affirmative Action. It does not require organizations to use hiring quotas, nor does it require that employers hire unqualified applicants (Lewis et al., 2001). Affirmative Action–related regulations do require federal contractors to hire a member of a protected group (women or people of color), but only in situations where two position finalists are equally qualified and only one of these applicants is a member of the protected group. In addition to hiring and recruitment requirements, some employers (those with more than 50 employees) must file annual Affirmative Action plans in which they compare a demographic profile of their current workforce to the availability of women, African Americans, Hispanics/Latinos, Asian/Pacific Islanders, and American Indians in local job pools (Kettner, 2002). If members of these groups are not represented in the organization's labor pool, the organization must make good faith efforts to recruit members of these groups (Billings-Harris, 1998).

In addition to Affirmative Action–related regulations, civil rights, age, and other antidiscrimination laws prohibit discrimination in treatment of staff members after they are hired or in promotions, layoffs, or terminations. Employers can be found in violation if affected employers can prove that workplace polices or practices have a "disparate impact" on specific demographic groups or classes of people. For example, if no African-American employee is promoted to manager over a period of years despite good performance evaluations, one or more African-American staff members could successfully bring a discrimination case to the EEOC for resolution or sue in court for monetary damages. Consequently, employers must have clear written policies for making promotions and other types of employee-related decisions and must be able to prove that these policies are implemented in a consistent manner.

Two particular problem areas for employers involve enforcement of the ADA and antisexual harassment policies.

The ADA prohibits employment discrimination against persons with disabilities and requires employers to provide reasonable accommodation in some situations to disabled employees (Pecora, 1998). Ambiguities in the ADA make it particularly difficult for employers to comply with the Act and for employees to successfully file complaints. Employers are expected to make efforts to accommodate employees who can perform a specific job unless such accommodation imposes an "undue hardship," such as a great deal of expense (Kettner, 2002). The law does not specify what undue hardship actually entails. In addition, the definition of disability in the Act is vague—interpretations of what constitutes a disability by the EEOC and the courts often change in response to new complaints. For example, in 1997 the EEOC defined mental illness as a protected disability (Pearlmutter et al., 2001). It is the employee's responsibility to provide verification of a disability that substantially limits his or her ability to engage in a major responsibility or his or her ability to perform certain types of work tasks.

Enforcement of state and federal regulations that prohibit sexual harassment can be difficult for employers. The Civil Rights Act of 1964 prohibits sexual harassment (Shank, 1994). As with other provisions of the Civil Rights Act, the employer can be held responsible for the behavior of supervisors, employees, or contractors who harass staff members or consumers. The law defines two types of sexual harassment in the workplace:

- *Quid pro quo harassment:* An employee is asked for sex in return for a job, promotion, or other type of workplace benefit or consideration. To be considered harassment, the victim must be able to establish that the advances made by the perpetrator were unwelcome or unsolicited (Kettner, 2002).
- *Hostile work environment harassment:* The presence of behaviors that create a workplace that is so hostile that it interferes with the victim's ability to work. This type of harassment can include repeated inappropriate comments, harassing phone calls, nude pictures posted in the workplace, inappropriate touching, indecent exposure, and explicit efforts to physically intimidate the victim or make it difficult for that individual to carry out a work assignment (Shank, 1994). Homophobic remarks are considered to constitute sexual harassment. To prove a hostile work environment case, the victim must be able to provide verification that any "reasonable" woman or man would find the same behavior offensive.

In order to limit legal liability for harassment claims, employers must be able to verify that they have a written antiharassment policy that is enforced in a standardized way. They also must be able to prove that staff members and supervisors have received sufficient training so that they are knowledgeable about definitions of inappropriate behavior, reporting procedures, and processes for handling complaints (Shank, 1994).

Problems With Enforcement

Although most employers would agree that harassment and discrimination are inappropriate, there is wide variation in how organizations actually comply with federal and staff laws that mandate fair hiring and treatment of staff. Organizations may not have written policies to guide the handling of complaints, or they may simply choose to ignore staff complaints. In some organizations, difficulties in interpersonal relations among staff may be handled appropriately through training, enforcement of standardized policies, or routine supervisory or arbitration processes. More problematic for organizations is harassment that originates within the administrative ranks or by outside contractors who may provide much needed resources for the organizations. Perpetuators may hold a great deal of power in the organization, and staff may be afraid to bring complaints. In some circumstances, organizations will fail to enforce antiharassment policies or retaliate against the injured party in order to protect these powerful individuals or the organization's reputation, or simply to maintain the organization's status quo. Some organizations simply fail to comply with government guidelines because it is difficult for government agencies to enforce and for organizations to take action under current legal guidelines for a number of reasons:

- Individuals or groups of people affected must bring complaints. This may require that the individual or group assume certain risks or costs. They may face demotion or termination by the employer, additional verbal harassment, and legal expenses associated with hiring a lawyer if the organization fails to take action.
- Government agencies will not know that a specific employer has failed to comply with antidiscrimination or antiharassment laws unless affected individuals or groups file complaints with these agencies.
- Harassment is considered a civil violation rather than a criminal act unless it involves violence.

- Federal government monitors federal contractors but primarily just ensures that contractors have workplace policies.
- For the most part, discrimination and harassment are addressed through either the federal EEOC or through the courts. The EEOC may fine employers if they verify discrimination complaints. Many victims may file EEOC complaints and sue employers for damages. Consequently, case (court) law often determines how the act is interpreted, and the determination changes constantly depending on rulings that may be appealed or overturned in state and federal courts.
- Because employers face few, if any, legal penalties for harassment or discrimination, lawsuits by filed by individuals or a group of individuals who experience the same type of discrimination or harassment often are the only recourse for addressing such problems. In addition to the ethical implications of such behavior, one of the primary reasons employers have written antiharassment or antidiscrimination policies is to protect the organization against lawsuits and the large damage awards or legal fees involved in defending the organization (Kettner, 2002; Perlmutter et al., 2001; Shank, 1994).

Because of ambiguities in the law, employers who wish to guard against harassment or discrimination complaints should take the following actions:

- Have written employment policies that are enforced.
- Ensure that hiring process takes place in a fair manner. A written job description with minimum qualifications and a recruitment plan should be developed. Standardized screening tools and tests should be used. Interview questions should be prepared in advance; all interviewees should be asked to respond to the same set of questions, and more than one person should be present at each interview.
- Provide ongoing training to staff and supervisors about inappropriate behavior that is defined as harassment in federal and state law.
- Require supervisors to report harassment complaints to superiors.
- Maintain a paper trail when harassment reports are made in order to verify that the organization has taken appropriate action to respond to complaints. Ensure that employees who file grievances do not experience retaliation (Pecora, 1998; Pearlmutter et al., 2001).

BOX 8.1 SAMPLE JOB DESCRIPTION FOR AN EXECUTIVE DIRECTOR'S POSITION IN A SOCIAL SERVICE ORGANIZATION

Position Title:	Executive Director of *EMPOWER NOW*
Job Description:	Chief administrator of a nonprofit organization providing counseling and employment services to women who have experienced domestic violence. The chief administrator will work with the organization's board of directors to develop policies, plan programs, and raise funds for the organization. In addition, the executive director will be responsible for recruiting, hiring, training, and evaluating the performance of paid employees and volunteers. The administrator is responsible for overseeing the organization's budget, preparing grant proposals, and negotiating service delivery contracts.
Qualifications:	Minimum educational requirement: Master's degree in a social service-related field. An MSW degree is preferred. A minimum of 5 years of administrative or supervisory experience in a social service organization is required. Previous experience in the field of domestic violence and working with diverse clients and staff members is desirable. The candidate is expected to be knowledgeable about empowerment-oriented and multicultural approaches to service delivery.
Starting Date:	January 1, 2007
Application Deadline:	October 15, 2006
Application Procedures:	Send a current resume and a list of three references to: Esmeralda Garcia Board President EMPOWER NOW 5310 Main Street Anywhere, California XXXXX

EMPOWER NOW is an Equal Opportunity, Affirmative Action Employer

SUPERVISING, ASSESSING, AND TRAINING STAFF

Once staff members are hired, it is imperative that the social service organization holds staff accountable for their actions. Consequently, the organization must provide appropriate supervision for employees and regularly assess staff performance. In addition, organizations must provide opportunities for staff members to learn new skills or improve their abilities. Consequently, social service organizations either help their employees attain additional education or provide them with in-service training.

Supervision

According to Shera and Page (1995), a critical aspect of empowerment-oriented social service organization is that supervisors "promote positive relationships and images through the development of positive language, help staff focus on client strengths, and model appropriate behaviors and values to staff" (p. 4). Peer consultation for staff members who need assistance with workplace issues may be an effective means to provide support and consequently increase a sense of personal empowerment and autonomy (Shera & Page, 1995). In their study of management practices in empowerment-oriented organizations, Gutierrez et al. (1995) found that the use of peer supervision techniques helped build relationships and support, resulting in a sense of shared philosophy and psychological safety among staff members. Workers can be organized into teams, or support groups can be established to facilitate peer consultation and information exchange.

Another method used to provide peer support involves mentoring. Mentoring has been found to be an effective method of orienting new employees to the workplace and helping them to develop appropriate workplace skills (Dreher & Ash, 1990; Hardina & Shaw, 2001). Kaminski et al. (2000) studied the use of mentors to train workers to act as workplace advocates and leaders. They found that the best mentors repeatedly praised student performance, gave trainees new tasks that involved greater levels of responsibility, and encouraged workers to develop their own goals and tactics for producing results. As discussed in Chapter 7, an additional benefit of the mentoring process is that mentors can help marginalized employees (e.g., women and persons of color) navigate difficulties in workplace culture that could limit their ability to secure promotions or become administrators (Burke & McKeen, 1990; Ragins, Townsend, & Mattis, 1998).

Good, supportive, and nurturing relationships between supervisors and employees and among staff members are critical for the creation of organizational structures that enhance the well-being of clients. However, most supervisory models are based on hierarchical models that rely on the use of power and authority to change worker behavior (Kaiser, 1997). Hierarchical models may be necessary to establish a system of accountability in organizations; by removing some of the supervisory layers, worker autonomy is increased.

Corsun and Enz (1999) conducted a study of service workers in private clubs to examine whether supportive relationships in the workplace were associated with dimensions of psychological empowerment (worker autonomy, feelings of self-efficacy, and commitment to the job) identified by Spreitzer (1996). They found that employee perceptions of the degree of helping behavior among staff members and the degree of organizational management support (trust, participation, orientation to employees) were highly correlated to each of the dimensions of psychological empowerment identified by Spreitzer. Based on these findings, Corsun and Enz argue, "Co-workers, customers, and management would do well to express and model supportive and helping behaviors. As these values come to be shared and lived, the quality of work and service provided are likely to increase among employees" (p. 221).

Gutierrez et al. (1995) propose that supervision in empowerment-oriented agencies be viewed as a parallel process model, similar to approaches used by clinical social workers. The basic assumption of this model is that positive and negative aspects of the relationship between supervisors and social workers often carry over into the relationship between worker and client. As applied in empowerment practice, the best way to ensure that workers respect client autonomy and focus on strengths-based solutions to problems is to apply these principles in the administrative and supervisory process. Workers who are given autonomy and have performance evaluations that focus on their strengths and opportunities to enhance their professional growth are more likely to interact with clients in an empowering manner.

Performance Evaluation

A standardized system of performance appraisal is critical for employers. Union contracts or civil service laws cover many social service employees. These employers can be fired only for "just cause," specific violations of workplace rules or policies. Such employees have the right to be given notice about the disciplinary action and a right to representation by a union or another representative. The employer must be able to verify that an objective investigation was made, that there was ample evidence of wrongdoing on the part of the worker, and that sanctions for poor behavior or performance are applied equally across members of different demographic groups. If these standards are not met, the employee may be able to sue for wrongful termination. In nonunionized workplaces, employers have much latitude to fire employees "at will," meaning at their own discretion. However, even "at will" terminations are restricted by federal and state laws such as the ADA and U.S. Civil Rights Act, which allow employees to sue if they can prove the employer exhibited a pattern of discrimination in disciplinary or termination decisions (Tambor, 1995).

Most employers develop mechanisms to protect themselves from such lawsuits by implementing clear written policies that guide personnel decisions, documenting inappropriate employee behavior, and establishing a "paper trail" to indicate what actions are taken to discipline employees (Pearlmutter et al., 2001). Some employers also require new "at will" employees to sign agreements stating that they will agree to take grievances against the organization to arbitration (Tambor, 1995). Such agreements usually mean that the employee has given up his or her right to sue the organization for wrongful termination or discrimination.

It should be noted, however, that termination of problem employees is not the only objective associated with performance evaluation. The primary purpose of evaluating performance is to enhance the skills and personal development of employees. Performance assessments help managers reinforce appropriate worker behavior and give objective feedback to workers who need to improve their skills (Weinbach, 1998). Organizations are best served by using standardized performance assessment tools and making routine evaluations of worker behavior and training needs (Pearlmutter et al., 2001). However, assessment also should take into account the individual needs of the worker and differences in job descriptions and responsibilities. Evaluations of worker performance should focus on goals established for and by individual workers in collaboration with supervisors (Kaiser, 1997). Goal setting and appropriate feedback (balanced with positive and negative comments) from supervisors increase staff member satisfaction with the supervisory process (Larson, Day, Springer, Clark, & Vogel, 2003).

Social service organizations typically use a number of different measures for performance assessment (Kettner, 2002; Lewis et al., 2001; Pearlmutter et al., 2001). These methods include the following:

- *Narrative assessments by supervisors using previously established criteria.* Evaluators can respond to a set of open-ended questions about the employee's behavior or document critical incidences (both positive and negative) that reflect the staff member's performance.

- *Traditional management by objective systems in which the supervisor determines if the employee has accomplished a predetermined set of objectives.* The supervisory process is then used to identify blocks to task accomplishment and to establish new or revised performance benchmarks.
- *Rating scales and checklists that require the supervisor to make an assessment of the worker's level of performance on a standardized scale.* In some cases, these scales contain explicit behavioral "anchors" that provide examples of good or bad performance as observed by the supervisor. For example, a behavioral anchor for "dressing professionally" on the low end of the scale could be, "Wears jeans or other nonprofessional attire at all times." Alternatively, the top end of the scale would be reflected in the statement, "Consistently dresses professionally at all times."
- *Comparisons of an individual worker's performance to those of other workers.* For example, workers could be compared in terms of the number of successfully closed cases or the number of clients served on average.
- *Multirater assessment systems in which more that one evaluator directly assesses the worker's skill or performance level.* In some social service agencies, the evaluators may listen to an audiotape or videotape of a session with a client and rate the worker in terms of the quality of interaction with the client. The rater's assessments are then compared to determine congruency among the various assessments made (Larson et al., 2003). Multirater assessments are generally considered to be more reliable (accurate, objective) than other types of performance evaluations.

Many organizations and professional associations now evaluate performance by developing lists of specific skills or competencies that professionally trained workers should possess. In addition, efforts have been made to create tools or systems of measurement to determine if workers in certain job categories have actually acquired these skills or if they need additional training. For example, the National Network for Social Work Managers (NNSWM) has developed a set of competencies to be attained by applicants for the Certified Social Work Manager (CSWM) credential. NNSWM grants these certificates to people who hold a BSW or MSW degree, who have 5 years of management experience, and who can demonstrate management competency in core areas that include advocacy, governance, community relations, planning, evaluation, staff development, human resource management, program development, policy practice, and financial development (Wimpfheimer, 2004).

BOX 8.2 LEADERSHIP

Pang has successfully persuaded her board of directors to allow her to restructure the organization, using elements of the empowerment and feminist management approaches. One of Pang's biggest challenges will be reassess the positions that staff members currently hold and to reassign them to positions that better match their strengths. One of the government grants that Pang has recently obtained requires that the organization document staff activities as well as the quality and effectiveness of their work. Pang realizes that she will need to establish a supervisory structure that can be used evaluate staff performance and provide opportunities to upgrade worker skills.

- What type of leadership approach should Pang take to address the problems in this organization?
- What aspects of this approach would be the most beneficial for the organization?
- What management tools or documents should Pang use to create new positions for the organization?
- What type of supervision should be offered to the staff?
- How should performance be evaluated?

Nationally, many schools of social work have developed child welfare competencies and curriculums under Title IV-E of the Social Security Action. Commonly referred to as Title IV-E, this act provides the largest federal funding stream for child welfare services such as foster care, subsidized adoption for children with special needs, and agency administrative costs. The act also provides resources to train agency staff and students in child welfare practice. These resources help to subsidize university social work programs to educate BSW and MSW students posed to enter careers in child welfare. These competency-based curriculums often are developed with significant input and participation by child welfare organization mandated or contracted by law to deliver child protection, family reunification, and permanent placements for children (adoption, guardianship, or other long-term care). Often these competency-based curriculums reflect the performance priorities of both schools and child welfare agencies. Graduating students must demonstrate practice competency in core areas such as ethics, interviewing, assessment, intervention, cultural competency, human behavior and the social environment, workplace management, policy, planning, and administration. Child welfare agencies that employ social work graduates often use elements or features of these competencies to

evaluate worker practice and performance (Briar-Lawson, Sc
Harris, 1997).

Training

Workers who receive poor or mixed assessment results are gene
sidered candidates for additional staff training. Lewis et al. (2
tify additional measurement strategies for the identification of staff training needs, including client satisfaction studies, employee opinion surveys, and traditional organization needs assessments that recognize new client problems or increases in demand for services. Organizations can review the "best practice" literature developed by other organizations and use these programmatic recommendations and performance standards to develop new policies and procedures for staff.

Training options can include providing in-service training to all or some employees, sending employees to workshops sponsored by professional associations or other organizations to attain specialized knowledge, and supporting (through stipends or release time) employees who wish to go to college or graduate school to attain a degree that will allow them to improve their skills and/or seek promotion (Kettner, 2002).

At minimum, most organizations provide new employees with some type of standardized orientation to the agency. Orientations generally consist of informing new employees about the organization's mission and purpose, leadership, culture, formal structure, legal basis for existence, client or consumer base, close collaborators, community supporters, and the organization's programs and services. Orientations provide an opportunity to communicate to new employees about the agency's expectations concerning good organizational citizenship and the consequences of inappropriate behavior. Legal requirements and agency personnel policies such as affirmative action, nondiscrimination, sexual harassment, and provisions of the ADA are introduced. Grievance procedures and disciplinary or termination polices are described. Formal written procedures, protocols, and rules for the delivery of services are provided.

Employee benefit packages, such as retirement, unemployment insurance, worker's compensation, and family leave, are often discussed. Some organizations consciously structure orientations to socialize new employees to the organization by pairing up new employees with veteran employees during the orientation process. This often has the effect of introducing the new employee to important social networks in the organization that are needed for long-term success in the organization (Lesser, 2000).

Most organizations either provide ongoing training to workers or seek opportunities to send staff members to workshops or training sessions offered by local organizations or state and national professional associations. Trainings may be oriented to dealing with common workplace problems and dilemmas or to improving worker knowledge or competency in specific skills and practices (Lewis et al., 2001). For example, an organization interested in improving the cultural competency of employees or implementing empowerment-oriented practice models for working with individuals, groups, and families could improve employee acquisition of these skills by designing and delivering training sessions for staff or contracting out for specialized workshops.

WORKING WITH VOLUNTEERS

Paid staff members are not the only individuals in the organization whom leaders must encourage and motivate. In addition to involving staff members and the clients in organizational decision-making, executive directors and other leaders must be prepared to recruit and train volunteers. Volunteers are unpaid workers and can include board members, fundraising coordinators, or members of organizational task forces that design or evaluate programs. Volunteers can perform clerical work for the organization, serve as publicists for the organization's activities, lobby on behalf of the organization, or participate in protests and demonstrations to support the organization's position on social issues. In some cases, volunteers are permitted to deliver organizational services, such as delivering meals to homebound seniors, tutoring students, or facilitating self-help groups.

Cnaan, Handy, and Wadsworth (1996) identify four dimensions that can be used to determine if an individual is a volunteer:

- Has the individual willingly volunteered to perform the activity?
- To what extent has the individual been rewarded for his or her work?
- Is the work performed within the context of a formal organization?
- Is the beneficiary of the volunteer activity someone who is a stranger to the volunteer?

Using these criteria, a volunteer can be defined as someone who is not rewarded for work provided in the context of a formal organization and who provides services or acts on behalf of people outside the volunteer's personal or professional network. Cnaan et al. (1996) note, however, that this definition is somewhat narrow and excludes much of the helping activity commonly found in low-income communities: informal help given to friends, relatives, and neighbors, or the reciprocal exchange of emotional support, goods, and services that takes place among members of self-help groups.

In many social service organizations, volunteers are generally regarded as a necessary supplement to, although not a substitute for, paid staff. In some organizations, organizational maintenance, fundraising, social action, and service delivery may be the almost exclusive domain of volunteers. All or predominantly volunteer organizations can include new organizations in the start-up phase who rely on volunteers to get the organization up and running or self-help oriented organizations (such as Alcoholics Anonymous) that philosophically are opposed to the delivery of services by professionals (Gidron & Hasenfeld, 1994; Smith & Shen, 1996). In addition, many social justice organizations rely on a small group of paid staff to keep the organization running and to recruit and train a cadre of volunteers to participate in lobbying and other types of social action (Minkoff, 1997).

In addition to philosophy and mission, social service organizations use volunteers to reduce the costs associated with service delivery (Handy & Srinivasan, 2004). Using one or more volunteers in lieu of a paid staff member eliminates expenditures for salary and fringe benefits. Consequently, nonprofit service delivery in an organization that makes substantial use of volunteer labor may be substantially less costly than government provision, especially taking into account higher staff salaries for unionized public sector employees.

There are some disadvantages to using volunteers. There may be hidden costs involved in using and retaining volunteers: the provision of training on specific aspects of organizational policy and service delivery; reimbursement for travel, food, and other expenses; and costs associated with providing recognition or awards (such as certificates, plaques, or parties) to volunteers (Weinbach, 1998). Volunteers are transitory, and keeping individual volunteers working with the agency for long periods may be difficult (Omoto & Snyder, 1993). Volunteer turnover often requires additional expenses related to recruiting and training replacements. In addition, volunteers often require supervision. Agencies may need to pay staff members simply to recruit and manage a large volunteer labor force (Edwards, Mooney, & Heald, 2001).

Social service agency managers often seek opportunities to recruit volunteers in the course of their other public activities. Participation in community task forces or coalitions, engagement with potential funders, and interviews with the media can be used as situations to both sell the organization's services and seek new volunteers and donors. However, success in recruiting new supporters for the organization means that the manager must understand how to motivate and mobilize new volunteers.

People want to volunteer for numerous reasons, including altruism, commitment to a cause, religious belief, or the opportunity to socialize with others (Chinman & Wandersman, 1999; Gronbjerg & Never, 2004; Hyde, 1994; Omoto & Snyder, 1993). Volunteering can help people establish both personal and professional relationships; consequently, volunteering helps people establish a sense of linkage with, and belonging to, a community (Putnam, 2000).

Volunteering may help individuals find ways to cope with personal issues, providing peer counseling and other support to people with similar problems. For example, many of the early volunteers in acquired immunodeficiency syndrome (AIDS) service organizations during the 1980s were people who also were positive for the human immunodeficiency virus (HIV) or were members of the gay community (Poindexter, 2002). Another way that people may personally benefit from volunteering is that they can use the experience to obtain job-related skills or contacts that may be helpful in future job searches (Metzendorf & Cnaan, 1992). In many organizations that serve marginalized communities, the recruitment of clients for volunteer positions serves multiple purposes:

1. It creates a sense of reciprocity in the act of receiving a service. The client feels less dependent on the organization if he or she can give something in return to the organization (Neysmith & Reitsma-Street, 2000).
2. The services provided to consumers are more likely to reflect their needs and preferences because members of the client group either have been involved in the delivery of services or have had the opportunity to give input on program design and evaluation (Hardina & Malott, 1996a).
3. The client develops a sense of self-competency because his or her input and insight about the delivery of services are valued (Zimmerman & Rappaport, 1988).
4. The organization serves as a portal that the former client or community resident can use to find employment. The organization may provide a job reference or an opportunity for the client to list the agency on his or her vita (Cooney & Weaver, 2001; Itzhaky, 1995).

Many agencies hire their volunteers, especially in circumstances where having a staff member who is a member of the target community is perceived to be important for enhancing the quality of the service provided or for helping the agency communicate with its clientele (Lowe, Barg, & Stephens, 1998). For example, a substance abuse agency might prefer to hire and train counselors who are recovering addicts.

An additional reason that people volunteer is that such service may be required or encouraged by their employer or school. Many corporations provide incentives to employees, such as flexible work hours or paid leaves of absence, to work with local nonprofit organizations (Puffer & Meindl, 1995). Such practices are believed to help businesses establish good working relationships with the community and to "give something back" to the public. In addition, many high schools and colleges require that students participate in service-learning courses (Edwards et al., 2001). Service learning requires that students give a predetermined number of hours to nonprofit and volunteer efforts in their communities in return for acquiring skills and learning about people in need.

Another important source of unpaid labor in social service organizations is student interns. The Council on Social Work Education requires that graduate social work students perform a minimum of 900 hours of practice experience in field agencies. Undergraduate students must complete 400 hours in a field agency. Field agencies must provide a BSW or MSW field instructor for undergraduate students and a MSW-level instructor for graduate students. There is an expectation that the field instructor will, in collaboration with the social work educational program, provide specific learning assignments that complement the program's curriculum and will monitor student performance (Council on Social Work Education, 2002). Psychology, public health, business, and public administration programs may seek to place student interns in social service organizations. All these various professional programs have different expectations and learning goals for students. As with other types of volunteers, internships provide a valuable supplement to agency staff, but they also require a commitment from the organization of time and staff resources (Netting, Nelson, Borders, & Huber, 2004).

One of the chief responsibilities of executive directors or those staff members responsible for volunteer recruitment and retention is understanding what motivates volunteers and how volunteer participation is sustained over time (Omoto & Snyder, 1993). Netting et al. (2004) identify a number of actions that a manager can take to minimize conflict between paid staff and volunteers:

- Develop policies that focus on the volunteers' support of staff activities.
- Ensure that volunteers are not assigned the same jobs as paid staff.
- Inform staff members about the contributions volunteers make to the organization.

In addition, the skilled chief executive officer (CEO) or volunteer administrator must strive to find the best mix of volunteer and paid labor and involve members of these and other key constituency groups (e.g., clients, board members, volunteers, community leaders, funders, and representatives from local institutions) in making decisions and supporting the work of the organization (McCauley & Hughes, 1991).

BOX 8.3 USING VOLUNTEERS

Pang has found that one source of conflict within the Northwest Women's Shelter that relates to the use of volunteers. Because this organization was founded by a committed group of feminists, some of the services are provided by volunteers. Although the organization routinely hires paid staff to operate the shelter, some of the services (such as rape counseling and weekly support groups for women about to leave the shelter) continue to be provided by volunteers who have little training and who receive little oversight from agency staff. Despite concerns about the quality of these services, the shelter would suffer financially if it had to suddenly replace all volunteers with paid staff.

- What steps should Pang take to decide what "jobs" in the organization should be completed by staff or volunteers?
- Who should be included in this type of decision-making?
- What factors should influence the decision-making process?
- Are there procedures that could be used to integrate volunteer labor with professional staff in the provision of rape counseling services and the running of support groups?
- If volunteers do leave the organization when they are assigned to other tasks, how could Pang recruit new volunteers for the organization?

MANAGER RESPONSIBILITY FOR FACILITATING COLLABORATION AND INTEGRATION AMONG STAFF, VOLUNTEERS, AND CLIENTS: EMPOWERING THE MANY RATHER THAN THE FEW

The skilled empowerment-oriented manager must be able to build working alliances among members of the various constituency groups within the organization as well as those entities represented in the organization's external environment (Martin, 1980). One challenge for the social service administrator is the different roles and responsibilities of staff members in the organization. The interests of professional staff (those who have received formal education in a specific area of expertise or practice) may be quite different from the interests and needs of paraprofessionals (those who have received some training in a specific area of practice and perform some of the tasks normally reserved for professionals). In most social service organizations, the workforce includes nonprofessional staff members and support staff, such as maintenance and clerical workers (Weinbach, 1998). One of the responsibilities of the administrator is to recruit an appropriate mix of workers so that the primary functions of the organization can be accomplished. Executive directors are responsible for mediating when the interests of these various groups conflict and for facilitating a decision-making process in which most, if not all, of the interest groups can engage in dialogue and reach a compromise that will serve at least some of the needs of the various competing interests.

What complicates decision-making is that administrators should not only attend to what is happening within the organization, but Schmid (1992) argues that executive directors also must be responsive to constituency groups and donors located outside the organization. One approach for effective management that balances internal and external demands is to create a decentralized decision-making structure in which responsibility for some types of decisions is delegated to staff and other organizational members. The director is not the sole authority for most types of decisions. According to Schmid, one of the primary advantages of decentralization is that "it relieves the director of routine management duties, enabling him or her to engage in innovative thinking and strategic planning, creating new challenges, and adopting patterns of management by exception" (p. 110).

Decentralization and power sharing allow the administrator time to respond to external demands while stimulating creativity and innovation inside the organization. Consequently, transformation of the organization and its administrators, staff, and clients becomes the main focus of the organization. The empowerment literature is very explicit about the responsibility of organizational managers in creating an atmosphere in which workers will feel empowered:

- Provide career and professional development opportunities (Gutierrez et al., 1995).
- Involve staff in policy-making, program planning, and evaluation (Rose & Black, 1985).
- Flatten organizational hierarchies by eliminating some levels of supervision and using team approaches (Spreitzer, 1995).
- Psychologically empower workers by giving them more autonomy over their work (Paul, Niehoff, & Turnley, 2000).

- Encourage workers to advocate for improvements in policies and client services (Bowen & Lawler, 1995; Reisch, Wenocur, & Sherman, 1981).

Facilitating such changes in the workplace requires that the executive director think and act "politically" both inside and outside the organization and encourage workers to do the same. Brenton (1999) argues that partnerships between administrators and staff members are critical for facilitating working partnerships among clients and staff members:

> At the present time, the power structure in many social work agencies is typical of that found in bureaucratic organizations and serves as a means of insuring authority, control, and hierarchies, while the division of labor or tasks serves often to protect "turfs" or particular sectors of action. The best strategy is to encourage practitioners to form partnerships with the members of a community (users of services and others) and create alliances and coalitions, is to give them access to partnerships within their own professional and organizational milieus. (p. 44)

Although internal and external alliances among staff members and other organizational participants are important for maintaining organizational stability, the executive director must be able to make some decisions quickly (in response to situational demands). Consequently, one of the primary skills for the transformative leader is the ability to differentiate between those decisions to be reserved for the director and those that should be made in consultation with other organizational participants. As Rago (1996) notes, the ability to leave some decisions to others may be the most difficult task undertaken by administrators in social service organizations.

SUMMARY

Effective administrative leadership requires a specific set of skills to recruit and maintain skilled staff members and volunteers. It also requires that the administrator function politically in interaction with the organization's external environment (Pearlmutter et al., 2001). In empowerment-oriented practice, it is imperative that the executive director establish a vision for the organization and that he or she make it clear that the organization and its staff is oriented toward bringing clients and other marginalized groups into the organization's decision-making process.

One critical component of transformative leadership to empower organizations, staff, volunteers, and clients is that the executive director can create an organizational culture in which staff members and volunteers are client oriented and committed to a set of values that supports power sharing. Therefore the executive director must have the ability to inspire and motivate paid as well as unpaid workers. In addition, they must be able to facilitate group-oriented decision-making processes. Chapter 9 describes specific management skills and techniques to motivate staff are described. Chapter 10 examines team approaches to organizational decision-making.

QUESTIONS FOR CLASS DISCUSSION

1. Describe the attributes of a good leader.
2. Is it necessary for a leader to be charismatic? Must someone be born "charismatic," or can this attribute be acquired? If so, how does someone become charismatic?
3. How would a leader go about establishing a vision for the organization?
4. How would leaders using the servant or transformative approaches work effectively with problem employees?
5. What are the benefits and disadvantages of federal and state employment regulations such as Affirmative Action and the Americans with Disabilities Act?
6. How would you differentiate between *quid pro quo* harassment and hostile work environment harassment? How can sexual harassment be prevented?
7. What are the attributes that you associate with a "good supervisor"? What are some of the reasons a supervisory relationship might be inadequate to improve the performance of an individual worker?
8. What tasks should be assigned to volunteers in social service organizations? Are there any responsibilities commonly held by social workers that are not appropriate volunteer activities?

SAMPLE ASSIGNMENTS

1. Conduct an analysis of the various constituency groups and types of job positions in the organization in which you are employed or in which you are an intern. Classify these jobs as professional, paraprofessional, nonprofessional, support staff, and volunteer. How would you assess the degree of diversity in this organization (age, social class, gender, ethnicity, mental/physical disabilities, or sexual orientation)? Are there differences between the

composition of the management team and the composition of the front-line staff or other workers? Are there demographic differences among staff members at various ranks, volunteers, and clients? How much power do volunteers and clients have in comparison to people who hold staff positions?

2. Identify task areas that are not currently addressed by staff members in your organization. Based on your analysis, write a job description for this new position and a rationale for hiring someone with these specifications for the job.
3. Develop a plan to recruit volunteers for your organization. List the types of activities that could be undertaken by volunteers, reasons why volunteers might be interested in volunteering, and appropriate recruitment methods that would appeal to these potential volunteers.
4. Interview executive directors from at least three social service organizations. Develop and administer an interview guide that focuses on the administrator's philosophy and model of management and/or leadership used by that administrator. Be sure to include questions on workplace diversity and empowerment of staff members and clientele. Write a three- to five-page paper on your findings. What did you find out about the administrators that you interviewed? Compare and contrast their philosophies about management and interaction with staff members and clients.

CHAPTER 9

Increasing Employee Motivation: Promoting the Psychological Empowerment of Workers

Social workers are employed in a variety of social service organizational settings, ranging from public and private nonprofits to for-profit organizations. Sometimes organizational structure, culture, policies, and procedures create a work environment where the nature of work becomes dull, routine, and mechanical. When work becomes monotonous, staff motivation suffers, and low motivation usually translates to poor-quality work, low commitment, and, more importantly, mediocre services to clients. Social work by its very nature is difficult work. High staff burnout and staff turnover are not uncommon in many social service organizations. Transformative social work leaders and managers need to find ways to keep their staffs highly motivated because low motivation is costly to both the organization and the clients its serves. This chapter discusses empowerment as a staff motivator. We describe

- The relationship between self-efficacy and empowerment, that is, the importance of self-efficacy in terms of job task and feeling empowered as a member of an organization.
- Why empowerment practice is both necessary and advantageous for social work managers and supervisors.
- Theories of and strategies for motivating staff.
- The relationship between empowerment and motivation.
- Staff job assignment and whether job assignments need to be restructured to better support an empowerment approach.

- The autonomy of work in an empowered organization.
- Limitations of staff involvement in decision-making.
- Employee benefits as a job motivator in the context of a changing diversified workforce.

EMPOWERMENT AS SELF-EFFICACY

Empowerment has been described as an awakening of personal and interpersonal power by which individuals, families, and communities can better manage and mitigate problems affecting their lives (Gutierrez, 1995). Power under empowerment is not seen as authoritative, manipulative, or a scare resource exercised to change the behavior of others for personal gain; rather, it is viewed as a positive inner resource that allows a person to

- Gain aptitude for managing one's life.
- Engage in expressions of self-worth.
- Acquire capacity to work with others to influence and manage community life.
- Access and participate in public decision-making (Gutierrez, Parsons, & Cox, 1998).

From this perspective of empowerment, individuals gain mastery, competence, and confidence to participate in democratic community life (Shera & Page, 1995). Central to this view of empowerment is the concept of self-efficacy, that is, the belief in one's own ability to perform specific tasks based on his or her perceptions of self-competence (Gist, 1987; Pearlmutter, 1998). A leading theorist on self-efficacy, Bandura (1997) describes self-efficacy as "beliefs in one's capacities to organize and execute the courses of action required to produce given attainments" (p. 3). Self-efficacy is a person's self-assessment of his or her aptitude and proficiency to successfully carry out tasks. Personal belief in one's self-efficacy influences the choices of actions he or she will undertake, the amount of effort he or she will exercise in a given action, and how well and how he or she will persevere in the face of obstacles and failures (Bandura, 1997). Advancing a sense of self-efficacy is critical to the empowerment process because it promotes actions on one's behalf, a belief in self-worth, and a sense of control (Gutierrez et al., 1998).

Empowerment and self-efficacy are often discussed in the literature in the context of social worker and client relationships. Social workers are taught and encouraged to empower clients by assisting them to discover and unleash their inner power. Clients are educated to become more aware of the true causes of their condition, thus increasing their sense of self-efficacy and control of their environment. Despite the emphasis on empowerment practice, little attention has been paid to the needs of social workers who may feel powerless working in traditional, highly centralized, top-down organizational settings commonly used to deliver social services (Cohen & Austin, 1997). Powerlessness and helplessness are fed by prescribed job tasks, routine methods of service, and little input into organizational decision-making. Powerless and helplessness often result in low morale, low motivation, and minimal levels of job performance. In this context, it is unrealistic to expect workers to be motivated to use empowerment practice and to be successful with clients if the workers themselves feel powerless in their work (Cohen & Austin, 1997). If empowerment practice is to be successful, workers need to experience empowerment in the workplace so that experience is transferred to their work with clients.

Organizations prefer hierarchical bureaucratic structures because of their ability to provide uniform and equitable services to clients free of employee bias or discrimination (Skidmore, 1995). For management, other advantages include a rational division of labor based on a specialized, clearly defined job task. From this perspective, one could easily conclude that self-efficacy would be high among staff because competence levels for the job usually are achievable and performance is repetitive. However, individuals, families, and communities are highly complex and heterogeneous. Social work practice with these groups requires different and personalized service approaches over long, nonroutine periods. A routine one-size-fits-all approach to services may actually lower self-efficacy among staff if they perceive that clients are not achieving positive outcomes, leading further to staff perceptions of powerlessness. Spreitzer (1996) suggests that self-efficacy actually is improved in highly complex, unpredictable social service environments where workers learn to experiment and have success with creative and customized approaches to servicing clients. In essence, social workers feel empowered to discover new solutions and make decisions that affect their work lives and how they do their job (Cohen & Austin, 1997). If social service managers are concerned about workers being more successful with clients, then increasing the staff's sense of self-efficacy through empowerment should be a major consideration. Self-efficacy and its relationship to motivation are discussed later in this chapter.

ENCOURAGING MANAGEMENT SKILL DEVELOPMENT AND STRENGTHS FOR EMPOWERMENT

The National Association of Social Workers (NASW) explicitly recognizes empowerment practice in its mission. "The primary mission of the social work profession is to enhance human well-being and help meet the basic human needs of all people, with particular attention to the needs and empowerment of people who are vulnerable, oppressed, and living in poverty" (NASW, 1999, Preamble para. 1). As discussed in Chapter 8, social workers need to acquire empowerment skills as part of their professional development and obligation to serving others. Social workers in supervisory and management positions need to promote, train, and consult with their staff on empowerment practice. However, empowerment can cause dilemmas for social services managers accustomed to traditional management practices and beliefs. After all, traditional management practices and hierarchical arrangements have produced desired results for controlling worker behavior (Kettner, 2002; Weinbach, 1998). In addition, career success and advancement for many managers are the result of being raised in an organization and taught traditional management approaches deemed successful and valued by the organization. Nonetheless, traditional top-down management approaches may not fit well with a professional workforce more concerned about professional autonomy, professional standards, quality of care, and successful outcomes for clients (Lewis, Lewis, Packard, & Souflée, 2001). When applied to a well-educated and professional workforce, poor results such as poor motivation, low morale, burnout, and high staff turnover are likely to ensue. Professional staff may feel that their knowledge and skills are not valued, creating an asphyxiating effect on productivity and achievement of organizational goals. From this perspective, one of the major tenets of management—maximizing staff productivity and performance—is compromised.

Weinbach (1998) has described the role of management as "functions performed by persons within the work settings that are intended to promote productivity and organizational goal attainment" (p. 12). Managers should seek to create and maintain an optimal work environment conducive to the effective and efficient delivery of services to clients and achievement of organizational goals. Empowerment management practices can be viewed as a departure from traditional management convention; however, concerns about efficiency, effectiveness, and productivity, as well as achievement of organizational goals, still remain central. To most empowerment theorists, management through staff empowerment is viewed as a better vehicle for achieving longstanding management ends. Literature on empowerment suggests management through staff empowerment increases employee satisfaction, management satisfaction, morale, motivation, productivity, and, more importantly, consumer satisfaction (Barnard, 1999; Bowen & Lawler, 1995; Shera & Page, 1995). In the world of business and market competition for customers, many private organizations have adopted empowerment management practices as a way of creating and maintaining a competitive edge in a free market economy (Bowen & Lawler, 1995). These organizations have become adaptive and recognize the power in tapping the energy, creativity, and ingenuity of empowered staff and its overall positive effect on their financial bottom line. The same cannot be said of most social service organizations, which are notoriously slow to adapt to changing environment conditions (Cohen & Austin, 1994). This inability to adapt may be deadly to some social services organization, especially in an era of increased accountability and performance expected by stakeholders, legitimators (i.e., legislators, advocates, licensing and accreditation bodies), funders, consumers, and the public at large (Austin, 2002). As described in Chapter 8, staff members often are the source of new ideas and ingenuity needed to meet the demands of organizational constituents.

The guiding philosophy of empowerment is nonbureaucratic and staff participation in organizational decision-making (Bowen & Lawler, 1995). It is the process of giving staff the authority to make major decisions and the accompanying responsibility for those decisions (Barnard, 1999; Paul, Niehoff, & Turnley, 2000). But more importantly, staff empowerment means pushing or transferring power to the lower levels of the organization (Forrester, 2000; Paul et al., 2000) where staff members exercise their skill and expertise consistent with organizational goals. Through this process of power sharing, staff orientation toward work is altered to reflect a greater sense of self-efficacy, commitment, and productivity (Barnard, 1999). As noted in Chapter 8, through shared leadership the organization becomes more adaptive to changing environmental conditions and more likely to engage in organizational learning and to devise better ways to serve clients (Cohen & Austin, 1994). To empower social work staff, and, by extension, the clients, existing and traditional organizational methods of providing social services must be modified (Gutierrez, GlenMaye, & DeLois, 1995). For too long, traditional hierarchical arrangements have created a service delivery system that treats clients and their culture as homogeneous, subjecting them to conformity and submission to agency services (Iglehart & Becerra, 2000). This type of service delivery is neither responsive nor empowering to clients. Social work staff easily recognizes the inherent contradictions and futility of this approach, which ultimately leads to demoralization, helplessness, and poor helping relationships between social workers and clients. What follows is a discussion of how staff empowerment can assist mangers in motivating their staff to serve clients and achieve the goals of their organization.

STRATEGIES FOR MOTIVATING STAFF

Managers have often wondered why some employees are more inspired than other employees to do their work. Early management thought viewed worker motivation rather simply: motivation was directly connected to pay and monetary rewards that increased worker production (Skidmore, 1995). Others viewed punitive measures, such as reprimands or reductions in pay, as a way of controlling unwanted or undesirable workplace behaviors (Kettner, 2002). Although monetary and punitive techniques can motivate workers to some degree, motivation is far more complex. Current understanding of motivation recognizes a diversity of worker needs coupled with workers' personal expectations about their work environment. Most motivational theorists would agree that nonmonetary incentives and rewards, such as challenging work or potential for growth, can be powerful work motivators. Managers must assess across a broader spectrum of what intrinsically motivates their employees and match incentives and rewards appropriately.

BOX 9.1 MOTIVATING STAFF

Emilio, MSW, has been a Social Work Supervisor in a public child welfare agency for about 4 months. Emilio's unit consists of nine social workers. His initial observations of his unit were that workers appear lethargic and detached from their work. In recent interactions with veteran supervisors to learn the "ropes," Emilio was told to assume command and control of his unit, otherwise senior management and workers would perceive him as weak. In reviewing performance reports from his unit, he concluded that his unit was one of the underperforming units in the agency, despite the fact that six unit members possess MSWs. In Emilio's first unit meeting, he laid out *his* plans for improving the unit's performance. Three months later, gains in unit performance were marginal, and complaints from clients and community were constant. Emilio reflected on his graduate days in the MSW program and recalled empowerment approaches to management and supervision as a way of motivating staff and improving services to clients. He decided that now was the time to put some of his graduate education to work and to apply an empowerment approach to his unit.

- What motivation theory or theories should Emilio consider as a way of stimulating worker motivation? Why?
- Identity some early and specific steps that Emilio should undertake to implement an empowerment approach to supervision.
- Describe how these steps might link to the motivational theory or theories you selected.

Employee motivation can be defined as the employee's willingness to engage in behaviors that are directed toward the achievement of the organization's goals (Franco, Bennett, & Kanfer, 2002). These behaviors are viewed as positively related to better work performance; therefore, the direction, intensity, and persistence of work-related behaviors are highly desired by the organization (Wright, 2001). The motivational process involves stimulating the employee to freely and purposefully take action to reach a desired goal (Montana & Charnov, 2000). Empowerment can function as an important stimulus to increasing employee motivation. But before we describe how empowerment functions to spur motivation, it would be wise to revisit a few classic theories on motivation.

Researchers have written extensively about motivation, and it is beyond the scope of this chapter to review them all; however, several motivational theories are important to note. Some authors have categorized motivational theories into two fairly broad categories for purposes of useful description and explanation. For example, Lewis et al. (2001) groups theories of motivation into *content theories* and *process theories*. Wright (2001) uses a similar conceptualization that he labels *humanistic* and *proximal theories* of motivation. Content theories refer to understanding motivation in a framework of human needs and fulfillment of those needs. Humanistic theories approximate content theories in that these theories examine the relationship between employee motives and their satisfaction that influences work behavior. Maslow's Hierarchy of Needs, which is based on a hierarchy of personal needs, exemplifies content theory. Maslow's Hierarchy of Needs and other classic content/humanistic motivational theories are briefly presented here.

- *Maslow's Hierarchy of Needs (1954):* Maslow portrays human needs as hierarchical, that is, human needs beginning with lower basic needs rising to higher level needs. The hierarchy of needs includes (1) physiological, which refers to basic requirements of life such as food, clothing, and shelter; (2) safety and security, which refer to being free from physical harm or threat; (3) social or belonging needs, which refer to social inclusion in a group to express human qualities such as love and caring; (4) esteem, which refers to seeking recognition and a sense of uniqueness; and (5) self-actualization, which refers to becoming what one is fully capable of based on unique personal qualities (personality, skills, education, etc.). Individuals must satisfy a lower level of need before moving on to the next. Working to satisfy the next need on Maslow's hierarchy functions as a motivator.
- *Herzberg's Motivator Hygiene Theory (1975):* Two primary factors, known as motivating and hygiene factors, play different roles in relating to job satisfaction and motivation. Hygiene factors are extrinsic to the job and function only to reduce levels of

job dissatisfaction. Examples of hygiene factors include salary, job security, and working conditions. Motivating factors are intrinsic to the job and stimulate employees to perform at higher levels. Examples include achievement, responsibility, and nature of work.

- *McClelland Needs Theory (1965):* This theory is based on three motivators: need for achievement, need for power, and need for affiliation. Each individual is strongly influenced by one of these three motivators. Persons motivated by achievement set high but attainable goals and seek frequent feedback on performance. Persons motivated by power seek to influence others for the good of the organization. Persons motivated by affiliation seek interpersonal relationships in a supportive, interactive environment and seek recognition of their contributions to organizational goals.

Process Theory refers to the interaction among needs, behaviors, and rewards. Employee needs are seen as being very diverse, reflecting individual differences placed in the value of rewards that influence work behavior. Closely related, proximal theory focuses on motivational constructs (i.e., desires) at the level of purposeful action and attempts to predict behavior or performance based on contextual factors in the workplace (i.e., rewards). Expectancy theory, whereby work behavior is influenced by perceived rewards, exemplifies process theory. Expectancy theory and other classic process/proximal motivational theories are briefly presented here:

- *Expectancy Theory (Vroom, 1964):* Expectancy theory explains work behavior in the context of individual goals and the expectation of achieving these goals. Expectancy theory has three main components. First, increased effort on the part of the employee will lead to increased performance. Second, increased performance is desired because it will lead directly to rewards. Third, the individual must have a preference for rewards that are given. Organizations need to directly connect rewards to performance and ensure that rewards are desired by the employee.
- *Behavior Modification (Skinner, 1999):* Somewhat related to expectancy theory, behavior modification suggests that worker behavior can be controlled through a system of rewards and punishments. Rewards act as positive reinforcement for desired behaviors, and punishment discourages undesired behaviors. Rewards are intrinsic, such as recognition and increased responsibility, as well as extrinsic, such as pay and other financial incentives. The net result is an operant conditioning of staff linked to

motivation and performance. The use of rewards results in more sustained desirable behavior, while the effectiveness of punishments diminishes overtime.

- *Goal Theory (Locke & Latham, 1990; Wright, 2001):* This theory suggests that setting specific goals, coupled with the rewards for goal attainment, significantly increases worker performance. This theory of work motivation contains two underlying processes that explain the effect of goals on work motivation: goal content and goal commitment. Goal content refers to characteristics of the goal, such as difficulty, specificity, and conflict, which can influence performance to attain that goal. Goal commitment refers to the attitude that a person holds to a goal and his or her determination to achieve it even when confronted by setbacks or obstacles. The extent to which the goal seems achievable is reflected in a person's sense of self-efficacy and in the procedural constraints inherent to the organization.

These classic theories of motivation suggest that intrinsic or internal influences are important in enhancing worker motivation. Factors such as fulfillment of needs, concepts of self, achievement, recognition, autonomy, and potential for growth are a few of the intrinsic variables linked to increased motivation. Empowerment approaches to management, such as broader distribution of power, participative decision-making, and greater staff responsibility and autonomy, emphasize and support many of these intrinsic determinants to motivation. Empowerment management practices allow workers to achieve an empowered psychological state stimulating motivation and better orientation toward work (Spreitzer, 1996).

In additional to internal determinants, worker motivation is influenced by organizational and external environment influences (Franco et al., 2002; Shera & Page, 1995). Rigid and controlling organizational structures are seen as hampering employee motivation because work must strictly conform to agency rules and policies. Empowerment practices seek to alter traditional organizational arrangements and culture by instituting more flattened reporting relationships, delegating authority and responsibility, supporting work autonomy, and using participative decision-making, practices all believed to more positively influence worker motivation. One example is an organization's use of self-directed teams entrusted with real responsibility, decision-making, and autonomy working to reach team and organizational goals (Barnard, 1999). *Environmental influences* refer to the nature of community and broader sociopolitical surroundings and the congruence between what workers believe is possible and what is expected and supported in the environment

(Franco et al., 2002). If agency outcomes are not supported in the environment, workers may be less motivated to produce desired results. Management through empowerment practice should include attempts to influence community by networking, public education, consciousness-raising legislative work, and soliciting broad-based community support (including clients) for support of empowerment and organizational goals (Cox & Joseph, 1998).

Strategies for increasing employee motivation through empowerment require an approach that is incremental and well thought out. Forrester (2000) suggests that many organizations have failed at implementing empowerment because attempts to put it into operation have occurred too abruptly or are not deliberately phased-in. Petter, Byrnes, Choi, Fegan, and Miller (2002) present a conceptual framework for empowerment that discusses the theoretical relationship between empowerment and employee motivation. An adaptation of their conceptual framework for empowerment and its relationship to employee motivation is presented in Figure 9.1. This adaptation of Petter et al.'s conceptual framework provides an underpinning for identifying effective strategies for implementation of empowerment practice to be discussed shortly.

Figure 9.1 postulates that certain organizational characteristics or antecedents, such as a supportive culture, must be present for empowerment to develop and remain successful. Once the psychological sense of empowerment is achieved, an increased sense of motivation can occur. Ultimately, an increased sense of empowerment and motivation is thought to be related to improved organizational performance. Petter et al. (2002)

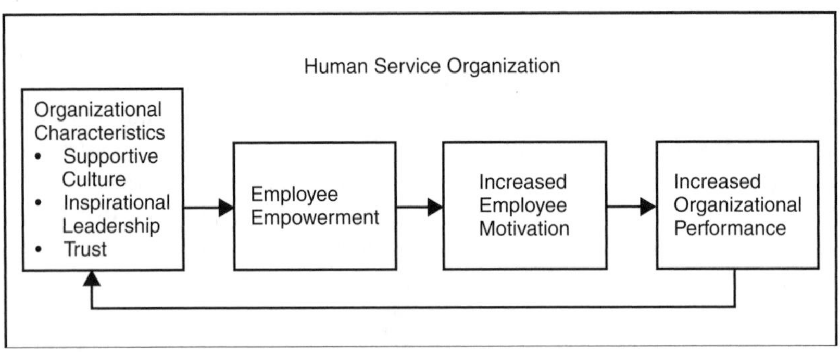

Figure 9.1 The theoretical relationship between empowerment and employee motivation. [Adapted from Petter, J., Byrnes, P., Choi, D.-L., Fegan, F., & Miller, R. (2002). Dimensions and patterns in employee empowerment: Assessing what matters to street-level bureaucrats. *Journal of Public Administration Research and Theory, 12,* 377–401.]

further propose that seven dimensions need to be addressed to move an employee to an empowered state. These dimensions can represent strategies that social service managers can adopt to empower their staff. These dimensions are as follows:

- *Power:* Grant power and authority to those doing the work while building in accountability.
- *Decision-making:* Allow more opportunities for staff to participate in decision-making to create more of an organizational democracy.
- *Information:* Increase information, especially information related to organizational mission and goals, so that workers have the necessary information to make decisions.
- *Autonomy:* Integrate choice and discretion into work performance with appropriate boundaries.
- *Initiative and Creativity:* Allow workers to initiate tasks and explore creativity consistent with organization goals.
- *Knowledge and Skills:* Encourage adequate knowledge and training not only in job skills, but also the philosophy, principles, and benefits of empowerment.
- *Responsibility:* Allow employees to track and evaluate their own performances in consultation with the supervisor rather than the supervisory oversight of the job task.

In addition, managers should consider three main areas of focus for implementing empowerment strategies suggested by Shera and Page (1995):

- *Structure:* The role of traditional supervision and leadership is changed to incorporate role-modeling empowerment values and behaviors, opening and broadening communication, and listening to the concerns of workers regarding job role and work. Supervisory duties become more egalitarian, such as sharing of unit responsibilities (i.e., chairing meetings, setting unit goals), team approaches to problem-solving and decision-making, two-way responsibility and authority rather than top-down management, and parallel use of power.
- *People:* This strategy involves working with staff to address client attitudes and identifying rewards for increasing motivation. Clients can often be viewed negatively by staff, in which case a conscience-raising effort to address the broader political and socioeconomic causes of client problems and issues should be undertaken. As previously mentioned, the use of more intrinsic

rewards is recommended as a way to increase motivation coupled with creating new organizational rituals (culture) that encourage recognition, group cohesion, and working relationships.

- *Technology:* Even with more egalitarian structures and improved worker attitudes and motivation, agency service technology needs to be compatible with the philosophy and principles of empowerment. This includes active client and community participation in developing, implementing, and evaluating organizational services. This also includes manager's use of research to identify more effective and appropriate service delivery methods and outcomes, as well as ongoing education and training of staff to enhance their skills and knowledge.

JOB ASSIGNMENT, JOB RESTRUCTURING, AND JOB AUTONOMY AS MOTIVATING STRATEGIES

As part of organizational structure, work tasks and duties are identified and organized into jobs. Jobs are positioned throughout the organization, with accompanying levels of authority and power. *Job assignment* refers to a particular set of tasks and duties strategically positioned in the organizational structure and occupied by persons capable of performing the job. If organizations and managers are committed to staff empowerment as a goal, then job assignments—that is, tasks, duties, authority, and power—should be consistent with empowerment practice. A strategy for evaluating job assignment consistent with empowerment practice is the job characteristic model. Similar to job assignment, the job characteristic model encompasses tasks specific to the job and the nature of the work (Wright, 2001). Under the model, improved job satisfaction and work motivation are present if workers are able to achieve three critical psychological states: (1) meaningfulness to their work, (2) a sense of responsibility for outcomes associated with their work, and (3) feedback on outcomes resulting from their work. Several job characteristics are seen as essential for achievement of these psychological states (Lewis et al., 2001; Wright, 2001):

- *Variety:* The extent to which one uses various activities and actions to carry out the job, coupled with the use of different knowledge and skills.
- *Task Identity:* The extent to which one associates with the job's finished product, from beginning to end.
- *Task Significance:* The extent to which the job is perceived as having a substantial effect on the lives of people.

- *Autonomy:* The extent to which the job permits choice, discretion, and independence in completing the work.
- *Feedback:* The extent to which the job activities provides the worker with information on his or her performance.
- *Challenge:* The extent to which the job is difficult and complex, but achievable.

Lewis et al. (2001) further state there are three moderating factors that may affect job characteristics and its effects on job motivation and performance. First, workers require basic knowledge and skills to increase the likelihood that work performance will lead to good outcomes. Second, worker growth and development needs vary from worker to worker. Third, contextual satisfaction, which refers to other aspects of the job, such as satisfaction with pay and working conditions (e.g., hygiene factors); otherwise, job enrichment may not make much difference. If these characteristics are not present in workers' job assignment, then organizations and managers should consider redesigning jobs or changing or reorganizing tasks and duties to better fit staff empowerment.

Kettner (2002) states that the purpose of job redesign is to better match worker skills and responsibilities to job tasks, thereby increasing efficiency and productivity. Redesign is also meant to introduce variability into job assignments as a way of improving overall quality of work life. Job redesign needs to be concerned about two levels: changes to the individual job tasks and duties and changes to the larger overall work environment, such as supervision, structure, and staff interaction (Kettner, 2002). The important issue for empowering practice is that job redesign pushes power and authority to the lower levels of the organization. Job tasks, duties, and roles are altered to increase staff participation, responsibility, and autonomy in organizational work. The intent is to alter the relationship between a person and his or her work, to change work behavior, and to rehumanize the workplace. The human resource model (Kettner, 2002) best exemplifies the rehumanizing potential whereby supervisors use the knowledge, skill, creativity, and participation of workers to achieve high performance levels.

Several strategies for job redesign offered by Lewis et al. (2001) but slightly modified to better incorporate empowerment practice are as follows:

- *Combining Tasks:* Promoting more egalitarian approaches for completing the work, such as staff identifying the tasks to be done and mutual agreements on how tasks will be carried out, including crossing over to do other's tasks or new tasks.

- *Forming Natural Work Units:* Creating self-directed teams entrusted with authority and responsibility to make decisions and to work autonomously.
- *Increasing Client Relationships:* Supporting workers partnering with clients so that workers see clients as a resource in solving their problems and issues versus expert, authoritarian, or one-size-fits-all approaches to services.
- *Vertical Loading:* Allowing more staff participation in problem solving and decision-making. Referred to as "high involvement" or "participative decision-making" management.
- *Opening the Feedback Channel:* Offering open feedback on work performance, not just from supervisors but also from peers (mutual accountability), organization, clients, and community.

Before embarking on job redesign, important issues must be anticipated and considered; for example, how job redesign will affect or change organizational culture. Additionally, communication is critical because staff need to understand empowerment, its goals, responsibilities, expectations, and anticipated outcomes. Job redesign effects on other operations of the organization must be identified and evaluated. The mechanics of the job redesign require that job analysis be performed to capture the new essence of the job, followed by new job descriptions and new job specifications (Dessler, 1998), all important features needed to institutionalize empowerment into the organization. All this suggests that empowerment does not come cheap; it requires commitment, leadership, energy, and resources to achieve. However, benefits to worker satisfaction, motivation, and performance are tangible (Bowen & Lawler, 1995). Some empirical research supports a positive correlation between employee satisfaction and customer satisfaction. Studies suggest that how employees feel about their jobs spills over to customers, increasing satisfaction with the services the customers receive (Bowen & Lawler, 1995).

BOX 9.2 EMPOWERING WORKERS: JOB REALIGNMENT AND BENEFIT REVIEW

The human resource specialist for the Northwest Women's Shelter recently resigned, and Pang has appointed Veronica to the position because of Veronica's knowledge of the organization and the community. Veronica knows that the last year has been a turbulent time for the agency. Although Pang has implemented many management reforms, clients still complain about the services, and many staff members seem to lack motivation. Recently, the agency board instructed Pang to have her staff investigate why services are disjointed and detached from the needs of clients. The board requested that the review include job assignments and tasks to determine their alignment and relevance to agency mission, goals, and objectives. Additionally, senior staff was directed to review employee benefits, because the board believes they are becoming a financial drain on the agency. The board is seeking justification for why the current benefit plan should continue or recommendations on alternative benefit plans. As human resource specialist for the agency, Veronica was appointed to lead this review; however, she is concerned that practitioners will fear and resist the review.

- How might Veronica explain the review to staff using an empowerment approach?
- What are some key empowerment characteristics that Veronica should consider in her review of job assignments and tasks? Why are they important?
- Veronica's findings suggests that some job assignments and tasks are redundant, disconnected, and fragmented, and are not meeting the needs of clients. What specific strategies might Veronica recommend to her director and board?
- How might Veronica pursue an assessment of the appropriateness of the employee benefit plan?
- How might Veronica link her recommendation for an employee benefit plan to staff and client empowerment?

AUTONOMY

Employee autonomy is often cited by workers as one of the beneficial features of empowerment (Petter et al., 2002). The freedom and independence to make decisions and the discretion to do the work provide workers with a sense of self-determination. Self-determination is seen as a motivator whereby workers express initiative and creativity. On the other hand, managers are sometimes reluctant to grant staff autonomy for fear that when things go wrong, the managers are responsible for poor outcomes and workers' performance. In essence, managers feel they are left to pick up the pieces, which reflects on their abilities as supervisors. To clarify, autonomy under empowerment does not mean that workers are free to work without any accountability and responsibility to the organization, to their supervisor and peers, or to clients and community. Most social service environments require a great deal of coordination and interaction with other personnel, units, and sections of an organization. To be totally autonomous in one's job is unrealistic and dysfunctional (Cohen & Austin, 1997).

Autonomy must be set within appropriate boundaries and with clear expectations directly connected to organizational goals. Staff must be informed of the extent of their authority, boundaries of decision-making, performance expectations, and, just as importantly, the potential for repercussions based upon decisions made outside the boundaries of granted authority (Spreitzer, 1996). Communicating clear task assignments and setting boundaries for autonomous work are consistent with empowerment, because certainty and understanding of tasks increase feelings of competency (self-efficacy). Role ambiguity is associated with low levels of intrinsic motivation (Spreitzer, 1996). Managers must be concerned with setting reasonable boundaries, and staff must understand their role in the overall system. Forrester (2000) suggests focusing on results as a way of establishing appropriate boundaries and managing autonomy. Results define expectations, accountability, and authority, and it concentrates power to achieve that end. Other boundaries appropriate for managing autonomy include ethical and behavioral boundaries such as values, standards, and professional conduct. Stated succinctly, staff autonomy is as follows: "This is the result you must produce, under these conditions; and within these terms you may exercise your power" (Forrester, 2000, p. 81).

LIMITATIONS OF STAFF INVOLVEMENT IN DECISION-MAKING

One of the tenets of empowering staff is increased staff participation in decision-making. Although such participation is desirable as a method of increasing staff motivation, several limitations exist that must be recognized by organizations and managers. As alluded to in Chapter 1, some decisions are not conducive to high levels of participation by organizational members. Decisions that must be made in times of crisis require quick decisions by organizations and cannot wait for slower and more time-consuming features of participative decision-making. Another limitation is that some employees are better prepared than are others to handle responsibility, authority, and power associated with empowerment and involvement in decision-making (Forrester, 2000). Others may be self-conscious about their lack of skill. Some workers may not wish to be empowered because empowerment represents too much work and uncertainty (Petter et al., 2002). Managers need to differentiate among employees with more or less skills who are reluctant to feel comfortable and confident about their contributions to work life. Closely related, quality and effectiveness of decision-making could be hampered if staff members do not have a rudimentary knowledge of decision-making theories, concepts, and processes. Staff education and training are important so that staff decision-making skills and knowledge are maximized.

High staff involvement in decision-making implies a collective or group process. Although group decision-making has many advantages, such as more diverse points of view, there are potential pitfalls as well. Some group members may feel that being a good member of the group means being silent about disagreements, so they are overly committed to consensus (Dessler, 1998). This type of group behavior may impede creativity and constructive dissent. Individual domination of the group's decision-making process is another real concern. A dominant individual can control or cut off discussion and heavily influence others to his or her point of view. In addition to individual domination, formal authority, political connections, and rhetoric capability frequently determine decisions rather than individual talents and knowledge (Sagie & Koslowsky, 2000). Gender bias can be present. Bhappu, Griffith, and Northcraft (1997) found that both male and female organizational members pay more attention to the suggestions of men than to the suggestions of women. Managers need to be aware that groups may divide into subgroups based on similar points of views and perceptions. This may take on the characteristic of a majority suppressing a minority within the group. If this occurs, the majority may ignore the contributions and thoughtful ideas of the minority (Sagie & Koslowsky, 2000). Last, the external political environment may limit participation in some social service settings when public perception is negative (Gutierrez et al., 1995). For example, public perception of child welfare services is extremely low, and the public is distrustful of child welfare agencies and their decisions. Public distrust is expressed as demanding more oversight and control over decisions as a way of managing the perceived egregious acts of these agencies.

EMPLOYEE BENEFIT PACKAGES

This chapter has discussed empowerment as an intrinsic motivator, but extrinsic incentives, such as financial rewards, can motivate employees if a clear and direct connection between behavior and the rewards is established (Kettner, 2002). Clearly, financial rewards, such as salary increases, bonuses, merit increases, and commissions, are desirable to many employees and may motivate them to increase their performance in anticipation of such rewards. Employee benefits play a similar role as financial rewards in stimulating employee motivation, because employees recognize a monetary value, in the form of a subsidy mostly paid by employers, for services used and directly benefiting them. Employee benefits are any supplements to salary or wages provided to the employee for working for the company (Dessler, 1998). Examples of common employee benefits are health insurance, paid vacations, and retirement plans. Employee benefit packages that meet or exceed employee expectations or needs are associated with a positive quality of work life, which employees interpret as supportive and reinforcing to empowerment principles. Said differently, if employees perceive their personal needs as being met as part of employers' commitment to empowerment, they are more likely to accept and engage in empowerment principles themselves.

The origins of required employee benefits can be traced to the Social Security Act of 1935. The federal government sought to provide social insurance to the nation's workforce, which was suffering from the economic devastation of the Great Depression. Unemployment insurance and worker's compensation are two examples of social insurance stemming from this era. Similarly, the National Labor Relations Act of 1935 authorized collective bargaining by unions, which increased employee benefit packages for its members. In the 1940s, companies began to widely expand the use of "discretionary benefits," benefits not covered by legal or union requirements, primarily as a way to bypass federal restrictions on wage levels in place at the time (Martocchio, 2003). Over time, discretionary benefits (e.g., retirement plans, life insurance) have been used as a substitute to wage increases as a motivational tool. However, there have always been questions about whether employee benefits truly stimulate motivation.

Martocchio (2003) reports that employees generally view employer-sponsored benefits as an entitlement, and employers have treated them the same way. Companies have not "questioned their role as social welfare mediators . . ." (p. 8); however, rising costs and foreign competition has caused companies to reexamine this role. Some companies are trying to reshape benefits as a reward for enhancing motivation and job performance (Barbeito & Bowman, 1998). Employee benefits as an entitlement may partly explain why many organizations do not view more commonly offered employee benefits, such as retirement, life insurance, and health insurance, as connected to motivation in everyday activities of staff (Kettner, 2002). Rather, these commonly provided employee benefits are seen as producing other desirable employee qualities, such as loyalty, commitment, and a favorable attitude toward the company (Dessler, 1998). For some organizations, commonly provided employee benefits are a way of attracting and holding good employees or relieving employees from the stresses of everyday life so that they are productive (Kettner, 2002).

Historically, organizations have structured employee health plans using a one-size-fits-all approach. All workers are given the same benefits, without much thought or consideration to individual differences and needs in their workforce. This approach has worked well in the past when the workforce was more homogeneous, mainly composed of white men who were the primary economic providers for families. Recent workforce trends and demographics show women moving more rapidly into workforce, especially into professional and technical fields, as well as greater representation of older workers (Barbeito & Bowman, 1998). Minorities, immigrants, and persons with disabilities also have made substantial gains into the workforce. The diversity of the workforce reveals a multiplicity of benefits that cannot be met by the more commonly provided benefit plans. The new workforce includes family structures with mostly single parents, parents who both are employed, multiple-generation families, domestic partnerships, and same-sex partnerships (Pynes, 1997). Single parents or dual working parents may desire benefits connected to child care. Multiple-generation families may desire benefits connected to elderly care. If benefits are to be more meaningful and valued in this changing workforce, then employees should have input into what benefits are more desirable and better able to meet their needs (Kettner, 2002). Employee input into benefit structuring would support employees' sense of psychological empowerment as they are able to make decisions about important personal issues, which affects their attitudes and orientation toward work. In this context, benefits are more closely linked to stimulating worker motivation.

Currently, some employees are able to make choices using employer-sponsored flexible benefits, sometimes referred to as *cafeteria plans,* in which different sets of benefits and levels of participation are offered (Martocchio, 2003). Cafeteria plans are designed to better meet the needs of the growing diverse workforce. Costs for legally required benefits are put aside and still provided by the employer, but a percentage of employer and employee contributions is used separately to fund other benefits under the cafeteria plan, such as child care, elder care, or extended health coverage to unmarried or same-sex couples (Pynes, 1997). Some evidence suggests good worker reaction to cafeteria plans, as well as worker job satisfaction (Martocchio, 2003). Employee service needs (Kettner, 2002), such as substance abuse counseling, wellness programs (e.g., smoking cessation), or financial planning are sometimes included as part of employee benefit packages. Some organizations provide educational monetary support to employees for job-related education and career advancement (Pynes, 1997). Organizations view service-related benefits as investments in their workforce because workers are healthier, more financially stable, and better skilled, which in turn lead to better productivity. Thus, flexible benefits, cafeteria plans, and employee services better meet the needs of today's workforce and improve quality of work life for a greater number of persons. Employees' ability to participate in these nontraditional benefit plans supports staff empowerment by allowing staff to better manage personal issues that may affect work performance and their ability to work successfully with clients and community.

SUMMARY

Empowerment can function as a powerful intrinsic motivator for organizational staff, and the benefits of high staff motivation have positive implications not only for staff and consumers of agency services but also for managers and supervisors. As part of an empowerment approach, managers must work with their staff to help them attain a higher sense of confidence and competence (self-efficacy) about the nature of their work. An empowerment approach calls for managers to relinquish traditional management practices and to establish a culture of shared power and participatory decision-making. Creating an organizational culture of empowerment may require examining job tasks and assignments and to consider restructuring jobs and levels of autonomy assigned to specific jobs. Although highly desirable within an empowerment framework, participatory decision-making in organizations has limitations that managers must consider, but they must not allow these limitations to discourage their commitment to shared decision-making. Last, employee motivation and retention are influenced by employee benefit packages offered by employers. Organizational leaders and managers may wish to consider more varied employee benefit packages for their staff in light of a changed and more diversified workforce that possesses different needs and desires than yesteryear's workforce. Chapter 10 describes another method for motivating staff and increasing performance: the assignment of staff members to work teams.

QUESTIONS FOR CLASS DISCUSSION

1. In their role as employees or students placed in an organization, in what areas of their work do employees or students feel powerless? What can be done to decrease their sense of powerlessness? Do feelings of low self-efficacy contribute to their sense of powerlessness?

2. Does the organization in which you are employed or are placed practice more traditional methods of management (i.e., hierarchical structure, centralized power, concentrated decision-making, etc.), or does it practice a more empowerment approach? What indicators do they observe that supports their conclusions?
3. What are some reasons or fears that managers and supervisors might have for not wanting to engage in an empowerment approach with their staff? Are these reasons and fears legitimate?
4. What kinds of things motivate you to do a better job at your work site or at your placement? Do you believe you receive these things as motivators now?
5. Do you believe that shared decision-making and job autonomy are always a good thing? What kind of fears or concerns, if any, would you have if you were asked to participate in shared-decision-making or work autonomy?

SAMPLE ASSIGNMENTS

1. Conduct an interview with a supervisor or manager in your organization. Ask him or her where he or she learned his or her supervisory and management skills. Ask which supervisory and management skills are highly prized by the organization. Try to differentiate which skills were learned through internal organizational transmission and training versus which skills were learned from outside the organization, such as in graduate school or at a management conference.
2. Interview three social workers who have been employed in an organization for at least 1 year. Ask them what tangible motivators they have experienced or received over the last year. Write a short essay on which motivational theories best describe the motivators at work with these three employees.
3. Join a work group at your place of employment or at your placement. Keep a journal on this experience, and track and record the following:

   - What instruction or training was provided to the work group?
   - Does the work group possess any real power?
   - How does decision-making work within the group?
   - How does the work group relate to the rest of the organization?
   - How do the members of the work group perceive themselves?
   - How autonomous is the work group?

- What kinds of limitations has management placed on the work group?
- How motivated is the work group to perform its tasks?
- In your mind, does the work group feel empowered? Why or why not?
- What other issues or observations related to empowerment practice have you experienced while a member of the work group?

CHAPTER 10

Team Building and Collaboration

One of the basic premises of the empowerment-oriented management approach is that organizational hierarchies that support decision-making by a small number of managers, and that require the use of power and authority to make people work, are harmful to the organization's members. Consequently, this management model contains a focus on power sharing, collaboration, and using workplace teams for decision-making and task accomplishment (Gutierrez, GlenMaye, & DeLois, 1995; Shera & Page, 1995). The primary purpose of this approach is to flatten organizational hierarchies and to empower workers through participation in organizational decision-making (Spreitzer, 1996). Empowerment-oriented management also requires that organizational leadership use a team approach to involving staff in setting goals, monitoring service quality and outcomes, and modifying the delivery of services (Barnard, 1999; Lawler, Mohrman, & Ledford, 1995).

In this chapter, organizational teams are defined and the importance of teams for the development of empowerment-oriented workplaces is described. We also examine

- The role of teams in social service organizations as well as the use of interdisciplinary teams in these settings.
- The attributes of effective teams.
- Common problems in teams.
- Skills for managing effective teams.
- Organizational structures that support team building.

- The use of online strategies to create virtual teams.
- Strategies for measuring team effectiveness.

DEFINING ORGANIZATIONAL TEAMS

The simplest definition of a *team* is a group of people who work to achieve a goal (Pearlmutter, Bailey, & Netting, 2001). Consequently, the term *team* can be applied to a sports team, a debate club, or a group of student volunteers. According to Johnson and Johnson (2003), there are three basic types of teams:

- Teams that make recommendations
- Teams that produce things or take action
- Teams that manage the organization

Mohrman, Cohen, and Mohrman (1995) believe that workplace teams can be differentiated from recreational groups based on a number of factors:

> A team is a group of individuals who work together to produce products or deliver services for which they are mutually accountable. Team members share goals and are mutually held accountable for meeting them, they are interdependent in their accomplishment, and they affect their results through their interactions with one another. Because the team is held collectively accountable, the work of integrating with one another is included among the responsibilities of each member. (p. 40)

Wheelan (1999) distinguishes between teams and other types of committees and tasks groups on the basis of effectiveness. A team is a group that has been able to identify shared goals, to develop a process to achieve those goals, and to accomplish the desired task. A team is also a group in which members "feel involved, committed, and valued" (p. 3). Consequently, it is the quality of interpersonal relations among members that is critical for goal achievement. According to Johnson and Johnson (2003), teams can also be distinguished from work groups in that members of a team are interdependent upon one another; that is, successful goal accomplishment depends on the performance of all group members working as a whole rather than on the actions of one member. A team makes joint decisions, and individuals can be charged with carrying them out. For the group to be successful, most, if not all, members must complete individual assignments. However, the success of each member is dependent upon the actions of the others.

THE IMPORTANCE OF TEAM BUILDING IN EMPOWERMENT-ORIENTED ORGANIZATIONS

Teams are used to produce products or deliver services in empowerment-oriented organizations for a number of reasons. Teams are believed to increase employee productivity and their commitment to the organization (Spreitzer, 1996). They are expected to reduce employee absenteeism and turnover (Paul, Niehoff, & Turnley, 2000). In industries such as manufacturing, team approaches are expected to reduce costs by flattening organizational hierarchies and transferring authority to make many production-related decisions to the staff members who are directly involved in production. Consequently, this type of managerial approach reduces the number of managerial staff and support workers needed by the organization (Dailey & Bishop, 2003).

Shifting power to lower level workers is one of the primary rationales for the team-based approach (Paul et al., 2000). Barnard (1999) describes team building as critical for the success of management strategies associated with total quality management (TQM):

> Management is becoming less of a top-down command, and more a process of giving employees authority to make important decisions and be responsible for the outcomes. The overriding goal of this sharing of power is to directly involve employees in decision making so that they can use their expertise to help increase the prosperity of the organization. (p. 73)

In addition to manufacturing, experts on organizational development have recommended that teams be used in industries with large numbers of staff members who are engaged in work that is not routine, that requires high levels of expert knowledge, and that requires collaboration among a number of professionals to achieve production goals (Mohrman et al., 1995). Teams are expected to raise productivity because they increase the individual worker's sense of psychological empowerment. A number of recent studies have documented the link between team building and other types of employee involvement strategies (such as employee profit sharing, management information sharing, and employee advisory councils) and feelings of psychological empowerment in the workplace. For example, Spreitzer (1996) surveyed 400 middle managers in a *Fortune 500* organization. She found that teams contribute to the individual worker's sense of personal empowerment. Dailey and Bishop (2003) examined the impact of a TQM-related employee involvement initiative in two automobile plants in Canada. They found that four characteristics of TQM management models—teamwork, training, management support, and rewards—increased employee feelings of personal empowerment and commitment to the organization.

TEAMS IN SOCIAL SERVICE ORGANIZATIONS

Social service organizations use teams to meet the needs of clients with multiple problems. Teams permit clients to be assessed from different perspectives and to have an intervention plan coordinated by a group of professionals rather than addressed in a fragmented manner when they are referred elsewhere for services. Teams also allow for the integration of two or more service systems within one agency or among a number of agencies that serve a specific geographic area or client population. For example, a team approach can be used in circumstances where a consortium of public and private agencies is responsible for making child welfare decisions and communication problems and other difficulties in coordinating care among providers have been encountered (Lewandowski & GlenMaye, 2002). For example, the Annie E. Casey Foundation's Family to Family program uses teams to make foster care placement decisions. These teams are composed of public welfare staff, community-based agencies, community leaders, and the parents of children in foster care (Annie E. Casey Foundation, 2001a).

Teams are used extensively in health and mental health settings to involve professionals representing a variety of disciplines in providing care to a single patient or client. For example, Reese and Sontag (2001) describe the use of teams that include doctors, nurses, clergymen, and social workers to provide supportive services to hospice patients. Mizrahi and Abramson (2000) have studied collaboration between physicians and social workers, acting as a team to provide services to patients as individual and family counseling, advocacy, treatment planning, and educational information. Teams are used extensively in psychiatric settings, the criminal justice system, and in school social work, settings in which social workers are likely to engage in collaborative decision-making with members of other professions (Guin, Noble, & Merrill, 2003; Vinokur-Kaplan, 1995).

INTERDISCIPLINARY COLLABORATION IN TEAMS

The process of creating teams that include members of a variety of disciplines is called *interdisciplinary collaboration.* Bronstein (2002) defines interdisciplinary collaboration as "an effective interpersonal process that facilitates the achievement of goals that cannot be reached when individual professionals act on their own" (p. 113). According to Abramson and Rosenthal (1997), such collaboration requires "a common vision; a joint development structure, and the sharing of work, resources, and rewards" (p. 1479). Although interdisciplinary teamwork is expected to improve the quality and effectiveness of client services, this approach is not an easy remedy for service fragmentation. Pearlmutter et al. (2001) describe the dilemmas associated with creating teams with members from a variety of disciplines:

> Just as persons need to be competent autonomous individual professionals trained in their respective disciplines, they must simultaneously function well in interdisciplinary groups that are interdependent, mutual and reciprocal. (p. 126)

Bronstein (2003) argues that for interdisciplinary collaboration to be effective, professionals must be able to differentiate between their own role and the roles of other professionals on the team. Mohrman et al. (1995) offer a rationale for the use of teams that seems to be particularly applicable to social service. Collaborative decision processes are needed in order to accomplish tasks that are often not routine or standardized. These types of complex activities may require that members of different professions share knowledge. In social service organizations, client systems (individuals, families, groups, and communities) have multiple or complex needs that cannot be adequately addressed by a professional from one discipline or organization. Therefore a framework for pooling information and expertise must be established in order to assist the client.

Bronstein (2003) has developed a model of interdisciplinary collaboration that identifies team characteristics that contribute to the group's ability to achieve its goals. In addition to interdependence, her model includes the following components:

- Team ownership of goals
- Flexibility or the capacity to alter member roles in response to situational demands
- The ability to reflect on group processes
- The development of new professional activities by the team that build on the existing strengths and expertise of each member

Bronstein (2003) argues that these elements are likely to characterize interdisciplinary collaboration in circumstances where members have a history of collaboration, participants are capable of establishing interpersonal relationships built on trust, respect, and understanding, and the agency's administrators provide sufficient resources and support for team development.

Abramson and Rosenthal (1997) identify two barriers that impede the ability of interdisciplinary teams to function effectively. One of the primary difficulties with interprofessional approaches is that members may be reluctant to surrender control over decision-making, resources, clientele, and practice roles. Such competition among professionals often is referred to in the social work and collaboration literature as *turf battles*. Workers often act in a manner that they perceive will protect their turf from encroachment by others. In addition, interdisciplinary teams may be adversely affected by traditional patterns of interpersonal domination and control by gender, ethnicity, or professional status. For example, patient care teams in hospital settings are most often headed by male doctors who have substantially more power and control over patient-related decision-making than do members of such female-dominated professions as social work and nursing (Mizrahi & Abramson, 2000).

CHARACTERISTICS OF EFFECTIVE TEAMS

Sundstrom et al. (1999) define team effectiveness in terms of "the extent to which a work team meets the performance expectations of key counterparts—managers, customers, and others—while continuing to meet members' expectations of working with the team" (p. 10). Lewandowski and GlenMaye (2002) argue that effective teams are those in which "professionals are aware of and have respect for model differences, and in which assumptions about good professional functioning and team interaction are understood and reconciled" (p. 25). Wheelan (1999) defines high-performance teams as cohesive and cooperative work units that can engage in problem-solving. Mohrman et al. (1995) identify three factors associated with effective team decision-making: high levels of coordination, the ability to make decisions in a timely manner, and a high level of personal self-efficacy among staff members.

A great deal of empirical research has been conducted to identify the components of effective teams. Barnard (1999) examined the problem-solving capacity of teams in for-profit corporations and large nonprofit organizations. She found that membership in teams was highly associated with improvements in product quality and organizational efficiency. She also found that teamwork improved social interaction among participations and consequently increased employee commitment to the organization. Nandan (1997) studied the degree of commitment among social service employees in nursing homes. She found that role clarity and an individual's receptiveness to the team approach were highly associated with commitment to the organization. In a study of interorganizational child welfare teams that included parents, Lewandowski and GlenMaye

(2002) identified three factors associated with member satisfaction with the functioning of the team: the degree of unity of purpose among group members, role clarity, and respect for other team members.

As discussed earlier in this chapter, teams can be effective mechanisms for increasing feelings of autonomy and personal empowerment among staff members under certain workplace conditions. In addition to the positive effects of teams on individuals, research on teams has documented their positive effects on organizations. Research by Kirkman and Rosen (1999) indicates that with sufficient management support, the provision of performance-related awards, and access to information, team members as a group will feel empowered. They also found that feelings of team empowerment increased the level of productivity for the team as a whole, stimulated employee initiative, and improved customer service. Team membership contributes to the ability of organizational staff to adopt service innovations and practice principles (Allen, Foster-Fishman, & Salem, 2002). A high degree of task and goal interdependence among team members increases job satisfaction, reduces conflict, and increases cooperation among staff members (Van der Vegt, Emans, & Van de Vliert, 2001).

PROBLEMS WITH TEAM FUNCTIONING

Using teams to coordinate programs or to integrate work units is not always an effective approach for making improvements in service delivery. Because teams are composed of a variety of different people who may represent different interests or professions, they do not always function smoothly. As with organizational boards and committees, leaders with good group work skills are needed to coordinate the team. In addition, teams should be composed of individuals who are committed to the team process and who can function well in a group (Johnson & Johnson, 2003; Nandan, 1997). The research literature on teams identifies a number of common problems that are likely to limit a team's ability to achieve its goals:

- Team members may have incompatible goals or levels of commitment.
- Team members may have hidden agendas that interfere with the process.
- Some members may simply not function well on teams.
- The team may lack a clear direction or a sense of purpose.
- Inexperience with teams may hinder the process.
- The leader may not be focused on the task or may not be concerned about outcomes or group functioning (Barnard, 1999;

Lewandowski & GlenMaye, 2002; Nandan, 1997; Pearlmutter et al., 2001).

Interdisciplinary teams may face a number of other barriers. According to Reese and Sontag (2001), members of the team may not be aware of the type of knowledge, theories, or values associated with the different professions represented on the team. Because of this lack of awareness, members of the team may view the performance of individual members as inadequate. The roles associated with the different professions may sometimes overlap, contributing to a sense of competition among participants. For example, The Annie E. Casey Foundation (2001a) describes issues associated with using family to family–related teams that include caseworkers, community partners, and parents to make child placement decisions:

> Expect a wide variety of reactions from staff about the team decision-making process, which will continue to change as the process becomes more embedded in the agency's regular course of business. Some staff object to what they see as a loss of control over their own cases or the potential for higher scrutiny of their work. The most common issues are caseworker fears of time drain, anxiety about the challenges of practicing straight talk in the presence of families and community partners, and a general fear that public discussion of the case may expose weaknesses in their skills. (p. 37)

In addition to the performance and perception of team members, organizational structure and leadership contribute to a team's failure to perform well (Mohrman et al., 1995). Managers who often use the power inherent in hierarchical relationships may feel threatened by the autonomy and influence of the team (Barnard, 1999). Consequently, they may try to limit the team's authority or may try to overrule decisions made by the team. Another common problem is that administrators may give less than full support to the team (Kirkman & Rosen, 1999; Pearlmutter, et al., 2001). They may fail to specify in writing the purpose or mission of the team. The resources provided for the team, such as staffing, information, funds, and appropriate meeting facilities, may be inadequate (Spreitzer, 1996; Wheelan, 1999). In some cases, the team may not be provided with adequate time to accomplish the designated tasks. In some circumstances, managers may fail to adequately reward individual participants or the team as a whole for their performance (Barnard, 1999).

Paul et al., (2000) identify two additional drawbacks associated with team approaches. Workers may limit improvements in performance and feelings of commitment to the team and fail to focus on the achievement of organizational goals. A second issue of concern is that in organizations that shift from a hierarchical to a team structure, high start-up costs may be associated with moving workers to new positions and training them to function in teams.

SKILLS FOR BUILDING AN EFFECTIVE TEAM

The literature on successful teams indicates that two levels of leadership are critical to the ability of the team to achieve its goals: team leaders and organizational management. Team leaders must be able to identify the group's goals, build cohesion, and ensure work is accomplished. Managers must decide when and how to use team approaches, provide adequate resources for team development, and select or recruit members. As with committee work, performing these tasks requires a mix of both interpersonal and task-oriented skills.

Skills for Team Leaders

Often the effectiveness of a team is dependent upon its leadership. Team leaders may be appointed by organizational managers or elected by members. Teams may be leaderless or autonomous. In these teams, a leader or leaders may emerge during the course of the team's work. In a study of leaderless teams, Taggar, Hackett, and Saha (1999) found that emergent leaders were those individuals who were able to exert significant amounts of influence over other team members. Personality traits associated with new emergent leaders included emotional stability, extraversion, and conscientiousness. However, Taggar et al. also note that teams are rarely effective unless many of the team members take some responsibility for leadership.

In those teams with a designated leader, certain responsibilities come with the job. The leader must serve as a link between organization or unit managers and team members. Often the leader is responsible for informing the members about the purpose of the team and presents a rationale for their recruitment to the team (Pearlmutter et al., 2001). The leader is responsible for scheduling meetings, finding an appropriate meeting space, and developing agendas. The leader must be able to assign appropriate tasks to each team member and ensure that the work is distributed equitably (Reese & Sontag, 2001). He or she must be an advocate for the team, securing any additional resources from the management that are needed to ensure the effectiveness of the team.

The team leader is responsible for actually running the group. Attention must be paid to both process and outcome. A feeling of psychological safety among team members contributes to the ability of team members to learn new tasks and improve their performance. Edmonson (1999) defines psychological safety as a "shared belief held by members of a team that the team is safe for interpersonal risk taking" (p. 350). Critical tasks for building effective teams include selecting and orienting team members, ensuring open communication, building mutual trust and support, and managing differences among members (Pearlmutter et al., 2001). Team leaders should foster knowledge of, and respect for, the skills and values of the different professional disciplines that are members of interdisciplinary teams (Reese & Sontag, 2001). Team leaders working with members of different disciplines may need to help members establish appropriate professional boundaries in circumstances where two or more members have the skills and knowledge to respond to the same client needs or circumstances. For example, in a hospice, both a social worker and a member of the clergy might be called upon to offer emotional support to a grieving family member. In such circumstances, Reese and Sontag suggest that workable interdisciplinary teams must be able to create appropriate ground rules that specify how and when individual members should engage with clients and provide services.

Teams experience the same process of development expected in most groups and organizations (Bailey, 1998). Applying these concepts to teams, Pearlmutter et al. (2001) identify the following developmental stages:

Stage 1. *Dependency on the Leader.* A new group is formed. Group members express concerns about who is included on the team and the rules for team governance.

Stage 2. *Counter Dependency and Fight.* Group members start to challenge the leader for control of the group.

Stage 3. *Trust and Structure.* The group concentrates on resolving conflicts among members and accomplishing tasks. The effective group will engage in cooperation and negotiation, and members will openly communicate with one another.

Stage 4. *Work and Productivity.* Goals are achieved.

Stage 5. *Termination.* An assessment is made of the work accomplished by the team, and the group disbands or takes on a new project.

Alternatively, team building has been examined with language used to describe the process of group development: forming, storming, norming, performing, and adjourning (Bailey, 1998). Each of these stages—from group formation, contesting the authority of the leader, developing rules for group maintenance (norming), completing the work, and disbanding the group—requires that the team leader develop skills that allow him or her to guide the developmental process. For example, in

Stage 1—Forming—the group leader schedules a time and location for team meetings, facilitates dialogue among team members, and sets a time-line for task accomplishment (Table 10.1).

Skills for Managers

Pearlmutter et al., (2001) argue that the manager who is responsible for overseeing the work of the team has a key role in ensuring its effectiveness.

Table 10.1 Leadership Roles to Build Effective Organizational Teams

Stage of Group Development	Developmental Activity	Leader's Role
Stage 1	Forming	Develops a structure for meetings (time and location of meetings, purpose of the team, time-lines for task completion). Encourages input and dialogue among participants.
Stage 2	Storming	Discusses how decisions will be made. Obtains the resources the team will need to complete its work. Helps the team develop appropriate decision-making rules.
Stage 3	Norming	Enforces the team's decision-making rules. Ensures that the team adheres to the goals and tasks that members prefer. Motivates and rewards team members. Keeps outsiders (including management) from interfering with the work of the team.
Stage 4	Performing	Follows up with individual members to ensure that tasks are accomplished. Mediates disputes among members. Modifies time-lines as needed. Secures any additional resources needed by the group.
Stage 5	Adjourning	Identifies group accomplishments. Thanks members for their participation Acts to disband the group or to identify new agenda items.

Source: Adapted from Bailey, D. (1998). Designing and sustaining meaningful organizational teams. In R. Edwards, J. Yankey, & M. Altpeter (Eds.), *Skills for effective management of nonprofit organizations* (pp. 185–199). Washington, DC: National Association of Social Workers.

The manager must meet with the team on a regular basis to guide its work, evaluate the performance of individual members as well as the team as a whole, and serve as a link between the team and other work units in the organization. Barnard (1999) recommends that managers share information with employees about how their work fits within the structure and purpose of the organization. She also advocates that managers foster work autonomy by actively collaborating with staff to clarify their role in the organization and their goals.

Kirkman and Rosen (1999) agree that the role of the manager in increasing team effectiveness is critical, but they believe that the manager should not make a habit of intervening in the group's work. They argue that a manager is more likely to increase team members' feelings of empowerment and self-competency if the manager sets high standards but allows the team to be self-managing: solving their own problems, taking on all responsibility for the delivery of some types of integrated services, and hiring, disciplining, and training new members.

Although self-managed teams have positive implications for employee empowerment, Dailey and Bishop (2003) argue that management support is critical:

> Managers can readily influence and control the design of teams to enhance the possibility of positive outcomes. They can ensure that teams have appropriate information access, that their membership is represented by diverse job functions and administrative backgrounds, and that the appropriate number of members is assigned to each team. (p. 399)

Resources can include tangible items such as meeting facilities, office supplies, technical training, and computer technology (Mohrman et al., 1995). Support also can be given in ways that are perhaps less tangible but more meaningful to participants: emotional support, a pleasing atmosphere in the work area, colocation of team members in one work area, provision of snacks for the work room, and certificates and other types of recognition for team performance (Barnard, 1999; Thomsett.com, 2004).

Wheelan (1999) recommends that team membership be limited to the minimum number of people needed for task accomplishment. Members should be selected simply because they can accomplish the task at hand and because they can be expected to contribute to goal achievement. According to Johnson and Johnson (2003), effective teams are those that contain fewer than 10 members. Consequently, the manager should conduct a careful assessment of prospective team members, focusing on individual skills and member ability to work as part of a team.

Training both team members and team leaders is important. Wheelan (1999) argues that much of the emphasis on training members to form cohesive units through exercises such as rock climbing or group "therapy" sessions is misguided. Instead, organizations should focus on the provision of training to group members and leaders on group processes, on goal setting, and on the provision and use of feedback on group performance. Reese and Sontag (2001) advocate for the use of team orientation and training methods that can be used to inform members about the professional skills and values of each discipline represented on the team in order to prevent turf battles among members.

According to Stevens and Yarish (1999), training should include information on how to conduct effective meetings and information on interpersonal communication skills, collaboration, and diversity. They advocate that an organization first conduct a needs assessment to prioritize the issues that can be addressed. Such an assessment should focus on the tasks to be accomplished by the team, the needs of individual employees, and the needs of the organization and its managers. A needs assessment can determine if organizational structure can be altered sufficiently to accommodate one or more teams or if the organization's hierarchy should be eliminated and reconfigured as a series of interlocking teams (Mohrman et al., 1995).

BOX 10.1 DEVELOPING AN INTERPROFESSIONAL WORK TEAM

Latonya is an MSW who is an employee of a public child welfare agency. The county government has recently acted to consolidate both child welfare and children's mental health into one umbrella agency. Part of the rationale for the merger is that child welfare and mental health staff seldom communicated with one another. Many of the children who were placed by child welfare services in foster care and group homes also needed mental health services from the county. However, referrals made by child welfare workers to children's mental health were often slow to be processed. The psychiatrists, psychologists, and licensed clinical social workers sometimes disagreed with the nonlicensed social workers and foster care workers without professional degrees about the type of services that could best be provided to the children. In addition, mental health services lacked adequate staff resources to adequately provide children's services; care for children often was contracted out to private providers. Both foster parents and birth parents had complained to the county about delays in obtaining treatment for their children. Parents also complained that they were seldom consulted about treatment options.

Latonya has just been asked by the director of the newly established Children's Services Agency to put together and lead a team charged with integrating foster care and children's mental health services. The director has not provided Latonya with a job description for her new role or a mission statement for the new team. Latonya is not sure about where the team will meet or what people should be invited to sit on the team.

1. What are the first steps Latonya should take to put together the team?
2. What constituency groups should be invited to sit on this team?
3. What types of challenges is Latonya likely to face in putting together this team?
4. What things can Latonya do to develop team consensus and cohesion?

TEAMS AND ORGANIZATIONAL STRUCTURE

Teams are often established simply to respond to situational demands on the organizations; for example, communication problems in different work units. However, some organizations may restructure themselves to eliminate traditional hierarchies and subsequently adopt an organizational model consisting entirely of teams. Such team approaches may be used to decrease decision-making delays that occur in situations where multiple levels of managers must provide approval for actions made by employees at lower positions in the organization's hierarchy (Thomsett.com, 2004). Teams can be established in response to the demand of funders for better collaboration between service units or organizations serving similar service areas or clientele. However, some organizations use team approaches to redesign the manner in which work is conducted and to eliminate organizational hierarchies that are viewed as less than adequate for maintaining productivity and retaining personnel (Dailey & Bishop, 2003).

The two primary approaches used to implement a team structure throughout the organization are the linking-pin approach and an organizational model that includes a system of teams that eliminates or flattens the organizational hierarchy (Thomsett.com. 2004). The linking-pin approach developed by Likert (as cited in Johnson & Johnson, 2003) involves the use of individual staff members who serve simultaneously on two teams and consequently serve as the communication link between these teams. These teams are organized on a hierarchical basis. The member who is the link is both the leader of a work team assigned to one

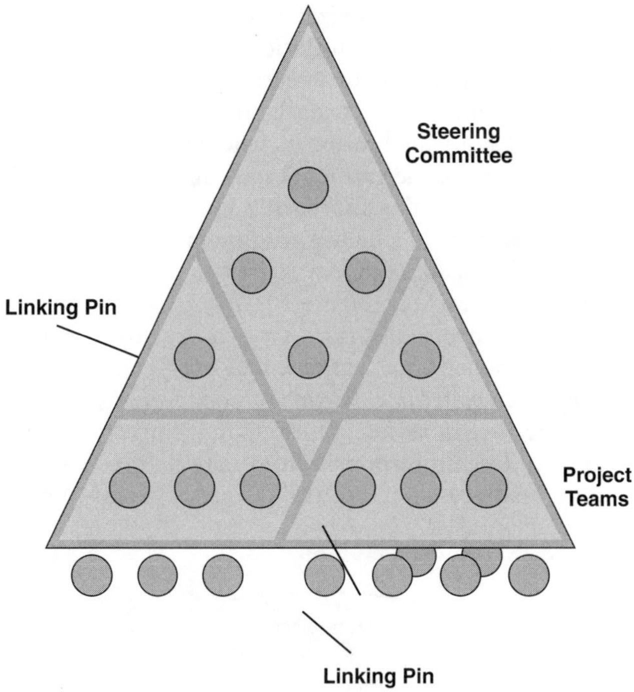

Figure 10.1 Alternative organizational structure: the linking pin approach.

level of an organization and a member of a team at a higher level that is responsible for managing the work of the subordinate team. Consequently, the entire organization is made of a series of interlocking teams that remain connected to one another by virtue of these key individuals (Figure 10.1). At the top of the organization is the management team that includes individual members with middle management responsibilities for different units in the organization (Kettner, 2002). These middle management teams include members who serve as a link to units lower in the organizational hierarchy. In addition, two organizational units at the same level in the hierarchy are linked through the inclusion of at least one person who is a member of both teams.

In the second team-based approach, the organization is structured as a system of teams that are located or "nested" within one another (Mohrman et al., 1995). This means that work teams located inside larger teams are also to be assessed in terms of the performance of the larger unit.

Individual teams within the organizational team system are responsible for the core functions of the organization: managing the organization, producing a product or service, or integrating the work of two or more teams. As with the linking-pin approach, an effective "system of teams" model must include individual members who participate in two or more teams so that the work of the various teams can be integrated. However, Mohrman et al. argue that this approach is unique in that no member of any team is required to hold a higher position in the organization than is any other member; instead, authority to make certain types of decisions is held by the team as a whole (Figure 10.2).

Kettner (2002) identifies a third type of organizational structure, generally used in smaller organizations, that uses a team approach. The *collegial model,* also called a *collective* or *cooperative,* requires that all members of the organization share management responsibilities. Decisions and leadership responsibilities may be made as a group or rotated among members. As with the system of teams approach, this

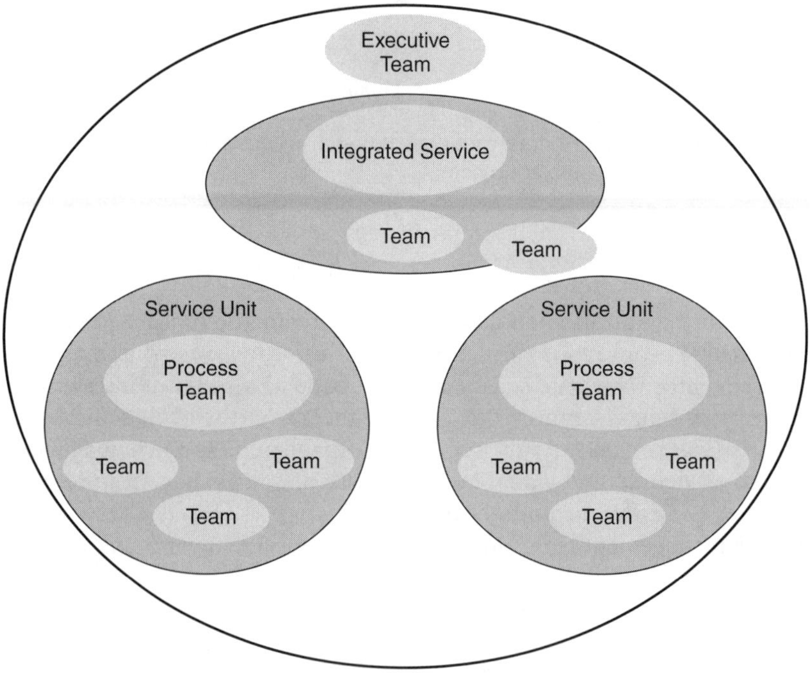

Figure 10.2 Alternative organizational structure: a team approach. Adapted from Mohrman, S., Cohen, S., & Mohrman, A. (1995). *Designing team-based organizations* (p. 49). San Francisco, CA: Jossey-Bass.

model is intended to eliminate most of the harmful effects associated with power and control in organizational hierarchies. One limitation of this model is that all members must be able to work independently but come together to work as a group as the situation requires. In addition, members may have little recourse when individuals fail to carry their fair share of the workload. This collective approach is often used in feminist social service agencies and is similar to decision-making structures found in informal organizations (Hyde, 1989).

MEETINGS IN CYBERSPACE: CREATING VIRTUAL TEAMS

Another variation of team structure includes teams in which membership includes people in different locations. Chapter 14 describes teams made up of representatives of two or more organizations who meet regularly to share resources or to deliver services. Task groups, coalitions, or service collaboratives often struggle to develop trusting relationships and group cohesion simply because member organizations have different interests and goals. However, it is not necessary for team members to actually meet face to face. Some intraorganizational teams, as well as teams that include members from a number of organizations, may do most or all of their work in cyberspace. Mittleman and Briggs (1999) define virtual teams as those supported by technology that allows members to "communicate and collaborate across time, distance, and departmental and organization boundaries" (p. 246). Teams in which members are located at some distance from one another are called *geographically dispersed teams* (GDTs). GDTs give a great deal of flexibility to organizations and permit integration of service delivery and production among a variety of widely dispersed organizational units. They also permit organizations to allow some employees to work from home while functioning as a part of a workplace team (Peterson & Stohr, 2000).

These teams depend on a variety of technological innovations, including a heavy reliance on e-mail and audio and video teleconferencing. Other online techniques used for team building include

- Internet chat rooms and bulletin boards
- Software that permits document sharing and meeting planning
- Voting keypad systems that compute voting tallies for all meeting participants
- Group support systems that allow team members to use computer-generated charts and matrices to brainstorm and problem-solve (Mittleman & Briggs, 1999)

Although virtual teams have many advantages for large corporations with dispersed work units, they also can be used successfully by public and nonprofit organizations to coordinate the delivery of social services. For example, Henrickson and Mayo (2000) describe the development of a "cybermall" to enhance health and social service delivery by 18 agencies in Los Angles County that provided support to people living with human immunodeficiency virus (HIV). The purpose of the project was to establish links among agencies serving this population and to assist case managers in securing resources for clients from among the agencies in the network. The cybermall included a private Intranet network for use by the agencies that allowed them to use a common application form, to schedule appointments, and to exchange confidential information about clients. Online meetings and case conferences were conducted using chat room technology and videoconferencing.

Virtual teams have many benefits and limitations. Some of the advantages of virtual teams are that they increase the size of the pool of eligible team members because location is not an issue. They also give workers more autonomy to manage their workloads and increase workers' sense of participation in organizational decision-making (Peterson & Stohr, 2000). Virtual teams increase cooperation among workers and decrease travel time and expenses. Other advantages of virtual teams are that information and data can easily be archived or distributed, that meetings can take place in a variety of time frames (chat rooms in real time versus information exchanged through e-mail or electronic bulletin boards), and that workers can participate from a variety of locations as they travel or work from home (Mittleman & Briggs, 1999). The limitations of this approach include difficulty establishing trust and cohesion among members, differences in agendas and expectations among individuals and dispersed work units, and high start-up costs associated with new technology and worker training.

MEASURING TEAM OUTCOMES AND PROCESSES

A number of factors can be considered when assessing whether teams are successful in achieving their goals. Mohrman et al. (1995) argue that an assessment of team effectiveness should examine the following factors:

- The performance of the team.
- The contribution of the team to the organization's overall performance.
- Improvements in the knowledge and skills of team members.
- Whether the team has met the needs of the employees. Such needs include feelings of self-competency and personal empowerment.

Wheelan (1999) argues that team dynamics should be assessed at three different levels: the ability of participants to function as members of a team, the ability of the leader to manage group dynamics and engage with both group members and organizational management, and the ability of managers to provide resources and support to the team. Vinokur-Kaplan (1995) has used Hackman's (as cited in Vinokur-Kaplan, 1995) framework for group effectiveness to assess teams. Hackman's framework has three primary components: the team's ability to produce a good product, the ability of team members to work together well into the future, and the ability of the team to stimulate professional growth among its members.

Team effectiveness can be assessed in terms of the positive attributes associated in the research literature with workplace teams: feelings of personal empowerment among individual members, job satisfaction, group cohesion, members' commitment to the organization, and role clarity (Barnard, 1999; Dailey & Bishop, 2003; Kirkman & Rosen, 1999; Nandan, 1997; Spreitzer, 1996; Van der Vegt et al., 2001). All or a mixture of these characteristics can be used to assess both team process and the outcomes produced by the team (Table 10.2).

Table 10.2 Instrument for Measuring Effective Teams

	Assessment Criteria	Yes	No
1	The team has a clear purpose.		
2	The team has identified tasks consistent with its purpose.		
3	Task assignment is consistent with the skills and abilities of members.		
4	There is a fair division of tasks and responsibilities among team members.		
5	The rules that govern the behavior of team members are clear.		
6	Most team members work cooperatively with one another.		
7	The team consists of people with an appropriate mix of skills and abilities.		
8	The various roles of team members, across different areas, work units, or organizations, are clear and distinct.		
9	Team members from different disciplines respect one another's work.		
10	I attend most team meetings.		
11	I work cooperatively with team members.		
12	I receive all the information and support I need from team members to accomplish my assigned tasks.		
13	I feel that I am an important member of the team.		

(*Continued*)

Table 10.2 Instrument for Measuring Effective Teams (Cont.)

	Assessment Criteria	Yes	No
14	I have received adequate training to prepare me for my work on the team.		
15	The team leader is effective in moving the team's agenda.		
16	The team leader engages with members to ensure participation from each person in the team.		
17	The team leader acts to enforce team rules.		
18	The team leader works to minimize conflicts among members.		
19	The team leader ensures that the team has all the resources it needs to meet its goals.		
20	The team leader takes responsibility for ensuring that the work of the team is completed.		
21	The team leader serves as an effective link between the team and the organization.		
22	Management provides adequate information to the team about its work.		
23	Management ensures that the team has all the resources it needs to complete its work.		
24	Management allows the team adequate autonomy to identify and solve problems.		
25	Managers have set high standards for work performance.		
26	Membership in the team has helped to increase my own knowledge and skills.		
27	I feel adequately rewarded by management for my work on this team.		
28	The team has achieved or is likely to achieve its primary goals.		
29	The team has contributed significantly to the organization's performance.		
30	I feel that my role in the team has contributed significantly to the organization's performance.		

Organizations can measure the degree to which representatives of various disciplines are able to work collaboratively. Bronstein (2002) has created an index of interdisciplinary collaboration that measures team member interdependence, commitment to team goals, member behaviors, and group processes. Her scale also assesses four factors associated with the development of successful teams: role expectations, personal characteristics of members, agency culture that supports collaboration, and whether individual team members have had a positive experience with collaboration in the past. Bronstein's scale, tested using a random sample of members of the National Association of Social Workers, was found to have a high level of reliability and correlated well with other measures of collaboration.

One final measure of team performance should be noted. As with organizational boards, the process of self-evaluation can be a valuable tool that teams can use to monitor group processes, improve the conduct of meetings, and assess whether goals have been achieved. The TQM approach relies heavily on team members to develop performance standards, assess their work, and take on responsibility for modifying workplace conditions and activities necessary for improvement. Adherents of the team approach suggest that regular assessments of performance and, as appropriate, celebrations of goal achievement and recognition of the work of individual members are critical for the success of these groups (Johnson & Johnson, 2003).

SUMMARY

The development of workplace teams is one of the primary methods used by organizations to empower staff members. It is believed that teams promote the integration of tasks among various work units, increase communication, and improve service effectiveness. Research on teams indicates that they improve employee morale, knowledge, skills, and interdependence with other workers. Team members should be chosen so that they hold a variety of skills and types of knowledge essential for completion of the task at hand. In many instances, team members will be recruited from across a number of professional disciplines. This will increase challenges associated with the leadership and management of teams. The inclusion on the team of members with differing perspectives and professional values requires interpersonal skills on the part of leaders to facilitate dialogue, establish appropriate boundaries associated with professional roles, and develop trust among members. Team members must be able to interact in ways that promote interdependence, that is, have the ability to build upon the work of others in order to achieve team goals. Organizational managers are critical to the success of the team. Management support, the provision of necessary resources, and the ability to generate commitment to the organization among team members are important elements of the team process.

QUESTIONS FOR CLASS DISCUSSION

1. What problems or issues have you experienced in working as a member of a team?
2. How does team membership conflict with or complement your autonomy to make decisions as a professional social worker?

3. How are teams used in your place of employment or field internship?
4. How would you put together an interagency team made up of individuals with different backgrounds and professional status? What are the first steps you would take?
5. What actions would a manager need to take to convince you to share information or task accomplishments with other members of an interdisciplinary team?

SAMPLE ASSIGNMENTS

1. Interview three or more members of an interdisciplinary team. Ask each member to identify the team's mission and goals, styles of decision-making, and outcomes achieved. To what factors do team members attribute the effectiveness or lack of effectiveness of the team?
2. Examine the organizational structure and goals of your field agency or place of employment. Identify areas in the organization and specific tasks that can benefit from a team approach. Provide a written rationale for integrating these tasks or units into a team.
3. For a team or group in which you are a member, complete the team member self-assessment tool (Table 10.2). Identify tasks that could be addressed by team members and leaders to make the group more effective and cohesive.
4. With a team of five members, prepare a presentation for this class that focuses on some aspect of organizational management. Select a team leader or coleaders for your group. The team leader will be responsible for conducting meetings, motivating team members, following up on tasks/assignments, and coordinating the production of the final product.

As a group, develop a set of rules for running each meeting, making task assignments, and sanctioning/rewarding members who do not complete tasks. (Meetings can be scheduled during and outside class). With your completed (written) presentation, also turn in a one- to two-page paper to your instructor that

A. Lists each team member.
B. Identifies the team leader.
C. Describes the team rules.

D. Lists the tasks assigned each team member and indicates whether the task has been completed.
E. Provides an overall assessment of how the team functioned. Use the stage model of team development described in Table 10.1 to make your assessment.

Be sure to include an assessment of the effectiveness of the team leader.

SECTION IV

Strategies for Managing the External Environment of the Empowering Organization

CHAPTER 11

Advocacy for Improvement in Services and Policies

Throughout the course of human history exist examples of man's inhumanity to man. History records the enslavement of people based on the color of their skin for economic gain, the mass murder of millions because of their religious beliefs, and the marginalization of people with physical and/or mental disabilities because of fear or their perceived lack of usefulness to society. The capacity of human beings to care and to destroy is reflected throughout history.

Advocacy is necessary when people are marginalized, when individuals are denied access to life-sustaining goods and services or are not offered services intended to sustain rather than to enrich life, when children go to bed hungry, and when families find they must live on the streets. These are a few of the many social problems facing society. These are issues for which there must be the recognition that something is amiss in the society. These are matters of social justice or perhaps the lack of it. These conditions call for change. To bring about change, people—individually and in concert with each other—must mobilize to address societal issues. In mobilizing for change, people engage in activities that are broadly defined as *advocacy.* This chapter defines advocacy, its relevance to empowerment organization practice, and its impact on organizational services and policies. We also address

- Internal and external advocacy.
- Advocacy as a component of ethical practice.
- Using a problem-solving approach to advocacy.

ADVOCACY DEFINED

Advocacy is action taken on behalf of a constituency or an issue that is intended to advance the group or cause. According to Barker (1999), advocacy is "1) The act of directly representing or defending others and, 2) In social work, championing the rights of individuals or communities through direct intervention or through empowerment" (p. 11). Advocacy requires action on the part of the advocate. Sometimes this is done in concert with those affected by problems; other times it is not. According to Ezell (2001), "Advocacy consists of those purposive efforts to change specific, existing, or proposed policies or practices on behalf of or with specific clients or group of clients" (p. 23). From an empowerment perspective, change not only is directed at the amelioration of problems but also is intended to "preserve [its] integrity only if the processes of social change lead us to an organization of society in which the interests of all are safe guarded through the participation of all" (Hartman, 1989, p. 387).

Advocacy activities can take many forms and range from interventions that include actions by an individual to collective involvement with people acting in concert to remedy a situation (Dobelstein, 1990). An advocate can act on behalf of an individual, in response to a social issue, and/or to remedy legislation and/or policies that serve to disadvantage specific populations. The need for collective action arises when it is impossible for individuals acting alone to bring about change (Ezell, 2001; Schneider & Lester, 2001). The process can require strategies aimed at radical transformation of values, consciousness, and social institutions (Middleton, 1985).

In this context, advocacy can take place at a variety of systems levels: individual, group, organization, community, and political. Single individuals or groups can be engaged in the process. Advocacy can take place within the practitioner's place of employment or be directed toward outside organizations, institutions, and political decision-makers. Although there are numerous definitions of advocacy and the context in which it takes place, most experts agree that advocacy practice includes the following activities:

- *Case Advocacy.* Action taken by practitioners to help individual clients obtain resources and services. Case advocacy can take place within the practitioner's own workplace, or it can involve helping the client obtain services from another agency (Hardina, 1995).
- *Self-Help Advocacy Training.* This approach involves the provision of information and technical skills training by practitioners to members of the client group in need of assistance. The purpose of self-help advocacy training is to empower the consumers of service to obtain the resources they need from service providers (Rose & Black, 1985). The rationale for this approach is that

consumers will remain dependent on social service professionals and powerless unless they develop the knowledge and skills to obtain the resources they need.

- *Class Advocacy*. This type of advocacy practice recognizes that most people who request services from social service organizations have common problems that may be rooted in institutional discrimination or social policies that have harmful effects. Consequently, class advocacy involves the joining together of people with common problems, social service professionals, and other concerned individuals who take action to resolve the problem (Ezell, 2001). The primary rationale for this approach is that groups of people coming together to take action have more power than a single individual acting alone.
- *Legislative Advocacy*. This approach to advocacy requires that individuals and groups interested in introducing or revising legislation and social policies engage in the process of persuading public officials to represent their interests when voting on legislation (Schneider & Lester, 2001). The process for affecting legislative change is called *lobbying*. Lobbying can involve visiting public officials, writing letters, attending rallies, analyzing policy impacts, disseminating this information to officials and the public, and testifying at government hearings.
- *Political Advocacy*. Social work involvement in the political process has also been identified as a type of advocacy practice (Ezell, 2001; Hardina, 2002; Haynes & Mickelson, 2005). Political advocacy can include registering voters, volunteering on a political campaign, managing a campaign, and running for office. The rationale for classifying involvement in politics as a type of social work advocacy is that electing public officials who support social work values is a good way to ensure that legislation will reflect the interests of both social workers and the people they serve.

Social workers may confine their advocacy practice to problems that occur within their place of employment, focus on ameliorating problems that have their origins in the community or the political structure, or practice a combination of internal and external advocacy.

INTERNAL ADVOCACY

Empowerment-based organizational advocacy relies upon a commitment by the organization to fulfill its obligations, as stated in its mission statement, through its service provision activities. It is essential that the organization be clear in its purpose for being and equally clear in the articulation of its goals and objectives. Although an empowerment-focused organization seeks to be inclusive of all its members, it continues to be accountable and must produce the outcomes promised to the funding source. The challenge for an empowerment-focused organization is to assure that in meeting programmatic goals and objectives it does not lose the essence of empowerment principles—respect for consumers and staff (see Chapter 1). It is important to note, however, that for advocacy efforts to grow and to have a program focus that furthers the primacy of the interactions among all persons involved in the organization, the organizational culture must promote such activities (see Chapter 5).

The manager in an empowerment-oriented organization serves a dual purpose with regard to advocacy. He or she must be prepared to act as an advocate on behalf of clients and staff (Menefee, 2000). However, the manager also must "set the tone," encouraging staff members to advocate for, or in partnership with, clients and encouraging clients to advocate for themselves or to "fight for their rights" (Gutierrez, GlenMaye, & DeLois, 1995). Both the social work literature and the business literature on empowerment-oriented management explicitly urge managers to encourage advocacy practice because it is believed to increase worker motivation and improve services for clients (Bowen & Lawler, 1995; Reisch et al., 1981). Research evidence that such advocacy does produce better service outcomes can be found in studies documenting the effectiveness of total quality management approaches (Lawler, Mohrman, & Ledford, 1995). However, the manager must be prepared to give up some degree of control over service delivery and may need to take action to either accommodate or, in some situations, oppose recommendations for change that originate with staff and clientele (Rago, 1996).

Case advocacy and self-help advocacy training are generally strategies used by staff members with or without the support of managers to increase client access to services. In addition, staff members may engage in advocacy to change organizational policies and practices that they believe are detrimental to clients. A fourth type of internal advocacy practice involves whistle blowing—identifying wrongdoing or fraudulent practices on the part of the organization or its staff.

Case Advocacy

Case advocacy is generally the least controversial type of advocacy practice. It is most often used when a direct service worker finds that a client is having difficulty obtaining a good or services that he or she needs. Barriers to service delivery may originate in organizational policies or practices, government regulations, failure of the service delivery system to produce desired outcomes, or the actions of individuals in the organization. The social worker may seek to correct the problem by contacting a coworker, making a referral, or requesting that an exception be made to organizational policy. However, one of the chief limitations of advocacy practice is that resolution of the problem requires a request from the client and action on the part of the social worker. Hardina (1990) has argued that case advocacy, in most instances, reinforces the power of the social worker (who possesses information, knowledge, authority, and professional status) to resolve the problem. Case advocacy also encourages feelings of powerlessness and dependency on the part of the client, who, without access to information or status, must continue to rely on the social worker to resolve the problem each time it occurs.

Self-Help Advocacy

Power-dependency issues inherent in the advocacy process can be addressed in two ways. Case advocacy can take place in the context of a partnership between client and worker who share information about the origins of the problem and its solutions. They also share responsibility for resolving the problem. Second, individual clients affected by similar problems can engage in self-help advocacy. Self-help advocacy is viewed as a situation in which people who have common needs or problems come together for mutual support in their attempts to address their common concerns (Sommer, 1990). These disenfranchised persons give voice to their concerns in their own words by telling their stories. Many consumers are perceived to lack sophistication or to have little understanding of how bureaucracies work and historically have been ignored by those in power. Unless the voices of the consumers are heard directly, the power will continue to reside elsewhere. This is not to say that social workers should not engage in advocacy; indeed they should, for surely the profession requires it. However, as consumers assume more responsibility for speaking for themselves, the role of the social worker changes. As described earlier, self-help advocacy groups formed by consumers of service provide an example of the partnership that can exist between the organization and the consumer. In supporting efforts to educate consumers, the organization actively engages in empowerment.

In consumer-focused advocacy training, the emphasis is on providing information regarding agency policies, consumer rights and responsibilities, and the overarching policies that sanction agency activities. There must be opportunity for consumers to speak freely among themselves regarding the issues about which they are concerned as well as an opportunity to reflect on the agency's responsiveness to those needs.

Policy Advocacy

Social workers engage in policy advocacy within organizations. Again, this is an activity that can be practiced by individual workers, can take place in partnership with clients, or can be undertaken by groups of workers. More often the focus is on policies that impede access to services or harm clients, or on workplace conditions that are detrimental to staff members. The role of the advocate in relation to administrative policies and procedures is to understand them. Based on his or her knowledge of policies, the advocate can determine if differential treatment exists and find ways that will maximize the input in policy formulation and interpretation. The advocate should know the facts (Fernandez, 1980). By knowing the facts, the advocate should be informed regarding the specific circumstances and should be able to answer the questions who, what, when, where, and how. The advocate can engage in the process of open and honest dialogue within the organization. Misinformation or flawed information is detrimental to the advocacy process.

Whistle Blowing

In some organizations, staff members may find it necessary to engage in "whistle blowing" activities. Greene and Latting (2004) describe whistle blowing as

1. An act of notifying powerful others of wrongful practices in an organization.
2. Motivated by the desire to prevent unnecessary harm to others.
3. The action of an employee or former employee who has privileged access to information (p. 220).

Advocacy within the organization, particularly when it deals with incompetence or maltreatment, can be a potential source of significant conflict. Although whistle blowing is primarily ascribed to employees, it would seem that consumers of services, particularly those who are well informed about their rights, potentially could engage in the same types of behaviors. Whether these behaviors are whistle blowing is subject to debate. Regardless, the input of such behaviors can yield significant repercussions for stakeholders and may require the social worker to advocate with forces outside the organization (external advocacy) as well as inside the organization (internal advocacy).

EXTERNAL ADVOCACY

In addition to whistle blowing, case and self-help advocacy can lead to the engagement of managers, clients, and staff members in external advocacy. For example, a worker may document that the organization does not have sufficient financial resources to serve all applicants or that some clients need more specialized services than the organization can provide. In such circumstances, organizational constituents may lobby the legislature for more funding or participate in a task group to design a new program or create a new agency. Therefore, class, legislative, and political advocacy require use of a set of practice activities outside the organization.

Managers in social service organizations typically engage in advocacy on behalf of their own organization, professional interest groups, or the people served by their organization. Staff members may, in some circumstances, engage in these practices as well. Class and legislative advocacy are routine activities for social workers employed in social movement and other types of advocacy organizations. The advocate may find that solutions to problems encountered by clients or staff require some degree of action outside the place of employment. For social workers, each of these activities should be used to promote social justice as specified in the National Association of Social Workers (NASW) *Code of Ethics* (see Chapter 3). The code, however, is ambiguous in its definition as to how social justice is to be achieved.

Most social workers would agree that social work practice should focus on changing laws and social policies that are harmful to clients or that place members of many demographic groups at some economic, educational, social, or political disadvantage. Reeser and Epstein (1990) distinguish between legislative advocacy that is conducted on behalf of clients or to acquire funding for social service organizations and lobbying activities that are conducted (usually in conjunction with the NASW) to enhance job opportunities, salaries, or working conditions for social workers. Advocacy to support the profession typically is conducted to obtain or revise laws related to social work licensure or title protection, limiting the use of the title "social worker" to those with professional degrees.

Political practice is believed to be an appropriate activity for many social workers. However, as noted in Chapter 12, state and federal laws preclude government and nonprofit organization employees from engaging in political campaigns or running for office while on the job. Consequently, social workers usually engage in such activities as volunteers. For many social workers and organization managers, this type of activity is a logical extension of legislative advocacy. Not only are people sympathetic to social work issues elected to office, but work on political campaigns helps advocates make personal connections with powerful people who can influence the process of policy change, introduce new legislation, or affect whether funding for social service provision is allocated to local organizations.

Class advocacy is much more controversial than are legislative and political advocacy. It often involves social action-related activities. Although legislative advocacy is regarded as a type of social action (Reeser & Epstein, 1990), other types of social change-related activities include rallies, media campaigns, boycotts, strikes, and civil disobedience. Occasionally such tactics are used to advance the interest of powerless groups or people who are not adequately represented in the political process (Mondros, 2005). Often strength in numbers provides an adequate substitute for people lacking authority, knowledge, information, professional status, personal contacts with decision-makers, and other sources of power (Hardina, 2002). In situations where negotiations fail or decision-makers simply refuse to meet with representatives of the group taking action, constituents may escalate their use of tactics, moving rapidly from cooperation to campaign to direct confrontation (Mondros, 2005). However, the use of some types of confrontation (such as civil disobedience) may drive away potential participants or increase difficulties with authorities. Decisions to use such tactical methods must be made carefully, weighing the risks, benefits, and ethical implications. As noted by Reisch (1990), engagement in social action may be actively discouraged or prohibited by employers, unless such activities fall explicitly within the purpose and mission of the organization.

ADVOCACY AS A COMPONENT OF ETHICAL PRACTICE

In practice, advocacy is closely linked to ethics, values, and social justice as discussed in Chapter 3. Advocacy also is associated with legal rights as well as human rights and entitlement. The advocate positions himself or herself in what Pearlmutter (2002) refers to as "between client and community. This ability . . . is essential if social work is to have an impact on our society and meet the challenges posed by current legislative and political realities" (p. 387). While appearing to be straightforward, advocacy in actuality is more complex than its definitions and approaches would suggest. Advocacy is sometimes perceived of as actions that result in outcomes that yield "win/lose" consequences rather than benefiting all parties involved. Consequently, social workers need to closely examine who benefits from the act of advocacy, the risks or losses that may affect either the advocate or the beneficiaries of advocacy practice, and the ethical implications inherent in the advocacy process.

Much of what guides the practice of social work is defined by the NASW *Code of Ethics*. The code prescribes the professional behavior of social workers and attempts to balance the interest of all parties by articulating the responsibility of the social worker to both the employer and the consumer of services. Unfortunately, many social service agencies require adaptation as a measure of success, often at the expense of cultural considerations. In adaptation, consumers are expected to conform to and accept the services provided them, often without consideration of the cultural appropriateness of the service. A primary example is the use of interpreters when working with persons whose primary language is not English. The shortage of bilingual practitioners and sometimes the use of young children to translate for their parents pose an ethical dilemma.

On the surface, advocacy and ethical practice appear to be noncontradictory. Each activity appears to speak to the greater good of individuals in need of services and to address issues such as disparity. However, in practice there is potential for conflict. Advocacy for one population over another when the needs of both are comparable can be perceived as creating a potential ethical dilemma. For many, advocacy, because of its inherent ability to be used in an adversarial manner, raises many issues. However, when the decision has been made regarding programmatic goals and objectives and when the funding for those selected issues and/or populations has been allocated, then the focus of advocacy must shift to meeting the mandate that has been established. There are a number of competing interests and populations in need. A program commits to providing services to a particular population or within specific geographic boundaries. Even if another equal or perhaps even greater need is recognized, the organization must serve those it agreed to serve. For example, an entity in the northeast part of the country established an agency to provide free comprehensive services to people residing in a specific geographic area. The boundaries established, by use of census tracts, excluded people in the same circumstance on the same street because residents on one side of the street fell outside the designated area. This example also demonstrates the lack of community input in the planning process, as residents of the community could have provided valuable information regarding the unintended consequences this program could have on their community. Even though this example does not reflect decisions made by the local agency, it nevertheless had to deal with fallout. As difficult as it may be when an organization fails to fulfill its commitment, regardless of the reason, the organization can be subject to a loss of funding as well as credibility within the community. In the example provided, community members believed that the program's focus had shifted, that is, the program was not really interested in helping poor people; rather, the community members believed that the program was solely interested in its research agenda. The agency did nothing to address this ethical dilemma.

A shift in focus creates a dilemma that can be of concern to both the employer and the employee. Ethical practice would suggest that one must be accountable to the organization, but at the same time there must be recognition of the obligation to provide for the consumer's need. Sometimes, what is best for the consumer of services is not necessarily what is best for the organization or employees. When such conflicts arise, it is imperative that an agreed upon protocol be in place to respond to the issue. In the absence of such a mechanism, conflicts can escalate to a higher level. Greene and Latting (2004) suggest that the following protocol be used to resolve such dilemmas:

1. Establish screening procedures to ensure that only ethical and morally responsible personnel are hired.
2. Establish a "no tolerance" policy against ethical violations.
3. Hold periodic meetings to identify situations ripe for ethical violations and provide periodic training.
4. Establish written policies regarding the organization's ethical standards.
5. Include in the policy the steps employees should take if they observe violations and the assurance that no retribution will occur.
6. Establish an organizational ethics committee to oversee an "ethics audit."
7. Evaluate employees' performance based partially on the treatment of clients and expand the reviews to include the input of both peers and clients.
8. Actively encourage peer monitoring and reporting of organizational wrongdoing or unethical practice (p. 226).

This type of protocol can be instrumental to the success of empowerment-focused practice. It may be not be prudent for an employee to engage in the entire list advocacy-focused initiatives, because there may be potential risks. Employees can be fired or demoted, they can be ostracized by colleagues, they can experience a loss of personal privacy, or they may receive verbal or physical threats as a consequence of the advocacy activities. Engagement in external advocacy activities can involve arrest or exposure to violence (Hardina, 2002).

The positive consequences of advocacy cannot be overemphasized. Advocates may see positive consequences of their action, such as improvements in client services and workplace conditions. The ability to foster social change also contributes to the worker's sense of personal efficacy and empowerment (Hardina, 1995). Consequently, the worker must carefully assess whether such risks outweigh the potential benefits of these activities and whether such actions are likely to produce positive results. Reisch and Lowe (2000) argue that social workers should examine whether it is actually their own responsibility or the responsibility of others to be the advocate. Greene and Latting (2004) offer commonsense criteria for assessing whether to advocate:

- Are the potential benefits for the client worth the risk?
- Is my evidence sufficient?
- Are my motives in terms of the organization unbiased?
- Can I live with myself if I do not act?
- Am I prepared to face negative consequences as a result of my advocacy?

Greene and Latting (2004) also suggest that advocates consult with mentors or other people outside the organization before engaging in any type of advocacy that may have negative consequences.

BOX 11.1 INTERNAL ADVOCACY

Ernestina has just received her MSW and has started working as a case manager at the Mission Street Anti-Poverty Organization. During Ernestina's first week at the agency, a client reports that she has been sexually harassed by a male supervisor. Ernestina is reluctant to report this information to the organization's administrators. There does not seem to be a written antisexual harassment policy or a set of grievance procedures. In addition, lines of supervisory authority are so unclear in this organization that Ernestina fears that this supervisor may have some input into her performance review and may be able to retaliate against her. A staff member to whom Ernestina has confided also raises an ethical issue: making a complaint could result in unjustly damaging the reputation of an employee who may be innocent of the charges. How should Ernestina handle the client's complaint? She should:

1. Inform her supervisor of the complaint.
2. Go straight to the shelter's executive director and inform her about the complaint.
3. Get more information from the client.
4. Take no action. Persuade the client to drop the complaint.
5. Advise the client that it is her responsibility to advocate for herself in this situation. Discuss options for resolving the problem with the client.

6. Take the complaint to the media before trying to resolve it in the agency.
7. Advocate within the agency for a clear antisexual harassment policy that contains a mechanism for making complaints.
8. Choose more than one of the above options.

- What are the likely benefits, risks, and outcomes associated with each of these options?
- If you were the executive director of this organization, how would you respond to Ernestina's complaint?

USING A PROBLEM-SOLVING APPROACH FOR ADVOCACY

Whenever an advocate engages in social change strategies, he or she is involved in a political process. In addition to identifying the risks and benefits, it is important to identify allies and to know the culture community and its history of receptivity to change. Knowing the importance of vigilance, persistence, follow-up, and oversight also is important. It is very easy to slip back into the status quo. How a person chooses to engage an issue is dependent upon the advocate and is a decision informed by self-reflection. It is important that the advocate understand his or her abilities and carefully consider the consequences of taking on the role of advocate. The advocate, the actor, cannot be separated from who he or she is as an individual. The style of practice must be consistent with things such as personality type, temperament, and disposition. The advocate brings to the practice of advocacy his or her past experiences, perceptions of the issue, and a sense of injustice, to mention a few considerations. The advocate must have a sense of purpose that mobilizes for action (Burghardt, 1979).

Advocates should possess certain generic skill sets regardless of the approach or the level at which the advocacy activities are directed, for example, organizational policy, legislation, or quality of services. Among the skills identified by a number of authors (Ezell, 2001; Fernandez, 1980; Schneider & Lester, 2001) are the following:

1. Know the facts regarding the situation and the people involved.
2. Understand the system.
3. Know the rights of the consumer.
4. Keep written documentation.
5. Research how the issue is handled in other venues.

6. Follow channels (particularly for internal issues).
7. Identify supporters.
8. Understand the opposition.
9. Provide options for resolving or addressing the issue.

We submit that it is imperative for all practitioners to engage in advocacy practice. Direct service workers, clinicians, have an excellent opportunity for advocacy in their work with the consumer. In their intervention approaches, they can move beyond traditional therapy to a better understanding of the "why" by giving greater credence to what the consumer sees as the problem. Every act of helping is not advocacy. Rather, advocacy practice is associated with the act of moving the system, making changes, and addressing what is sometimes the "invisible" nature of oppression and marginalization. Advocacy practice is committed to change. This approach looks at those we serve as having rights to quality services and input into those decisions that will affect their lives. The person who engages in advocacy should

1. Believe in his or her own abilities and skills.
2. Appreciate past accomplishments.
3. Need little outside recognition or approval.

This is not to say that the advocate is a "lone ranger"; rather, the advocate should take a stand, even if so doing involves risk or sanctions. In many instances, the advocate may be able to solicit support from supervisors, colleagues, or individuals and groups from outside the organization. For example, if the advocate has determined that there is a need for a homeless shelter in the community, it may be fairly easy to identify potential allies: government officials, religious leaders, representatives from social service and health care agencies, housing advocacy groups, and members of the target population.

The advocate must be prepared to work within the confines of existing organizational structures. The process of working within an organization often means that someone must remain cognizant of those aspects of the system that can disadvantage or unwittingly harm the persons for whom services are provided. Protection of client confidentiality when complaints are made is an important consideration. Also, most organizations expect that grievances or efforts to suggest organizational reforms will be made in a manner consistent with organizational structures and protocols. For example, a worker should first discuss issues or concerns with his or her immediate supervisor. In situations where this is not feasible (for example, when the complaint or concern is about the supervisor), the worker should seek counsel from the next person in the organization's chain of command. Only when internal options have been exhausted should the advocate attempt to use external resources (such as professional organizations, legal counsel, or the media) to resolve the problem.

BOX 11.2 EXTERNAL ADVOCACY: ACHIEVING SOCIAL JUSTICE

After working in the Mission Street Anti-Poverty Organization for several months, Ernestina finds that many of the residents have difficulty finding a place to live after they leave the organization's homeless shelter. There is no transitional housing in the community, especially for persons with disabilities and households that include children. Rents are extremely high; welfare grants and wages from the retail and service industry jobs that many of the women obtain are insufficient to help them save for making a deposit on an apartment. Consequently, some of the clients find a way to stay at the shelter longer than the 30-day maximum. Larry Littlefeather, the executive director, intends to end this practice. Long stays at the shelter add to the agency's expenses and prohibit the shelter's ability to accept new clients. Ernestina knows that some of the families with children that the shelter has helped in the past are living on the streets.

Given these circumstances, what are Ernestina's options? She should:

1. Do nothing. Preventing homelessness is not part of her job description.
2. Advocate internally against a change in the shelter's residency policy.
3. Help the shelter find more funding so that the shelter can expand its services to women and children in need.
4. Form a task force made up of clients and local social service professionals to develop transitional housing programs.
5. Join NASW in order to advocate for more funding and services for women and children.
6. Start a social justice campaign to increase public recognition of domestic violence and homelessness. Go to the state legislature to increase welfare grants and fund job training programs that will help women obtain adequate wages. Advocate for other laws and policies that will improve living conditions for homeless people and women who experience domestic violence.
7. Provide information and support to help current and former clients campaign for better housing and wages.

8. Choose more than one of these options.

   - What components should Ernestina include in her advocacy plan?
   - Who are her likely allies in this advocacy campaign?

SUMMARY

This chapter attempts to define advocacy and to set the context in which advocacy takes place. Although advocacy can be associated with helping an individual consumer, it can be much more. Advocacy provides the strategies for addressing many issues of social injustice in society. Advocacy is a process in which all professionals must act. The action can be as simple as writing a letter or as complex as engaging the public in demonstrations. The key is that one must act. In order for organizations to advocate or for organizations to encourage staff members to advocate on behalf of, or in collaboration with, clients, the organization must have sufficient resources. The process of obtaining funds and monitoring expenditures is examined in Chapter 12.

QUESTIONS FOR CLASS DISCUSSION

1. In what advocacy activities have you been involved?
2. How did you experience the act of advocacy?
3. How might case or self-help advocacy lead to class advocacy?
4. How would you approach getting an agency policy changed that you thought might be detrimental to recipients of services?
5. Discuss the connection between social justice and advocacy.

SAMPLE ASSIGNMENTS

1. You are a new practitioner in a mental health facility. You notice that all the mirrors in the facility give a distorted image. What do you do?
2. Have members of the class break into groups. Group members should be assigned the role of funders, the executive director, community persons at large, consumers, and practitioners. The funders have determined that the agency is no longer meeting its mandate and that they intend to cease funding. What do you do?

CHAPTER 12

Securing Resources for the Organization: Funding and Budgeting

One of the more difficult aspects of organizational life for social workers to grasp is how social services organizations are funded and how organizations develop and manage social services budgets so vital to the organization's ability to work toward its mission and to serve clients. Many individuals are initially drawn to the social work profession because of their desire to work directly with individuals, families, and communities. As such, there is a propensity among social workers to view matters related to funding and budgeting as outside the purview of social work practice. However, it does not take long for most practitioners to soon realize that their ability to serve clients at any level of practice (individual, family, community, etc.) is largely dependent on the financial resources available to the organization in which they are employed. Securing funding and administering budgets requires skill and expertise that are directly related to social work practice, but in the past had largely been relegated by social work to other professions such as business and public administration. Ignoring this area of practice has had tremendous negative implications for social work, especially related to social welfare policy and administrative decisions that ultimately shape and define the nature of social services and how social service organizations deliver these services.

Social workers, especially those practitioners who have adopted an empowerment approach, provide a unique and insightful perspective on the lives of disadvantaged and oppressed populations. It is imperative that social workers be at the table when policy and administrative decisions are made so that they can offer their perspectives and advocate for persons who are not present to advocate for themselves. Discussions and decisions made at the policy and administrative level often include how and which social services to fund and at what levels. As social workers move into managerial and administrative roles in social service organizations, funding and budgeting expertise has become increasingly important in the repertoire of skills needed by social work practitioners. By combining funding and budgetary skills along with empowerment practice, social workers better position themselves within an organizational context to more effectively serve disadvantaged populations. In this chapter, we discuss

- Major sources of funding available to social services organizations.
- A process for identifying funding sources.
- The development of funding proposals, the primary vehicle used by nonprofit agencies to obtain funds.
- Procedures for developing and monitoring an agency budget.
- Funding restrictions and limitations imposed on organizations by funders and the implications of these restrictions for empowerment practice.

HOW SOCIAL SERVICE ORGANIZATIONS ARE FUNDED

Government is the biggest funder of social services, funding in excess of $200 billion annually (Martin, 2001). Government is also a large provider of social services usually authorized and mandated under legislation. The federal government provides the bulk of funding that is passed on to public agencies at the state and local levels. These funds often are restrictive and are intended only for the purposes identified in the legislation. Examples include funding for mental health, child abuse, substance abuse, services to the aged, and disability services. Federal funding for social services administered by public agencies is complex, but some of the more common mechanisms include the following:

- *Entitlements:* In accordance with regulatory rules, every eligible person receives the service along with federal financial participation to support the service.
- *Block Grants:* Based on prescribed funding formulas, states or localities receive a set amount of funding for services, which they must manage along with other revenue sources to meet state and local needs.

- *Grants/Cooperative Agreements:* These are funds awarded to other government agencies as well as nonprofit organizations to support social service activity. Grants funds usually are "granted" to the agency to support these social services activities, whereas in cooperative agreements, the federal government is a partner in support of social service activities (Martin, 2001).
- *Purchase of Service Contracts:* Some government agencies buy services from nonprofit agencies and for-profit organizations on behalf of individual clients. For example, job training for welfare recipients is often delivered by nonprofit organizations that have contracts with county welfare departments. These organizations are reimbursed for the services they deliver. Reimbursement is often contingent upon achieving successful outcomes (Austin, 2002; Hefetz & Warner, 2004).

Federal funding for organizations to support social services often comes with the requirement that state or local agencies match federal funding. This match is based on either a prescribed formula that can include a dollar-for-dollar match by state and local entities for every federal dollar or a sharing ratio. For example, 75% federal share and 25% local share for the cost of services. Sometimes agencies are allowed to use an *in-kind* match, meaning they can contribute personnel time, administrative overhead, space, and equipment, which are assigned monetary values and used as matches.

Government funds also support many nonprofit agencies that provide social services in the United States (Gronbjerg, 1992; Hardina, 2002). Despite large government expenditures in the billions of dollars, most private nonprofits do not view government funds as a steady and dependable source of revenue. Large amounts of government funding come in the form of grants and contracts that are time limited and not embedded in legislative mandates. Private nonprofits often manage several government grants or contacts along with other sources of funding to maintain their financial and service integrity.

Foundations are a large source of revenues for social services, especially for private nonprofits; however, even the public sector competes for these funds. In 1999, more than 44,000 foundations with assets over $230 billion existed in the United States (Martin, 2001). On average, foundations award $15 billion in grants each year. Social services organizations are likely to solicit funds from three primary types of foundations:

1. *Community Foundations:* These funds usually are held in trust from donors who represent a variety of interests and priorities connected to a geographic region, such as a city, county, or other

defined geographic area. Funds and grant-making activities are administered by a governing board or committee that distributes these funds in accordance with the interests and priorities of donors.

2. *Independent Foundations:* An individual, a family, or a group of individuals contribute funds for purposes of financially supporting programs or services, usually in the form of grants. The individual, family, or group can be closely or loosely connected to governance and administration of funds, but this varies from foundation to foundation.
3. *Corporate Foundations:* These are company-sponsored foundations set up as separate legal entities for the purpose of charitable giving. Corporate members, sometimes including managers and workers, are involved in governance and administration of the charitable fund (Brody & Nair, 2003).

Foundations are limited to making grants to tax-exempt agencies such as private nonprofits organizations and government bodies. Foundations establish their own priorities for funding, which has the effect of excluding or underfunding some social service activities. Social services agencies are in a competitive environment when pursuing these funds. Foundation funding awards are time limited, typically ranging from 1 to 3 years. Some foundations limit their funding for administrative overhead and capital expenditures; others do not fund these costs at all.

Out of necessity, many social service organizations develop other funding sources as a way of ensuring financial viability and sustainability for the organization. Some traditional methods include pursuing charitable donations as part of a collective annual campaign, such as working with the local United Way. Other methods include pursuing monetary or in-kind donations from individuals. Some organizations use a fee-for-service method in which clients pay for services provided to them, with poorer clients paying on a *sliding scale.* With a sliding scale, poorer clients pay for only a portion of the actual cost of the service based on their income. Third-party payments have become more popular with social services providers, especially for behavioral services that are provided as part of *managed care.* Other developing and creative fund development strategies now being used by social service providers include the following:

- *For-Profit Corporation Subsidies:* Establishing a separate commercial profit-making entity controlled by the private nonprofit organization. Profits are taxed as with any private commercial business or venture.

- *Commercial Venture:* As part of a business venture, the organization provides goods and services to other organizations or to the public to generate a profit, but the organization does not establish a separate profit-making entity. Goods and services are sold under the auspices of the nonprofit. In order for organizations to maintain their nonprofit or Internal Revenue Service (IRS) 501 (c) (3) status, IRS rules restrict their ability to compete in the open market, and the venture cannot be directly related to the tax-exempt purpose of the nonprofit organization.
- *Affinity Marketing:* This is a joint venture between a social service provider and a business in the form of a promotional campaign. Three main types are common. In *sales promotion,* a business donates money to a social service organization in relation to sales over a period of time. Similarly, *credit card promotions* provide donations to a social service organization every time a credit card is used to purchase goods and services. Last, the *charity mall* uses e-commerce via the Internet. The social service organization is part of a registry or has an exclusive association with a for-profit business selling goods over the Internet, and the business contributes a small percentage of its earnings to the private nonprofit (Martin, 2001).

Charitable donations, fee-for-service, and the other funding mechanisms listed tend to provide more discretionary and flexible funding for social service organizations, which is critical for their survival among private nonprofits.

IDENTIFICATION OF APPROPRIATE FUNDING SOURCES

Social services provided by the government can rely on more predictable and stable sources of funding because government provision of social services is supported by legislative enactments and mandates. Further, legal authorization for government social services typically is codified into statue and financially supported by yearly appropriations. Yearly appropriations are supported by taxes levied by government on its citizens (Austin, 2002). The leadership of public social services must work to maintain appropriate levels of community, legislative, and other executive approval for their programs and services. The leadership often works with community constituents, legislative members, and key executive officials to safeguard their funding levels and minimize reductions in appropriations for their programs during fiscal shortfalls. Although government providers of social services have access to more reliable funding, it is not unusual for them to compete with the private sector for government and private foundation funds to support other programming not support by legal mandates.

Private social service organizations often do not possess steady and reliable sources of funding and often seek government contracts and grants to improve their financial viability. As such, private social service organizations are continuously searching for funding to support their services and, by extension, their organizations. For all organizations, locating funding sources requires research and organization. Once an organization identifies an appropriate funder, inquires must be made and relationships with funders cultivated in order to assess the compatibility between each funder's priorities, philosophy, and values and those of the organization seeking the funds. The better the compatibility between the funder and organization, the better the likelihood the funder will consider financially supporting the organization's programs and services. For many organizations, especially in the private sector, locating funding sources and establishing relationships with funders is a full-time endeavor, requiring strong knowledge of topic areas and good human relations skills.

Fortunately, the ease and accessibility of the Internet now allows organizations to identify funders and to access their information quickly. In some cases, funding applications can be completed or downloaded online. Organizations looking for government funding sources might begin with the *Federal Register,* which regularly announces funding opportunities. The *Federal Register* contains funding opportunities for government and private social services organizations (available at *http://www.gpoaccess.gov/fr/index.html*). The *Catalog of Federal Domestic Assistance* is another good source of federal grant making (available at *http://www.gsa.gov/fdac*). The United States Department of Health and Human Services (DHHS) provides information on federal funding opportunities on its *GrantsNet* web site administered by the DHHS Office of Grants Management (available at *http://www.os.dhhs.gov/grantsnet/*). Similar to DHHS, some states have consolidated state funding opportunities administered by different state agencies onto a single web site. For example, California has established the *GetGrants* web site, which identifies grant programs within the state. At the local level, city and county governments also provide opportunities for organizations to help address local social service needs. Organizations should check with local governments to identify public funding opportunities that may be available in their communities.

A number of web sites contain information on foundation grant giving. One good source for foundation grant giving is the Foundation Center.

The Foundation Center has established a web site that organizations can use to locate a funder based on their interest and organizational profile (available at *http://fdncenter.org/funders/*). A source for community foundations and their service area is the Council on Foundations (available at *http://www.cof.org*). At this site, community foundations are listed by state so that locating a nearby potential funder is easy. In addition to these sites, many foundations post their own individual web sites that provide useful information on their mission, funding priorities, recent awards, amount of giving, assets, and board membership. This information can be useful for approaching funders and tailoring one's request for financial support. Many communities engage in federated or collective fundraising, such as United Way or Catholic Charities, which in turn is used to support a variety of local social service activities. Although this source of revenues has decreased in recent years (Austin, 2002), it remains an important source of income for many agencies providing social services. Finally, some organizations now make direct appeals to donors via their own web sites (Hardina, 2002). With this method, individuals can contribute directly to those organizations that are most appealing to them, for example, organizations working to combat domestic violence.

PROPOSAL WRITING

Unless organizations are receiving funds through government appropriations, agencies often find themselves engaged in proposal writing to supplement other revenue sources. For some agencies, grant awards are their major source of revenues. Lohmann and Lohmann (2002) describe *grantsmanships* or proposal writing as an important skill needed by social service organizations for social administration. As such, an organization's ability to survive may be contingent on its ability to write funding proposals as a way of securing new revenues. Writing funding proposals consumes a great deal of organizational time and resources, and competition among social service agencies for funds often is fierce. The success of these efforts often is low: 80% to 95% of all proposals are not funded (Henry, 1998). Therefore, organizations should give considerable thought and planning to the development and writing of funding proposals in order to increase their ability to secure funding. This includes assessing whether the project is wanted and feasible, assessing the capacity of the organization to carry out the project, identifying whether funders are interested in the project, and determining the consequences of securing the funding in relationship to the organization's mission and purpose (Brody & Nair, 2003). Because of the lure and attraction of funding, organizations sometimes forget that their reputations and credibility can be seriously damaged if they are unable or incapable of carrying out the terms of their proposal.

Most funders have specific proposal requirements, formats, and guidelines that they make available to organizations as part of their applications for funding. Organizations should review these materials carefully to ensure their proposals comply with the funder's requirements and requests. Generic elements or sections of proposals are described in the following. Most proposals contain similar elements, but individual funders may request less or more information, depending on their application requirements. Generic components of a funding proposal include:

- Cover letter
- Executive summary
- Statement of need
- Organizational overview
- Goals and objectives
- Program components
- Budget
- Evaluation
- Program continuation
- Appendices and attachments

Cover Letter

The cover letter should be a brief introduction to the proposal; it also can serve as an introduction to the organization submitting the proposal. The cover letter should contain information on why the proposal was written and what the organization hopes to address and accomplish. In some cases, the cover letter mentions supporters or collaborators working on the proposal. Typically the cover letter is signed by the chief executive officer or chairperson of the governing board.

Executive Summary

The executive summary should be a brief overview of the material contained in the proposal. Important information to consider including in the executive summary are the following:

- Information about your organization, its tax exempt status, and why the organization is interested and capable of carrying out the proposal.
- Why you selected the funder for support of your project.

- The purpose of the proposal, the problem or need, the target population, and the timeframe associated with the funding request.
- What it will cost to fund the project (being careful not to sound exacting or demanding) and other funding sources for the project if appropriate.
- How your program will work on the problem or need.
- How the proposal is consistent with the organization's purpose and mission.
- How the proposal will complement other organizational and community services.
- Community supporters or collaborators connected to the proposal.

Statement of Need

In this section of the proposal, expand on the problem or need that your organization is interested in addressing. Many communities and localities experience similar social problems and issues, such as unemployment or teen pregnancy. When describing the problem or issue in the proposal, give a compelling reason why the condition must be addressed now and the consequences if the problem were to be left untreated. The description of the problem should not be inflated, but the issue should be well researched. A literature review of the problem in its current state should be included. Provide information and data so that the funders can grasp the seriousness of problem and its effects on the local community. A common mistake made in this section of the proposal is overwhelming the funder with data and information as a way of demonstrating knowledge of the issue. Data and information presented are meant to educate the funder about the problem or issue, and this can be accomplished with more limited amounts of information that is presented strategically and coherently. The problem identified and described must relate directly to the organization's purpose and mission. Describe past efforts and current community efforts to resolve the issue. If the problem is outside of the organization's scope, the proposal must address why the agency has decided to pursue a resolution and why the organization is qualified to do so (Hardina, 2002).

Organizational Overview

Funders are very interested in knowing more about an organization they may financially support. Funders want to know if the organization is trustworthy, is legitimate, and has the capacity and community support to carry the project if funded. In most cases, funders need to know the organization's tax-exempt status in order to legally fund the project.

It is in the agency's best interest to provide as much information as possible about the organization, including its purpose and mission, its experience in delivering services, the number of years it has been in existence, and its reputation in their community. Funders will want to know past and current financial supporters of the agency, the qualifications of the organization's staff, especially its leadership, and the composition of its governing board, including the roles they execute on behalf of the organization. Past evaluations of agency services and copies of financial audits and statements should be provided as a way of demonstrating credibility and competency with financial administration and service delivery.

Goals and Objectives

The proposal should state the goals the program is working to achieve. The goals are connected to the proposed solution to the problem or issue identified in the statement of need. Goals usually are given as broad statements on a condition that requires remedy or change, such as reducing child abuse or increasing racial tolerance. Objectives relate directly to goals but are quantifiable and measurable so that they can be evaluated or measured against actual achievements. As described in Chapter 6, objectives can focus on the processes necessary to achieve program outcomes or on specific tasks. *Process objectives* focus on improving internal operations in the organization; for example, providing 16 hours of training on computer software applications is a process or operational objective. The three types of *task-related objectives* are as follows:

- *Service Objectives:* These objectives relate to units of services provided to clients or populations served by the program, for example, providing 10 units (hours) of counseling to each client served by the program.
- *Product Objectives:* These objectives relate to tangible goods or items developed by the program, such as survey instruments, written reports, or curriculum manuals.
- *Impact Objectives:* These objectives refer to actual outcomes achieved as the result of program activities. Examples are a 20% reduction in teen pregnancy or 20 adults remaining drug-free for 6 months. Sometimes programs measure actual changes in clients through the use of scales or well-being inventories (Brody & Nair, 2003).

Objectives alert the funder as to what the funder can expect in return for its investment in the program. Objectives should be clear, realistic, and achievable for the organization, and the funder should have confidence that the results can be achieved. Organizations should periodically measure their progress toward objectives, monthly or quarterly, to ensure that satisfactory progress is being made. As noted in Chapter 6, other evaluation criteria should be included in the lists of objectives, for example, pretest and posttest outcome measures on quality indicators. In addition, funders often require quarterly or midyear progress reports to assess any potential problems in meeting the objectives as stated in the funding proposal.

Program Components

This section of the proposal states the work plan or activities that will be completed by the staff working on the project. It must relate directly and support the objectives mentioned in the proposal. The proposal should describe in detail the specific tasks, duties, process, and procedures that will be undertaken so that the project can achieve the objectives, including applicable timelines. Include details of the management and supervisory structure, oversight, and responsibility for the project. Describe service technologies and practice methods the project will use. Explain relationships and interfaces with other agency units or community organizations that may be connected to the project (i.e., source of referrals). Describe how data will be collected for monitoring, reporting, and evaluation. Some funders request information on how the organization plans to secure and limit access to case files or other sensitive data for purposes of confidentiality and privacy of clients.

As described in Chapter 6, some authors recommend adding a *theory of action* to this section, describing cause-and-effect relationships or why certain activities will lead to results (Chambers, Wedel & Rodwell, 1992). Specifying cause-and-effect relationships will explain why the program should have the anticipated effect on the problem or group and will help focus the evaluation section of the proposal. A theory of action should be written or framed in research terms, with the program's intervention cast as the independent variable and the projected outcomes as the dependent variable. This process requires that writers have a good grasp on theories and causal relationships concerning social problems and how solutions to these problems are being framed by other theorists and researchers.

Preparing a Proposal Budget

As with most organizational budgets, the proposal's budget represents the plan of action for achieving the proposal's goals and objectives. Based on the amount of the proposal's request, organizations must provide a detailed plan for expending these funds that is consistent with the proposal's goals and objectives. Funders have different requirements for budget details and other information needed to evaluate this section. Organizations should check with individual funders regarding their requirements. Some funders simply require a budget specific to the project. Funders likely will request financial information on how any funds from other funding sources will be used to support the project. Other funders will request an entire agency budget in addition to the proposal budget. Funders use this information to determine how the project fits into the overall operation of the organization and whether the project is consistent with the organization's mission and goals. Usually funders require a budget narrative or written budget justification that explains the purposes of the expenditure, such as salaries and benefits related to staff or cost of telephones for communication purposes.

Two types of expenditures usually are provided in proposals: direct costs and indirect costs. *Direct costs* include items more closely associated with the direct provision of program and services, such as staff salaries and benefits, telephones and fax machines, photocopying, utilities, and rent and leases. *Indirect costs* are viewed as more removed or distant from the direct provision of services but still important to the support of the program. These costs can include part of the director's salary or salaries connected to support functions such as accounting and personnel. Capital costs, such as building and equipment depreciation, often are calculated as part of indirect costs. Funders typically review closely all costs and requests for more expensive items such as computers. Atypical costs, such as financial incentives for clients served by the project, usually draw the attention of funders. Consequently, agencies must be prepared to explain the importance of the atypical costs to the project's success. Some funders will clearly state that they will not fund certain items or will state that there is a maximum allowance for a certain item, for example, a $5,000 per year limit on travel expenses.

Evaluation

Evaluation should be directly linked to the proposal's objectives. Evaluation compares the proposal's intended objectives with the actual outcomes achieved. If objectives are clear and measurable, the evaluation section can be easily developed and written. Evaluation should occur not only at the end of the project or funding year but throughout the life of the program. Good evaluation plans typically schedule evaluation activities at regular intervals, such as bimonthly or quarterly, in order to assess progress toward objectives and to monitor activities. Good evaluation plans also incorporate qualitative approaches to evaluation as well as quantitative approaches. Qualitative approaches can include interviewing clients about their perceptions of services or interviewing staff about the project's processes and procedures. Both qualitative and quantitative evaluations are important so that problems can be detected and corrected early and in timely fashion. Some funders require that an organization write-in the name of an independent evaluator so that evaluation is more objective and credible. Some funders request that you incorporate, either as part of the evaluation or as a separate proposal section, a written dissemination plan for the evaluation. Dissemination can include electronic distribution, written reports, and oral presentations provided to community members, media, conference attendees, universities, and professional journals. Findings determined as part of the evaluation usually cover a complete funding cycle or report year-end results. In recent years, evaluation has received more attention from funders and the public as social service organizations are increasingly called upon to demonstrate results compensatory to financial investment.

Program Continuation

Because many grants are time limited, funders may ask the organization to address how the project will be sustained after the funders' support is terminated. Options that may be available to organizations include third-party payment for services, fees, fundraisers, or assumption of cost by other local funding agencies (Brody & Nair, 2003). This section of the funding proposal often is difficult to address because of the uncertainty of future events, but organizations applying for funding must present a viable estimation of how the project will be maintained over the long term.

Some funders are rethinking the wisdom of short-term funding cycles for worthwhile proposals and projects. These funders now are viewing their funding as long-term investments in communities and organizations, and they may be more willing to support a project over the course of 3 to 5 years and sometimes even longer. The rationale behind this type of approach is that it allows sufficient time for an organization to institutionalize and develop needed infrastructure for the project while the organization simultaneously works on gaining broader community support for the project, including financial support. After a few years, the funder begins to slowly detach its financial support from the organization as other funding is cultivated and secured.

Appendices and Attachments

This section contains documents that describe the structural, legal, and financial status of the organization. Other supporting documents specific to other sections of the proposal, such as documentation of the organization's tax-exempt status, organizational charts, information on board membership, and recent financial audits, typically are included. Letters of support for the proposal, job descriptions, salary structures, and resumes of organizational leadership or key personnel are included in this section. Charts, tables, and other summary data may be included. Measurement instruments or scales, if used as part of the proposal, may be included. If requested, written agency procedures and policies, such as affirmative action or sexual harassment policies, would be included in this section.

BOX 12.1 PROPOSAL WRITING

The young mothers group at the Mission Street Anti-Poverty Organization has decided to submit a proposal to fund a Child Care Resource and Advocacy Center that will be operated using feminist and Afro-centered principles and practices. They have identified at least two funding sources, the Brown Family Foundation and the Rosa Parks Society, an African-American women's service club, as potential funding sources. They have identified one primary goal for the organization. They want to help low-income families obtain affordable child care through the provision of information, referral, and advocacy services. Initially, they would like to provide at least 40 referrals and have a part-time staff member make at least two presentations on affordable child care resources per month. Other activities include lobbying the state legislature for increased funding for child care subsidies and changes in regulations that would help more low-income women become certified home child care providers. Keisha has been asked to help draft the proposal.

Keisha must make a number of decisions:

1. Who should be involved in proposal writing?
2. What are possible sources of information for the needs assessment section of the proposal?
3. What components of a fundraising proposal should be included in the draft?
4. What seems to be the theory of action for this program?

At least one goal and several objectives are suggested in the recommendations made by the young mothers group. Write these objectives in a way that ensures that they are measurable and time limited. How should the success of this program be evaluated?

DEVELOPING BUDGETS

One of the major areas of function and responsibility of management in social services organizations is development of the agency budget. Developing an agency budget is a time-consuming and labor-intensive process. For many, as one budget development cycle is "put to bed" another begins almost immediately. Kettner (2002) describes the agency budget process as actually encompassing a 3-year period. As the organization is implementing the current year budget, it is developing next year's budget and evaluating the budget year just completed. One can easily see how social service administrators become consumed by managing an agency.

The budget defines, in monetary terms, the agency's priorities and intentions for a budgetary period, usually defined in yearly increments. Martin (2001) states that "budgeting can be thought of as the process by which resources are allocated to a social service agency's various programs and activities" (p. 76). Budgets also function as a vehicle for monitoring and controlling agency operations and serve as mechanism for future program planning and services. Anthony and Young (2003) identify three types of budgets for most organizations. The first is the *capital budget.* The capital budget is concerned with expenditures needed to purchase fixed long-term assets for the organizations based on available revenues. The second is the *cash budget,* which is concerned with planned cash receipts and disbursements. The third and most familiar to many is the *operating budget.* The three main components of the operating budget are revenues, expenses and expenditures, and outputs measures.

Revenues

Sources of revenue were discussed in the section "How Social Service Organizations Are Funded." In the budget development process, anticipating the amount of revenues is generally recommended first (Anthony & Young, 2003). However, this is not always the case, as sometimes budget managers begin by first developing expenditures rather than anticipating or exploring potential revenue sources. This can be a flawed process because the organization may budget for items or programs it cannot afford. Anticipation of revenue often is based on several years of experience with prior revenues. To better estimate revenues, government organizations providing social services must follow activities regarding governmental appropriations for their program and services. Most government social service organizations use conservative estimates of appropriations. This approach avoids the need to severely reduce programs and services in midyear in the event appropriations are not increased or remain constant.

The process is similar for private social services, but in addition to public appropriations they may receive, private social services must estimate revenues from third-party payers, fees, donations, grants, and other sources of funding common to their agency. Most organizations can forecast fairly accurately based on prior years, but unforeseen events, such as a decline in donations, certainly are possible. In some years, revenue sources will grant increases for cost of living or for inflation. Generally these increases are communicated to the organization in advance and can be incorporated into the budget development process. Once estimated revenues are established, expenditures should flow from the revenues in order to establish a balanced budget, meaning expenditures do not exceed revenues. If the agency is pursuing additional sources of funding, revenues should not be increased until an organization is absolutely sure that a new revenue source is established and that new revenues clearly are forthcoming, as evidenced by a signed agreement.

Expenditures

At a basic level, expenditures are developed using budget categories such as personnel, operating expenses, and travel. Each budget category contains a number of budget items that further detail expenses under that category. For example, the budget category for personnel lists all job classifications employed by the agency and their corresponding salaries and benefits. An example of typical budget categories and budget items is given in Table 12.1.

Generally, personnel costs, which include salaries and fringe benefits, consume the largest portion of the agency's budget, sometimes up to 80% (Hardina, 2002). Fringe benefits include Social Security, unemployment and workers compensation, and company-sponsored health and incentive benefits (see Chapter 9). Operational costs, both direct and indirect, are estimated and included as expenditures in the agency budget. Direct or indirect costs in an agency budget are similar to what was mentioned earlier in this chapter for the budget section of funding proposals. Direct costs includes items more closely associated with the direct provision of program and services, such as salaries and benefits, telephones and fax machines, photocopying and printing, rent and leases, and utilities. Indirect costs, sometimes called *overhead costs,* are viewed as more removed or distant from direct program and services, but these costs are necessary for the general operation of the agency. Examples of indirect costs are insurance for theft, loss, and liability, external financial services (i.e., audits), and the director's salary applied proportionately across all programs. Indirect costs can be listed as a budget item or as a percentage of the overall agency budget.

Table 12.1 Agency Expenditures

Budget Category	Budget Item	Cost
Personnel		
	Director	$62,000
	2 Supervisors	$156,000
	16 Case Managers	$720,000
	2 Clerical	$60,000
	Total salaries	$998,000
	Benefits × 28% of total salaries	$279,440
	Total salaries & benefits	$1,277,440
Operating Expenses		
	Rent	$25,000
	Utilities	$4,800
	Telephone	$3,600
	Printing	$3,000
	Office supplies	$2,700
	Postage & shipping	$2,160
	Membership dues	$675
	Insurance	$3,100
	Audits	$2,700
	Total operating expenses	$47,735
Travel		
	In-state travel	$4,000
	Out-of-state travel	$6,000
	Conferences	$2,000
	Total travel	$12,000
Total Agency Expenditures		$1,337,175

Similar to revenues, budget expenditures are developed by analyzing the history of expenditures in prior years. Changes for the upcoming budget year, such as termination of grants or contracts, will need to be anticipated and deleted from revenues and expenditures, along with loss of indirect costs that will need to be absorbed by other programs (see "Preparing a Proposal Budget" below). Expenditures for each budget item for new programs may be more difficult to estimate, but many funding sources allow small or modest corrections to budget items once more is known about how expenditures are proceeding. In anticipating expenditures, costs known in advance are known as *fixed costs* and have the effect of reducing uncertainty when making estimates of expenditures. Fixed costs can include the cost of salaries and benefits, lease or rent, and office supplies. *Variable costs* apply to costs that fluctuate according to market conditions and are difficult to predict. Examples are the cost of fuel for vehicles and the cost of health insurance premiums for employees.

BOX 12.2 BUDGETING

The young mothers group at the Mission Street Anti-Poverty Organization has, with Keisha's help, completed its grant proposal. The only section that remains is the budget. They have asked Keisha to calculate how much it would cost to operate a child care resource and advocacy center, staffed by a half-time worker with a BSW degree with assistance from volunteers. Keisha has promised to conduct research on what should be included in the budget and to estimate the dollar amounts for specific items.

- What resources could Keisha use to make budget estimates? What line items should be included in this budget?
- How should Keisha go about obtaining estimates of expenditures?
- If the Child Care Resource and Advocacy Center is funded and money is spent on services, to whom are board members and staff accountable?
- Fiscal agent agreements specify that a 501 (c) (3) organization must take responsibility for monitoring budget expenditures and revenues for the unincorporated organization. Once the Child Care Resource and Advocacy Center becomes an independent organization, what budget tools will staff and board members need to keep track of expenditures and revenues?

Outcome Measures

As a result of the accountability movement (Martin, 2001), some social service agencies either commit or are required by the Government Performance and Result Act (GPRA) of 1993 to connect budget information to planned outcome measures. The resulting information provides a measure of both budgetary and programmatic performance assessed against intended and actual results.

MONITORING EXPENDITURES

A competent manager will monitor revenues and expenditures throughout the budget year to check for problems in the budget (Skidmore, 1995). Frequent and periodic checks of the budget will allow the manager to correct detected problems early enough to avoid serious financial difficulty for the agency. A useful tool for assessing financial problems and the overall fiscal condition of social services organizations is the financial statement. Financial statements provide periodic and year-end financial information on the financial health of the agency to end users, such as directors, board members, funding sources, constituents, and the public. Organizations generally use four types of financial statements: operating statements, balance sheets, cash flow statements, and annual reports. *Operating statements* are essentially point-in-time statements that reflect agency revenues and expenses. Based on a complete funding cycle such as budget year, operating statements can be generated monthly, quarterly, or for any time-frame that meets the monitoring needs of the organization. For example, a monthly operating budget can display revenues received and expenditures paid for that month and for year to date (YTD) in line-item format. These monthly and YTD revenues and expenditures are then compared to revenues and expenditures budgeted for the entire year. Percentages are used to compare the YTD revenues and expenditures to the overall agency budget. Table 12.2

Table 12.2 Agency Operating Statement

	Budgeted Fiscal Year 2004–2005	Current Month	Year to Date	Received to Date
Revenues				
County	$278,938	$23,245	$139,469	50%
State	$204,400	$20,440	$136,267	67%
Federal	$149,899	$12,492	$62,458	42%
Local grants	$127,888	$10,657	$63,944	50%
Foundation grants	$348,990	$29,083	$203,578	58%
Fee for services	$12,636	$1,053	$5,792	46%
Fundraising	$119,000	$9,917	$29,750	25%
Donations	$89,000	$7,417	$51,917	58%
Interest	$6,424	$535	$2,141	33%
Total Revenues	$1,337,175	$114,838	$695,315	52%
Expenditures				
Salaries	$998,000	$83,167	$457,417	46%
Benefits	$279,440	$23,287	$128,077	46%
Rent	$25,000	$2,083	$12,500	50%
Utilities	$4,800	$369	$2,400	50%
Telephone	$3,600	$277	$2,100	58%
Printing	$3,000	$273	$2,000	67%
Office supplies	$2,700	$245	$1,800	67%
Postage & shipping	$2,160	$196	$1,440	67%
Membership dues	$675	0	$675	100%
Insurance	$3,100	0	$1,550	50%
Audits	$2,700	0	0	0%
Travel	$12,000	$2,400	$8,000	67%
Total Expenditures	$1,337,175	$112,297	$617,958	46%

shows an example of an agency budget using the format described. In this way, managers can detect whether the agency is within its budget or is over its budget, and they make necessary corrections before the end of the budget year.

The *balance sheet* is similar to the operating budget in that it captures the revenue and expenditures for the agency. However, the balance sheet also includes owned assets (such as property and equipment) and liabilities (money owed by the organization) and net assets (the difference between all assets and liabilities). Balance sheets usually cover an entire fiscal year and are meant to report on the agency's overall financial health or net worth. Balance sheets can contain information from previous years so that the agency can track its net worth over time.

The purpose of the *cash flow statement* is to assess whether sufficient funds exist to cover current operating expenses. In simpler terms, the cash flow statement alerts the end users as to whether the agency has enough cash to pay its bills. Cash flow problems may be more of a problem for private nonprofits than for government agencies; however, both can experience problems with cash flow, especially if governmental appropriations are late. For private nonprofits, delays in reimbursement can severely undermine the agency's financial condition because private nonprofits are legally limited in their ability to build up reserves (Smith & Lipsky, 1993). If case of a cash shortfall, an agency may be forced to take out short-term loans, temporarily lay off workers, or cut services pending reimbursement from funders. Cash flow statements are retrospective and may provide information too late to head off serious financial problems. As such, some organizations now use a *cash flow forecast statement* to predict cash inflows against cash outflows so that the agency can better respond to potential problems (Martin, 2001).

Social service organizations publish *annual reports* that typically include both programmatic and financial information. In addition to monitoring, the annual report is useful for evaluating the agency's year-end performance and for future planning. Publication of the annual report often coincides with the organization's annual planning meeting, which is attended by the board of directors, agency leadership, and other stakeholders (Lohmann & Lohmann, 2002). The financial information should contain an independent audit report that objectively assesses the organization's financial integrity (Strachan, 1998). The IRS also requires nonprofit organizations to annually file Form 990 covering organizational activities for the fiscal year, which is part of the annual report. Other important information often included in the annual report are agency programs, organizational charts, and identification of staff and roles, board membership, and major donors (Hardina, 2002). The annual report is available to the public upon request and is free of charge except for reasonable duplication expenses (Martin, 2001).

RESTRICTIONS AND LIMITATIONS ON THE USE OF FUNDS: IMPLICATION FOR EMPOWERMENT

Every funding stream comes with restrictions and constraints on how the receiving organization can use the funds. For example, some funding sources dictate what kind of expenditures are allowed and which are not. In this case, the agency will have to repay expenditures that do not conform to the funder's rules and policies (Green, 1998). Most funding sources possess strict rules regarding mingling of funds obtained from different sources. This policy may restrict an agency's ability to temporarily cover budget shortfalls in one area or may negatively impact some agency operations even though the overall fiscal resources of the agency are sufficient. Other restrictions may include limiting who is eligible for services, placing requirements on how services are provided, or dictating practice methods the agency can use (Austin, 2002). Categorical funding can limit services to specific populations or problem types.

As described in Chapter 2, resource-dependency theory suggests that social service organizations primarily dependent on governmental and foundation funding will more likely possess less autonomy and will be more obliged to conform to the rules, requirements, and demands of the funder (Blau, 1964; Gronbjerg, 1992). This situation becomes problematic if a funder does not share an empowerment perspective. Changes in political wind and new legislative priorities can radically change the characteristics of funding streams. This will have implications on programs and services provided by social services organizations. Organizations may have to change, adjust, or delete the scope of their programs and services. New governmental priorities may or may not be consistent with the agency's original mission and goals, resulting in goal displacement that substitutes part or all of the agency's goals in order to acquire new revenue sources. Smaller private nonprofits are especially vulnerable to shifting priorities that may result in wholesale organizational changes. For example, Smith and Lipsky (1993) cite attempts by government officials to deprofessionalize staff (use volunteers or low-paid staff without professional degrees) within private nonprofit social service agencies under the guise of minimum standards, despite the fact that many of the agencies had a long history of providing quality services using professional staff.

During times of national and state budget shortfalls, private nonprofit sectors take a disproportionate share of budget cutbacks meant to address revenue deficits (O'Connell, 1996). Following multiple years of budgetary deficits, these agencies may experience difficulty in sustaining and controlling programs and services. Additionally, the loss or reduction of overhead and indirect costs paid by various funding sources inflates the agency's weakened financial status (Smith & Lipsky, 1993). A heavy dependence on one funder's resources likely means that an agency must conform to new funding policies or requirements in order to remain financially viable. In doing so, organizational innovation and creativity may be lost. In the case of overreliance on governmental funding, pressures to conform to funding rules may result in some private nonprofits becoming a form of shadow government, that is, they assume the bureaucratic and legal characteristics of government agencies (Schmid, 2004). An overreliance on governmental funding also can result in government shifting their own shortcomings to the private sector, including reductions in the quality of services, bureaucratic methods of service delivery, and unfairly bearing cuts during fiscal shortfalls. As a result, private organizations become part of the *organizational sink* typically associated with government programs (Gronbjerg, 1992).

Purchase of service contracts is especially problematic for many nonprofit organizations. Funds for program start-up are seldom available from government. If the service delivered does not produce the desired result (for example, job attainment by a participant in a training program or placing a child in foster care), the nonprofit organization will not recover the full cost of providing the service. This may place nonprofit organizations providing service to disadvantaged populations with complex needs at a financial disadvantage if they cannot demonstrate success (Austin, 2003).

Grant funds often represent an infusion of new revenue to an organization. Although welcome by most organizations, these funds often come with limitations. Almost all funders place limits on the use on these funds for administrative overhead. This can result in inadequate administrative support, which often is necessary to manage and monitor these revenues and programs. Many funders will not finance capital projects or physical facilities. As a result, agencies are limited to leasing or renting space that may not be optimal for the provision of services or may not be located in areas most accessible to clients. Grants are time limited, typically from 1 to 3 years, and are not a source of long-term sustainability for programs and services. Agencies must continuously engage in writing and securing new grants, a process that is time consuming, is labor intensive, and consumes a great deal of agency resources. Kramer and Grossman (1987) refer to this process of endlessly pursuing grants as *goal deflecting*, meaning that less time is spent on services, evaluation, and improving programs. Lohmann and Lohmann (2002) report that a 2% to 3% success rate for funding proposals submitted to federal grant makers is not uncommon. The cost of grant making itself typically is an expense not allowed by funders and is absorbed by the agency. Not all grant funding cycles and reporting requirements are the same. Management of even a few grants requires skill and attention to ensure new revenues are secured and existing ones meet funder management and reporting requirements. The very nature of grants often means dealing with unavoidable cash flow problems, fronting start-up costs, working with slow reimbursement processes, and dealing with unforeseen expenses.

Finally, government and private funders have the ability to restrict certain activities that organizations deem important to their mission or to their organizational sustainability, such as advocacy, political action, and lobbying. For example, IRS regulations restrict most nonprofits from using a substantial portion of their revenues for lobbying purposes. Only 20% of the first $500,000 of their budget can be used to directly lobby government. Smaller proportions of the organization's revenue over $500,000 can be used for direct lobbying; restrictions are also placed on the amount of funds organizations can use to appeal to the public to lobby on the organization's behalf. Organizations incorporated under section 501 (c) (3) of the tax code may risk losing their nonprofit status if they violate these standards (Hardina, 2002). Nonprofit organizations are restricted from making donations to political campaigns. In addition, the Hatch Act prohibits governmental employees, such as social workers in public agencies, from engaging in some forms of political activity, such as being involved in political campaigns while they are at work.

Advocacy, political activity, and lobbying activities are often associated with an empowerment perspective, but the sources of funding can put limits on these types of activities. O'Connell (1996) states that the traditional value of nonprofits has been their ability to be an independent force for service, advocacy, and empowerment. However, funding for nonprofits tends to reflect more of a value on service rather than on advocacy or empowerment. Social service organizations interested in an empowerment approach will have to develop a variety of funding sources and strategies, especially unrestricted private funds to protect against funding uncertainties, as a way of better protecting organizational autonomy and purposes.

SUMMARY

Knowledge of how social services organizations are funded and how budgetary processes operate has become an increasingly important skill for social work practitioners to possess, especially for those practitioners in supervisory and managerial roles. Restrictions placed by funders and the types of budgetary priorities made by decision-makers can influence a social services organization's ability to adopt and practice an empowerment approach. Government and foundations are major sources of funding for social services organizations, but many other traditional and creative approaches to securing funding are available to organizations. Identifying and developing relationships with funders, as well as the ability to draft funding proposals, are critical roles for social service managers. Securing funding through funding proposals is labor intensive, and organizations should weigh both the benefits and detriments of pursuing and securing funding. Although every funder has different requirements for the funding proposals submitted to it, organizations must submit as part of their request the problem they wish to address, their goals and objects, how funding resources will be spent if secured, and how they will evaluate their program activities. Monies secured from funding proposals often complement agency budgets, and the overall agency budget represents the agency's service priorities and plan for providing services. Managers and other staff in the organization have a responsibility to the agency budget to ensure that expenditures do not exceed revenues, and they must continually monitor the financial health of their organization. Almost all funding, except for unrestricted funds generated by the organization, come with restrictions and limitations that can impede the organization's ability to engage in an empowerment approach with their staff and consumers. Organizations interested in an empowerment approach must weigh these restrictions and limitations and diversify their funding portfolio in order to better support an empowerment approach. In addition to securing funds, organizations must be able to maintain grants and contracts over a period of years. In order to do this, they must be able to prove to funders that funds are used to provide programs that actually work. Methods for evaluating the effectiveness of programs and determining how and why they work are discussed in Chapter 13.

QUESTIONS FOR CLASS DISCUSSION

1. As a staff member or student in a social service organization, how do you see funding and budgeting relating to your organization's mission and goals?
2. In thinking about the organization at which you are employed or in which you are placed as a student, who are the major funders of the organization's programs and services? Why do you think that is?

3. In thinking about a problem that you would like to address in a funding proposal, what sources and processes would you use to document the problem in the funding proposal?
4. If you were asked to develop an agency budget for the upcoming fiscal year, where would you begin and what factors would you consider in the development of the budget?
5. In which ways do you think empowerment practice could be limited by funding sources and budgetary practices? How might you address limitations?

SAMPLE ASSIGNMENTS

1. Interview someone knowledgeable about your organization's finances (e.g., director, fiscal officer, program manager, or supervisor). Ask him or her to identify the organization's major sources of funding. Try to identify which of these funding sources are government or foundation sources and which are funding sources from donations, charitable contributions, fees, fundraising, etc.
2. Identify a social problem that you would like to address in your community. Using the Internet, identify two government funding sources and two private foundation sources likely to support a funding proposal to address the problem you identified. Review the funding requirements for each of these funding sources. How are they similar? How are they different?
3. Form a student group consisting of no more than five members and develop a funding proposal as part of a class project. Discuss and agree on a social problem your group would like to address. Organize and assign sections (statement of need, goals and objection, evaluation, etc.) to members of the group to develop and write. After the funding proposal is written, do a group presentation to your classmates and discuss each section of the funding proposal and the overall merits of the proposal. Ask them to provide feedback on your project.
4. Ask your supervisor or a manager in your organization for copies of your organization's financial reports (operating statements, balance sheets, cash flow statements, or annual reports). Review and try to interpret these reports, for example, what services, goals, and priorities do these reports reflect? Write down questions you have regarding these reports and meet again with your supervisor or manager to discuss and obtain answers to your questions.

CHAPTER 13

Using the Evaluation Process to Empower Workers and Clients

Evaluations are used to assess a variety of program characteristics and functions. The most important questions addressed focus on program effectiveness and how or why programs work. Organizations vary in terms of whether they choose to conduct evaluations in-house, using their own staff members, or they hire an outside evaluator to assess the programs. However, one of the basic assumptions of an empowerment-oriented approach to management practice is that organizational clients, staff members, and other key constituents should be involved in conducting program evaluations. In this chapter, we discuss the importance of program evaluation for improving organizational services. We also examine

- The role of clients and staff members in the evaluation process.
- Specific evaluation approaches used to involve clients, workers, and others in program assessment.
- Techniques for conducting evaluations of program outcomes and program processes.
- Ethical issues in program evaluation.
- Components of an evaluation report.

THE IMPORTANCE OF ONGOING EVALUATION IN SOCIAL SERVICE ORGANIZATIONS

Program evaluations measure program effectiveness, quality, and efficiency. Program evaluation can examine an entire organization, one program within the organization, or a component of a program. It is not used to measure the performance of individual workers or teams. Consequently it differs from performance evaluation and is different from single and multisystems designs used by social work practitioners to measure their own performance.

Evaluations can be conducted using either qualitative or quantitative methods. Some evaluations require the use of both methods. However, the evaluator's choice of methodology should be based on the type of evaluation to be conducted and the research questions to be addressed. *Quantitative methods* are used to answer "what" questions; for example, what outcomes are produced by the program? In other words, was the program successful, effective, or efficient? *Qualitative methods* are used to determine how and why the program works or why the program fails. Evaluations can be summative or formative. A *summative evaluation* generally focuses on program outcomes. A summative evaluation is generally quantitative and is conducted at the conclusion or at a logical end point of an intervention or project. A *formative evaluation,* on the other hand, is conducted as part of an ongoing process during program implementation. A formative evaluation generally uses a mixture of qualitative and quantitative methods to determine what is happening in the program, with the expectations that the problems will be addressed before the conclusion of the project. A formative evaluation assumes that the process of evaluating the program during the implementation phase will contribute to the effectiveness of the intervention (Royse & Thyer, 1996).

Given the variety of purposes for evaluation, methodologies can range from formal experimental designs in which people are randomly selected for participation to simple pre-test and posttest studies that measure the impact of an intervention on one or more groups of people to comprehensive case studies to observations of program participants to focus group interviews (Table 13.1). Decisions about evaluation methods are based on a number of factors, including the purpose of the study, the

Table 13.1 Types of Evaluation Approaches

Quantitative Methods	Qualitative Methods
Experimental designs	Constructivist evaluation
Quasi-experimental designs with control groups	Implementation analysis
Pre-test and posttest studies	Process evaluations and case studies
Social indicator analysis	Case studies
Caseload and case record analysis (quantitative)	Case record analysis (qualitative)
Longitudinal studies	Observational studies
Surveys	Qualitative interviews with program participants
Goal attainment	Focus group interviews

time and resources available to conduct research, ethical concerns about how data should be used, and the relationship between researchers and participants (Hardina, 2002). One of the first issues that should be addressed in any evaluation is whether an outside consultant or an agency staff member is responsible for coordinating the evaluation.

INTERNAL VERSUS EXTERNAL EVALUATIONS

Organizations may conduct evaluations simply because they are interested in improving the services they offer. However, most organizations conduct evaluations because they are required to do so by the foundations and government agencies providing their funding. Organizations that are licensed by government agencies or are accredited by independent industry regulatory boards must conduct regular evaluations in order to maintain licenses or accreditation status. These outside bodies focus on whether organizations accomplish program goals and objectives, whether programs produce the outcomes specified by the organization, and whether quality standards are achieved. In some cases, funders and other regulatory groups examine whether sufficient program inputs are available to effectively deliver services.

Funders and accreditation bodies are less often interested in program processes or whether services are implemented in the manner intended. However, collecting information on organizational throughput, how programs operate, and the barriers to successful service delivery can be essential for addressing goal attainment failures. For example, Cohen (1994) conducted a formative evaluation of an organization serving the homeless. This organization had tried to create an empowerment-oriented consumer advisory group. After several successful meetings, consumer attendance declined. Barriers to group formation in the agency included staff resistance to change, use of group coordinators who were not full-time staff members, difficulties in recruiting clients for participation and notifying them about meetings, and failure to include organizational staff in planning the intervention. Cohen's findings were used to develop a more appropriate plan for group formation.

THE ROLE OF CLIENTS AND STAFF IN THE EVALUATION PROCESS

Rose and Black (1985) identify client involvement in program evaluation as an essential component of empowerment-oriented practice in mental health settings. Involvement in evaluation has several benefits.

Information about how clients experience the program can be used to make needed improvements in services. According to Rapp, Shera, and Kisthardt (1993), consumer involvement in evaluation helps minimize the power differential between clients and workers. Without consumer involvement, staff perspectives on service delivery and preferred outcomes would dominate the research process. Information obtained from and, in some circumstances, collected by the consumers ensures that services are responsive to their needs. In addition, clients learn some of the skills needed to conduct evaluations (such as data collection), needed to participate in formal decision-making, and associated with self-advocacy (such as assertiveness). The acquisition of skills, in turn, increases the participant's sense of personal self-efficacy and self-esteem. It also gives clients a sense of control over agency practices that often render them powerless. Consequently, involvement in evaluation as well as participation in other types of agency decision-making becomes a component of intervention in working with individuals. The long-term impact of evaluation and other participation-oriented activities is to empower people and alleviate the effects of internalized oppression.

A similar rationale for empowering staff members through participation in agency evaluation can be found in the literature. Staff participation in evaluation of services increases staff motivation, improves performance, and increases service quality (Bowen & Lawler, 1995; Shera & Page, 1995). It also gives staff members more information about what they are doing and how they do it. Consequently, it increases worker autonomy to make decisions and increases feelings of personal self-efficacy and control of the workplace.

USING PARTICIPATORY EVALUATION APPROACHES

Participatory methods of program evaluation increase feelings of constituent ownership of the research process and the social service programs in which they participate. These methods ensure that the program will be assessed from the point of view of participants rather than the preferences of the evaluator. Chambers, Wedel, and Rodwell (1992) describe these research approaches as "constructivist," an inherently political process in which evaluation team members use their own knowledge and experience to explain how the program works and what is going on in the program. According to Rodwell (1998), participatory approaches are effective because

> There is a give and take between the researcher and the researched, between the data and the theory. There is mutual negotiation of meaning and power in the process and the product or inquiry, based on reciprocity, dialectical theory building, and a questioning of all elements of the research process. This negotiation involves recycling descriptions and emerging analysis and conclusions with the participants. As praxis, research is used to help participants (including the researcher) understand and change their situation. The result is empowerment of the researched because they are involved in a collaborative theorizing. (p. 79)

At least three types of evaluation approaches involve organizational constituents:

1. Agency self-evaluation
2. Empowerment evaluation
3. Participatory action research

Agency Self-Evaluation

The self-evaluation process for social service organizations requires that a variety of organizational constituents, staff members, administrators, clients, board members, and community residents be recruited for membership in a task group specifically charged with examining the organization's programs (Meier & Usher, 1998). In some cases, self-evaluation is conducted as an ongoing process by work teams in organizations that adopt a total quality management (TQM) approach. For some self-evaluations, an outside consultant acts as a facilitator, leading members of the task group through a process that requires that they identify research questions and data collection strategies. The consultant also assists the task group in identifying the program's theory of action. Most organizations experience a certain amount of goal "displacement." Consequently, the actual goals addressed by the organization and the manner in which the program actually works may be quite different from what the organization has described on paper (Patton, 1997). In the final stage of the process, the consultant helps participants make sense of the data collected and to make recommendations for improvements in the program (Meier & Usher, 1998). It should be noted, however, that because of interplay among task force members and dialogue between the consultant and the task force, each agency self-evaluation will be quite different.

The second approach to agency self-evaluation is much more structured. A national organization or a foundation may distribute a protocol that includes specific procedures or standardized instruments to be used for conducting the self-evaluation by affiliates of the national organization or local groups that receive funding from a specific source. One rationale for this practice is that it allows for outcome data to be obtained and comparisons to be made across the different sites. For example, the Annie E. Casey Foundation (2001b) requires that public child welfare agencies that participate in its Family to Family program conduct agency self-evaluations to assess the achievement of program objectives. The purpose of the self-evaluation is "to use child and family outcomes to drive decision-making and to show where change is needed and where progress has been made" (p. 9).

The U.S. Office of Juvenile Justice and Delinquency provides the following justification for providing the agencies it funds with a self-evaluation workbook:

> The Office of Juvenile Justice and Delinquency Prevention (OJJDP) strongly believes in the need for community-based projects to conduct local self-evaluations, which provide information about project-specific goals and objectives. Local evaluations are useful for program planning and management, mentor recruitment and retention, publicity and community awareness and resource development. (Information Technology International, Inc., 2002, p. 1)

Another reason for using agency self-evaluation as an approach for assessing the effectiveness of programs is that it is a good method for involving staff in the process of changing the organization in order to increase staff motivation and improve their performance (Shera & Page, 1995). Patton (1997) argues that a primary rationale for self-evaluation is that, as an end result, participants develop feelings of internal self-accountability. Agency self-evaluation builds feelings of cohesion among evaluation team members and helps to give staff and other constituents a feeling of personal ownership of the organization and its services (Meier & Usher, 1998). Participation in agency evaluation helps ensure that findings from the evaluation study are used and that recommendations made by the evaluation team actually will be adopted (Patton, 1997).

Empowerment Evaluation

Empowerment evaluation is an approach that can be used to examine the impact of a social service organization or program. Community coalitions, collaborative partnerships, or task groups can use empowerment evaluation to identify service gaps and improve program coordination.

As designed by anthropologist David Fetterman, the approach can be used to increase the ability of marginalized groups to make the programs that serve them more effective. One of the primary focuses of this method is capacity-building, providing a vehicle through which members of oppressed groups can develop skills and the capacity to address the problems that affect their lives (Fetterman, 2001). However, this technique often includes other constituents (such as staff members and administrators) in the process. In addition, it often requires an external evaluator to help participants agree on research goals, methodology, and interpretation of results (Coombe, 1999). Fetterman (1996) describes the evaluator as a coach who provides training on self-evaluation techniques and decision-making. The evaluator is expected to act as an advocate, disseminating the evaluator report and lobbying for the adoption of program changes recommended by the stakeholders. However, Fetterman also stresses that the evaluator and the participants are equal partners in the research process and that mutual learning is expected to take place during the evaluation. Fetterman (2001) identifies four primary steps in empowerment evaluation:

1. Developing a mission statement or vision
2. Examining the program's strengths and weaknesses
3. Establishing goals for the future and establishing strategies to achieve these goals
4. Dialoguing between the evaluator and constituents to determine the type of research evidence needed to document progress in achieving the goals

Fetterman (2001) also notes that an essential part of the evaluation process is developing a clear theory of action that describes program operation (see Chapter 6). He recommends that the theory of action not be totally derived from the theoretical literature but that it be grounded in the experiences of the program's participants.

A factor that differentiates the empowerment evaluation process from other types of participatory evaluation techniques is that participants are expected to develop research and evaluations skills that they can use to conduct program evaluation and monitoring on an ongoing basis (Secret, Jordan, & Ford, 1999). Patton (1997) notes that empowerment evaluation is particularly appropriate when one of the goals of the social service organization is to help people increase their own feelings of self-competency. In such situations, the participation of clients and other constituents in evaluation is actually one component of the intervention and consequently will increase the program's effectiveness.

Empowerment evaluation techniques can be applied in a number of different ways. Secret et al. (1999) describe an empowerment evaluation conducted for an human immunodeficiency virus (HIV) prevention street outreach program. Both staff members and clients were included in the evaluation team. In addition to an outcomes assessment, the purpose of the project was to identify problems in program implementation (formative evaluation) and to recommend solutions. Team members examined how outreach services were provided and conducted research into alternative models of service delivery. They designed a new outreach model that required staff members to conduct an assessment of the prospective client's readiness to change before selecting an appropriate outreach method to fit client needs. Team members also developed an evaluation plan to test the effectiveness of the intervention using an experimental group and a control group, selected appropriate tools to measure outcomes, and pretested the measurement instruments.

Participatory Action Research

The purpose of participatory action research (PAR) is to minimize power differences between researchers and constituents, to increase the knowledge of participants, and to promote social change (Sohng, 1998). PAR is associated with two aspects of learning theory: Kurt Lewin's action research principles (Lewin, 1951) and the work of Freire (1970). The basic assumption of these approaches is that academic research should be used to reduce the harmful effects of oppression by involving members of powerless groups in the construction of knowledge, a critical examination of the world around them, and action to address social problems (Stringer, 1999). PAR also draws upon social constructionism and the work of postmodern theorists, such as Michel Foucault, who maintain that scientific knowledge often has little relevance in people's everyday lives but instead serves to maintain existing institutional arrangements that limit power to members of economic, social, and political elites (Rodwell, 1998). PAR generally does not focus on agency operations but addresses a social problem that affects constituency group members. Stringer describes this approach as one in which

> Knowledge acquisition/production proceeds as a collective process, engaging people who have previously been the subjects of research in the process of defining and redefining the corpus of understanding on which their community or organizational life is based. As they collectively investigate their own situation, stakeholders build a consensual vision of their life-world. Community-based action research results not only in a collective vision but also in a sense of community. It operates

> at the intellectual level as well as at social, cultural, political, and emotional levels. (p. 11)

The purpose of PAR is to transform both individual participants and society. Research partnerships are established between experts (external consultants or agency staff) and community constituents. There is an expectation that most of the members of the research team will be members of low-income or other marginalized groups. As with other applications of the transformative approach, PAR is based on the idea of mutual learning and equalitarian relationships among members. The two primary approaches to PAR projects are the *parallel process model,* in which the researcher simply acts as a methodological consultant for the group, and the *deep entry model,* in which the researcher simply becomes a member of the evaluation team that is lead by a member of the constituency group (Johnson, 1994). Smith (1997) describes a PAR model in which an external researcher/facilitator uses a five-stage process for goal attainment:

1. The researcher collects information about the community and its problems.
2. The researcher uses dialogue to engage the group in a process of problem identification.
3. Group members develop an understanding of the social, economic, and political context or origins of the problem. They identify questions that they want answered.
4. The group identifies theories about problem origins, designs data collection methods, and generates possible solutions to address the problem.
5. The group takes action.

Action generally goes beyond just the collection and interpretation of data. PAR assumes that participants will participate in program development and social action to resolve common problems and to change the social institutions in which their problems originate. Lewis (2002) describes how the Highlander Research and Education Center, a training institute for community organizers in Tennessee, used a participatory action approach to empower local residents adversely affected by chemicals and other pollutants used by local employers in the mining industry. Residents conducted research on the hazardous effects of the chemicals used in mining. They then used this information to lobby state government to regulate the industry. PAR can also be used to conduct needs assessments and plan interventions. For example, Yoshihama and Carr (2002) used a participatory research action model to work with a group of Hmong immigrant women to identify community needs and to plan educational workshops that addressed these needs.

Limitations of Participatory Approaches

Participatory methods have a number of disadvantages. Distrust and conflict among participants can limit their ability to move forward with the evaluation, particularly in groups that include a variety of people. In addition, time may be needed to develop consensus about goals, mission, and research methods, and many research projects are time and funding limited. The inability of participants to reach a consensus in a timely manner can result in an incomplete project, a project in which data analysis and conclusions are based on incomplete evidence, or a project in which only a handful of participants are responsible for producing the final report (Chambers et al., 1992).

A number of conditions must be met if participatory evaluations are to be successful. Members must develop trusting relationships in order to reach a consensus on project goals, data collection methods, analysis of findings, and recommendations. Participants must be provided with training about research methods, data collection, and analysis. Establishment of a good organizational structure that supports the work team, provides strong administrative support and adequate resources for the project, and selects a skilled facilitator to coordinate the process can address many potential problems (Alvarez & Gutierrez, 2001; Chambers et al., 1992; Telfair & Mulvihill, 2000). Probably just as important as the technical skills, if not more so, are the interpersonal skills necessary to establish trusting relationships among members, individual commitment to the progress, group cohesion, and consensual decision-making (Schmuck, 1997).

Yoshihama and Carr (2002) note that community power dynamics and patterns of decision-making may foster tensions between traditional community decision-makers and people traditionally excluded from the decision-making process, such as women and persons of color. There likely exist, even within oppressed communities, in-groups and people who have not previously held power or had the ability to make decisions. Participatory approaches can require long periods in order to resolve preexisting conflicts among participants, and difficulties in developing consensus may delay or frustrate the collection of data and the use of the findings for program modifications and collective action. In addition, the different purposes behind each of these methods (capacity-building, improvements in service delivery, and social/personal transformation) may frustrate the users of participatory processes if they try to accomplish multiple goals with the adoption of these methods (Table 13.2).

Table 13.2 Comparing Empowerment-Oriented Evaluation Approaches

	Self-Evaluation	Empowerment Evaluation	Participatory Action Research
Role of the researcher	Consultant; works for agency or funder	Consultant; works for agency or participants	Consultant; partner with participants
Purpose	Evaluate agency services Increase service effectiveness Enhance internal and external accountability	Self-determination Capacity-building and skill development Enhance internal accountability of the program	Capacity-building Develop a critical consciousness among participants Social change
Process	Internal agency work teams; may or may not include clients	Internal agency work teams; includes agency clientele Method can be used by collaborative partnerships or service networks	Work team, task force, or coalition, most often located outside the parameters of one agency Most of the participants are members of an oppressed group Can be used for intra-agency improvements but more often focuses on community problems, new agency start-ups, or as a means to address the effects of institutionalized oppression
Outcome	Improves service quality	Increases participant skills and control	Alleviates oppression

OUTCOME EVALUATION

Regardless of whether evaluations are conducted by experts or by program participants in data collection or analysis, they are primarily used to assess the impact of a program *(outcomes)* or what happens in the program *(process)*. Outcome evaluations are conducted, often at the request of program funders, to establish whether programs have achieved the desired results. It is assumed that if the program does not produce the intended results, the program will be modified to make it more effective. Consequently, outcome evaluation can focus on one or several measures of achievement: program objectives, outcomes, or the relationship of program costs to benefits produced. Outcome evaluations must be rigorous enough to produce results that can be disseminated to program funders to verify program effectiveness or can be used to justify program modifications or termination.

Measuring Objectives

The program's objectives serve as the starting place for program evaluations. As described in Chapter 6, objectives must be measurable, be time limited, and contain an evaluation mechanism. They must be developed in relation to a specific program plan and specify processes and tasks to be completed. Program objectives must incorporate the program's theory of action and describe how the program works and what the program is expected to do (outcomes). Program objectives can be explicit or implicit, shifting in relation to demands of external funders, constituents, and the social, economic, or political environment. However, most government and foundation donors use objectives specified in funding proposals and performance-based contracts as benchmarks for program accomplishment. Determination of the program's success will be based on the degree to which these objectives are achieved. Objectives can be either absolute or relative. An *absolute objective* is one in which a predetermined standard is to be attained. A *relative objective* specifies that a proportion of a problem is to be addressed or a percentage of a population is to be served (Hardina, 2002). Because of the difficulty in measuring social service outcomes, many of the objectives to be measured actually are immediate program outputs, such as the number of people served or the actions taken by staff rather than long-term outcomes or changes in individuals, groups, families, organizations, and communities (see Chapters 6 and 12). Case records and data from the organization's management information system may be sufficient to track and report the accomplishment of objectives. Objectives can include indicators of program quality as well as measures of consumer satisfaction with services.

BOX 13.1 OBJECTIVES FOR AN EMERGENCY SHELTER PROGRAM

Goal: To reduce the number of women sleeping on the streets

Program: Outreach and Advocacy Network for the Homeless

Objective 1: To place 50 women in emergency shelter beds each night by March 31, 2006. (Absolute Objective)

Evaluation criteria: Number of women placed in shelter beds each night.

Objective 2:	To provide counseling services to 15% of the homeless women in the downtown area by June 30, 2006. (Relative Objective) **Evaluation criteria:** Number of women who receive counseling services.
Objective 3:	To place 10 women per month in transitional housing by September 30, 2006. (Absolute Objective) **Evaluation criteria:** Number of women who receive transitional housing placements.
Objective 4:	To reduce the number of homeless women in the downtown area by 25% by December 31, 2006. (Relative Objective) **Evaluation criteria:** Pre-test and posttest measures of the number of homeless women in the downtown area.

It is important to note that objectives, outputs, and outcomes in empowerment-oriented organizations should also address issues identified in the empowerment model. Rapp et al. (1993) argue that outcomes should focus on consumer strengths, consumer-driven definitions of improvements in their quality of life (for example, friendships, access to education and employment, or improvements in the surrounding community), and increases in political participation. McKenzie (1999) suggests that social justice-related outcomes, such as reducing power inequities between members of the elite and members of the marginalized groups, also should be evaluated.

Measuring Outcomes

Outcome evaluations focus on whether the program has produced long-term changes in individuals, groups, families, or communities. Many organizations specify formal evaluation procedures in conjunction with the establishment of goals and objectives. For example, an organization that conducts home visits to improve child health and development might choose to assess effectiveness using a number of different measures, including the number of home visits made in a timely manner, the characteristics of family members, and child abuse risk factors as well as improvements in child health and development (Duggan, Windham, McFarlane, Fuddy, Rohde, Buchbinder, & Sia, 2000).

Standardized measurement tools are often used to determine success rates in programs that provide mental health services or that otherwise focus on changing individual attitudes, knowledge, or emotional status.

However, agencies should use these tools with caution. Many instruments are copyrighted, meaning that agencies must pay a fee in order to use them. In addition, some of these tools may not be culturally, gender, or age appropriate for agency clientele (Salahu-Din, 2003).

Another issue of concern about standardized scales is that they must be both reliable and valid. *Validity* refers to the degree to which the instrument actually measures the desired concept. *Reliability* refers to whether the instrument is consistent and accurate. Will the scale, if conditions remain the same, measure the same concept the same way upon repeated measurement? The validity and reliability of scales can be statistically assessed in several ways. Most scale developers provide psychometric information about their instruments. We can say that a scale has *face validity* if the general public or experts in the field would agree that the scale does in fact measure the intended concept. *Concurrent validity* pertains to whether the instrument can be correlated with similar measures of the same concept for which validity has been determined. *Construct validity* pertains to whether there is a correlation between the concepts in question and other indicators that measure concepts that in theory should be related to one another (Royse, 2004). For example, we would expect that a new scale to measure the degree to which social workers feel empowered in the workplace should be highly correlated with previous scales that were designed to measure worker empowerment. We also would expect a high, positive correlation between two scales designed to measure worker empowerment and related concepts such as personal feelings of control or job satisfaction.

Measures of reliability commonly used to assess scales are *test–retest reliability* (will the test produce the same measurement over time?) and *split-half reliability* (locating scale items in two different parts of a survey or study and assessing whether the answers correlate with one another; Royse, 2004). We also can assess *internal consistency reliability,* or Cronbach's alpha. This is a statistical test of whether respondents who answer one question in a specific manner will be consistent in their responses to items that measure a similar concept. Often the items assessed for internal reliability are responses to questions that make up a single scale. For example, research on empowerment indicates that there is a positive relationship between feelings of personal control in the workplace and job satisfaction. Therefore, if a respondent answers a question on an empowerment scale in a way that indicates that he or she feels a high degree of personal control over the workplace environment, we would expect that person to indicate that he or she also has a high degree of job satisfaction.

An additional method used to establish reliability is *interrater reliability,* in which two or more people conduct either an observation or a content analysis of qualitative data or an already produced product (such as a case record) to determine the degree to which each of the raters agrees on the assessment (Neuman, 2003).

Measures of reliability and validity are considered to be good or adequate, as measured on a scale from 0.00 (low) to 1.00 (high), if they exceed .70 (Royse, 2004). Reliability and validity measures have been established for a number of empowerment scales. For example, Leslie and Holzab (1998) tested their empowerment scale against Rotter's locus of control scale (personal sense of ability to control one's personal environment) as well as measures of job satisfaction. All three measures were highly correlated with one another. They also established, through repeated tests administered to social workers, that items on these scales had a high degree (>.70) of interrater reliability.

Parsons (1999) developed a measure of client empowerment that included three subscales: personal (self-awareness; self-esteem), interpersonal (assertiveness; problem-solving), and community/political participation (joining organizations; voting). Repeated testing using a population of 95 mental health consumers indicated that each of the subscales was highly correlated with the others. The interitem reliability of the scale (Cronbach's alpha) was .89. Study participants who had received the empowerment-oriented agency services for more than 2 years scored higher on the empowerment scale than clients who had received services for less than 2 years.

Standardized tests can be found in books (such as *Measures for Clinical Practice* by Fischer & Corcoran, 1994) that feature a compilation of scales that can be used in a variety of outcome studies. Research articles in professional journals and well as web searches can be used to identify appropriate measurement instruments. However, given that standardized scales may not be sufficient to establish the effectiveness of an intervention or to adequately measure complex concepts across a number of ethnic or other cultural groups (see Cultural Competency), evaluators should consider using a variety of measures such as behavioral indicators, interviews, or surveys to supplement their findings. An additional type of reliability, *convergent analysis,* is established when multiple measures produce similar results (Hardina, 2002).

It should be noted that appropriate indicators do not exist for many outcome studies. Consequently, evaluators may need to develop standardized tools and surveys for measuring outcomes. Time and financial resources often limit the degree to which evaluators conduct statistical analysis of the reliability and validity of these measures. Easy-to-use tests of reliability and validity include pretesting instruments on a small group of people with characteristics similar to people included in the study and using multiple measures of the same concept. Qualitative researchers argue that consulting potential respondents on the design of instruments, data collection methods, or data analysis are good methods for ensuring that instruments adequately reflect the experiences of the people studied and are sufficiently accurate to measure program outcomes (Patton, 1997; Secret et al., 1999).

A range of research designs can be used to determine program success. Often research studies are conducted to control for confounding variables that might exaggerate or mask the real effect of the intervention. Demographic characteristics of participants often are confounding variables. For example, women often respond to alcoholism treatment differently than do men (Weisner & Schmidt, 1992). In addition, threats to internal validity inherent in the research design can affect results. Problems with internal validity can include the following:

- *Selection:* The sample is not representative of the population. Some groups are overrepresented or underrepresented in the sample.
- *History:* Participants may differ in terms of their personal history, which can affect the way they respond to research procedures.
- *Maturation:* People develop at different rates, which can affect the way they respond during a study. Maturation is especially a problem in studies with children. A 6-year-old will respond in a much different way than will an 8-year-old. However, maturation also can refer to natural states in adults during the course of a study. For example, a person's reaction time during a day-long study of agility may be greater during the morning than during the afternoon as a result of the passage of time, fatigue, or hunger.
- *Testing:* People react to the testing instrument and may alter their responses, especially if the test is repeated a number of times during the course of the study.
- *Statistical Regression:* Extreme scores on a testing instrument may move closer to the mean scores for all participants upon repeated testing. In pre-test and posttest studies, statistical regression can make the intervention appear more or less effective than it actually is.
- *Mortality:* People drop out of studies conducted over long periods. Therefore, the group of participants at the beginning of a study may differ from the group of participants at the conclusion of the study.
- *Instrumentation:* The way in which the research instrument measures a phenomenon may change over time. Generally, problems with instrumentation occur as a result of human error. Procedures used to administer the study may be altered (for example, distribution of the instrument or inclusion of people meeting specific criteria). Human observers may fail to see some aspect of the event under study because of fatigue or hunger (Royse & Thyer, 1996).

The best method for controlling for confounding and other extraneous variables uses a random experimental design (Williams, Unrau, &

Grinnell, 1998). Participants are randomly selected and assigned to an experimental group or a control group. The intervention is withheld from the control group. Participants are tested or measured on a particular attribute, perception, or behavior; the intervention is given to the experimental group; and then both groups are tested a second time and their scores compared. If the scores from both groups are the same on the posttest study, the intervention is judged to be ineffective. If the experimental group's scores are significantly different (as verified through statistical analysis), the intervention is judged to be effective.

Although random experimental designs are ideal for determining program effectiveness and controlling for extraneous variables, organizations seldom have sufficient resources to establish formal experiments. Funders seldom provide additional funds that can explicitly be used to determine whether programs actually work. Withholding treatment from people in need can be an ethical violation (Neuman, 2003). In addition, most social service programs have a small number of clients enrolled in a single program, and randomly selecting clients and placing some in a control or alternative treatment group would not be feasible. In another research dilemma, randomization is also not possible because some programs are "full coverage," that is, they are expected to benefit everyone in a community or region, or they cannot exclude participants or select people for participation in either a control group and or an experimental group (for example, a campaign to increase child safety seat use in cars).

Consequently, most program evaluations implement quasi-experimental designs, such as one-group pretest and posttest studies or comparisons of a group of people under treatment to a control group that was not necessarily chosen at random. For example, a control group can be constructed from people who are on the waiting list for service. Children in a child development program can be compared to older brothers and sisters on key development indicators. Research designs that can be used effectively with small populations or where creation of a control group would be difficult include the following:

- Comparisons of the pretest and posttest scores for each participant on one or more outcome indicators.
- Using all members of preexisting groups to serve as the experimental and the control groups.
- Using social indicator data collected by government agencies (for example, using U.S. Census on poverty rates in a specific community to determine if an economic development program has been successful in increasing the income of neighborhood residents).
- Time series analysis, using repeated measures over a number of time periods to track social indicators or caseload data (Figure 13.1).

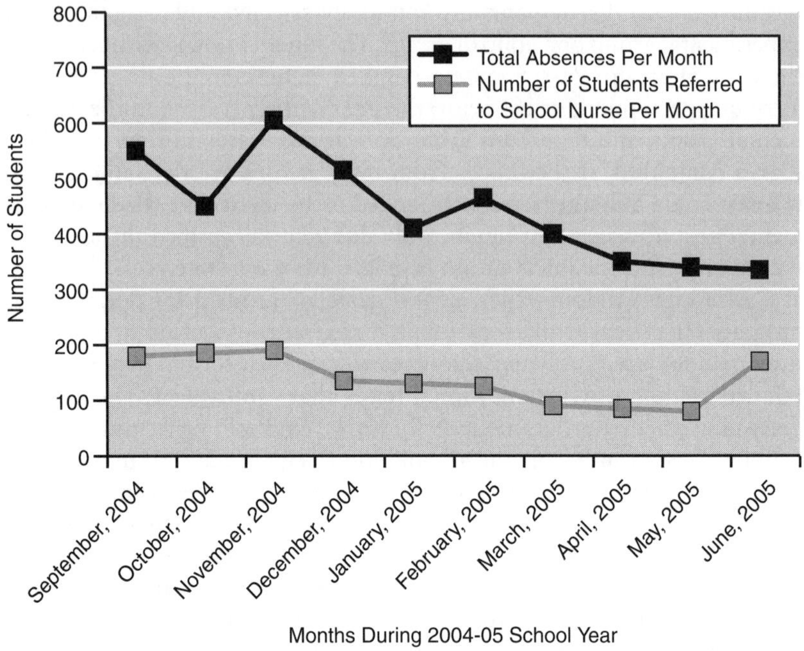

Figure 13.1 Interrupted time series analysis for a full-coverage school breakfast program. All children in a small school district began to receive a free school breakfast in December 2004. The program's theory of action was that ensuring access to school breakfast for all children enrolled in the school district would reduce the total number of absences and referrals to the school nurse each month. Trend lines for each outcome measure indicate that the program appears to be effective. However, time series analysis cannot control for environmental factors and unexpected events that may affect the results.

- Using statistical controls to hold constant the effects of confounding variables (such as cross-tabulation or regression analysis, Table 13.3).
- Using a quasi-experimental design in which participants are separated into groups and different levels of the intervention are compared (Chambers et al., 1992; Royse & Thyer, 1996).

Table 13.3 Annual Income for Graduates of a Job Training Program by Gender and Education

	Male			Female		
Education Level	H.S. Dropout	H.S. Graduate	Some College	H.S. Dropout	H.S. Graduate	Some College
None	6 (15.0%)	4 (7.0%)	0 (0.0%)	10 (19.2%)	6 (12.0%)	1 (1.6%)
≤$9,999	9 (22.5%)	6 (10.5%)	2 (3.1%)	18 (34.6%)	12 (24.0%)	4 (6.6%)
$10,000–$19,999	18 (45.0%)	12 (21.1%)	5 (7.8%)	11 (21.2%)	20 (40%)	8 (13.1%)
$20,000–$35,999	5 (12.5%)	25 (43.9%)	36 (56.3%)	8 (15.4%)	3 (6.0%)	42 (68.9%)
≥$36,000	2 (5.0%)	10 (17.5%)	21 (32.8%)	5 (15.4%)	9 (18.0%)	6 (9.8%)
Total	40 (100.0%)	57 (100.0%)	64 (100.0%)	52 (100.0%)	50 (100.0%)	61 (100.0%)

Note: Table allows for comparisons by both education level and gender. In addition to the number of people who fit into each category, percentages are calculated to allow for direct comparisons across subsamples that do not have an equal number of participants. The table clearly shows that women and high school (H.S.) dropouts had lower annual wages than men and high school graduates and people with some college education.

These designs can be used effectively to measure the impact of empowerment-oriented interventions on clients, community residents, and organizational staff. For example, Itzhaky and York (2002) used a quasi-experimental, pretest and posttest design to measure the impact of their community empowerment model (described in Chapter 6). The study included a number of outcomes measured before and after the intervention: the number of community volunteers, scores on a test that measured self-esteem and feelings of mastery of the surrounding environment, and scores on measures of family, service, and community empowerment. The researchers verified substantial increases in the number of community volunteers during the course of the project. They also found significant increases in self-esteem and empowerment scores among the community activists who participated in the study.

In developing new interventions, evaluators try to maximize the external validity of their research or the degree to which results are generalizable to other respondents, organizations, population groups, communities, or regions of the country (Neuman, 2003). Threats to external validity can include the fact that people will change their behavior if they know they are under study (reactivity), the use of multiple treatments (the impact of a single treatment cannot be assessed), and the combined impact of selection bias and the intervention. Because some demographic groups respond to interventions differently than do other groups, the underrepresentation or overrepresentation of one or more demographic groups can significantly alter the results of the study and make it difficult to generalize findings.

Many agency-based evaluation studies use preexisting groups of people or include the entire population of clients in their study. This practice often is necessary because the agency has limited resources available for evaluation and because client populations are small. Consequently, many program evaluations use nonprobability sampling (Royse & Thyer, 1996). Evaluators will need to assess whether the people who actually participate in the study are representative of client population, staff, key informants, and other constituents who may be included in the study.

To actually generalize findings, a representative, randomly selected sample is needed. To generalize findings to a group of clients, the sample must be drawn from the entire group of clients. To generalize findings to a group of agencies, participants must be selected from each of these agencies, or a portion of the participating agencies must be randomly selected for participation in the study. If we intend to generalize our findings to every empowerment-oriented social service organization in the United States, we would need to construct a list of the population of these organizations and randomly select participants from the list, a time-consuming and costly process. In most cases, generalizability is not an issue of concern in evaluation studies. Most often evaluators are interested only in the impact of one program or the impact of several similar programs (Royse & Thyer, 1996).

The main reason why external validity has limited importance for outcome evaluations is that organizational staff and client characteristics vary so much from site to site that it is difficult to say that what works in one organization will actually work in another. Evaluators should, however, disseminate their findings. Evaluation reports and "best practices" literature provide guidance to other social service professionals who want to choose from among a variety of program options or determine what program components are likely to be effective (Chambers et al., 1992).

Looking at Costs and Benefits

One method for examining organizational outcomes involves an economic analysis of the costs of service delivery. However, the two techniques commonly used, cost–benefit analysis and cost–efficiency analysis, move beyond a simple examination of program expenditures (Royse & Thyer, 1996). These methods require that costs be examined in relationship to the outcomes or benefits associated with the program. Cost–benefit analysis requires that a dollar value be placed on program benefits and assumes that the best program will be the one in which benefits outweigh the costs. Cost–efficiency analysis compares the quantity of benefits associated with various program options to program expenditures. For example, Zhou, Euler, McPhee, Nguygen, Lam, Wong, and Mock (2003) conducted cost–benefit analysis and cost–effectiveness analysis of media and community mobilization approaches to increase the number of hepatitis B vaccinations among Vietnamese children and adolescents in Houston and Dallas. They found that both approaches were somewhat effective in increasing the number of children who received all three doses of the vaccine. The cost of each approach per child vaccinated (cost-effectiveness) was $339 for the media campaign and $420 for community mobilization. The media campaign was more expensive than the community mobilization campaign but was more cost-effective because it persuaded more families to have their children vaccinated. The benefits of each approach were measured in terms of cost savings. The researchers found that the cost savings associated with both approaches were significant; the cost savings per child for the media campaign was $5,300 and for community mobilization was $5,034. Cost savings was calculated based on estimates of the dollar value of years of lives saved as a consequence of receiving the vaccine.

Government agencies and private corporations often use cost–benefit and cost–efficiency analysis methods to choose from among a number of options for new programs. In some situations, nonprofit organizations and government organizations use these analysis methods to "sell" program options to the public, emphasizing that the costs of social service programs outweigh potential costs to taxpayers. Cost–benefit analysis and cost–efficiency analysis have some important limitations, however. Translating the benefits or even all of the costs of many social services into dollar amounts may be difficult (Royse & Thyer, 1996). For example, cost–benefit analysis sometimes uses figures from insurance actuarial tables to estimate the cost of a life. These figures vary substantially by gender and occupation and are based on estimates of lifetime earnings. Many people would argue that such assumptions are biased toward high-income earners and are essentially unfair. Also, estimating the positive benefits of counseling services (for example, increasing feelings of self-efficacy or reducing depression) can be especially difficult. Instead, many cost–benefit analyses use estimates of cost reduction in lieu of benefits (for example, tobacco prevention programs are expected to reduce hospitalization costs for smokers paid by government or private insurers). Another issue associated with cost–benefit analysis is projecting anticipated benefits over time. Estimated rates of inflation (called *discount rates*) are used to calculate future costs and benefits (Patton & Sawicki, 1993). Consequently, analysts cannot accurately anticipate these costs. In addition, many programs have unintended effects (called *externalities*) or spillover effects (impacts on other programs or people) that could increase either the cost or benefits of a particular project. For example, a new job training program used to place 18-year-olds in construction jobs could result in the displacement of older workers who receive higher wages. This in turn could increase government costs associated with unemployment benefits.

The biggest concern about using cost–benefit analysis from a social work perspective is related to the distributional effects of specific programs (Prigoff, 2000). Many nonprofit, public, or corporate projects may benefit one group while disadvantaging another. For example, a group home for ex-offenders would have beneficial effects for residents of the house but could reduce the real estate value of neighboring homes. Many projects tend to produce benefits for people who already have resources and have negative impacts on people in poverty or those otherwise disadvantaged. Cost–benefit analysis uses the assumption that no program option should be pursued if the potential benefits for one group do not exceed the costs to others. This is called the *principle of pareto-optimality* (Patton & Sawicki, 1993). However, some economists believe that a project could be authorized if it provides potential rather than actual benefits to target groups. Cost–benefit analysis also provides limited guidance on how to make distributional decisions (Prigoff, 2000). Although estimates of the impact of project costs and benefits on different ethnic groups or people at different income levels can be made, the actual decision about who would benefit and who should experience negative consequences of any program option usually is determined through the political process (Table 13.4).

Table 13.4 Cost–Efficiency and Cost-Benefit Analysis and Distributional Issues

Purpose: To compare the costs and benefits of outreach programs to enroll community residents in treatment programs for chemical dependency. The analysis assumes benefits are increased work earnings and decreased health care costs.

	Cost	No. of People Contacted	Percent Enrolled in Treatment Program	Cost per Contact	Cost per Person Enrolled	Percent of Low-income Enrollees
Cost–efficiency analysis						
Door-to-door outreach	$500,000	400	25%	$1,250.00	$5,000.00	75%
Media campaign	$250,000	10,000	10%	$25.00	$250.00	25%

	Cost	Benefit	Benefit/Cost Ratio	Percent of Low-Income Beneficiaries	Benefits for Low-Income Residents
Cost–benefit analysis					
Door-to-door outreach	$500,000	$5,000,000	10	25%	$1,250,000.00
Media campaign	$250,000	$3,000,000	12	10%	$300,000.00

	Door-to-Door Outreach	Media Campaign
Net benefits to groups in society		
Low-income families	$1,250,000	$300,000
Middle- and upper-income taxpayers	$3,250,000	$2,450,000
Net benefit to society	$4,500,000	$2,750,000

Note: This analysis assumes that the low-income group pays no taxes. The program costs (paid in taxes) are subtracted from the program benefits for middle- and upper-income taxpayers. Option 2 (the media campaign) is clearly superior to option 1 (door-to-door outreach) in terms of both cost-efficiency and the benefit/cost ratio. However, option 1 (door-to-door outreach) provides more benefits to low-income residents. Door-to-door outreach also provides greater net benefits to society.

EXAMINING THE PROGRAM'S INPUT AND THROUGHPUT: PROCESS EVALUATION AND IMPLEMENTATION ANALYSIS

Process evaluations and implementation analysis assume that the program is a "black box," with input, throughput, and output (see Chapter 2). These modalities usually require use of a number of data collection methods, including interviews, document analysis, observations, or surveys. Data typically are gathered from a variety of organizational participants: administrators, front-line staff, and clients. These evaluations also can be used to examine communication patterns, program policies, and interaction between program staff and clients or representatives of other organizations. Process evaluations are often published in the professional literature as case studies that use interviews, observation, and document analysis to examine an organization's efforts to perform specific interventions.

A process analysis examines how a program works and why the program is or is not effective. Many process evaluations are formative, taking place during the intervention phase of the process. Formative evaluations often rely on data obtained using management information systems and the perceptions of program participants about what they are doing, whether they have the resources they need, and their roles in the organization (Patton, 1997). Formative evaluations also examine the characteristics of program participants and whether services and other resources are distributed equitably in the organization. Are some client groups receiving services while others are not? Are some staff members more likely to be promoted than others? If disparities are present, one purpose of a formative evaluation is to examine why differences in resource distribution or service use occur and the effect of these disparities on the organization's ability to deliver the service (Chambers et al., 1992). The evaluator and the evaluation team will then recommend modifications to the way resources are distributed. Other questions addressed in a formative evaluation pertain to clients' perceptions about the strengths and weaknesses of the program, staff perceptions of their interactions with one another, and whether the program is doing what it has been designed to do (Patton, 1997).

Process analyses are undertaken when outcome evaluations indicate that programs are not achieving their goals or when researchers are interested in replicating the success of new programs but cannot explain why the programs are successful. Consequently, these types of evaluations try to explain what has happened in the program, often relying on qualitative data (including observations, in-depth interviews with clients, staff, and other key informants) and focus groups to paint a picture of how the program is working. One main concern of a process evaluation is determining whether the program was offered in a manner consistent with the intentions of program planners. If the offering was not consistent, what happened in the program to alter the previous plans? Did unexpected events or differences in client characteristics affect what the program accomplished? For example, Linhorst and Eckert (2003) conducted a study to determine whether a mental hospital had the appropriate structures and processes in place to adequately empower patients. They used agency documents and focus groups with staff members and clients to conduct the evaluation. They found that many clients were involved in decisions that pertained to their own care. However, barriers to client involvement included limited treatment options available to some clients as well as the severity of illness among some client groups.

Implementation analysis focuses on whether policies and procedures have actually been implemented in the organization in the manner intended by decision-makers. Program implementation differs from process analysis in that it is primarily concerned with how policies mandated by a source external to the organization are actually carried out or how the implementation of policies vary across different organizations or locations. In most cases, the programs in question are mandated by government agencies or are implemented as a condition of foundation funding. Many factors can affect the way a program is implemented, including organizational culture, staff resistance, inadequate funding, improperly trained staff, the personal characteristics of program participants (for example, gender, age, and ethnicity), and local or regional variations in how organizations are operated and maintained. Many of the questions examined by implementation analysis are similar to those addressed in a process evaluation. According to Patton (1997), additional types of implementation studies can include the following:

- *Component Evaluation:* This method of evaluation focuses on one particular aspect or part of a program (for example, intake services, referrals, intervention planning, staff–client interaction, or a specific type of intervention that can be differentiated from other services).
- *Effort Evaluation:* The primary focus of this type of evaluation is the amount of activity or work that is put into the program and the quality of that work. Effort evaluation can simply look at the number of qualified staff hired for the program, client/staff ratios, and the number of clients actually served. It also can examine the resources (money, facilities, worker time, training modules, etc.) that are devoted to the program.
- *Treatment Specification:* This type of evaluation is used to precisely identify the components of an intervention and the theory of action used to deliver the service and produce outcomes.

Program implementation analysis also examines the degree to which a program has "drifted" from its original intent and program specifications or the degree of compliance with the expectations of program sponsors or funders. Common implementation problems include failing to deliver the intended intervention, using the wrong intervention to produce the intended outcome, or providing the intervention inconsistently over time (Chambers et al., 1992).

Implementation analysis usually is intended to provide concrete information on how to make a program more effective. It also can be used to develop and understand issues related to the delivery of new interventions. For example, Bartle, Couchonnal, Canda, and Staker (2002) conducted an implementation analysis of Project EAGLE, a federally funded child development program that used an empowerment approach to deliver services. The researchers used methods associated with organizational ethnography to understand the experiences of program clients and staff members: observations of service delivery and staff meetings, focus groups, and content analysis of agency documents. During the initial stages of the 7-year study, the funding agency, the U.S. Administration on Children, Youth, and Families (ACYF), provided research guidelines and questions for each of the child development programs it funded. The evaluators found that the funding source often emphasized economic self-sufficiency as an outcome rather than improvements in child development or increases in the self-esteem or problem-solving ability of parents. They also found that staff members needed to feel empowered before they could engage clients in the empowerment process. During the course of the study, staff members developed successful strategies to facilitate feelings of empowerment in their clients. According to evaluators:

> Empowerment became viewed as a collaborative effort in which staff and families engaged in activities and relationships to actualize strengths and mobilize community resources. Although staff had professional expertise, they did not wish to be imposers of service goals; the families' self-knowledge was considered an equally important experience. Thus, dialogue and mutual decision making between families and staff was crucial to the process of empowerment. (p. 39)

BOX 13.2 CHOOSING AN EVALUATION DESIGN

Charles has been asked to conduct an evaluation of the male batterer's program affiliated with the Northwest Women's Shelter. He serves as the coordinator for this program. Pang, the executive director, has requested the evaluation for two reasons:

1. The primary funding source, the County Probation Department, wants concrete information about the program's effectiveness in order to reauthorize funding.
2. The shelter is reimbursed by the county based on the number of people who successfully complete the male batterers program. Reimbursements currently do not cover the organization's costs, and many of the participants drop out before they complete the program.

The executive director wants the evaluation to address the following questions:

A. Is the program effective?
B. Why do participants drop out?
C. What actions could be taken in the future to decrease the dropout rate?

Charles has been given 2 weeks to prepare an evaluation plan. He needs to make the following decisions.

- What type of research methodology should be used to address each of these questions?
- Who should be involved in conducting the evaluation?
- What are the potential advantages or disadvantages if Charles conducts the evaluation himself?
- If Charles does not conduct the evaluation, who should be recruited from inside or outside the organization to design the evaluation, collect data, and analyze the results?
- What potential ethical issues is Charles likely to encounter in the evaluation process?

ETHICAL ISSUES

In empowerment evaluation, using mutual dialogue to identify client problems and involving constituents in the evaluation process are components of ethical practice. Conducting evaluations of programs also requires that social workers comply with ethical standards required of all researchers (Reamer, 1998). Issues of importance when either in-house staff performs an evaluation or an outside consultant conducts an assessment include confidentiality, anonymity, and informed consent. In outcome evaluation, a determination must be made as to whether interventions can ethically be withheld from the client. In addition, the security of data, ensuring that case records and other information about respondents are not accessible to anyone other than the researcher or authorized staff members, is a concern. Although these ethical issues most often involve outcome data, evaluation approaches such as implementation analysis, which can involve observation of organizational participants and face-to-face interviews, can pose challenges for the researcher. Participatory approaches to research may require that researchers think creatively about how to address ethical issues.

Confidentiality

The confidentiality of respondents must be protected. No information that could identify respondents should be released to anyone. Protecting confidentiality is critical to persuading clients, particularly those who are members of socially stigmatized groups (for example, the homeless, persons with HIV, or welfare recipients), to participate in a research study and to reply accurately to research questions. Most researchers distinguish between confidentiality and anonymity. In the case of *anonymity,* the researcher does not know the identity of participants or is not able to match the response with the participant (Rubin & Babbie, 2001). Obviously when people are interviewed for a study, the researcher has direct contact with them and therefore knows who has participated. Therefore, *confidentiality* requires simply that the researcher does not release the identity of participants to others.

In some situations, protecting confidentiality requires that the researcher implement procedures to restrict access to the names of participants. Often researchers must track who in their sampling frame actually participated in both the pre-test and posttest studies or replied to a survey. This process often is necessary so that follow-up letters requesting participation can be sent to prospective participants. The general practice used to track respondents while protecting their identities is to assign a code number to each respondent who will be placed on surveys or standardized instruments. However, this practice requires that only the researcher have access to the list, that the list be kept in a secure location, and that the list be destroyed at the conclusion of the study.

Implementation analysis, process evaluations, and participatory approaches often make the protection of confidentiality more difficult for the researcher. An outside evaluator working extensively with agency participants or agency staff conducting an internal evaluation may find that they have personal knowledge that allows them to connect individuals to their responses. In these situations, it is particularly important that clients and staff members who could be at risk of losing services or their jobs be protected from retaliation if they give negative assessments of the organization. Surveys should be collected without any identifying information. Demographic information should be collected with caution, especially in small agencies. For example, in an agency that employs a handful of African Americans, a question on the respondent's ethnic identity may make possible the identification of an individual employee, and then other responses (negative or positive) made by that employee could be attributed to him or her. The respondent, fearing that he or she could be identified, may respond to additional questions in a less than candid manner, limiting the reliability of the data collection instrument.

Protection from Harm and Informed Consent

Participation in a study can have both benefits and risks for participants. Participants can be persuaded to be interviewed, tested, or surveyed by providing them with a cash stipend, meal coupons, bus tokens, and other financial incentives. They also may be informed that their participation can help test the effectiveness of an intervention or that the data will be used to improve programs or help others. The principle of informed consent requires that participants be told before the beginning of a study about the benefits and possible risks involved (Chambers et al., 1992). Situations in which a participant could be adversely affected include physical harm, social stigma, loss of employment, or possible loss of services from a public program or nonprofit organization (Royse, 2004). Some research studies can potentially cause emotional harm or psychological distress by requiring that respondents disclose personal information or recall painful memories (for example, studies of posttraumatic stress disorder or sexual abuse).

The responsibility of the researcher is to minimize potential harm to research subjects. Efforts should be made to minimize physical harm or emotional distress by providing appropriate services (medical care or counseling) to participants who are adversely affected by participation in the study. To ensure that participants are not placed at unnecessary risk, all evaluation studies should be reviewed by institutional review boards (IRBs) located at the agency or the university where the research originates (Royse, 2004). IRBs are panels whose explicit function is to examine the ethical implications of studies and their potential impacts on participants. These boards make recommendations about the types of procedures that researchers should use to comply with ethical standards.

One of the responsibilities of the IRB is to review how the researcher complies with the requirement that all participants be fully informed about risks and benefits. In most studies, participants are asked to sign either a consent form or a letter that provides details about human subjects procedures. This material includes information on potential risks to the participant, strategies used to minimize the risk, and benefits that are expected to accrue to the participant, future program beneficiaries, and/or the public at large (Royse, 2004). Procedures to protect confidentiality or to preserve the anonymity of respondents should be described. Respondents should be assured that no information that could be used to identify them will be used in written reports that may be read by agency staff or the public. Respondents also should be assured that information that potentially could identify them will be available only to the researcher and will be stored in a secure location; tapes and other information that could be used for identification purposes will be destroyed at the conclusion of the study. Cover letters should give the name of the IRB that assessed the study for human subjects protections. Letters should include contact information for the researcher in case the respondent wants more information or would like to withdraw from the study.

Voluntary Participation

One of the basic premises of human subjects protections is that participation in research studies should be voluntary (Royse, 2004). Participants have the right to refuse to participate in the study, and they can withdraw from the study at any time. The researcher should include this information in the cover letter and consent form. Although it may seem obvious that participants are able to freely give consent to participate, this may not be the case in instances where participants are mandatory clients (for example, prisoners or parents who have children in foster care) or are receiving a service from the agency that is evaluating its programs (Maeve, 1998). People may feel compelled to participate even in situations with possible substantial harm or perception of harm associated with participation. For example, a welfare recipient may feel compelled to answer questions in an evaluation of a welfare reform initiative if his or her refusal to participate is perceived to be associated with termination from the program. Information provided by the researcher should assure participants that no penalty is associated with nonparticipation or refusal to respond to any research question.

Cultural Competency

Cultural competency in the conduct of research can be defined as "including different perspectives [and] values" and "being aware of cultural blinders and biases" (Patton, 1997, p. 151). Researchers should make every effort to ensure that research design, data collection, and analysis are culturally appropriate to the populations being studied in order to maximize the degree to which the evaluation is representative of the population studied (Chambers et al., 1992). Much of the empirical research used to develop theories was based on western culture (Europe, the United States, and Canada) and often included only white male participants (Harding, 1998). One reason why qualitative methods and ethnographic research are used in social work practice is to gain knowledge about the lifestyles of people who are not part of the dominant culture (Lum, 1996). Program evaluators need to use cultural knowledge in designing studies that include all organizational clientele regardless of gender, age, sexual orientation, social class, language preference, religious background, and race. A representative sample of organizational clientele is needed for program evaluations so that treatments can be designed that are effective for all segments of the client population (Salahu-Din, 2003).

Culturally appropriate practices should be used to recruit participants and to provide incentives for participation. They also should be used during the development of cover letters, consent forms, and research instruments. For example, in some Asian immigrant cultures it is not appropriate for a man to interview a woman in her own home without the presence of a male relative. In such cases, interviews may need to be conducted by women or by a male/female team. Alternatively, the interview could include both the female and a male relative.

Researchers should make an effort to determine if the language used in research material is appropriate in terms of literacy level and dialect. It goes without saying that some research instruments and other materials must be translated into languages other than English. It should not be taken for granted that word-for-word translations are always appropriate; in most cases, a literal word-for-word translation will not provide adequate context to transmit the original meaning of the English language instrument. The translation process must ensure that the appropriate dialect and education level are used. Some professional translators focus on formal language (suitable for business exchanges or legal proceedings) rather than the informal language used in most ethnic cultures among friends, relatives, and neighbors. Translators used in the research process should be knowledgeable about the appropriate style language that can solicit accurate responses from participants. One additional safeguard that can be used to ensure good translations is "back translation," which involves translation (usually by someone other than the original translator) of the instrument back into English (Royse, 2004). The second translation should be close in content to the original English version. In addition, the researcher should pretest any instruments or consent forms and should consult extensively with research participants (using participatory methods) before implementing the study.

Evaluators should be aware that standardized instruments sometimes are inadequate to measure diversity in behaviors and beliefs (Royse, 2004). Most of these instruments were developed to measure psychological states and attitudes among members of the dominant culture. Consequently, cross-cultural comparisons made using these instruments may put persons of color or people for whom English is a second language at a disadvantage. For example, an instrument designed to measure self-esteem could result in lower scores for Asian Americans because humility is considered a positive social value in Asian cultures but sometimes is associated with low self-esteem in western cultures.

Trust is an issue of concern in evaluation studies with people from marginalized groups (Reisch & Rivera, 1999). Low-income people have often been the subject of numerous research studies conducted by members of the dominant culture. Sometimes participation in such studies has been required in exchange for medical care, mental health treatment, and social services. In some cases, people have not been adequately informed about possible risks of participation and may have been harmed as a consequence of a medical experiment or other type of intervention. One example of this occurrence is the Tuskegee experiments conducted on African-American men in Alabama between 1932 and 1968. The original treatment for syphilis offered to the participants was ineffective and may have caused them harm. When penicillin, which was effective, was introduced as a treatment in the 1940s, it was not given to the participants (Salahu-Din, 1993). As a result, many participants in this experiment became seriously ill or died of the disease. Similar studies conducted in low-income people and communities of color have involved deception about interventions and have failed to adequately provide for informed consent. In most instances, misrepresentation and deceit are considered unethical practices in research. However, double-blind studies (a placebo or sugar pill is given to a control group of participants while the intervention is available to others; neither group is aware of which pills they receive) and studies in which participants are not informed that they will be observed by a researcher may be acceptable in some instances. Such studies should undergo rigorous IRB assessment.

One of the processes used to establish trusting relationships is a method primarily used in qualitative research, called *entry* (Berg, 1998). In ethnographic studies, researchers must familiarize themselves with the community through observation, conversational interviews with members, and participation in cultural events and the daily life of the community. Successful entry into the community often requires an explicit invitation from community members and the use of informal social networks to gain access to research subjects (Neuman, 2003).

BOX 13.3 CULTURALLY COMPETENT RESEARCH

Maribel has been hired by the Chinese Aid Society to conduct a needs assessment that will focus on the prevalence of depression among elderly Chinese immigrants. Maribel knows from her past experience as a geriatric researcher that elderly people often live in isolation and may be reluctant to participate in formal research studies. She has identified several research instruments that are commonly used to measure depression among adults. During the first stage of her study, Maribel pretests her depression scale using several respondents whom she believes are representative of the target population for this study. Most of the instruments are returned blank or with missing responses.

- What steps should Maribel take to address this problem?
- What information should she gather about her respondents before she starts her study?
- What information sources could she use to learn more about her potential respondents?
- What should Maribel do to ensure that her research instruments, methodology, and data collection methods are culturally competent?

DATA ANALYSIS AND REPORT WRITING

Once the data have been collected, an analysis must be made and a report disseminating the findings written. Analysis of data by constituents or participatory research–related work teams will make the process more difficult and time consuming but will ensure that results reflect the day-to-day experiences of program participants. Participatory methods also help ensure that the research actually "fits" with the information needs of organizational decision-makers. Consequently, it becomes more likely that the recommendations made by the researchers or evaluation team will actually be used to improve the program (Fetterman, 2001; Patton, 1997).

Participatory research studies or reports that will be disseminated to a wide audience should include funding sources, key informants, staff members, and constituents. The report should include data analysis and presentation methods that can be easily understood by nonacademic audiences. Study findings should be presented in a manner that is respectful of the knowledge and experiences of the key beneficiaries and decision-makers (Hardina, 2002).

Reports should focus exclusively on the research questions that program constituents want answered and should be packaged in such a way that administrators can easily use the information to make good decisions about changes in program operation. Data analysis methods probably should be limited to descriptive statistics (frequencies, means, and standard deviations) and narratives, based on qualitative interviews and observations that describe common themes and patterns. Inferential statistics may be appropriate in some instances when formal hypotheses have been tested in outcome studies. However, the report should provide the reader with information about what these numbers mean and how they should be interpreted. The report should include some numerical information about how the program affects the various demographic groups it serves. Is the intervention more effective for men or for women? Is the success rate the same for members of all ethnic groups served by the organization? Use of qualitative data, obtained through personal interviews, observations, or focus groups, may be necessary to determine whether members of some demographic groups experience the program (access to services, cultural competency, and job satisfaction) differently from members of other groups. This information is important because it can point out disparities in the way people are treated by the organization and its programs and consequently will provide detailed information that can be used for program modifications.

Reports that list key findings, use graphs and tables to present results, and briefly summarize the implications of the results may be sufficient to inform participants, funders, and the public about the effectiveness or quality of services. It is essential, however, that these reports also offer concrete recommendations about how the information collected should be used to start new programs, modify current services, or terminate program services that are ineffective or not heavily used. In some cases, information in the report can help organizations struggling with fiscal restraints choose from among a number of options for reducing service delivery or eliminating some program components.

The structure of the research report may vary with the intended audience, the types of data collected or approaches to evaluation (process or outcome), and the purpose of the study (Hardina, 2002; Williams et al., 1998). However, key components of evaluation reports include the following:

1. *Introductory Information:* The first few pages of the report should include a title page with the title of the report and author credits, an abstract or brief summary of the purpose of the report, methodology, and major findings. In long reports, substitute an executive summary for the abstract. The executive summary

should contain a list of major findings and recommendations, usually formatted as an outline with bullet points. Reports longer than five pages should include a table of contents.

2. *Problem Statement:* This section of the report should include information on the background and purpose of the study as well as a description of the problem to be addressed by the program/intervention, its scope, and its impact on the target population or community. A description of the organization, group of people, or coalition that is conducting the study should be provided. Information about the purpose of the evaluation and the type of information needs addressed by the study should be included. The goals and objectives of the program evaluated and the evaluation criteria should be provided in this section.
3. *Literature Review:* This section should contain a review of the theoretical, empirical, or "best practice" literature in relation to the type of program offered and its intended outcome. However, if the audience is the public at large or program constituents, this section need not be extensive or overly technical. If the purpose of the report is to convince funders to renew a grant or contract, the inclusion of technical information that verifies the effectiveness of the program model examined would be beneficial. Be sure to include information about the program's theory of action—how the program is expected to work, and what outcomes the program is expected to produce. Remember that in an outcome evaluation, the intervention (program) is always the independent variable and the outcome measures the dependent variables. This should be made explicit in the literature review.
4. *Methodology:* This section should include information on the evaluation methodology used: sampling, data collection, research design, and data analysis methods.

    The primary evaluation questions addressed and their links to outcome measures and objectives should be restated in this section. Key concepts examined should be clearly defined. A description of measurement tools and steps used to assess validity and reliability should be included. The report should contain a description of how human subjects will be protected and the methods used to ensure that research instruments and data collection techniques are culturally appropriate. This section of the report should include a plan for data analysis that explains statistical or qualitative data analysis procedures in language that can be understood by a member of the intended audience (for example, someone with a limited education, a high school graduate, or a college-educated professional).

5. *Results:* This section of the report should contain the most important study findings. The report should contain a demographic profile of participants and address the major research questions identified earlier in the report. Charts and graphs should be used to display quantitative findings as clearly as possible. For qualitative studies or when reporting on findings that were obtained through open-ended interviews and unstructured observations, a written narrative summarizing the values and perspectives of respondents and/or conclusions drawn from the observations of the evaluation participants is needed.
6. *Conclusions:* The final section of the body of the report should include a brief summary of the most important findings. Are these findings consistent with previous research or best practice literature? If not, how do they differ? The report should contain recommendations for change that are directly tied to the research questions and that are based on the data analysis. There should be an implementation plan for putting recommendations into action. This section should contain a brief description of the limitations of the study and any remaining research questions that should be addressed in future studies.
7. *Appendices:* Appendices for a typical research report can include copies of research instruments, copies of consent forms, and a list of organizations or individuals who served on the evaluation team.

As Fetterman (2001) notes, evaluation findings can be disseminated using nontraditional methods. Reports can be converted to PDF documents and posted on the Internet. Alternatively, a list of key findings can simply be posted on the organization's web site. Copies of the report can be e-mailed to interested recipients. Videoconferencing technology as well as Internet chat rooms and bulletin boards can be used to distribute information from evaluation studies. As opposed to advanced technology, research findings can be presented orally or with Power Point presentations at small group meetings or issued in the form of a press release.

SUMMARY

Evaluations provide information to justify continuing effective programs, to modify programs that need improvement, and to terminate services that do not work or that are underused. Whereas outcome evaluations can be conducted effectively using data to verify whether program objectives are achieved, process or implementation analysis requires data from multiple sources. Involving program participants often is the best way to pinpoint what is happening in the program or to document effectiveness. Participatory methods, self-evaluation, empowerment evaluation, and PAR are often used to involve staff members, clientele, and other constituents in the research process. Each of these methods has its strengths and weaknesses. Involvement of program participants helps motivate staff to improve performance and make efforts to improve program quality. Conducting evaluations with input from clients helps ensure that programs meet client needs and that services will be used. Each of these methods consumes a great deal of time and resources. It may be difficult to obtain a consensus among members for the identification of project goals, methodology, data analysis, and recommendations for action. Participatory evaluation coordinators must have good technical skills in order to put basic research concepts and ethics into action. However, they also need good interpersonal skills, the ability to establish trust among group members, the ability to move the agenda, and the willingness to engage in a process of dialogue with participants on research methods and data interpretation. Conducting research studies that will document the effectiveness or quality of social service programs is one of a number of essential skills needed to "sell" the program to potential clients, funders, and the public at large. Skills and techniques needed to market services to people, funders, organizations, and government are described in Chapter 14.

QUESTIONS FOR CLASS DISCUSSION

1. How would you "sell" your agency on using participatory research methods? Why would such methods be an advantage or disadvantage for your agency?
2. Describe some of the situations in which participatory action research should not be utilized.
3. How should ethical issues (for example, confidentiality) be addressed in participatory research?
4. How should issues of cultural competence in the use of standardized indicators and methods be addressed by an evaluator who has limited resources or options for choosing procedural methods?
5. In what ways would the lack of a representative sample limit the interpretation of evaluation results?

SAMPLE ASSIGNMENTS

1. Identify an ethnic population (preferably one outside the dominant culture) that you want to study. Do several interviews or read several articles about this population group and their customs and norms. Find a standardized instrument that measures a particular behavior, attitude, belief, or perception. Make an assessment as to whether this indicator can appropriately be used to measure the concept addressed by the scale. Analyze the psychometric data and determine how and on what populations the instrument was tested. Are you convinced that this instrument is appropriate for measuring the concept among members of the group that you have identified? Why or why not?
2. Join an internal agency committee or a task force of organizations outside your agency that is currently engaged in a joint research project. Write a three- to four-page paper that describes group composition, the degree to which the group represents its constituency base, its leadership and decision-making structure, the group's goals, and the degree to which the goals have been addressed. Was this group successful, or do you think it will be successful in completing the research, making recommendations for action, and ensuring that the recommendations are implemented?
3. Working with a group of four or five classmates, develop a plan that includes a research design, a sampling method, and an instrument for measuring empowerment, cultural competence, or a commitment to social justice among social work students. Implement your study. Write a brief research report on your findings that includes a problem statement, a brief literature review, a methodology section, human subjects protections, results, and conclusions. As an addendum to the report, analyze the group process. Describe how a facilitator was chosen, how decisions were made, how tasks were assigned, the degree to which tasks were completed, and member satisfaction with the group process.
4. Identify a program objective in your field agency or place of employment for which there is currently no evaluation plan. In consultation with your field instructor and agency administrators, make an assessment as to whether participatory approaches are appropriate for this evaluation. Working by yourself or with organizational participants, develop an appropriate evaluation plan and develop or select an appropriate measurement instrument.

5. Conduct a brief process analysis of one program in your field agency or place of employment. Use at least two of the following methods: program documents, observation, case record or management information system data, and personal or group interviews. Describe the program's intended theory of action and its goals. Are the goals that are being achieved actually the same as the goals specified in program documents? Describe how the program actually works as opposed to descriptions offered in agency documents or described by managers.

CHAPTER 14

External Relations: Developing Organizational Power

The chief limitation of many theories that explain how organizations function is that they focus exclusively either on what happens inside the organization or on how the organization engages with and adapts to the external environment (Hasenfeld, 1992). Much of empowerment theory pertains to facilitating skill development, self-competency, and the ability to influence social change among organizational clientele and staff. However, one of the basic premises of empowerment-oriented management practice is that stimulating individual change also increases the ability of the organization to control its external environment. Organizations need to recruit clients, market their services, obtain funding, and establish cooperative relationships with other organizations and groups in their task environment.

Empowerment theory also assumes that the organization will contribute positively to efforts to change social policies and institutional arrangements associated with oppression. Nearly all social service organizations lobby the government in an attempt to obtain either new or continued funding for services or to influence the development of new policies and regulations. Although staff members, especially executive directors, engage in lobbying on a regular basis, the organization's influence is enhanced when it can engage its constituents in lobbying efforts. Consequently, it is in the organization's best interest to provide training and opportunities for constituents to lobby. An additional component of the empowerment model is that constituents increase their own political power by electing to office those candidates who support policies that will benefit the constituents. Therefore, an empowerment-oriented organization will engage in activities, such as voter education and registration, that will help its constituents acquire political power. This chapter discusses activities that can be used by the organization to increase its own mastery over the external environment and increase the political power of constituents:

- Marketing services
- Using informal networks to recruit clients
- Serving as a mediating institution to link informal community networks to formal organizations
- Establishing interagency collaborations with other groups and organizations
- Increasing the political power of the organization its constituents

MARKETING SERVICES

The process of promoting an organization's services, recruiting clients, obtaining influential board members or supporters for the organization, and raising funds is called *marketing*. Organizations use a number of techniques for promoting their services, including direct mail campaigns, advertising, holding special events, and media coverage. Hardcastle, Wenocur, and Powers (1997) define markets as "composed of people who have some need, desire, or preference and are willing to exchange something in order to have that need, desire, or preference met" (p. 310). According to Lohmann and Lohmann (2002), the process of marketing "can be used by social agencies to enhance relations with existing stakeholders and to identify new target groups that may become supporters" (p. 334).

One of the difficulties for social service organizations, nonprofit, public, or for-profit, is that they have more than one constituency group to which they must "sell" their services (Lohmann & Lohmann, 2002). Methods for recruiting clients may not be as effective in trying to find individual donors or to convince a government agency to award a grant. Organizations may use a process of trial and error to find out what works or conduct market research to find out what types of products and services constituency group members want. For example, focus group interviews can be conducted with current or former clients of the organization to determine how the organization can better serve their needs. Surveys of local residents or key people in the community who are likely to refer clients to the organization also can be used to determine what types of services are needed and how they should be offered (Hardcastle et al., 1997).

Marketing can include a variety of activities aimed at the different constituency groups. For example, promotional brochures can be designed to encourage potential clients to use agency services. Other written material, such as annual reports, can be produced in such a way that their primary purpose is to convince funders that the organization provides quality programs. Organizations can take out advertisements in local media and in professional journals to promote the use of their services and to solicit referrals from doctors, teachers, or social workers who are likely to refer clients to the organization. Many organizations make extensive use of media (newspapers, radio, and television) to inform the public about the good work that they are doing. One way to do this is to collaborate with local media to produce public service announcements that inform the public about social problems and the services provided by the organization (Lohmann & Lohmann, 2002). Although the organization may have to pay some or all of the costs of producing the radio or television spots, no charge is associated with broadcasting the public service announcement (Cohen, 1998).

Effective use of media requires that the organization's leaders maintain extensive contact with journalists who are likely to provide coverage of the organization and the public issues addressed by its programs (Cohen, 1998). One caution about using media to promote the organization is that the type of coverage provided by media sources is just as likely to be unfavorable as it is favorable. The organization may not be able to control the contents of the articles produced. One way to ensure positive coverage is to actively seek opportunities to cultivate media sources by serving as an expert for journalists interested in examining issues related to the organization's mission. Organizations can influence coverage by issuing press announcements, holding press conferences to announce significant achievements or new programs, and writing op-ed pieces for the local newspaper (Cohen, 1998; Hardcastle et al., 1997).

Other types of marketing also involve fundraising for the organization. For example, most nonprofit organizations send direct mail solicitations to potential donors. Some of these individuals will have donated to the organization at least once; organizations frequently maintain extensive lists of donors. In addition, some organizations purchase mailing lists used by groups that have similar missions or that market their programs to a similar demographic profile of donors. Letters sent to prospective donors give detailed information about the mission of the organization and the activities it undertakes to accomplish its goals. Organizations may contact potential donors by phone. In some cases, commercial fundraising firms are hired to run telephone solicitations for donors. Most fundraising events sponsored by nonprofits have a marketing aspect, bringing the organization to the attention of potential donors who may be interested in attending a dinner, listening to a concert, or meeting a celebrity (Lohmann & Lohmann, 2002). As noted in Chapter 12, many nonprofit organizations are aggressively marketing their services using Internet technology. To some extent, e-mail solicitations for funds or new members have replaced fundraising letters sent by postal mail (Boland, Barton, & McNutt, 2002). Organizations find that keeping in touch with previous donors by e-mail is less costly than corresponding by postal mail.

In short, social marketing is not only about providing information about the organization to various constituencies, such as clients, community residents, funders, the public at large, and other organizations in the task environment. Social marketing requires that the organization build strong relationships with both the people it serves and the decision-makers who can influence the survival of the organization. Political economy theory tells us that the effective organization must be able to strategically manage both its internal constituency groups and relationships with external entities that can affect, positively or negatively, the organization's ability to acquire resources and operate programs.

Outreach is a method that many organizations use to obtain clients. Although advertising, web page design, and public service announcements have a role in bringing clients to an organization, one of the most effective recruit mechanisms is "word of mouth." This involves informal processes in which current and former clients, community leaders, and other key people in the community (for example, doctors, teachers, and social service personnel) refer clients to the organization based on its reputation or the perceived quality of its services.

In addition to reliance on "word of mouth," many social service organizations conduct outreach activities to locate potential clients. Hardcastle et al. (1997) define outreach as "systematically contacting isolated people in their homes or wherever they reside (institutions, streets), or in the neighborhoods where they congregate, and linking them to services" (p. 180). Outreach workers may use community institutions such as schools, churches, and health clinics to promote services and screen people for eligibility. For-profit businesses can serve as meeting places or information sources for some marginalized communities and can be used effectively to recruit specific types of populations at risk. For example, human immunodeficiency virus (HIV) prevention work often focuses on bars where gay and bisexual men are expected to gather (Fisher, Ryan, Esacove, Bishofsky, Wallis, & Roffman, 1996). Such outreach methods also are effective in ethnic communities when appropriate places for delivering information and referral services can be identified. Melvin Delgado (1996, 2000) has written extensively about how for-profit businesses such as small grocery stores and restaurants in Puerto

Rican communities function as social service agencies, providing some types of services and credit to their regular customers.

To ensure that clients and other key people in the community know about agency services, organizations use a variety of outreach methods, including handing out flyers, displaying posters, distributing promotional materials (such as pens, t-shirts, and buttons), and participating in community events or fairs. Agencies that take a more aggressive approach to outreach often launch door-knocking campaigns in which every household in target communities is contacted by agency workers and screened for eligibility for services. Many agencies hire people from the community to conduct door-to-door outreach and to deliver services to their neighbors. For example, health prevention or promotion programs often rely heavily on paraprofessional staff who live in the community and have extensive, informal ties with friends, relatives, and neighbors in the target community (Lowe, Barg, & Stephens, 1998; McFarlane & Fehir, 1994). Additional approaches to attracting difficult-to-reach people to the social service organization include the establishment of telephone hotlines and the use of street theater to illustrate the impact of social problems on the community and how organizational services can be used to address those problems (Hardcastle et al., 1997).

BUILDING RELATIONSHIPS IN THE COMMUNITY: USING INFORMAL NETWORKS

Outreach initiatives are particularly effective if social service organizations use informal helpers from the neighborhood they serve. Community organizational practice in impoverished communities often requires that organizers identify "natural" leaders in communities, people to whom others often turn for help (Kahn, 1991; Kretzmann & McKnight, 1993). These natural leaders serve as links between the nonprofit agency and community residents in need, putting the "word out" in the community about the availability of services and informing the agency about the needs of the community. Often informal leaders are recruited for positions on organizational boards and serve as a cadre of potential activists who can be mobilized to lobby and engage in social action on behalf of the organization and its constituents (Zachary, 2000). Informal leaders help connect organizations to informal helping networks that often are prevalent in low-income neighborhoods (see Chapter 4).

Different communities may establish different types of networks that vary in terms of member inclusion, leadership structure, and decision-making patterns (Yoshihama & Carr, 2002). Use of these networks will require a substantial amount of time and effort on the part of the organization, not only to identify natural helpers but also to gain insight into how these networks operate and sustain themselves.

Informal networks are important for enhancing the quality of life in the community. Wilson (1996) and Figueira-McDonough (2001) have argued that poverty, gang membership, and substance abuse are highly related to the absence of social ties and informal networks in urban, inner-city neighborhoods. Consequently, they have recommended that efforts to alleviate these problems should focus on creating local networks and strengthening bonds among community members. It should be noted, however, that the term *community* should not be applied only to geographic neighborhoods. It can include communities delineated by ethnicity, culture, social class, or common interests and problems (Hardina, 2002). What is essential to the formation of community is a sense of "collective identity," or recognition that one belongs to a specific group or entity that can be distinguished from others. Often, threats or dangerous situations that impact individuals within the community result in people coming together to address the problem and consequently helps to create a sense of inclusion and identification in a specific neighborhood or population group.

Much of the recent literature on community organization has identified efforts to strengthen informal support networks as an integral part of empowerment-oriented practice (Brenton, 2001; Miley, O'Melia, & Dubois, 2004). Brenton argues that practice in impoverished communities should focus not on community problems but on making the neighborhood resilient so that "after experiencing adverse exogenous shocks, it can bounce back to its initial equilibrium" (p. 21). Such a community will contain strong informal community network organizations that can mobilize residents to fight for social change. Miley et al. recommend that empowerment practice with individuals should rely heavily on identification and use of the client's own social support network. This network can be "mapped," identifying individuals and institutions with which an individual client may receive, give, or exchange resources on a regular basis. More comprehensive maps can be created to examine the existence and strength of community networks and to identify natural leaders or helpers. Murty (1998) defines a network as "a set of actors linked by a specific set of relations" (p. 22). Social network analysis is conducted using individuals or organizations as units of analysis or is used to examine linkages between individuals and organizations.

Information for a social network analysis can be obtained through informal "conversational" interviews with community residents about who they can turn to for help or through formal, structured interviews with residents and other key informants in a neighborhood about the individuals and organizations with whom they exchange help (Hardina, 2002). The second stage of social network analysis requires that the researcher create a "map" of the relationships among individuals or organizations in the network. The map can be used to answer questions about the strength of relationships among network members, the resources given or exchanged, and the density of networks. *Density* refers to the number of interrelationships that can be found among network members. Other attributes of relationships that can be measured are frequency, duration, intensity, and importance as well as negative and positive aspects of the relationship (Murty, 1998). The smallest unit represented is the *dyad,* or the relationship between two actors. Graphs illustrate the complexity of relationships among network members. One component of the graph may be the *primary egonet,* or the group of actors that interact with a focal individual or organization. These maps can include information about the strength of the relationship between two actors (dark lines indicate strong relationship; light lines indicate weak relationships) and the degree of reciprocity in the relationship (Figure 14.1).

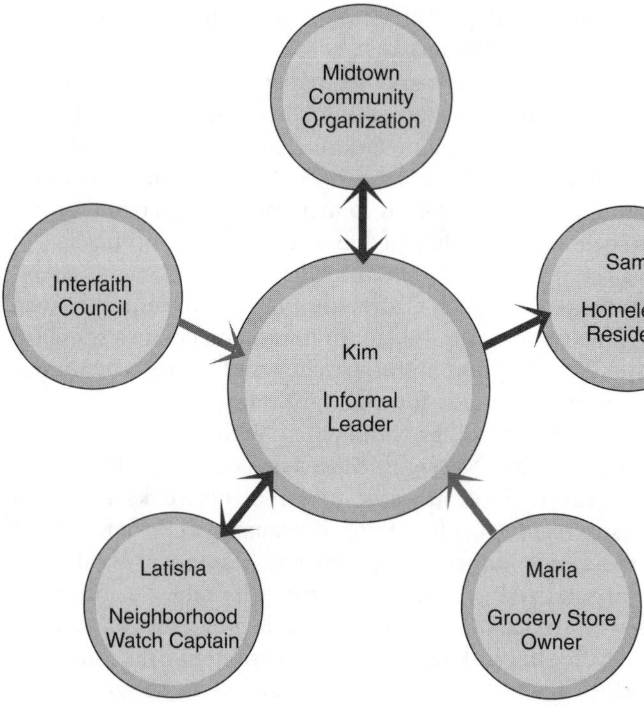

Figure 14.1 Map of an informal community network. Arrows indicate if the relationship is one way (only one of the actors receives support, goods, or services) or if the actors participate in activities that suggest mutual exchange. Dark lines indicate strong interpersonal ties.

MEDIATING INSTITUTIONS

Strengthening interpersonal ties among community residents is only the first step in establishing community linkages that will empower organizational clients and community residents. In *To Empower People: From State to Civil Society,* Berger and Neuhaus (1977) argue that neighborhood organizations, such as religious institutions, neighborhoods, and nonprofit organizations, should "mediate" between the individual and government and help transmit social values. The link between these structures and government would facilitate the development of public policy beneficial to members of oppressed groups. Individuals who participate in organizational decision-making and the public policy debate are "empowered," and consequently they feel less alienated from government. According to Berger and Neuhaus, mediating institutions are particularly beneficial in low-income minority neighborhoods. Local control of neighborhood decision-making strengthens neighborhood ties and helps ethnic minorities defend themselves from the effect of discriminatory practices such as redlining.

Recently, the government and a number of national and local nonprofit organizations have promoted informal help giving and participation in volunteer activities as a method for helping people to form strong social bonds (Fabricant & Fisher, 2002). In addition, participation in nonprofit organizations is believed to increase individual and group productivity as well as the quality of life in communities (Putnam, 2000). Putnam uses the term *social capital* to describe the benefits associated with civic participation. Such efforts are believed to improve social ties among individuals and groups in communities and create a sense of "collective identity" among community residents. The use of volunteers to deliver services or raise funds for a nonprofit organization has beneficial effects for the organizations, providing them with resources at little or no cost to the organization (Neysmith & Reitsma-Street, 2000).

Another way to look at these informal networks relates to the strengths perspective (Delgado, 1996). Kretzmann and McKnight (1993) argue that most communities, even extremely impoverished neighborhoods or marginalized groups, have strengths that can be effectively mobilized to resolve local problems. Strengthening informal helping networks and developing linkages between these networks and nonprofit organizations provides both parties with access to new resources, the means to employ the skills possessed by local residents, and helps the community develop its own capacity to resolve problems rather than relying on help from outside the community.

An additional concern is that although linking with an informal network can have advantages for social service organizations, such relationships must be reciprocal, bringing resources and services to community residents. According to Backman and Smith (2000):

> Nonprofit organizations in distressed communities may encounter difficulty creating durable, supportive social networks unless they can demonstrate effectiveness and the ability to return benefits to their participants. Given that social networks are important to the development of community capacity, potential disruptions to these networks may undermine the ability of a community to address local problems. (p. 360)

Organizations can use a number of techniques to link with informal networks and small, informal groups and organizations in communities. These techniques range from very informal, supportive relationships with the community to formal, contractual relationships between the organization and individuals or the organization and other service providers. At the informal level, organizational administrators can engage in ongoing dialogue with community leaders and encourage their staff to develop working partnerships with client support networks and community leaders. The organization can provide resources (such as facilities, information, or technical assistance) that help maintain support groups or stimulate the development of new organizations that serve community needs. Formal links between organizations and informal networks can include hiring informal helpers to deliver services, developing Internet links to assist with the delivery of information and referral services, and contracting with smaller grass-roots organizations to deliver services to hard-to-reach populations or groups of people with specific needs that cannot be addressed by the larger organization (see Table 14.1).

One of the primary hazards associated with links between formal organizations and informal networks is that the organization that provides monetary resources may try to impose its own agenda on members of marginalized communities. Empowerment practice requires that all parties involved in any intervention retain decision-making capacity. As noted by Delgado (1996), the use of informal networks requires a commitment to establishing real partnerships between community residents and the organization.

> These resources must not undermine "natural helping systems" and instead must be provided as adjuncts to or in collaboration with indigenous resources. Government intervention/resources, as a result, cannot succeed in helping undervalued communities without taking into account a "community's capacity" to help itself; however, a community cannot be expected to rely totally upon itself without outside resources. (p. 59)

Table 14.1 Types of Organizational Links to Informal Networks

Informal Relationships	Formal Relationships
Organizational staff engages in informal discussions with community residents to identify leaders and obtain information about community needs.	Organization holds community forums and conducts focus group interviews to identify community needs.
Informal relationships are established between neighborhood leaders and organizational staff to identify people in need and exchange information.	Neighborhood leaders are recruited for the organizational board, advisory committee, and task groups.
The organization uses informal networks to provide social support to clients.	Informal helpers are hired to deliver services to hard to reach clients.
The organization informally provides facilities and other resources to nonaffiliated self-help groups in the community.	The organization facilitates the development of self-help groups for its clients and provides training and other resources to encourage leadership development and problem-solving.
The organization partners with informal and grass-roots organizations to coordinate events and other community activities.	The organization participates in collaborative partnerships and coalitions with informal neighborhood groups and grass-roots organizations.
The organization provides information and training to community members via e-mail and web page technology.	The organization establishes formal Internet links to community agencies and informal leaders to enhance information sharing and referrals.
The organization informally provides technical assistance and other services to help new organizations develop service capacity.	The organization contracts with smaller organizations with specialized programs for the delivery of services.

INTERAGENCY COLLABORATION

In order to attain legitimacy and funding, nonprofit organizations and their leaders must establish working relationships with a large number of entities in their task environment: donors, political decision-makers, accreditation bodies, state licensing boards, local residents, and the clients who seek assistance from the organization. These working relationships can be collaborative or grounded in conflict. Schmid (2000) identifies five different approaches for managing the task environment:

1. Bargaining for the exchange of resources
2. Developing coalitions or cooperative partnerships among organizations
3. Co-optation, the process of recruiting rival organizations and absorbing them into the organization
4. Using authority and power to obtain resources from others
5. Disruption, the process of threatening rivals to prevent resource acquisition or pressuring government and other funders for resources

Each of these strategies can be used by the organization to secure financial survival. For example, most organizations engage in bargaining and negotiation when they work with funders to set the parameters of a grant or of a purchase of service contract. Organizations can establish relationships with other organizations in their task environments to share or exchange information, clients, facilities, and other resources. Some of these exchange relationships are established within the context of collaborative partnerships to deliver resources or coalition groups that are organized to lobby for legislation, funding, or civil rights and other resources for members of marginalized groups. Collaborative partnerships and the process of subcontracting for resources can result in one-way, rather than mutual, exchanges, in which the more powerful organization benefits while the second organization is co-opted. In addition, organizations may use their power (ability to acquire resources, legitimacy, or political support) to coerce resources from others (Table 14.2).

Arrangements made among a number of organizations serving one community or a specific population group to share resources, information, or responsibility for a program or activity are characterized as collaborations. The term *collaboration* usually implies the existence of an agreement among a number of organizations to undertake a joint activity. Collaborations may involve lobbying for changes in legislation or policies, starting a new program, or coordinating the delivery of a service among a number of programs.

The term *collaboration* also implies that such partnerships are based on consensus and the mutual, reciprocal exchange of resources among the parties. Not all collaborative agreements are entirely cooperative ventures, however. Government and foundation funders often mandate that organizations collaborate with other organizations and groups that provide similar services. For example, the Ryan White Act mandates that acquired immunodeficiency syndrome (AIDS) service providers serving the same community work collaboratively if they are to qualify for federal funding (Rundall, Celetano, Marconi, Bender-Kitz, Kwait, & Gentry, 1994).

Table 14.2 Types of Relationships Between Social Service Organizations and Funding Sources

Relationship Type	Activity
Bargaining for the exchange of resources	The organization exchanges resources, information, clients, or personnel with another organization.
	The organization negotiates the parameters of grants and contracts with funders.
Developing coalitions or cooperative partnerships	The organization establishes a formal process with a number of organizations to deliver services or lobby for policies and legislation.
	The organization joins an already established network or group of agencies that collaborate to deliver services
Co-optation	The organization supports the inclusion of network individuals, groups, or organizations in a network in order to obtain access to the resources they possess.
Using authority and power to obtain resources from others	Ability to control the distribution of resources within the service delivery network and can restrict the entry of new organization.
	The organization subcontracts for services with smaller organizations and groups in order to acquire access to and control of their resources.
	The organization uses political power to obtain government funding.
Disruption	An organization representing marginalized groups threatens to withhold resources or political support or stage public protests unless resources are allocated.

Many organizations pursue membership in collaborative efforts in order acquire scarce resources or to protect their niche or "turf" from encroachment by other organizations (Graham & Barter, 1999). These partnerships carry with them varying degrees of power and resources and vastly different decision-making structures. Some common types of collaborative structures include, but are not limited to, collaborative service networks, coalitions, case management systems, and service coordination networks. All of these structures require that partners share some responsibility for service inputs (clients, technology, information, facilities, and funds) and goal achievement (influencing a piece of legislation, screening and referring clients for service, developing a new service, delivering a program, or reducing duplication of services).

Organizations enter into these arrangements for a variety of reasons. Most often the reason is perceived advantages in the acquisition of political power and financial resources. Participation in a service partnership or coalition consolidates resources, making the group as a whole better able to control the external environment, thus increasing the ability of these organizations to lobby for legislation or deliver comprehensive services. In many cases, collaboration, case management, and coordination of services are perceived to have advantages for both the organization and the clients it serves. Processes such as making one case manager responsible for referring a client to a number of agencies for service or the joint delivery of services by two or more agencies at one site are thought to increase access to service for most clients. However, case management and service coordination are controversial in that one of the main goals of such processes is to reduce the costs associated with duplication of services by two or more agencies. Reducing duplication also reduces client access to services (Hardina, 1993).

A social service organization may also perceive collaborations as requiring risk. It may risk losing information, clients, its status in the community (if the effort fails), autonomy to make its own decisions, and any technological superiority it may hold over other member agencies as a consequence of joining the partnership (Alter, 2000). Other costs associated with membership in any collaborative or coalition includes the organization's contribution of time and resources to the partnership and potential conflicts with other organizations over goals and responsibilities.

For many small organizations that serve unique or traditionally oppressed populations, the road to survival requires that they establish collaborative relationships with local service delivery networks or subcontract with larger organizations in order to deliver services (Iglehart & Becerra, 2000). Such interorganizational relationships provide a degree of power to the social service organization by virtue of their ability to reach populations that often are inaccessible to mainstream organizations. However, large, well-funded organizations have a competitive advantage in obtaining funds and consequently may dominate any collaborative arrangement with new organizations, setting rules of engagement for the collaborative and controlling access to resources and decision-making (Tucker, Baum, & Singh, 1992). However, smaller organizations that provide specialized services to ethnic or other difficult-to-reach communities may achieve some competitive advantages, especially in instances where there are no service alternatives, demand for these services is great, and inclusion in community service networks is mandated by legislation or prescribed by government or foundation grants and contracts as a precondition of funding.

The advantages of service partnerships are generally believed to outweigh the disadvantages. They assist in the creation of new organizations, help identify unmet needs or social problems, help disseminate innovative technology or programs, and expand the supply of services. According to Provan and Milward (2001), service delivery networks can be judged effective if

- The network provides most essential services.
- Strong relationship ties exist among organizational members.
- New agencies are incorporated into the network as others drop out.

Collaborative partnerships also can be judged to be successful based on how they function internally. Do partners share resources? How are funds allocated? Who sets the agenda and ensures that tasks are accomplished? As with successful teams, effective collaborations require that some attention be paid to group processes. Graham and Barter (1999) identify four stages in establishing partnerships among organizations:

1. Problem-setting and identification of participants
2. Direction-setting, allowing participants to establish principles for action and set common goals
3. Implementing of the action plan
4. Setting up a formal structure to continue collaborative efforts

It should be noted that in the process of establishing a structure for the collaborative effort, partners must also form trusting relationships. This can be easily accomplished when members have established good working relationships with one another or when group members have similar economic, ethnic, professional, or occupational backgrounds. Diversity of experience and background as well as lack of familiarity with one another can require a longer period of preparation in setting up the group or establishing joint goals. Often responsibility for facilitating the group process is assigned to one lead agency or to one or two group leaders.

BOX 14.1 ESTABLISHING COLLABORATIVE PARTNERSHIPS

Molly is the Associate Director for the Northwest Women's Shelter. The shelter has received a letter from the state's department of social services indicating that the shelter will receive a large contract to establish a women's services network for the local community. In order to qualify for the contract, the shelter must serve as the lead agency and coordinate a collaborative service delivery partnership among six community-based agencies. The shelter's partners in the collaborative will consist of a women's health center, a faith-based agency that provides food and clothing to low-income people, two small ethnic organizations, and the local public welfare agency. The purpose of the government contract is to establish a system to provide case management services to low-income women and children who are victims of domestic violence.

- What types of things must Molly do to establish the collaborative structure?
- What types of problems is Molly likely to encounter?
- What actions can be taken to address these problems?

According to Schopler (1994), the structure of interorganizational groups varies based on how they were developed. Collaboratives in which organizations are required to participate as a precondition of funding or legitimacy and that are created in response to institutions outside the community can be expected to have few participants, and decisions will be made simply to comply with the expectations of the funding agency. Such groups are unlikely to be effective. Alternatively, a collaborative partnership in which membership is voluntarily and the decision to form the group comes from within the community are more likely to be characterized by conflict in the decision-making process but are more likely to achieve their goals (Table 14.3).

Table 14.3 Group Dynamics in Mandated Versus Voluntary Interorganizational Structures

Origin	Externally Determined	Internally Determined
Mandated	*Constrained Compliance* Little formation time Few problems; low participation Conflict suppressed Low member satisfaction Low-quality output High compliance with funder	*Frustrated vs. Responsive* Brief formation stage Low level of problems Covert conflict Low/moderate satisfaction Moderate-quality output High/medium compliance with funder
Voluntary	*Focus vs. Conflicted* Long formation stage High participation Open conflict High satisfaction and output quality Low compliance with funder	*Creative Commitment* Long formation stage High level of problems Open conflict High satisfaction and output quality Low compliance with funder

Source: Schopler, J. (1994). Interorganizational groups in the human services. *Journal of Community Practice, 1*(3), 12.

Yamatani, Soska, and Baltimore (1999) have identified a number of characteristics associated with effective collaborations and networks (see Table 14.4). The partners must be recognized as community leaders. Members must have a common stake in producing an agreed-upon outcome and share a vision for achieving that goal. The decision-making

Table 14.4 Characteristics of Interorganizational Groups and Collaboratives

Component	Positive Characteristics	Negative Characteristics
Collaborative environment	Members are perceived as community leaders	Members have no track record as community leaders
Collaborative membership characteristics	Understanding and trust Diverse members Collaboration in best interest of members	Limited trust among members Membership does not reflect community diversity Participation in the collaborative threatens the resources or reputations of members
Collaborative process and structure	Common stake in process/outcomes Layers of decision-making Clear roles and policies Flexibility and adaptability	Members have differing agendas and goals Decisions are made by one or a small group of leaders No rules have been developed to guide group decision-making The group lacks the capacity to alter plans to fit situational demands
Communication	Open and frequent communication, both formal and informal	Little communication among members
Collaborative purpose	Attainable goals Shared vision Unique purpose	Unattainable goals or no real goals specified Members cannot agree on a purpose for the group
Factors related to resources	Distribution of funds Good leaders All necessary service providers are included in the partnership	Funding is available to only a few members of the group Leaders are not effective Some organizations are excluded from the partnership

Adapted from Yamatani, H., Soska, T., & Baltimore, T. (1999). *A study of community collaboratives*. Paper presented at the conference of the Council on Social Work Education, New York, New York.

structure must be spelled out and not be assigned only to one or a small group of individuals. Roles and responsibilities should be clearly specified. Ineffective partnerships, on the other hand, can be characterized as those in which there are disputes about group goals, hidden agendas, exclusion of key members based on arbitrary criteria, unspecified ground rules, and only one or a small group of people have power and the authority to make decisions. These ineffective groups may actually decrease the power of organizational members to influence policies and legislation or limit their ability to acquire the resources they need for financial survival.

INCREASING THE POLITICAL POWER OF THE ORGANIZATION

If the organization is to have the ability to acquire resources using power, authority, or disruption (the ability to stop or impede the actions of others using tactics such as protests or civil disobedience), it must have a number of resources at its disposal. Such an organization may have power because it offers a specialized service and has few competitors. It may be powerful because it has established legitimacy in the community: clients, competitors, government decision-makers, and the public at large recognize the agency as providing quality services, having expertise in a specific field, or having the ability to influence policy and legislation. Organizations can derive power from being well established, from providing services over a long period, from constantly expanding their service capacity, or by acquiring a large number of donors that can be expected to provide a continuous funding stream for the organization. Organizations also develop power by lobbying for legislation that will benefit the organization and its constituents or for causes for which the organization advocates (for example, the rights of children or protection of the environment). Many pieces of legislation may have funding implications for both public and nonprofit social service organizations. Reductions or increases in yearly government budget allocations for social service programs have implications for both public and nonprofit social service organizations. Because most social service organizations receive much of their funding from federal, state, and local governments, tracking the status of legislation and developing appropriate mechanisms for intervening in the legislative process is essential for the survival of these organizations.

Large social service organizations may employ a government-relations specialist or a grant writer to track legislative developments and to lobby on behalf of the organization. In smaller organizations, government relations may be part of the responsibility of the executive director. In any case, this job can involve a number of activities:

- Keeping track of the status of proposed legislation as it moves through the legislative process.
- Analyzing the impact of proposed legislation and changes in government budget on the organization and its clients.
- Maintaining relationships with legislators in order to have input in the development of legislation. Organizational staff may be asked to testify at public hearings or give input on the development of new legislation.
- Lobbying legislators through face-to-face meetings, letters, e-mail, or demonstrations to support or oppose legislation.
- Asking constituents or the public at large to lobby or engage in social action to support or oppose legislation (Hardina, 2002; Jansson, 1999).

Organizations can use a number of techniques to help them lobby. Many organizations join associations or coalition groups that work jointly to track legislation and plan lobbying campaigns. An organization's power to influence legislation is increased if it has a large number of partners who take the same position on the issue and who can pool their resources to make a large impact on the legislative process. Many of these coalitions, as well as independent advocacy groups, provide ongoing information about the status of pending legislation and the expected impact of policies. Some of these organizations send regular e-mail alerts to organizations advising them to take action (write a letter to the local newspaper, send an e-mail, attend a meeting with a legislator) as legislation is introduced, reviewed in committee, and sent to a legislative body for a vote. Advocacy organizations and coalition groups maintain web pages that contain a great deal of information about legislation and its impact. Many political decision-makers post information about their own legislative interests and their positions on the issues on their own web sites. Social service organizations can allocate time for their own staff to research legislation and make reports. Currently a vast amount of information about legislative processes is available on web sites maintained by federal, state, and local governments (Hardina, 2002).

In addition to lobbying, another source of power for social service organizations is the acquisition of a large membership base that can be counted on to make donations and to volunteer to assist with service delivery, fundraising, or lobbying activities (Mueller, 1992). For organizations that engage in social action, having a base of constituents that can be mobilized for action—to lobby for legislation, join a protest, or attend a meeting with an elected official—can be an important source of power. Strength in numbers can be an effective source of power that to some extent serves as a counterbalance to limited financial resources. As noted previously, in some cases funding sources can try to restrict the organization's participation in social action activities that threaten the political establishment. Having a powerful constituency base consisting of clients, community residents, and prominent people in the community can serve to mediate against attempts by funding sources to control organizational activities (Hardina, 1993).

BOX 14.2 INCREASING ORGANIZATIONAL POWER FOR LOBBYING

Shawn has just been hired as an outreach coordinator for the Mission Street Anti-Poverty Organization. His director has asked him to coordinate the organization's annual lobbying day in the state capital. Traditionally, the executive director and board members identify several issues of concern to the organization and then schedule visits with lawmakers on their annual trip. Often two or three clients accompany these organizational "leaders" on their lobbying visits. Discussions are limited to lobbying for more funding for the organization or against cuts in the state's welfare program. These visits produce few long-term results. As a result, clients seem to be reluctant to participate in lobbying activities.

What concrete steps can Shawn take to

- Identify issues and legislation that are more relevant to both the organization and its clientele?
- Involve more clients in lobbying activities?
- Increase the power and influence of the organization in the legislative process?

As described in earlier chapters, the recruitment of clients and other constituents for participation on the organization's board or in other decision-making roles benefits both the organization and the individuals who participate in these activities. Leadership roles within the organization prepare low-income people to become political activists and provide them with a greater sense of inclusion in mainstream society (Checkoway & Zimmerman, 1992; Zachary, 2000). In addition, the empowerment model encourages participation of clients and other constituency groups in social action activities. Empowerment-oriented

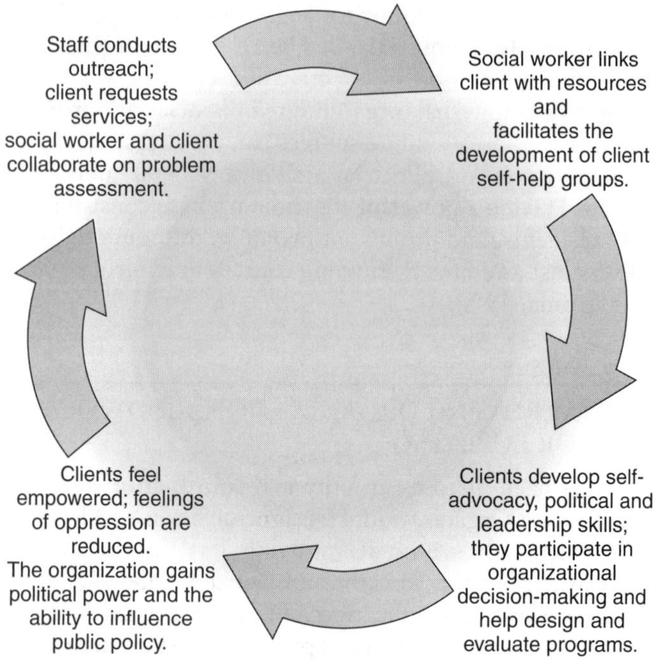

Figure 14.2 Cycle of empowerment.

organizations and their constituents are expected to participate in social movements (Reisch, Wenocur, & Sherman, 1981). There is a dual purpose for such participation. It helps members of historically marginalized populations to develop specific types of self-advocacy skills and to perceive themselves as sufficiently competent to be part of the political process (Figure 14.2).

Zimmerman and Rappaport (1988) define *psychological empowerment* as including both a sense of personal competence and participation in social change-oriented activities. In one of the first empirical studies on empowerment, they compared college students and community activists and found that individuals who were involved in community organizations were more likely than those not involved to score higher on measures of perceived competence to influence social change. Competency was measured in terms of a "greater sense of political efficacy, competence and mastery, a greater desire for control, more civic duty, and a general belief that their success is a result of internal rather than external factors" (p. 746).

INCREASING THE POWER OF ORGANIZATIONAL CONSTITUENTS

Participants in social action attain a sense of mastery over their own environments in situations where they have been able to influence the political process. One of the primary assumptions of the empowerment approach is that such participation will contribute to the adoption of public policies that will benefit low-income communities and help members of marginalized groups improve their status in society. This, in turn, should reduce feelings of internalized oppression among low-income and other disadvantaged people served by the organization—the very thing that empowerment practice was designed to address (Rose, 2000; Solomon, 1976).

Two complementary approaches can be used to increase the power of constituents to influence social change. One approach involves traditional models of community organizational practice, most often involvement in community development, social planning, or social action. Each of these models focuses on improvements in community life and increasing the power of marginalized groups to influence government decision-making through bargaining with political decision-makers, lobbying, and social protests. The second approach used to increase the power of constituents is through participation in electoral politics. Low-income people and members of marginalized groups often vote less often than do middle- and upper-income people (Piven & Cloward, 2000). Consequently, they are limited in their ability to influence the development of policies that will benefit their community.

Community Organizational Strategies

Rothman (1995) has identified three primary models for organizing communities: community development, social planning, and social action. Each of these models uses very different assumptions about the origins of social problems and appropriate interventions for addressing these problems. Strategies and tactics for promoting social change are the primary components of these intervention plans. *Strategies* are long-term plans of action used to achieve a goal. *Tactics,* on the other hand, are short-term activities that are used to carry out a strategy (Hardina, 2002).

In *community development,* the primary strategy is collaboration. All groups in the community, even people who have traditionally taken opposite positions on an issue, power brokers, and people who have limited power, are brought together to identify an issue of concern in the community. The group as a whole decides on a plan of action and appropriate tactics. Tactical methods associated with this approach are consistent with some of the basic premises of the empowerment model: increasing the capacity of the community and individuals to take action and solve problems, building consensus, and helping individuals develop a sense of self-competency, decision-making ability, and feelings of personal empowerment (Rothman, 1995). An additional advantage of the community development approach is that it focuses on strengthening informal community networks and linking these networks to the organization's partners, who have the capacity to mobilize resources needed for social change (Kretzmann & McKnight, 1993). One disadvantage of this approach is that it does not address issues related to power inequities; people without power have limited ability to pressure decision-makers to come to the bargaining table and to work with them on addressing issues. In addition, use of this model requires time and access to resources if participants are to reach a consensus about goals and methods used to achieve the desired outcomes (Hardina, 2002).

A second community model, *social planning,* is a process in which a social problem affecting a geographic community or members of a demographic (and often marginalized) group is identified and a plan or program is developed to address the problem (Rothman, 1995). This method assumes that a problem can be resolved by gathering facts, collecting data, and choosing the best method to address the problem. Traditional approaches to planning assume that these decisions can best be made through a rational process by experts, hired by government or private agencies, who have the technical skills necessary to make the best decision. However, innovative planning approaches assume that plans are most likely to be put in operation and lead to better outcomes when the people who are assumed to benefit from these plans are included in the decision-making (Forester, 1989).

As noted in Chapter 5, some of these approaches are effective in allowing clients and other constituents to have their voices heard in the planning process. Government agencies, politicians, and wealthy interests who have the most to gain or lose from the plan under consideration tend to dominate decision-making (King, Feltey, & Susel, 1998; Tauxe, 1995). Two models of planning practice emphasize the role of clients and other constituents in the planning. The *advocacy planning* model assumes that planners are actually the employees of constituents or interest groups and that the planner will aggressively advocate for plans that benefit their interest. However, achievement of the planning goal is predicated not on the planner's skill but on his or her ability to influence the political process (Hardina, 2002). The *transactive* model of planning assumes that plans should be made in the context of dialogue between planning experts and beneficiaries. It is further assumed that those plan beneficiaries, regardless of social class and education, are the best experts about their own lives and can make informed decisions about the plans that can best meet their needs (Friedmann, 1987). This model has its origins in the transformative model of community organization associated with Paulo Freire (1970). The partnerships that emerge between the experts and constituency group members benefit both groups and increase community capacity to resolve social problems that have their origins in oppression.

The third model of community organization identified by Rothman (1995) is *social action*. Social action assumes that power—money, authority, information, strength in numbers—must be used to achieve a goal. It also assumes that people with little access to power and other social resources must fight to pressure decision-makers to adopt policies and legislation that will benefit oppressed communities. Social action strategies include campaign and contest. A *campaign* is a series of planned actions used to influence the public and bring decision-makers to the bargaining table. Campaigns can include public education, union organizing drives, media exposure, lobbying, and political campaigns. *Contest* involves tactics that require direct confrontation—such as protests, boycotts, and direct action—with decision-makers. These tactics are generally used in situations where people with power have little contact with, or little interest in conducting dialogue with, members of powerless groups. Contest-related tactics are also most likely to be used in situations where people have been harmed by institutional practices and change is unlikely unless members of powerless groups come together to pressure decision-makers (Hardina, 2002). A disadvantage of this model is that it can exacerbate conflict among groups, result in policy changes that actually harm intended beneficiaries, and alienate some of the decision-makers whose input is essential if programs and policies are to be changed.

People can be engaged in social action in a number of ways. Most often people are engaged in dialogue to identify community problems and take action. Organizations may attempt to mobilize constituents and other community residents around a specific issue of concern or piece of pending legislation. Flyers, phone banks, e-mail announcements, or door-knocking campaigns are often used to recruit people for social action (Kahn, 1991). One essential component of social action organizing is the ability to assess the power resources of your opponents (Community Tool Box, 2003). Traditional ways of achieving this include personal interviews with community leaders and reviewing media accounts of key individuals who have influenced policy changes (Hardina, 2002.). Constituents can use a variation of the mapping project used in community development work to examine social networks to develop a pictorial illustration of links among major decision-makers (for example, connections between corporate-affiliated donors to political campaigns and legislators who will cast their votes to benefit these donors). Constituents can use power analysis to examine their relationship to policy-makers and the impact of their decisions on the community (Brutus, 1999). Such a map can be used to fully involve constituents in conducting assessments of the origins of problems contributing to the oppression of marginalized groups and choosing strategies and tactics to address these problems.

Strategies and tactics from each of the three models can be used effectively to address social problems. Rothman (1995) suggests that mixed strategies, conducted in different phases of the intervention process, may be most effective. In working in low-income communities, all three models of community organization may be needed to bring people together across race, ethnic, income, and gender-related boundaries, to develop solutions to problems, and to put pressure on decision-makers to allocate the resources needed for problem resolution (Hardina, 2002). For example, if lack of recreational space in a community is perceived to be a problem, community development-related methods can be used to bring people together to come to an agreement about a solution for this problem and to select members for appointment to a task group to develop a plan. Social planning techniques can be used to develop an appropriate plan for acquiring recreational space or programs. Social action then can be undertaken to pressure the city to release resources that can be used for recreational facilities (Table 14.5).

The *transformative model*, a fourth model of community organization, is based on the work of Freire (1970) and consequently is one of the theoretical components of the empowerment model of practice (see Chapter 2). The model, also referred to in the literature as *popular education*, requires that partnerships be established between the organizer and constituents that are grounded in mutual exchange and learning. Participants acquire skills and knowledge as they examine sources of oppression and develop action plans. The use of this model requires that consensus and collaboration be used to establish solidarity among participants and that contest strategies be used to confront the powerful and to demand changes in legislation and policies that sustain

Table 14.5 Organizational and Constituent Roles in Community Change

Community Organization Model	Role of the Organization	Role of the Constituent	Outcomes
Community development	Brings diverse groups together to identify needs Links informal networks with formal organizations Facilitates agenda setting Partners with other organizations and groups to bring about community change	Participants in the change process Citizens	Helps individuals develop leadership and other skills Strengthens networks Increases community capacity to facilitate change Leads to improvements in the quality of community life
Social planning	Identifies community problems Creates structures to facilitate change Partners with other organizations to develop new programs and services	Consultants Decision-makers Consumers of services Beneficiaries of change	Develops new programs or makes improvements in existing services Reduces social problems
Social action	Helps to identify problems experienced by community residents or marginalized groups Provides resources and information for organizing campaigns Forges coalitions that can be used to pressure political decision-makers and the public at large	Members of oppressed groups Constituents Lobbyists Employers Political activists Leaders	Increases power among members of oppressed groups Obtains changes in programs and policies Decreases institutional oppression
Transformative models	Creates working partnerships for social change with constituents Provides skills education and helps constituents gain knowledge about the origins of oppression	Experts on own lives Change agents Learners Teach others about oppression Political activists	Personal and social transformation

Adapted from Rothman, J. (1995). Approaches to community intervention. In F. Cox, J. Erlich, J. Rothman, & J. Tropman (Eds.), *Strategies of community organization* (5th ed., pp. 26–63). Itasca, IL: F. E. Peacock.

oppressive conditions. Subtypes of this model are multicultural and feminist approaches to community organizational practice (Gutierrez & Lewis, 1994; Hyde, 1994; Rivera & Erlich, 1999).

These models assume that social and economic institutions marginalize women and persons of color and that gender- or culture-specific practice methods are needed to build in-group capacity to resolve problems and confront oppressive conditions. For example, as noted in Chapter 2, feminist organizations often explicitly reject the hierarchical structures and use of authority associated with traditional organizations developed by white males. Instead they use consensus-style decision-making structures in which all organizational participants (administrators, board members, clients, and staff) participate in developing strategies and fighting for policies that enhance the status of women in society. *Multicultural organizing* can refer to either organizing within one ethnic community or bringing together a variety of ethnic groups to take action (Rivera & Erlich, 1999). An example of using the transformative approach in ethnic communities involves the use of informal community leaders as volunteers or paid staff members to deliver services. For example, some programs that target specific ethnic communities have focused on teaching new mothers about proper child-rearing procedures or health promotion activities (Duggan et al., 2000; McFarlane & Fehir, 1994). These programs require that the informal helpers first receive training in these methods before they are sent door-to-door to train others. Merideth (1994) describes a program called *Casa en Casa,* a popular education project operated in the Latino community in Oakland, California:

> . . . the staff emphasized their commitment to promoting critical reflection on the root causes of health problems in order to uncover and challenge oppressive structures, thus providing the basis for social action. Following Freire, the staff strongly believed in basing the educational process on people's life experiences, developing horizontal relationships between educators and learners and linking education to action for social change. Rather than merely providing information or facts about a subject, the staff had as their primary goal the formation of critical actors who would be able to analyze sources of powerlessness and work collectively to transform the conditions of their lives. (p. 358)

Consequently, the purpose of these programs is not only to change people through education but to develop a critical consciousness among participants and change society through social action. However, education in itself does not bring about social transformation. Participants also need to acquire political power.

Political Empowerment

One of the more critical activities needed to empower low-income communities is voter registration. Currently, only two thirds of all U.S. citizens age 18 and older are registered to vote (Alliances for Better Campaigns, 1998). Turnouts in recent campaigns of approximately 40% to 50% indicate that less than 30% of all U.S. adults actually vote. Voters are substantially more likely to be white, age 50 or older, college graduates, and have higher incomes than nonvoters (Jackson, Brown, & Wright, 1998; Verba, Schlozman, & Brady, 1997). The disparity in voting patterns is believed to contribute to the success of legislation that primarily benefits people who already have access to social resources such as good schools, jobs, and income. Consequently, many advocates believe that increasing voter turnout in low-income neighborhoods will help reduce feelings of alienation from government institutions and increase the likelihood that legislation that actually benefits these communities will be adopted (Piven & Cloward, 2000).

One of the reasons for the limited participation of low-income individuals and persons of color is that laws in many states have made voter registration difficult. The registration period may end 30 days prior to the election. New registrations are needed when the individual changes his or her residence or last name (because of marriage or divorce). Poor people typically have difficulty with registration requirements: they may be transient, changing residences on a regular basis (Piven & Cloward, 2000). Some demographic groups may be systematically excluded from the voting process. For example, at least 13% of all African-American men are in prison, on parole, or on probation because of disparities in drug sentencing laws. In some states, ex-felons have difficulty restoring their voting rights once they have served their sentences (Allard & Mauer, 1998). Consequently, the voting power of the African-American community has been reduced.

Other factors that can discourage voters include the limited availability of ballots in languages other than English, ballot wording that may confuse elderly or inexperienced voters, and the limited number of polling places that are fully accessible to disabled voters (Constitution Project, 2002, League of Women Voters, 2002a; National Association for the Advancement of Colored People [NAACP], 2002; U.S. Commission on Civil Rights, 2002; U.S. General Accounting Office, 1998). The institutional barriers that make voting difficult for some U.S. citizens is in stark contrast to the situation in Canada, Australia, and many European countries, which send registrars door-to-door or that require compulsory voting (Piven & Cloward, 2000).

Interest groups such as the League of Women Voters (2002b) and the NAACP (2002) have argued that low rates of participation are the result of limited efforts to educate potential voters about the electoral process and voting rights. They advocate additional voters' rights training for citizens, poll workers, and the general public. Empowerment-oriented, community-based organizations can play an important role in conducting voter registration drives and educating their constituents about the voting process and their choices at the polls.

As noted in Chapter 12, federal and state laws limit the participation of public and nonprofit employees and nonprofit organizations in most types of electoral activities on the job. These restrictions do not, however, limit the activities of employees off the job. Indeed, Section 6.04 of the National Association of Social Workers (NASW) *Code of Ethics* (NASW, 1999) explicitly calls for social work participation in politics:

> Social workers should engage in social and political action that seeks to ensure that all people have equal access to the resources, employment, services, and opportunities they require to meet their basic human needs and to develop fully. Social workers should be aware of the impact of the political arena on practice and should advocate for changes in policy and legislation to improve social conditions in order to meet basic human needs and promote social justice. (Section 6.04a, ¶ 1)

In addition, many nonprofit advocacy organizations set up special organizational structures called *political action committees* (PACs) to legally raise money for political candidates. PACs make it possible for many small donors to pool funds and consequently make large donations to candidates who they believe will represent their interests. Although PACs originally were intended to increase the power of small donors to influence political campaigns, business, unions, and other powerful groups use PACs to influence legislation that will benefit them. The NASW is one of many interest groups that operate a PAC. The NASW's Political Action for Candidate Elections donates the funds it raises to candidates who support social work positions on welfare reform, third-party reimbursement, and other issues that will benefit social workers and the people they serve (Colby & Buffum, 1998).

Even if a nonprofit organization chooses not to set up a PAC, a number of legal activities can be undertaken to increase the political power of clients and other constituents. Both nonprofit and public social service organizations can engage in nonpartisan voter registration. In fact, the National Voter Registration Act, passed by Congress in 1993, requires that states implement "motor voter" procedures for voter registration. People are encouraged to register when they apply for driver's licenses. This legislation mandates that people be allowed to register at public assistance offices, military recruitment offices, and in agencies that serve people with disabilities. People also are permitted to update names, addresses, and party affiliation at these sites (Piven & Cloward, 2000).

Many interest and advocacy groups, including NASW, consider it advantageous to encourage their members to register to vote with the expectation that the new voter will support candidates for office who agree with the organization's position on important issues. In addition to voter registration, nonprofit organizations are permitted to conduct nonpartisan analyses of candidate position on issues and to distribute this information to potential voters. They can engage in efforts to educate people about their voting rights and appropriate procedures for casting their votes. Nonprofits can sponsor candidate forums in which constituents have the opportunity to listen to and question candidates from all political parties. Some nonprofit organizations monitor the voting process to ensure that their constituents have access to the polling place and advocate for reforms in voting procedures. For example, organizations serving people with disabilities may be particularly concerned that polling places be made wheelchair accessible.

SUMMARY

Public and nonprofit social service organizations cannot survive without extensive links to their clientele, the community served, other organizations with similar missions, and/or government agencies and other local institutions. A substantial part of the job of an organization's executive director is to establish and maintain these linkages. As in micro practice, relationship skills—the ability to engage with and communicate effectively with a variety of people—is essential. Organizational directors need to be knowledgeable about how to access various decision-making structures and the impact of these decisions on the organization and its clientele. Although social service organizations must compete for scarce resources, one of the dilemmas faced by administrators is that a healthy, empowerment-oriented organization also must be prepared to share resources and information with others, establish collaborative partnerships and networks, and form coalitions and participate in social movements to lobby for legislation and fight for social change. The capacity to influence legislation and social policies and the ability to mobilize constituents to work on behalf of the organization are essential to the survival of social service organizations operating in a turbulent funding environment. Constituent mobilization is beneficial only if the constituents are able to participate in and have influence on the political process. Consequently, nonprofit organizations must find ways to support the political participation of low-income people and others who will lend their support to progressive social policies. Although one of the primary tenants of empowerment practice is that political action increases feelings of personal empowerment and self-efficacy among low-income and other marginalized people, it may not always produce positive effects. Both the limitations and the advantages of the empowerment model are discussed in Chapter 15.

QUESTIONS FOR CLASS DISCUSSION

1. What are some of the possible advantages and disadvantages to using informal support networks to deliver services?
2. What role do you think nonprofit and public social service organizations should play in mediating between community residents and government or other large institutions?
3. Are there situations where it would be appropriate for an organization to use co-optation, power, authority, or disruption to obtain funding? Why?
4. What are the advantages and disadvantages to an organization of forming collaborative partnerships or joining coalitions?
5. Do you think it is ethical for an organization to encourage clients to become politically involved? Why?
6. What are the consequences to a social service organization if it is unable to accumulate political power?

SAMPLE ASSIGNMENTS

1. Design a brochure, fundraising letter, or web page for your field agency or place of employment. Include information on the organization's mission, the target population, the social problem addressed by the organization, the services provided, organizational leaders, and procedures for contacting the organization.
2. Develop a map of a social network. The map can pertain to helping relationships among community residents, links between informal leaders and the organization, or links among organizations serving the same target population or community. On your map, identify a focal actor and portray the direction, strength, and density of relationships. Use information obtained through informal interviews, web sites, organizational documents, and media reports to develop your map.
3. Attend NASW lobby day and plan to meet with your state legislators. In advance, identify an issue of concern that you wish

to address with one or more legislators. Write a brief description of your meeting, your presentation to the legislator, and the outcome.

4. Analyze a piece of legislation. Examine its content. Describe how you think this legislation will impact social work practice in public or nonprofit organizations.
5. Develop an intervention plan using one of the community organizational models identified in this chapter. Describe the issue to be addressed, the model of practice to be used, the desired goal, and appropriate strategies and tactics for meeting this goal.

CHAPTER 15

The Empowering Model of Management: Is It Realistic?

In the final chapter of this textbook, we examine the empowerment model in terms of intervention processes and intended outcomes for organization clients, staff members, the organization, the community served by the organization, and society as a whole. We identify specific skills and actions that must be undertaken by organizational managers to facilitate empowerment in social service organizations. The strengths and limitations of the empowerment model of management practice are explored. We identify future trends in the management of social service organizations that require managers to adopt creative and innovative approaches to empowering practice. At the end of this chapter, we appeal to our readers to contribute to the knowledge base and further development of empowerment-oriented management practice in organizations by conducting qualitative and quantitative assessments of empowerment processes and outcomes.

TOWARD A DEFINITION OF EMPOWERMENT-ORIENTED MANAGEMENT IN SOCIAL SERVICE ORGANIZATIONS

As described in this textbook, the empowerment approach to social service management can be explicated from the theoretical and practice literature in social work, business, social psychology, and other disciplines. The practice of empowerment in organizations involves both process and outcomes. The process of empowerment involves creating opportunities for people to develop skills that can be used to influence others, to participate in organization decision-making, and to take action (through lobbying, electoral campaigns, and other types of activism) to influence social change. The acquisition of actual power, the development of feelings of personal self-competency, and actual changes in social policies and institutions are the outcomes associated with empowerment practice in organizations. As noted in Chapter 1, this model of practice focus on five distinct change targets:

1. Clients and community residents served by neighborhood-representing organizations
2. Staff members
3. The organization as a whole
4. The geographic community served by the organization
5. Social, economic, and political systems (Gutierrez, Parsons, & Cox, 1998)

Social workers, constituents, and organizations have specific roles to play and tasks to perform that contribute to the effectiveness of the empowerment model. These tasks are explicitly spelled out in the citizen participation and empowerment literature. For example, the social worker should engage in nondirective practice in the role of a facilitator (Gutierrez et al., 1998). Activities to be carried out include providing information for self-advocacy to clients, providing leadership and other skills training to members of the constituent group, and establishing self-help groups (Mackelprang & Salsgiver, 1999; Rose & Black, 1985; Zachary, 2000). Workers should assist constituents by identifying informal networks that can be used to recruit new members, enhance community cohesion, and resolve community problems (Brenton, 2001; Miley, O'Melia, & Dubois, 2004). The role of constituents in empowerment practice is to engage in self-advocacy, to develop skills for problem resolution, and to become politically active in order to gain influence to change systems that have oppressed them (Solomon, 1976; Zimmerman & Rappaport, 1988).

To make empowerment practice effective, the organizations that implement empowerment practice must provide opportunities for community residents and constituents to engage in organization decision-making and the political process. Constituents must be recruited for membership on the board and for other decision-making roles on task groups and advisory boards (Brown, 2002; Parker & Betz, 1996). The organization must assist constituents in linking with, and advocating for changes in, larger institutions such as school systems, lending institutions, and local government agencies that have historically oppressed the community (Berger & Neuhaus, 1977). The empowerment-oriented organization must provide resources to facilitate the acquisition of political power by its constituents. Actions to increase political activism among constituents include engagement in lobbying activities and social action as well as voter registration and education (Checkoway & Zimmerman, 1992; Verba, Schlozman, & Brady, 1997).

The outputs that accrue from the model are associated with each of the target groups (Table 15.1). For example, empowerment-oriented practice that incorporates the view and preferences of service users can be expected to make service delivery more responsive to program beneficiaries (Rose & Black, 1985). Constituent involvement in self-help groups, organizational leadership, and political action provides constituents with a sense of control over environmental conditions that foster personal problems and helps them to overcome a sense of powerlessness associated with internalized oppression (Solomon, 1976; Zimmerman & Rappaport, 1988).

Logically, participatory decision-making structures in organizations should have a dual function: to empower both service users and staff members (Gutierrez, GlenMaye, & DeLois, 1995). Consequently, organizational management should provide more opportunities for staff to participate in policy decisions and offer appropriate training and support to staff. In turn, staff members should be able to enhance their own skills, learn to change organization policies, and consequently gain a sense of mastery over their own work environment (Reisch, Wenocur, & Sherman, 1981).

Both the empowerment and citizen participation literature identify numerous benefits for the organization that establishes participatory structures. Service delivery becomes more effective as programs and policies are developed in response to local needs (Checkoway & Zimmerman, 1992). Organizational goals and mission are clear-cut; team approaches are used to improve intrastaff relations and establish partnerships among staff members, clientele, and other constituents. Clients, local residents, and volunteers serve as a constituency base for the organization and provide resources to the organizations (not just money, but skills, volunteer hours, and links to informal networks and local institutions). Consequently, efforts to empower organizational participants increase the power of the organization as well as the local community (institutions and residents) to acquire resources and affect changes in government policies. These organizations can serve as mediating structures, providing an avenue for participation in the larger society as well as a means to learn leadership skills and engage with the political system (Kretzmann & McKnight, 1993; Putnam, 2000).

The intent of an empowerment approach to managing social service organizations is to foster social change at all levels: individual, group, organization, community, and society. Consequently, an intermediate

Table 15.1 Empowerment Model of Service Delivery: Practice Activities and Outcomes

	Social Worker/ Organizer	Constituent	Organization	Community	Political/ Economic Systems
Role	Facilitator	Change agent	Provides opportunities for decision-making		
Practice activities	Provides information	Self-advocacy	Provides resources and trained staff		
	Facilitates self-help groups	Group member	Provides support for new groups		
	Identifies informal networks	Establishes strong networks	Links networks to community institutions		
	Leadership training	Member of the board	Provides leadership opportunities		
	Skills training	Program planner/ researcher	Redesigns service using consumer input		
	Raises critical consciousness	Lobbyist	Engages constituents in policy advocacy		
		Political activist	Encourages sustained political action		
Outcomes	Increases own skills	Increases own skills	Recruits skilled constituents		
	Personal empowerment	Personal empowerment	Better response to client needs		
	Delivers effective service	Acquires resources	Improves service effectiveness and use		
	Power to change organization	Power to change organization	Increases its power to change community	Community change	Reduces oppression
	Participation in social action	Participation in social action	Increases its ability to influence policy		
		Increases own ability to change systems			

Source: Hardina, D. (2004). Linking citizen participation to empowerment practice: A historical overview. *Journal of Community Practice, 11*(4), 11–38.

goal of empowerment-oriented organizing should be to foster real social and economic change in low-income communities. Empowerment efforts should focus on improvements in community life, moving beyond the development of social capital or the creation of informal networks and formal links with institutions. Expected outcomes should include the development of business and job opportunities, reductions in crime and substance abuse, and improvements in the health or educational status of clients and residents of the surrounding community. Finally, the ultimate goal of an empowerment approach that increases the political participation of clients and other constituents should be to bring about changes in legislation or institutional policies that improve the economic, social, and political status of community residents (Table 15.2).

SKILLS NEEDED BY THE TRANSFORMATIVE LEADER IN EMPOWERMENT-ORIENTED SOCIAL SERVICE ORGANIZATIONS

To facilitate the development of an empowerment-oriented social service organization, the manager must have many of the skills associated with transformative leadership. The leader must be able to articulate the mission and goals of the organization and to garner the support and commitment of staff. According to Jaskyte (2004), it is the leader's responsibility to shape organizational culture because

> Their beliefs, values, and assumptions form the core of the organization's culture from the start and are taught to new members. Leaders can transmit and embed organizational culture through deliberate teaching, coaching, role modeling, reward allocation, recruitment, selection, promotion, and other mechanisms. (p. 154)

Consequently, a transformational leader should serve as a role model, illustrating the empowerment approach in working with staff, clients, and other constituents. In this capacity, the leader should create an organizational structure that supports participation in decision-making by clients. According to Linhorst, Eckert, and Hamilton (2005), the empowerment-oriented manager should work to adopt inclusive decision-making structures that contain multiple avenues for participation, seek opportunities to interact with clients on committees and boards, and "promote meaningful client participation by sharing decision-making power and respectfully considering and acting on client preferences" (p. 28). The effective manager must recognize that only in instances where staff members feel empowered themselves will they proactively share power for service-related decision-making with the

Table 15.2 Organizational Characteristics and Intended Outcomes

Organizational Characteristics	Intended Beneficiaries of Change	Increases Participant Skill Development and Feelings of Self-Efficacy	Improves Organization or Community Cohesion	Improves Service Delivery	Successfully Advocates for Social Change
Includes clients/consumers in organizational decision-making	Clients/constituents Organization Society	√	√	√	
Creates partnerships to design and evaluate programs	Clients/constituents Staff members Organization Society	√	√	√	√
Delivers culturally appropriate services	Clients/constituents Staff Organization	√	√	√	
Minimizes power differentials between clients and staff	Clients Staff Organization	√	√	√	
Promotes team building and collaboration among staff members	Staff Organization	√	√	√	
Promotes psychological empowerment of workers by giving them more autonomy to make decisions that affect their work	Staff Organization	√	√	√	

Creates an administrative leadership structure that is ideologically committed to empowering clients and staff members	Administrators Organization	√	√	√	√
Increases employee job satisfaction through the provision of fringe benefits and other incentives	Staff Organization	√	√	√	
Encourages staff to advocate for improvements in service delivery and client resources	Staff Organization	√	√	√	√
Increases the political power of organizational constituents	Constituents Organization Society	√	√	√	√

people they serve. The transformational leader should actively explore new avenues to increase staff participation in organizational decision-making, including team approaches and task groups that flatten organizational hierarchies and reduce artificial barriers between administrators and front-line staff and between staff and program beneficiaries.

The empowerment-oriented, transformational leader should encourage members of the organization to engage in ongoing professional/personal development, increasing their knowledge and skills. The administrator should encourage participants in organizational decision-making to be innovative in applying new technology, theories, or program models to the social problems addressed by the organization. Participants should be actively encouraged to advocate for programs, policies, and services that will improve working conditions for staff and the effectiveness and quality of service delivery. At the same time, clients, staff, and other participants should be supported in their efforts to improve the quality of life of the organization's clientele, the conditions in the surrounding community, and the social, economic, and political institutions that limit opportunities and choice for individuals and marginalized communities. As noted in previous chapters, the best way for the leader to encourage organizational constituents to advocate for themselves or in partnership with others is by serving as a strong advocate for the rights of clients and staff members inside the organization. She or he must be prepared to advocate for the continued well-being and maintenance of the organization with program funders, organization partners, and social institutions that contribute to or potentially restrict the organization's ability to serve its clients. The leader must be a strong advocate for social justice, fighting for programs and policies that improve working conditions and professional development opportunities for staff and changes in policies and regulations that harm clients or limit their access to resources or their social or political rights.

In addition to empowerment and social justice, this management practice model incorporates the principles of cultural diversity and cultural competency among agency staff and in the implementation of organization policy. Managers must be able to hire and retain a diverse workforce able to communicate effectively with clients, to understand their language and cultural customs, and to engage in ongoing dialogue with these consumers in order to identify needs and deliver appropriate services. When hiring staff from the same cultural backgrounds as the clients is not possible, organizations must provide continuous cultural competency training to staff members and establish organizational structures that support the participation of consumers from a variety of backgrounds, cultures, and life experiences in program planning and evaluation. Managers should act as role models, illustrating the practice of nondiscrimination by showing respect for individuals and groups regardless of age, social class, gender, sexual orientation, culture, and religious beliefs. Nondiscrimination should be one of the primary values articulated within the organization and in interactions with clients, volunteers, collaborative partners, local organizations, and funders.

STRENGTHS OF THE EMPOWERMENT MODEL

In addition to the incorporation of core social work principles such as self-determination, social justice, empowerment, and cultural competency, use of the empowerment model by social service managers has numerous advantages. It provides the manager with a uniform approach to his or her work with clients, staff, volunteers, board members, key constituency groups, and external entities that influence and are influenced by the organization. The empowerment approach as practiced by organizational managers contains a specific set of practice activities and specifies expected outcomes if the model were to be implemented properly.

Many of the management practices associated with this model (team building, client involvement, and delegation of power and authority to staff) have been tested empirically. Consequently, many of the hypothetical assumptions contained in this model about the impact of these practices (such as improvements in service quality and effectiveness or increased feelings of self-efficacy among clients and staff) have been confirmed (Bryant, 2003; Checkoway & Zimmerman, 1992; Dailey & Bishop, 2003; Itzhaky & York, 2002; Lewandowski & GlenMaye, 2002; Nandan, 1997; Petter, Byrnes, Choi, Fegan, & Miller, 2002; Spreitzer, 1996; Zimmerman & Rappaport, 1988). Managers have access to a number of standardized measures and tests that will help them document the effects of this model and provide concrete evidence to funders that their programs work. Qualitative research has been conducted to identify effective methods for implementing this model in social service organizations (Bartle, Couchonnal, Canda, & Staker, 2002; Boehm & Staples, 2002; Cohen, 1994; Latting & Blanchard, 1997).

Another benefit of the empowerment model is that its purpose is not simply to serve the needs of funders, managers, or professional staff. Instead, the main purpose of this approach is to make the needs of clients paramount in the delivery of services. However, the emphasis of this model on self-determination and client autonomy reduces the likelihood that the organization will foster dependency on the organization for services among the agency's clientele. The client-centered focus of management practice helps foster a sense of commitment, loyalty, and organizational pride among staff members and other organization constituents. In the course of service delivery, this approach is also expected to improve the client's quality of life and the quality of services offered to the client. The process of establishing client-staff-administrator partnerships for decision-making and service may have a significant impact on reducing conflicts among the various interest groups that can be found within the confines of most social service organizations.

LIMITATIONS OF THE MODEL

A number of issues may adversely affect the use of the empowerment model in social service organizations. One of the primary issues of concern in any social service organization is whether funding is adequate for the effective operation of programs and the adoption of innovative service delivery strategies. Political economy theory suggests that organizations that serve unique or traditionally oppressed population groups may experience difficulty in obtaining adequate funding streams (Alexander, 2000). In order to function financially, organizations must establish legitimacy—public recognition that the organization has the ability to carry out its mission in an appropriate manner. The acquisition of funding for new or established programs can be especially difficult for organizations that provide services to marginalized groups or that engage in social action. Although fundraising for many social service organizations often originates within the community served, the monies raised may be insufficient to address the complex needs prevalent in many low-income or historically oppressed communities (Hardina, 1993). Government, corporations, and some foundations are reluctant to fund social action or untested, innovative programs (Delgado, 1997). Consequently, empowerment-oriented programs that serve low-income communities may have difficulty raising funds from a variety of donors. Executive directors and board members will need to find creative solutions to prevent funding shortfalls and find new sources of funds for social service programs.

A second issue related to funding is the time and money required for effective use of citizen participation and staff consultation approaches in social service organizations. In order to involve additional people in decision-making, extra time must be dedicated to fully informing people about the ramifications of the decision and ensuring that they can be heard. Altering traditional decision-making structures and adopting team or other participatory approaches also takes time. Simply introducing a new approach requires "buy in" from staff and other constituents. Staff members will require an orientation on the new model and training during the start-up phase. The organization may need to recruit new personnel with the skills necessary to implement the new approach. Clients, collaborating organizations, and funders will need to be "sold" on the new model; the organization may need to take a new approach to marketing its services.

A third limitation of the model is that its implementation requires a strong manager who can articulate a vision for the organization. The executive director must be an advocate for the organization, staff, and clients, representing their interests with funders, organizational partners, and government policy-makers. Staff members can be made to feel powerless as they begin to transfer some of the organizational decision-making authority to clients. As noted by Gutierrez et al. (1995), it is especially critical that the executive director be able to provide support, nurturing, and guidance to individual staff members as they put these values in action and work in partnership with client/constituents to transform their lives.

IMPLICATIONS FOR THE FUTURE OF MANAGEMENT PRACTICE IN THE SOCIAL SERVICES

Although we believe that the empowerment approach can be used effectively to manage most social service organizations, a number of recent trends and developments may limit its effectiveness in the future. For example, empowerment-oriented management approaches in for-profit organizations have sometimes been used in conjunction with efforts to downsize the workforce. Flattening the hierarchy may simply be a ploy to reduce the number of supervisory staff and increase the productivity of the remaining workforce. According to Corsun and Enz (1999),

> These efforts lack grounding in a philosophical belief in enabling or empowering employees, and are not reinforced by strong communities based on supportive relationships. Efforts to reduce hierarchy and enrich work jobs may experience failure if the relationships are unsupportive, distrusting, abusive, or manipulative. (p. 222)

Employment opportunities for social workers and other social service personnel can be affected by economic and political conditions. In 2005, Congress approved numerous cuts in programs that served the poor, such as food stamps and home heating subsidies (Inside Politics, 2005). As indicated by some of the empirical research and case studies that describe empowerment in social service organizations, this approach works best when organizations contain formal structures for participation and sufficient funds to pay adequate wages to staff and to provide clients with a variety of service options (Hardina, 1993; Julian, Reischl, Carrick, & Katrenich, 1997; O'Neill, 1992; Silverman, 2003).

Efforts to create a diverse, culturally competent workforce may be affected by recent trends. As noted in Chapter 8, voter referendums in a number of states have resulted in prohibitions against the use of affirmative action in the hiring of state employees and university admissions. However, federal contractors still must meet Affirmative Action requirements. Recent attempts to bring legal challenges against federal Affirmative Action laws have been unsuccessful. However, it is likely that opponents of equal opportunity may yet prevail, based only on ideology, on the courts to suspend, modify, or terminate these programs (Kahlenberg, 2000). One argument that can be made in support of diversity is that many corporate employers have actually found economic advantages in hiring new employees with a variety of perspectives and life experiences that can contribute to the development of innovative products and promote sales to underserved groups ("How HR can make a business case for diversity initiatives," 2003). In addition, the National Association of Social Workers (NASW) *Code of Ethics* reminds us that we as social workers have a responsibility to fight for social justice, cultural diversity, and equal access to resources for all. Consequently, social workers must continue to lobby for legislation that prohibits discrimination in hiring and be proactive in implementing internal organization policies that encourage the recruitment of a diverse group of talented employees and ensure that all staff and clients are treated fairly.

In Chapter 12, we noted that organizations are increasingly using the Internet to raise funds and recruit new members. The Internet and other technological advances will continue to play a role in how social service organizations are linked to the world around them. The Internet has many positive and some negative connotations for citizen involvement and client participation. It helps us disseminate information to others, conduct research, recruit organization members, and raise funds. Creative use of the Internet also allows public and nonprofit decision-makers to consult with a wide range of people when developing plans or evaluating the effectiveness of services. However, we must keep in mind that many low-income or otherwise marginalized people who benefit from social work services do not have access to the Internet and consequently may not be adequately informed about service delivery options or have an opportunity to participate in on-line discussions (Culver & Howe, 2004; McNutt & Boland, 2003).

DIRECTIONS FOR FUTURE RESEARCH ON EMPOWERMENT IN SOCIAL WORK PRACTICE IN ORGANIZATIONS

As noted previously in this chapter, numerous studies in the business and social or organizational psychology literature have examined the impact of empowerment-oriented management, workplace teams, and the total quality management approach. However, empirical studies that focus on the overall impact of empowerment-oriented management in social service organizations have largely been limited to the testing of instruments (Leslie & Holzab, 1998; Parsons, 1999) and qualitative studies about the process of empowerment in organizations (Bartle, et al., 2002; Gutierrez et al., 1995; Latting & Blanchard, 1997).

Therefore, future research on empowerment-oriented management should replicate research already conducted in for-profit industries. Studies should be conducted to determine whether the empowerment model improves service quality, productivity, and job satisfaction, and especially whether empowering management techniques actually improve the lives of our clientele. Are the people we serve more satisfied with the services they receive? Are these services more likely to be accessible and used by those with the greatest need? Have we succeeded in helping our clients increase their personal feelings of psychological empowerment and self-efficacy? Do they feel politically empowered? Have we provided them with the assistance they needed to change some aspect of their personal lives, their communities, or the government policies that have negatively affected them?

BOX 15.1 CRITERIA FOR SUCCESS

Today is the 1-year anniversary of Pang's first day on the job at the Northwest Women's Shelter. Staff and clients have thrown a surprise party for her, complete with cake and decorations. Pang thinks back on her first year as Executive Director with a sense of accomplishment. Significant changes have been made at the shelter, although there are still areas of conflict and difficulty. The empowerment model has proved to be effective in creating a new management structure and guiding decisions about financial planning, service delivery, and external relations.

- What practice principles did Pang most likely put into operation?
- What changes would you expect in the organization's overall structure?
- What are some of the criteria that Pang should use to assess whether her management approach was successful?

- Is it sufficient that Pang should assess whether she has been a successful manager? What other people, inside and outside the organization, should be involved in making this assessment?
- What evaluation techniques could be used to assess both the process of change and the outcomes produced?

Measuring outcomes should not be the only reason to conduct research. We also want to determine how and why empowerment-oriented organizations work. What aspects of these organizations are effective? What things do not work? In addition, we must try to measure the degree to which staff and clients actually are involved in decision-making. How much power do people actually have? We need to document "best practices" for inclusion and personal empowerment so that this information can be disseminated to other organizations.

SUMMARY

In this textbook, we described the parameters of empowerment practice in social service organizations. We believe that this model of practice is the best available. Implementation will help social workers to deliver services that actually empower individuals, marginalized communities, and organizational staff in a manner consistent with values identified in the NASW *Code of Ethics,* such as self-determination and social justice. The model also promotes cultural competency, diversity, and social justice in the delivery of services. Given recent trends in funding and management of social service organization, a model of management practice that incorporates basic practices associated with advocacy and empowerment is our best hope for meeting needs and providing appropriate services. The empowerment-oriented management approach can be fully integrated with, and used to support, empowerment practice with individuals and groups by front-line workers in social service organizations. The social service manager serves as a role model for staff members and clients, illustrating how values should be reflected in practice and how good working partnerships can be established with all organizational constituents, including clients.

QUESTIONS FOR CLASS DISCUSSION

1. In what situations would you as a manager use the empowerment model to guide your practice? Are there situations in which the empowerment model would not be appropriate?

2. What types of things can a manager do to foster commitment and loyalty among staff members?
3. How can organizations evaluate whether empowerment-oriented management has been effective?
4. What types of things could you as an individual practitioner do to promote organizational changes that empower clients and staff members?
5. What types of things could you as an individual social worker do to influence social change? What things can you ethically do as a social worker to encourage your clients to lobby for services or protest against cuts in social service funding?
6. What types of problems would you expect to see in a social service organization if the workforce becomes less diverse or if substantial cuts are made in the organization's budget?

APPENDIX

Web Resources for Nonprofit Managers

PROFESSIONAL ORGANIZATIONS

Association for Community Organization and Social Administration (ACOSA)	http://www.acosa.org/
National Association of Social Workers (NASW)	http://www.naswdc.org/
National Network for Social Work Managers	http://www.socialworkmanager.org/

INFORMATION ABOUT MANAGEMENT PRACTICE IN NONPROFIT ORGANIZATIONS

Carnegie Library of Pittsburgh	http://www.clpgh.org/subject/nonprofits/indexes.html
Idealist.org	http://www.idealist.org/
Independent Sector	http://www.indepsec.org/
Management Assistance Program for Nonprofits	http://www.mapnp.org/library/
National Center for Charitable Statistics/Urban Institute	http://www.guidestar.org
OMBWatch	http://ombwatch.org/

NEEDS ASSESSMENT, PROGRAM EVALUATION, AND PARTICIPATORY RESEARCH METHODS

Action Evaluation Research Institute	http://www.aifs.org.au/sf/actionresearch.html

American Evaluation Association (AEA)	http://www.eval.org
AEA Topical Interest Group on Collaborative, Participatory, and Empowerment Evaluation	http://www.stanford.edu/~davidf/empowermentevaluation.html
Annie E. Casey Foundation	http://www.aecf.org/
Community Tool Box	http://ctb.ku.edu
Guide to Program Evaluation	http://www.mapnp.org/library/evaluatn/fnl_eval.htm
National Neighborhood Partnership	http://www.urban.org/nnip/
Needs Assessment Guide	http://hab.hrsa.gov/tools/assessment.htm

FEDERAL LEGISLATION

Congressional Budget Office	http://www.cbo.gov/
Directory of Federal Agencies	http://www.lib.lsu.edu/gov/fedgov.html
Thomas Legislative Information	http://thomas.loc.gov/
U.S. House of Representatives	http://www.house.gov/
U.S. Senate	http://www.senate.gov/
White House	http://www.whitehouse.gov/

VOTER REGISTRATION

League of Women Voters	http://www.lwv.org
National Association for the Advancement of Colored People (NAACP)	http://www.naacp.org
Project Vote	http://www.projectvote.org
Rock the Vote	http://www.rockthevote.org
Southwest Voter Registration Project	http://www.buscapique.com/latinusa/buscafile/sud/svrep.htm

FUNDRAISING AND PHILANTHROPY

Catalog of Federal Domestic Assistance	http://12.46.245.173/cfda/cfda.html
Federal Register	http://www.gpoaccess.gov/fr/index.html
Foundation Center	http://fdncenter.org/
American Institute of Philanthropy	http://www.charitywatch.org/
Internet Nonprofit Center	http://www.nonprofits.org/
Better Business Bureau (BBB) Wise Giving Alliance	http://www.bbbonline.org/wise/wgadonate.asp
Network for Good	http://www.networkforgood.org/npo/

References

Abramson, J., & Rosenthal, B. (1997). Interdisciplinary and interorganizational collaboration. In *Encyclopedia of social work* (19th ed., Vol. 2, pp. 1479–1489). Washington, DC: National Association of Social Workers.

Abzug, R., & Galaskiewicz, J. (2001). Nonprofit boards: Crucibles of expertise or symbols of local identities. *Nonprofit and Voluntary Sector Quarterly, 30,* 51–73.

Agnes, M. (Ed.). (2002). *Webster's new world dictionary* (2nd ed.). New York: Hunger Minds, Inc.

Alexander, J. (2000). Adaptive strategies of nonprofit human service organizations in an era of devolution and new public management. *Nonprofit Leadership and Management, 10*(3), 287–303.

Allard, P., & Mauer, M. (1998). *Regaining the vote: An assessment of activity relating to felon disenfranchisement laws.* Retrieved August 6, 2000, from http://www.hrw.org/reports98/vote/usvote98.htm.

Allen, N., Foster-Fishman, P., & Salem, D. (2002). Interagency teams: A vehicle for social delivery reform. *Journal of Community Psychology, 30,* 475–497.

Alliances for Better Campaigns. (1998). *Voter turnout.* Retrieved August 1, 2002, from http://www.bettercampaigns.org/documents/turnout.htm.

Almeleh, N., Soifer, S., Gottlieb, N., & Gutierrez, L. (1993). Women's achievement of empowerment through activism in the workplace. *Affilia, 8*(1), 26–39.

Alter, C. (2000). Interorganizational collaboration in the task environment. In R. Patti (Ed.), *The handbook of social welfare management* (pp. 283–302). Thousand Oaks, CA: Sage Publications.

Alvarez, A., & Gutierrez, L. (2001). Choosing to do participatory research: An example and issues of fit to consider. *Journal of Community Practice, 9*(1), 1–20.

Annie E. Casey Foundation. (2001a). *Implementing the values and strategies of family to family.* Baltimore: Annie E. Casey Foundation.

Annie E. Casey Foundation. (2001b). *The need for self-evaluation: Using data to guide policy and practice.* Baltimore: Annie E. Casey Foundation.

Anthony, R., & Young, D. (2003). *Management control in nonprofit organizations.* Boston: McGraw-Hill/Irwin.

Arnstein, S. (1969). A ladder of citizen participation. *Journal of the American Institute of Planners, 35*(4), 216–224.

Arons, D. (1999). *Teaching nonprofit advocacy: A resource guide*. Washington, DC: Independent Sector.

Association of Community College Trustees. (2004). *Board self-evaluation*. Retrieved July 18, 2004, from http://www.acct.org/center/selfeval.htm

Austin, D. (2002). *Human service management: Organizational leadership in social work practice*. New York: Columbia University Press.

Austin, M. (2003). The changing relationship between nonprofit organizations and public social service organizations and public social service agencies in the era of welfare reform. *Nonprofit Sector Quarterly, 32*, 97–114.

Backman, E., & Smith S. R. (2000). Healthy organization, unhealthy communities. *Nonprofit Management and Leadership, 10*, 355–73.

Bailey, D. (1998). Designing and sustaining meaningful organizational teams. In R. Edwards, J. Yankey, & M. Altpeter (Eds.), *Skills for effective management of nonprofit organizations* (pp. 185–199). Washington, DC: National Association of Social Workers.

Baines, D. (2000). Everyday practices of race, class and gender: Struggles, skills, and radical social work. *Journal of Progressive Human Services, 11*(2), 5–27.

Bandura, A. (1997). *Self-efficacy: The exercise of control*. New York: W. H. Freeman and Company.

Barbeito, C., & Bowman, J. (1998). *Nonprofit compensation and benefits practices*. New York: John Wiley & Sons.

Barker, R. (1999). *The social work dictionary* (4th ed.). Washington, DC: National Association of Social Workers.

Barnard, J. (1999). The empowerment of problem-solving teams: Is it an effective management tool? *Journal of Applied Management Studies, 8*, 73–82.

Barrera, I., & Corso, R. (2002). Cultural competency as skilled dialogue. *Topics in Early Childhood Special Education, 22*, 103–113.

Bartle, E., Couchonnal, G., Canda, E., & Staker, M. (2002). Empowerment as a dynamically developing concept for practice: Lessons learned from organizational ethnography. *Social Work, 47*, 32–43.

Bendick, M., Egan, M. L., & Lofhjelm, S. (2001). Workforce diversity training: From anti-discrimination compliance to organizational development. *Human Resource Planning, 24*(2), 10–25.

Beresford, P., & Croft, S. (1993). *Citizen involvement: A practical guide for change*. London: Macmillan.

Berg, B. (1998). *Qualitative methods for the social sciences* (3rd ed.). Boston: Allyn & Bacon.

Berger, P., & Neuhaus, R. (1977). *To empower people: From state to civil society* (2nd ed.). Washington, DC: American Enterprise Institute.

Bernal, G., & Enchautegui-de-Jesus, N. (1994). Latinos and Latinas in community psychology: A review of the literature. *American Journal of Community Psychology, 22*, 531–557.

Bhappu, A., Griffith, T., & Northcraft, G. (1997). Media effects and communication bias in diverse groups. *Organizational Behavior and Human Decision Processes, 70*, 199–205.

Billings-Harris, L. (1998). *The diversity advantage: A guide to making diversity work*. Greensboro, NC: Oakhill Press.

Blau, P. (1964). *Exchange and power in social life.* New York: John Wiley & Sons.

Block, S., & Rosenberg, S. (2002). Toward an understanding of founder's syndrome. *Nonprofit management and leadership, 12,* 353–368.

Bobic, M., & Davis, W. (2003). A kind word for Theory X: Or why so many newfangled management techniques quickly fail. *Journal of Public Administration Research and Theory, 13*(3), 239–264.

Boehm, A., & Staples, L. (2002). The functions of the social worker in empowering. The voices of consumers and professionals. *Social Work, 47,* 337–480.

Boland, K., Barton, J., & McNutt, J. (2002). Social work advocacy and the Internet: The knowledge base. In S. Hick & J. McNutt (Eds.), *Advocacy, activism, and the Internet* (pp. 19–31). Chicago: Lyceum Books.

Bowen, D., & Lawler, E. (1995). Empowering service employees. *Sloan Management Review, 36*(4), 73–84.

Bradshaw, P., Murray, V., & Wolpin, J. (1996). Women on boards of nonprofits: What difference do they make? *Nonprofit Management & Leadership, 5,* 241–254.

Brenton, M. (1999). Sharing power. *Journal of Progressive Human Services, 10*(1), 33–50.

Brenton, M. (2001). Neighborhood resiliency. *Journal of Community Practice, 9*(1), 21–36.

Briar-Lawson, K., Schmid, D., & Harris, N. (1997). Improving training, education and practice agendas in public child welfare. *Public Welfare, 55*(2), 5–7.

British Columbia Ministry for Children and Families. (2005). *Cultural competency assessment tool.* Retrieved June 3, 2004, from http://www.mcf.gov.bc.ca/publications/cultural_competency/assessment_tool/tool_index1.htm.

Brody, R., & Nair, M. (2003). *Macro practice: A generalist approach.* Wheaton, IL: Gregory Publishing Company.

Bronstein, L. (2002). Index of interdisciplinary collaboration. *Social Work Research, 26,* 113–126.

Bronstein, L. (2003). A model for interdisciplinary collaboration. *Social Work, 48,* 297–306.

Brown, W. (2002). Inclusive governance practices in nonprofit organizations and implications for practice. *Nonprofit Management and Leadership, 12,* 369–385.

Brutus, C. (1999). Building community: Community-level power analysis. Retrieved August 4, 2003, from http://www.uwex.edu/ces/buildingcommunity/htm_files/clpa-tools.htm.

Bryant, S. (2003). The role of transformational and transactional leadership in creating, sharing and exploiting organizational knowledge. *Journal of Leadership and Organizational Studies, 9*(4), 32–44.

Burch, H. (1996). *Basic social policy and planning.* New York: Haworth.

Burghardt, S. (1979). The tactical use of group structure and process in community organization. In F. Cox, J. Erlich, J. Rothman, & J. Tropman (Eds.), *Strategies of community organization* (pp. 113–130). Itasca, IL: F. E. Peacock.

Burghardt, S., & Fabricant, M. (1987). Radical social work. In A. Minihan (Ed.), *The encyclopedia of social work* (18th ed., Vol. 2, pp. 455–62). Silver Springs, MD: National Association of Social Workers.

Burke, E. (1983). Citizen participation: Characteristics and strategies. In R. Kramer & H. Specht (Eds.), *Readings in community organization practice* (pp. 105–127). Englewood Cliffs, NJ: Prentice-Hall.

Burke, R., & McKeen, C. (1990). Mentoring in organizations: Implications for women. *Journal of Business Ethics, 9,* 317–322.

Carver, J. (1990). *Boards that make a difference.* San Francisco: Jossey-Bass.

Center for Faith-based and Community Initiatives, U.S. Department of Health & Human Services. (2001). Unlevel playing field: Barriers to participation by faith-based community organizations in federal social service programs. Retrieved October 4, 2004, from http://www.whitehouse.gov/news/releases/2001/08/unlevelfield1.html.

Chambers, D., Wedel, K., & Rodwell, M. (1992). *Evaluating social programs.* Boston: Allyn & Bacon.

Chambon, A. (1999). Foucault's approach: Making the familiar visible. In A. Chambon, A. Irving, & L. Epstein (Eds.), *Reading Foucault for social work* (pp. 51–81). New York: Columbia University Press.

Checkoway, B., & Zimmerman, M. (1992). Correlates of participation in neighborhood organizations. *Administration in Social Work, 16*(3/4), 45–64.

Chernesky, R., & Bombyk, M. (1995). Women's ways and effective management. In J. Tropman, J. Erlich, & J. Rothman (Eds.), *Tactics and techniques of community intervention* (pp. 232–239). Itasca, IL: Peacock Publishers.

Chinman, M., & Wandersman, A. (1999). The benefits and costs of volunteering in community organizations: Review and practical implications. *Nonprofit and Voluntary Sector Quarterly, 28,* 46–64.

Chow, J. (1999). Multiservice centers in Chinese American immigrant communities. *Social Work, 44*(1), 70–87.

Cnaan, R. (1991). Neighborhood-representing organizations: How democratic are they? *Social Service Review, 65*(4), 614–634.

Cnaan, R. (1999). *The newer deal: Social work religion in partnership.* New York: Columbia University Press.

Cnaan, R., Handy, F., & Wadsworth, M. (1996). Defining who is a volunteer: Conceptual and empirical considerations. *Nonprofit and Voluntary Sector Quarterly, 25,* 364–383.

Cohen, B., & Austin, M. (1994). Organizational learning and change in a public welfare agency. *Administration in Social Work,* 18, 1–19.

Cohen, B., & Austin, M. (1997). Transforming social service organizations through the empowerment of staff. *Journal of Community Practice, 4*(2), 35–50.

Cohen, M. (1994). Overcoming obstacles to forming empowerment groups: A consumer advisory board for homeless clients. *Social Work, 39*(6), 742–749.

Cohen, M. (1998). Perceptions of power in client/worker relationships. *Families in Society, 79,* 433–443.

Cohen, T. (1998). Media relationships and marketing. In R. Edwards, J. Yankey, & M. Altpeter (Eds.), *Skills for effective management of nonprofit organizations* (pp. 98–114). Washington, DC: National Association of Social Workers.

Colby, I., & Buffum, W. E. (1998). Social workers and PACs: An examination of National Association of Social Workers P.A.C.E. Committees. *Journal of Community Practice, 5*(4), 87–93.

Combs, G. (2002). Meeting the leadership challenge of a diverse and pluralistic workplace. Implications of self-efficacy for diversity training. *Journal of Leadership Studies, 8*(4), 1–16.

Community Tool Box. (2003). *Conducting advocacy research.* Retrieved September 13, 2003, from http://ctb.ku.edu/tools/en/sub_section_main_1214.htm.

Community Tool Box. (2004). *Developing an ongoing board of directors.* Retrieved July 5, 2004, from http://ctb.ku.edu/tools/en/sub_section_main_1095.htm.

Constitution Project. (2002, April). *Election reform briefing. Voter identification.* Retrieved August 9, 2002, from http://www.electionline.org.

Coombe, C. (1999). Using empowerment evaluation in community organizing and community-based health initiatives. In M. Minkler (Ed.), *Community organization and community building for health* (pp. 291–307). New Brunswick, NJ: Rutgers University Press.

Cooney, K., & Weaver, D. (2001). The implementation of a "work first" welfare-to-work program in a changing environment. *Journal of Community Practice, 9*(3), 33–54.

Cornelius, L., Booker, N., Arthur, T., Reeves, I., & Morgan, O. (2004). The validity and reliability testing of a consumer-based cultural competency inventory. *Research on Social Work Practice, 14,* 201–209.

Cornelius, L., & Ortiz, L. (2004). What will ensure Mexican Americans equal access to health care? In K. Davis & T. Bent-Goodley (Eds.), *The color of social policy* (pp. 155–168). Alexandria, VA: Council on Social Work Education.

Corsun, D., & Enz, C. (1999). Predicting psychological empowerment among service workers: The effect of support-based relationships. *Human Relations, 52,* 205–224.

Council on Social Work Education. (2002). *Accreditation and educational policy standards.* Retrieved December 29, 2004, from http://www.cswe.org.

Cox, E., & Joseph, B. (1998). Social service delivery and empowerment: The administrative role. In L. Gutiérrez, R. Parsons, & E. O. Cox (Eds.), *Empowerment in social work practice* (pp. 167–185). Pacific Grove, CA: Brooks/Cole Publishing Co.

Cox, E., & Parsons, R. (2000). Empowerment-oriented practice. In P. Allen-Meares & C. Garvin (Eds.), *The handbook of social work direct practice* (pp. 113–130). Thousand Oaks, CA: Sage.

Cox, L., Rouff, J., Svendsen, K., Markowitz, M., & Abrams, D. (1998). Community advisory boards: Their role in AIDS clinical trials. *Health and Social Work, 23,* 298–297.

Cross, T. (2001). *Cultural competence continuum.* New York State Citizens' Coalition for Children. Retrieved on June 3, 2005, from http://www.nysccc.org/T-Rarts/CultCompCont.html.

Cross, T., & Friesen, B. (2005). Community practice in children's mental health: Developing cultural competence and family-centered services in systems of care models. In M. Weil (Ed.), *The handbook of community practice* (pp. 442–459). Thousand Oaks, CA: Sage.

Culver, K., & Howe, P. (2004). Calling all citizens. The challenges of public consultation. *Canadian Public Administration, 47,* 52–75.

Dailey, B., & Bishop, J. (2003). TQM Workforce factors and employee involvement: The pivotal role of teamwork. *Journal of Management Issues, 15,* 393–412.

Daley, J. (2002). An action guide for nonprofit board diversity. *Journal of Community Practice, 10*(1), 33–54.

Davis, K., & Bent-Goodley, T. (2004). *The color of social policy.* Alexandria, VA: Council on Social Work Education.

Day, P. (2003). *A new history of social welfare* (4th ed.). Boston: Allyn & Bacon.

DeHoog, R. (1984). *Contracting out for human services.* Albany, NY: State University of New York.

Delgado, G. (1997). *Beyond the politics of place: New directions in community organizing.* Berkeley, CA: Chardon.

Delgado, M. (1996). Puerto Rican food establishments as social service organizations: Results of an asset assessment. *Journal of Community Practice, 3*(2), 57–77.

Delgado, M. (2000). *Community social work practice in an urban context.* New York: Oxford University Press.

Dessler, G. (1998). *Management: Leading people and organizations in the 21st century.* Upper Saddle River, NJ: Prentice Hall.

Devore, W., & Schlesinger, E. (1981). *Ethnic-sensitive social work practice.* St. Louis, MO: C. V. Mosby Company.

Dobelstein, A. (1990). *Social welfare policy and analysis.* Chicago: Nelson-Hall.

Dreher, G., & Ash, R. (1990). A comparative study of mentoring among men and women in managerial, professional, and technical positions. *Journal of Applied Psychology, 75,* 539–546.

Dressel, P. (1992). Patriarchy and social welfare work. In Y. Hasenfeld (Ed.), *Human services as complex organizations* (pp. 205–223). Newbury Park, CA: Sage.

Dropkin, M., & LaTouche, B. (1998). *The budget-building book for nonprofits.* San Francisco: Jossey-Bass.

Drucker, P. (1954). *The practice of management.* New York: Harper.

Duggan, A., Windham, A., McFarlane, E., Fuddy, L., Rohde, C., Buchbinder, S., & Sia, C. (2000). Hawaii's healthy start program of home visiting for at-risk families: Evaluation of family identification, family engagement, and service delivery. *Pediatrics, 105*(1, Pt. 3), 250–259.

Durst, D., MacDonald, J., & Parsons, D. (1999). Finding our way: A community needs assessment on violence in native families in Canada. *Journal of Community Practice, 6*(1), 45–59.

Dworkin, R. (1978). *Taking rights seriously.* Cambridge, MA: Harvard University Press.

Eadie, D. (1998). Managing for quality. In R. Edwards, J. Yankey, & M. Altpeter (Eds.), *Skills for effective management of nonprofit organizations* (pp. 453–468). Washington, DC: National Association of Social Workers.

Edmonson, A. (1999). Psychological safety and learning behavior in work teams. *Administrative Science Quarterly, 44,* 350–367.

Edwards, B., Mooney, L., & Heald, C. (2001). Who is being served? The impact of volunteering on local community organizations. *Nonprofit and Voluntary Sector Quarterly, 30,* 444–461.

Edwards, R., Austin, D., & Altpeter, M. (1998). Managing effectively in an environment of competing values. In R. Edwards, J. Yankey, & M. Altpeter (Eds.), *Skills for effective management of nonprofit organizations* (pp. 5–21). Washington, DC: National Association for Social Workers.

Englund, S. P. (2003). The tax-exemption in-a-day workbook. Retrieved July 9, 2004, from http://www.nonprofitlaw.com/taxworkbook.shtml

Ezell, M. (2001). *Advocacy in the human services.* Belmont, CA: Wadsworth.

Fabricant, M., & Fisher, R. (2002). Agency based community building in low income neighborhoods: A praxis framework. *Journal of Community Practice, 10*(2), 1–22.

Farling, M., Stone, A., & Winston, B. (1999). Servant leadership: Setting the stage for empirical research. *Journal of Leadership Studies, 6*(1/2), 49–72.

Fernandez, H. C. (1980). *The child advocacy handbook.* New York: Pilgrim Press.

Ferris, J. (1993). The double-edged sword of social service contracting. *Nonprofit Management and Leadership, 3,* 363–376.

Fetterman, D. (1996). Empowerment evaluation: An introduction to theory and practice. In D. Fetterman, S. Kaftarian, & A. Wandersman (Eds.), *Empowerment evaluation: Knowledge and tools for self-assessment and accountability* (pp. 3–48). Thousand Oaks, CA: Sage.

Fetterman, D. (2001). *Foundations of empowerment evaluation.* Thousand Oaks: CA: Sage.

Figueira-McDonough, J. (2001). *Community analysis and praxis: Toward a grounded civil society.* Philadelphia: Taylor & Francis.

Finn, J. (2000). A survey of domestic violence organizations on the World Wide Web. In J. Finn & G. Holden (Eds.), *Human services online: A new arena for service delivery* (pp. 83–102). New York: Haworth.

Fischer, J., & Corcoran, K. (1994). *Measures for clinical practice.* New York: Free Press.

Fisher, D., Ryan, R., Esacove, A., Bishofsky, S., Wallis, J., & Roffman, R. (1996). The social marketing of Project ARIES: Overcoming challenges in recruiting gay and bisexual males for HIV prevention counseling. *Journal of Homosexuality, 31*(1/2), 177–202.

Fix, M., & Passel, J. (1999). *Trends in noncitizens' and citizens' use of public benefits following welfare reform, 1994–97.* Retrieved March 27, 2005, from http://www.urban.org

Flynn, F., Chatman, J., & Spataro, S. (2001). Getting to know you: The influence of personality on impressions and performance of demographically different people in organizations. *Administrative Science Quarterly, 46,* 414–442.

Fong, L., & Gibbs, J. T. (1995). Facilitating services to multicultural communities in a dominant culture setting: An organizational perspective. *Administration in Social Work, 19*(2), 1–24.

Forester, J. (1989). *Planning in the face of power*. Berkeley, CA: University of California Press.

Forester, J. (1999). *The deliberative practitioner: Encouraging participatory planning processes*. Cambridge, MA: Massachusetts Institute of Technology.

Forrester, R. (2000). Empowerment: Rejuvenating a potent idea. *The Academy of Management Executive, 14,* 67–80.

Franco, L., Bennett, S., & Kanfer, R. (2002). Health sector reform and public sector health worker motivation: A conceptual framework. *Social Science & Medicine, 54,* 1255–1266.

Freire, P. (1970). *Pedagogy of the oppressed*. New York: Continuum.

Friedmann, J. (1987). *Planning in the public domain: From knowledge to action*. Princeton, NJ: Princeton University Press.

Galambos, C. (2003). Moving cultural diversity forward: Cultural competency in health care. *Health and Social Work, 28*(1), 3–7.

Gallagher, R. (1997). *Elements of empowerment in organizations*. Retrieved July 3, 2004, from http://www.orgdct.com/elements_of_empowerment_in_an_or.htm

Gamble, D., & Weil, M. (1992, March). *Theory construction for citizen participation in community organization practice*. Paper presented at the Annual Program Meeting of the Council on Social Work Education, Kansas City, MI.

Gant, L. (1996). Are culturally sophisticated agencies better workplaces for social work staff and administrators? *Social Work, 41,* 163–171.

Gant, L., & Gutierrez, L. (1996). Effects of culturally sophisticated agencies on Latino social workers. *Social Work, 41*(6), 624–631.

Garcia, B., & Van Soest, D. (1997). Changing perceptions of diversity and oppression: MSW students discuss the effects of a required course. *Journal of Social Work Education, 33,* 119–129.

Gardner, J. (1999a). Quality in services. In J. Gardner & S. Nudler (Eds.), *Quality performance in human services* (pp. 3–18). Baltimore: Paul H. Brookes Publishing Co.

Gardner, J. (1999b). Quality in services for people with disabilities. In J. Gardner & S. Nudler (Eds.), *Quality performance in human services* (pp. 21–42). Baltimore: Paul H. Brookes Publishing Co.

Gellis, Z. (2001). Social work perceptions of transformational and transactional leadership in health care. *Social Work Research, 25,* 17–25.

Gibelman, M., & Demone, H. (2003). The commercialization of health and human services: Natural phenomenon or cause for concern. *Families in Society, 83,* 387–397.

Gibelman, M., & Gelman, S.R. (2002). Should we have faith in faith-based social services? Rhetoric versus realistic expectations. *Nonprofit Management and Leadership, 13,* 49–65.

Gidron, B., & Hasenfeld, Y. (1994). Human service organizations and self-help groups: Can they collaborate? *Nonprofit Leadership and Management, 5,* 159–172.

Gilbert, D., & Franklin, C. (2001). Developing culturally sensitive practice evaluation skills with Native American individuals and families. In R. Fong & S. Furuto (Eds.), *Culturally competent practice: Skills, interventions, and evaluations* (pp. 396–411). Boston: Allyn & Bacon.

Gilbert, N., Specht, H., & Terrell, P. (1993). *Dimensions of social welfare policy* (3rd ed.) Englewood Cliffs, NJ: Prentice-Hall.

Gilligan, C. (1988). Adolescent development reconsidered. In C. Gilligan, J. Ward, & J. Taylor, with B. Bardige (Eds.), *Mapping the moral domain: A contribution of women's thinking to psychological theory and education* (pp. vii–xxxix). Cambridge, MA: Harvard University Press.

Ginsberg, L. (2001). *Social work evaluation: Principles and methods*. Boston: Allyn & Bacon.

Gist, M. E. (1987). Self-efficacy: Implications for organizational behavior and human resource management. *The Academy of Management Review, 12*, 472–485.

Gittell, M. (1980). *Limits to citizen participation: The decline of community organization*. Beverly Hills, CA: Sage.

Goodban, N. (1985). The psychological impact of being on welfare. *Social Service Review, 58*, 403–422.

Gopaul-McNichol, S. (1997). *A multicultural/multimodal/multisystems approach to working with culturally different families*. Westport, CT: Praeger.

Graham, J., & Barter, K. (1999). Collaboration: A social work practice method. *Families in Society, 80*(1), 6–13.

Graham, M. (1999). African-centered worldview: Developing a paradigm for social work. *British Journal of Social Work, 29*(2), 251–267.

Green, J. (1999). *Cultural awareness in the human services: A multi-ethnic approach*. Boston: Allyn & Bacon.

Green, R. (1998). Maximizing the use of performance contracts. In R. Edwards, J. Yankey, & M. Altpeter (Eds.), *Skills for effective management of non-profit organizations* (pp. 78–97). Washington, DC: National Association of Social Workers.

Green, R., Kiernan-Stern, M., Bailey, K., Chambers, K., Claridge, R., Jones, G., Kitson, G., Leek, S. Leisey, M., Vadas, K., & Walker, K. (2005). The Multicultural Counseling Inventory: A measure for evaluating social work student and practitioner self-perceptions of their multicultural competencies. *Journal of Social Work Education, 41*, 191–209.

Greene, A., & Latting, J. (2004). Whistle-blowing as a form of advocacy: Guidelines for the practitioner and organization. *Social Work, 47*, 219–229.

Gronbjerg, K. (1992). Nonprofit human service organizations: Funding strategies and patterns of adaptation. In Y. Hasenfeld (Ed.), *Human services as complex organizations* (pp. 73–97). Newbury Park, CA: Sage.

Gronbjerg, K., Chen, T., & Stagner, M. (1995). Child welfare contracting: Market forces and leverage. *Social Service Review, 69*, 583–613.

Gronbjerg, K., & Never, B. (2004). The role of religious networks and other factors in types of volunteer work. *Nonprofit Management and Leadership, 14*, 263–289.

Guin, C., Noble, D., & Merrill, T. (2003). From misery to mission: Forensic social workers on multidisciplinary mitigation teams. *Social Work, 48*, 362–371.

Gulati, P. (1982). Consumer participation in decision-making. *Social Service Review, 55*, 403–422.

Gummer, B. (1997). Public versus business administration: Are they alike in unimportant ways? *Administration in Social Work, 21*(2), 81–98.

Gummer, B. (2002). The socio-economic context of organizational behavior. *Administration in Social Work, 26*(3), 71–88.

Guo, C. (2004). *When government becomes the principal philanthropist: The effect on public funding on patterns of nonprofit governance.* Tempe, AZ: Center for Nonprofit Leadership and Management, College of Public Programs, Arizona State University.

Gutierrez, L. (1990). Working with women of color: An empowerment perspective. *Social Work, 35*(2), 149–153.

Gutierrez, L. (1995). Understanding the empowerment process: Does consciousness make a difference? *Social Work Research, 19,* 229–237.

Gutierrez, L., & Alvarez, A. (2000). Educating students for multicultural community practice. *Journal of Community Practice, 7*(1), 39–56.

Gutierrez, L., Fredricksen, & Soifer, S. (1999). Perspectives of social work faculty on diversity and societal oppression content: Results from a national survey. *Journal of Social Work Education, 35,* 409–420.

Gutierrez, L., GlenMaye, L., & DeLois, K. (1995). The organizational context of empowerment practice: Implications for social work administration. *Social Work, 40*(2), 249–258.

Gutierrez, L., Kruzich, J., Jones, T., & Coronado, N. (2000). Identifying goals and outcomes measures for diversity training: A multi-dimensional framework for decision-makers. *Administration in Social Work, 24*(3), 53–70.

Gutierrez, L., & Lewis, E. (1994). Community organizing with women of color: A feminist approach. *Journal of Community Practice, 1*(2), 23–44.

Gutierrez, L., Lewis, E., Nagda, B., Wernick, L., & Shore, N. (2005). Multicultural community practice strategies and intergroup empowerment (pp. 341–359). In M. Weil (Ed.), *The handbook of community practice.* Thousand Oaks, CA: Sage.

Gutierrez, L., Parsons, R., & Cox, E. (1998). *Empowerment in social work practice: A source book.* Pacific Grove, CA: Brooks/Cole.

Hacker, S., & Roberts, T. (2004). *Transformational leadership: Creating organizations of meaning.* Milwaukee, WI: Quality Press.

Handler, J. (1992). Dependency and discretion. In Y. Hasenfeld (Ed.), *Human services as complex organizations* (pp. 276–297). Newbury Park, CA: Sage.

Handy, F., & Srinivasan, N. (2004). Valuing volunteers: An economic evaluation of the net benefits of hospital volunteers. *Nonprofit and Voluntary Sector Quarterly, 33,* 28–54.

Hardcastle, D., Wenocur, S., & Powers, P. (1997). *Community practice: Theories and skills for social workers.* New York: Oxford University Press.

Hardina, D. (1988). *Consumer-inclusive versus client-exclusive strategies of service delivery.* Unpublished dissertation, College of Urban Planning and Policy, University of Illinois at Chicago.

Hardina, D. (1990). The effect of funding sources on client access to services. *Administration in Social Work, 14*(3), 33–46.

Hardina, D. (1993). The impact of funding sources and board representation on consumer control in organizations serving three low-income communities. *Nonprofit Management and Leadership, 4*(1), 69–84.

Hardina, D. (1995). Do Canadian social workers practice advocacy? *Journal of Community Practice, 2*(3), 97–121.

Hardina, D. (1997). Empowering students for community organization practice: Teaching confrontation tactics. *Journal of Community Practice, 4*(2), 51–63.

Hardina, D. (2002). *Analytical skills for community organization practice.* New York: Columbia University Press.

Hardina, D. (2004). Linking citizen participation to empowerment practice: A historical overview. *Journal of Community Practice, 11*(4), 11–38.

Hardina, D., & Malott, O. (1996a). Strategies for the empowerment of low-income consumers on community-based planning boards. *Journal of Progressive Human Services, 7*(2), 43–61.

Hardina, D., & Malott, O. (1996b). Community empowerment: Past experience and future trends. *Canadian Review of Social Policy, 37,* 1–19.

Hardina, D., & Shaw, K. (2001). *Evaluation of the Merced County peer mentor program.* Fresno, CA: Department of Social Work Education, California State University, Fresno.

Harding, S. (1998). *Is science multicultural?* Bloomington, IN: Indiana University Press.

Hartman, A. (1989). Still between client and community. *Social Work, 34,* 387–388.

Hasenfeld, Y. (1992). *Human services as complex organizations.* Newbury Park, CA: Sage.

Hasenfeld, Y., & Weaver, D. (1996). Enforcement, compliance, and disputes in welfare-to-work programs. *Social Service Review, 70,* 235–256.

Hawkins, F., & Gunther, J. (1998). Managing for quality. In R. Edwards, J. Yankey, & M. Altpeter (Eds.), *Skills for effective management of non-profit organizations* (pp. 525–554). Washington, DC: National Association of Social Workers.

Haynes, K., & Mickelson, J. (2005). *Affecting change: Social workers in the political arena* (6th ed.). New York: Longman.

Hefetz, A., & Warner, M. (2004). Privatization and its reverse: Explaining the dynamics of the government contracting process *Journal of Public Administration Research and Theory, 14,* 171–180.

Hein, J. (2000). Interpersonal discrimination against Hmong Americans. *The Sociological Quarterly, 41,* 413–429.

Henrickson, M., & Mayo, J. (2000). The HIV cybermall: A regional cybernetwork of HIV services. In J. Finn & G. Holden (Eds.), *Human services on-line* (pp. 7–26). New York: Haworth.

Henry, C. (1998). Effective grant writing. In R. L. Edwards, J. A. Yankey., & M. A. Altpeter (Eds.), *Skills for effective management of nonprofit organizations* (pp. 45–58). Washington, DC: National Association of Social Workers.

Hoefer, R. (1995). Desired job skills for human service administrators. In J. Tropman, J. Erlich, & J. Rothman (Eds.), *Tactics and techniques of community intervention* (pp. 272–276). Itasca, IL: Peacock Publishers.

Holland, T. (1998). Strengthening board performance. In R. Edwards, J. Yankey, & M. Altpeter (Eds.), *Skills for effective management of nonprofit organizations* (pp. 425–452). Washington, DC: National Association of Social Workers.

"How HR can make a business case for diversity initiatives." (2003). *Human Resource Department Management*, p. 6.

Hummel, J. (1996). *Starting and running a nonprofit organization* (2nd ed.). Minneapolis. MN: University of Minnesota Press.

Hyde, C. (1989). A feminist model for macro practice: Promises and problems. *Administration in Social Work, 13,* 145–181.

Hyde, C. (1994). Commitment to social change: Voices from the feminist movement. *Journal of Community Practice, 1*(2), 45–63.

Hyde, C. (2003). Multicultural organization development in nonprofit human service agencies: Views from the field. *Journal of Community Practice, 11*(1), 39–59.

Hyde, C. (2004) Multicultural development in human service agencies: Challenges and solutions. *Social Work, 49,* 7–16.

Iannello, K. (1992). *Decisions without hierarchy.* New York: Routledge.

Iglehart, A., & Becerra, R. (2000). *Social services and the ethnic community.* Prospect Heights, IL: Waveland Press.

Independent Sector. (2001). *New nonprofit almanac in brief: Facts and figures on the independent sector 2001.* Retrieved September 29, 2004, from http://www.independentsector.org/PDFs/inbrief.pdf

Information Technology International, Inc. (2002). *Self-evaluation workbook.* Retrieved June 15, 2004, from http://www.itiincorporated.com/sew_dl.htm

Inglis, S., Alexander, T., & Weaver, L. (1999). Roles and responsibilities of community nonprofit boards. *Nonprofit Management & Leadership, 10,* 153–167.

Inside Politics. (2005, February 5). *Dramatic cuts part of Bush budget.* Retrieved February 13, 2005, from http://www.cnn.com/2005/ALLPOLITICS/02/05/bush.budget.ap/

Itzhaky, H. (1995). Effects of organizational and role components on job satisfaction: A study of nonprofessional women. *Administration in Social Work, 19*(3), 1–16.

Itzhaky, H., & York, A. (2002). Showing results in community organization. *Social Work, 47*(2), 125–131.

Jackson, D., & Holland, T. (1998). Measuring the effectiveness of nonprofit boards. *Nonprofit and Voluntary Sector Quarterly, 27,* 159–182.

Jackson, R., Brown, R., & Wright, G. (1998). Registration, turnout, and the electoral representativeness of U.S. state electorates. *American Politics Quarterly, 26*(3), 259–272.

Jansson, B. (1999). *Becoming an effective policy advocate.* Pacific Grove, CA: Brooks/Cole.

Jaskyte, K. (2004). Transformational leadership, organizational culture, and innovativeness in nonprofit organizations. *Nonprofit Leadership & Management, 15,* 153–168.

Jasper, J., & Paulsen, J. (1995). Recruiting strangers and friends: Moral shocks and social networks in animal rights and anti-nuclear protests. *Social Problems, 42,* 493–513.

Johnson, A. (1994). Linking professionalism and community organization: A scholar/advocacy approach. *Journal of Community Practice,* 1(2), 65–86.

Johnson, D., & Johnson, F. (2003). *Joining together: Group theory and group skills.* Boston: Allyn & Bacon.

Julian, D., Reischl, T., Carrick, R., & Katrenich, C. (1997). Citizen participation-lessons from a local United Way planning process. *Journal of the American Planning Association, 63,* 345–355.

Kahlenberg, R. (2000). Affirmative action should be based on class, not race. In B. Grapes (Ed.), *Affirmative action.* San Diego, CA: Greenhaven Press.

Kahn, S. (1991). *Organizing: A guide for grass-roots leaders.* Washington, DC: National Association of Social Workers Press.

Kaiser, T. (1997). *Supervisory relationships: Exploring the human element.* Pacific Grove, CA: Brooks/Cole.

Kaminski, M., Kaufman, J., Graubarth, R., & Robins, T. (2000). How do people become empowered?: A case study of union activism. *Human Relations, 53,* 53–63.

Kelly, M. (2001). Management mentoring in a social service organization. *Administration in Social Work, 25*(1), 17–33.

Kettner, P. (2002). *Achieving excellence in the management of human service organizations.* Boston: Allyn & Bacon.

Kettner, P., Moroney, R., & Martin, L. (1999). *Designing and managing programs: An effectiveness-based approach* (2nd ed.). Thousand Oaks, CA: Sage.

King, C., Feltey, K., & Susel, B. (1998). The question of participation: Toward authentic public participation in public administration. *Public Administration Review, 58*(4), 317–327.

Kirkman, B., & Rosen, B. (1999). Beyond self-management: Antecedents and consequences of team empowerment. *Academy of Management Journal, 42,* 58–73.

Knuttilia, M. (1992). *State theories: From liberalism to the challenge of feminism.* Halifax, Nova Scotia: Fernwood.

Kramer, R. (1985). Toward a contingency model of board-executive relations. *Administration in Social Work, 9,* 15–33.

Kramer, R., & Grossman, B. (1987). Contracting for social services: Process and management and resource dependencies. *Social Services Review, 61,* 32–55.

Kretzmann, J., & McKnight, J. (1993). *Building communities from the inside out.* Chicago: ACTA.

Larson, L., Day, S., Springer, S., Clark, M., & Vogel, D. (2003). Developing a supervisor feedback rating scale: A brief report. *Measurement and Evaluation in Counseling and Development, 35,* 230–238.

Latting, J., & Blanchard, A. (1997). Empowering staff in a poverty agency: An organization development intervention. *Journal of Community Practice, 4*(3), 59–75.

Lawler, E., Mohrman, S., & Ledford, G. (1995). *Creating high performance organizations.* San Francisco: Jossey-Bass.

League of Women Voters. (2002a). *Mail registration-identification and first time in-person voting requirements.* Retrieved July 7, 2002, from http://www.lwv.org/elibrary/pub/ear_photoid.html.

League of Women Voters. (2002b). *Election reform survey.* Retrieved July 7, 2002, from http://www.lwv.org.

Lee, J. (2001). *The empowerment approach to social work practice.* New York: Columbia University Press.

Lee, M., & Greene, G. (1999). A social constructivist framework for integrating cross-cultural issues in teaching clinical social work. *Journal of Social Work Education, 35*(1), 21–37.

Leslie, D., & Holzab, C. (1998). Measuring staff empowerment: Development of a worker empowerment scale. *Research on Social Work Practice, 8,* 212–223.

Lewandowski, C., & GlenMaye, L. (2002). Teams in child welfare settings: Interprofessional and collaborative processes. *Families in Society, 83,* 245–256.

Lewin, K. (1951). *Field theory in social science: Selected theoretical papers.* New York: Harper & Row.

Lewis, H. (2002). Participatory research and education for social change: Highlander Research and Education Center. In P. Reason & H. Bradbury (Eds.), *Handbook of action research* (pp. 356–362). Thousand Oaks, CA: Sage.

Lewis, J. A., Lewis, M. D., Packard, T., & Souflée, F. (2001). *Management of human service programs* (3rd ed.), Belmont, CA: Wadsworth/Thomson Learning.

Lesser, E.L. (2000). *Knowledge and social capital: Foundations and applications.* Boston: Butterworth-Heinemann.

Lindblom, C. (1959). The science of muddling through. *Public Administration Review, 19,* 79–88.

Linhorst, D., & Eckert, A. (2003). Conditions for empowering people with severe mental illness. *Social Service Review, 77,* 279–305.

Linhorst, D., Eckert, A., & Hamilton, G. (2005). Promoting participation in organizational decision-making by clients with severe mental illness. *Social Work, 50*(1), 21–30.

Lipsky, M. (1980). *Street-level bureaucracy.* New York: Russell Sage Foundation.

Locke, E., & Latham, G. P. (1990). *A theory of goal setting and task performance.* Englewood Cliffs, NJ: Prentice Hall.

Lohmann, R., & Lohmann, N. (2002). *Social administration.* New York: Columbia University Press.

Lopez, S., & Guarnaccia, P. (2000). Cultural psychopathology: Uncovering the social world of mental illness. *Annual Review of Psychology, 51,* 571–598.

Lowe, J., Barg, F., & Stephens, K. (1998). Community residents as lay health educators in a cancer prevention program. *Journal of Community Practice, 5*(4), 39–52.

Lowenberg, F., & Dolgoff, R. (1996). *Ethical decisions for social work practice* (5th ed.). Itasca, IL: F. E. Peacock.

Lum, D. (1996). *Social work practice and people of color:* A process-stage approach. Pacific Grove, CA: Brooks/Cole.

Lum, D. (1999). *Culturally competent practice: A framework for growth and action.* Pacific Grove, CA: Brooks/Cole.

Mackelprang, R., & Salsgiver, R. (1999). *Disability: A diversity model approach in human service practice.* Pacific Grove, CA: Brooks/Cole.

Maeve, M. K. (1998). Methodological issues in qualitative research with incarcerated women. *Family and Community Health.* Retrieved July 12, 2002, from http://www.findarticles.com/cf_dls/m0FSP/3_21/53578837/print.jhtml.

Manning, S. (1999). Building an empowerment model of practice through the voices of people with serious disabilities. In W. Shera & L. Wells (Eds.), *Empowerment practice in social work* (pp. 102–118). Toronto, Canada: Canadian Scholars' Press.

Marris, P., & Rein, M. (1982). *Dilemmas of social reform.* Chicago: University of Chicago Press.

Marti-Costa, S., & Serrano-Garcia, I. (1995). Needs assessment and community development: An ideological perspective. In J. Rothman, J. Erlich, & J. Tropman (Eds.), *Strategies of community intervention* (5th ed., pp. 257–67). Itasca, IL: F. E. Peacock.

Martin, L. (2001). *Financial management for human service administrators.* Boston: Allyn & Bacon.

Martin, P. Y. (1980). Multiple constituencies, dominant societal values, and the human service administration: Implications for service delivery. *Administration in Social Work, 4*(2), 15–27.

Martocchio, J. (2003). *Employee benefits: A primer for human resource professionals.* Boston: McGraw-Hill Irwin.

Marx, K. (1965). *Capital* (Vol. 1). Moscow: Progress. (Original work published in 1867).

McCarthy, J., & Walker, E. (2004). Alternative organizational repertories of poor people's social movement organizations. *Nonprofit and Voluntary Sector Quarterly, 33*(3 Suppl.), 97S–117S.

McCauley, C., & Hughes, M. (1991). Leadership challenges for human service administrators. *Nonprofit Leadership and Management, 1,* 267–281.

McFarlane, J., & Fehir, J. (1994). De Madres a Madres: A community, primary health care program based on empowerment. *Health Education Quarterly, 21,* 381–394.

McGregor, D. (1969). The human side of enterprise. In W. Eddy, W. Burke, V. Dupre, & O. South (Eds.), *Behavioral science and the manager's role* (pp. 157–166). Washington, DC: NT: Institute for Applied Behavioral Science.

McKenzie, B. (1999). Empowerment in First Nations child and family services. In W. Shera & L. Wells (Eds.), *Empowerment practice in social work* (pp. 198–219). Toronto, Canada: Canadian Scholars' Press.

McNamara, C. (2004). *Board of directors' self-evaluation.* Retrieved July 14, 2004, from http://www.mapnp.org/library/boards/brd_eval.htm.

McNutt, J. (1995). The macro practice curriculum in graduate education: Results of a national study. *Administration in Social Work, 19*(3), 59–74.

McNutt, J., & Boland, K. (2003, November). *Will they come if we build it? Levels of electronic government development and citizen use of the Internet for public policy change.* Paper presented at the 32nd Annual Meeting of the Association for Research on Nonprofit Organizations and Voluntary Action, Denver, Colorado.

McPhatter, A. (1997), Cultural competence in child welfare. *Child Welfare, 76,* 259–260.

Meenaghan, T., Washington, R., & Ryan R. (1982). *Macro practice in the human services.* New York: Free Press.

Meier, A., & Usher, C. (1998). New approaches to program evaluation. In R. Edwards, J. Yankey, & Altpeter, A. (Eds.), *Skills for effective management of nonprofit organizations* (pp. 371–405). Washington, DC: National Association of Social Workers.

Menefee, D. (2000). What managers do and why they do it. In R. Patti (Ed.), *The handbook of social welfare management* (pp. 247–266). Thousand Oaks, CA: Sage.

Merideth, E. (1994). Critical pedagogy and its application to health education: A critical appraisal of the casa en casa model. *Health Education Quarterly, 21,* 355–367.

Metzendorf, D., & Cnaan, R. (1992). Volunteers in feminist organizations. *Nonprofit Leadership and Management, 2,* 255–269.

Middleton, E. J. (1985). *A view from the field.* Ann Arbor, MI: School of Social Work, University of Michigan.

Miley, K., O'Melia, M., & Dubois, B. (2004). *Generalist social work practice: An empowering approach* (2nd ed.). Boston: Allyn & Bacon.

Miller-Millesen, J. (2003). Understanding the behavior of nonprofit boards of directors: A theory-based approach. *Nonprofit and Voluntary Sector Quarterly, 32,* 521–547.

Milofsky, C. (1988). *Community organization: Studies in resource mobilization and exchange.* New York: Oxford University Press.

Minkoff, D. (1997). Producing social capital: National social movements and civil society. *American Behavioral Scientist, 40*(5), 606–621.

Miringoff, M. L., & Opdycke, S. (1986). *American social welfare: Reassessment and reform.* Englewood Cliffs, NJ: Prentice-Hall.

Mittleman, D., & Briggs, R. (1999). Communication technologies for traditional and virtual teams. In E. Sundstrom & Associates (Eds.), *Supporting work team effectiveness* (pp. 246–270). San Francisco: Jossey-Bass.

Mizrahi, T., & Abramson, J. (2000). Collaboration between social workers and physicians: Perspectives on a shared case. *Social Work in Health Care, 31,* 1–24.

Mizrahi, T., & Rosenthal, B. (1993). Managing dynamic tensions in social change coalition. In T. Mizrahi & J. Morrison (Eds.), *Community organization and social administration* (pp. 11–40). New York: Haworth.

Moffat, K. (1999). Surveillance and government of the welfare recipient. In A. Chambon, A. Irving, & L. Epstein (Eds.), *Reading Foucault for social work* (pp. 219–245). New York: Columbia University Press.

Menefee, D. (2000). What managers do and why they do it. In R. Patti (Ed.), *The handbook of social welfare management* (pp. 247–266). Thousand Oaks, CA: Sage.

Mohrman, S., Cohen, S., & Mohrman, A. (1995). *Designing team-based organizations.* San Francisco: Jossey-Bass.

Mondros, J. (2005). Political, social, and legislative action. In M. Weil (Ed.), *The handbook of community practice* (pp. 276–286). Thousand Oaks, CA: Sage.

Mondros, J., & Wilson, S. (1994). *Organizing for power and empowerment.* New York: Columbia University Press.

Montana, P., & Charnov, B. (2000). *Management* (3rd ed.). Hauppauge, NY: Barron's Educational Series.

Mordock, J. (1996). The road to survival revisited. Organizational adaptation to the managed care environment. *Child Welfare, 75,* 195–219.

Morgen, S. (1994). Personalizing personnel decisions in feminist organizational theory and practice. *Human Relations, 47,* 665–684.

Moynihan, D. (1969). *Maximum feasible misunderstanding.* New York: Free Press.

Mueller, C. (1992). Building social movement theory. In A. Morris & C. Mueller (Eds.), *Frontiers in social movement theory* (pp. 3–25). New Haven, CT: Yale University Press.

Murray, V., Bradshaw, P., & Wolpin, J. (1992). Power in and around nonprofit boards: A neglected dimension of governance. *Nonprofit Management & Leadership, 3,* 165–182.

Murty, S. (1998). Network analysis as a research methodology. In R. MacNair (Ed.), *Research methods for community practice* (pp. 21–46). New York: Haworth.

Nagda, B., Harding, S., & Holley, L. (1999). Social work and multicultural organization development: Toward empowering and empowered organizations. In W. Shera & L. Wells (Eds.), *Empowerment practice in social work.* Toronto, Canada: Canadian Scholars' Press.

Nandan, M. (1997). Commitment of social services staff to interdisciplinary care plan teams: An exploration. *Research in Social Work, 21,* 249–259.

National Association for the Advancement of Colored People. (2002). *Defending the vote: Holding officials accountable–NAACP 2001 election report.* Retrieved July 30, 2002, from http://www.naacp.org/news/releases/ElectionReformJuly02.pdf.

National Association of Social Workers. (1999). *Code of ethics.* Retrieved June 6, 2004, from http://www.naswdc.org/pubs/code/code.asp.

National Association of Social Workers. (2001). *NASW standards for cultural competence in social work practice.* Retrieved June 12, 2005, from http://www.socialworkers.org/sections/credentials/cultural_comp.asp.

National Respite Network and Resource Center. (1993). *Advisory boards and boards of directors.* Retrieved July 6, 2004, from http://sabes.org/resources/advisoryboards.htm.

National Technical Assistance Center for State Mental Health Planning. (2004, September). *Cultural competency: Measurement as a strategy for moving knowledge into practice in state mental health systems.* Retrieved June 9, 2005, from http://www.nasmhpd.org/general_files/publications/cult%20comp.pdf.

Neighbors, H., & Taylor, R. (1985). The use of social service agencies by Black Americans. *Social Service Review, 59,* 266–269.

Netting, F. E., Nelson, H. W., Borders, K., & Huber, R. (2004). Volunteer and paid staff relationships: Implications for social work administration. *Administration in Social Work, 28*(3), 69–89.

Netting, F. E., & O'Connor, M. K. (2003). *Organization practice: A social worker's guide to understanding human services.* Boston: Allyn & Bacon.

Neuman, W. L. (2003). *Social research methods.* Boston: Pearson Education.

Neysmith, S., & Reitsma-Street, M. (2000). Valuing unpaid work in the third sector: The case of community resource centres. *Canadian Public Policy, 26*(3), 331–346.

Norlin, J., & Chess, W. (1997). *Human behavior and the social environment: Social systems theory* (3rd ed.). Boston: Allyn & Bacon.

O'Connell, B. (1996). A major transfer of government responsibility to voluntary organizations? Proceed with caution. *Public Administration Review, 56,* 222–225.

Okayama, C., Furuto, S., & Edmondson, J. (2001). Components of cultural competence: Attitudes, knowledge, and skills. In R. Fong & S. Furuto (Eds.), *Culturally competent practice: Skills, interventions, and evaluations* (pp. 89–100). Boston: Allyn & Bacon.

Oliker, S. (1998). The proximate contexts of workfare and work. *Sociological Quarterly, 36,* 251–272.

Omoto, A., & Snyder, M. (1993). AIDS volunteers and their motivations. *Nonprofit Sector Quarterly,* 4, 157–176.

O'Neill, M. (1992). Community participation in Quebec's health system. *International Journal of Health Services, 22*(2), 287–301.

Orlandi, M. A. (1992*). Cultural competence for evaluators: A guide for alcohol and other drug abuse prevention practitioners working with ethnic/racial communities.* Rockville, MD: Office for Substance Abuse Prevention.

Ouchi, W. (1981). *Theory Z: How American business can meet the Japanese challenge.* Reading, MA: Addison Wesley.

Padilla, Y., Lein, L., & Cruz, M. (1999). Community-based research in policy planning: A case study addressing poverty in the Texas-Mexico border region. *Journal of Community Practice, 6*(3), 1–22.

Parker, L., & Betz, D. (1996). Diverse partners in planning and decision making. *Partnerships in education and research.* 2000. Retrieved September 8, 2002, from http://cru.cahe.wsu.edu/CEPublications/wrep0133/wreip0133.html.

Parsons, R. (1999). Assessing helping processes and client outcomes in empowerment practice: Amplifying client voice and satisfying funding sources. In W. Shera & L. Wells (Eds.), *Empowerment practice in social work* (pp. 390–417). Toronto, Canada: Canadian Scholars' Press.

Parsons, T. (1971). *The system of modern societies.* Englewood Cliffs, NJ: Prentice-Hall.

Patterson, S., & Marsiglia, F. F. (2000). "Mi casa es su casa": Beginning exploration of Mexican Americans' natural helping. *Families in Society, 81*(1), 22–31.

Patti, R. (2000). *The handbook of social welfare management.* Thousand Oaks, CA: Sage.

Patton, C., & Sawicki, D. (1993). *Basic methods of policy analysis and planning* (2nd ed.). Englewood Cliffs, NJ: Prentice-Hall.

Patton, M. (1997). *Utilization-focused evaluation: The new century text.* Thousand Oaks, CA: Sage.

Paul, R., Niehoff, B., & Turnley, W. (2000). Empowerment, expectations, and the psychological contract—Managing the dilemmas and gaining the advantages. *Journal of Socio-Economics, 29,* 471–485.

Pearlmutter, S. (1998). Self-efficacy and organizational change leadership. *Administration in Social Work, 22,* 23–38.

Pearlmutter, S. (2002). Achieving political practice: Integrating individual need and social action. *Journal of Progressive Human Services, 13*(1), 31–51.

Pecora, P. (1998). Recruiting and selecting effective employees. In R. Edwards, J. Yankey, & M. Altpeter (Eds.), *Skills for effective management of nonprofit organizations* (pp. 155–184). Washington, DC: National Association of Social Workers Press.

Perkins, D. (1995). Speaking truth to power: Empowerment ideology as social intervention and policy. *American Journal of Community Psychology, 23,* 765–794.

Perlmutter, F. (1988). *Alternative social agencies: Administrative strategies.* New York: Haworth.

Perlmutter, F. (1990). *Changing hats: From social work practice to administration.* Silver Springs, MD: National Association of Social Workers.

Perlmutter, F., Bailey, D., & Netting, F. (2001). *Managing human resources in the human services.* New York: Oxford University Press.

Peterson, S., & Stohr, V. (2000, March). *Virtual teams.* Retrieved August 6, 2004, from http://www.managementhelp.org/grp_skll/virtural/virtual-htm#anchor5002.

Petter, J., Byrnes, P., Choi, D. -L., Fegan, F., & Miller, R. (2002). Dimensions and patterns in employee empowerment: Assessing what matters to street-level bureaucrats. *Journal of Public Administration Research and Theory, 12,* 377–401.

Pinderhughes, E. (1989). *Understanding race, ethnicity, and power: The key to efficacy in clinical practice.* New York: Free Press.

Pine, B., Warsh, R., & Maluccio, A. (1998). Participatory management in a public child welfare agency: A key to effective change. *Administration in Social Work, 22*(1), 19–32.

Piven, F. F., & Cloward, R. (1971). *Regulating the poor.* New York: Patheon.

Piven, F. F., & Cloward, R. (2000). *Why Americans still don't vote.* Boston: Beacon Press.

Poindexter, C. (2002). "Be generous of spirit": Organizational development of an AIDS service organization. *Journal of Community Practice, 10*(2), 53–70.

Poindexter, C., & Lane, T. (2003). Choices and voices: Participation of people with HIV on Ryan White Title II consumer advisory boards. *Health and Social Work, 28,* 196–205.

Prigoff, A. (2000). *Economics for social workers.* Belmont, CA: Brooks/Cole.

Prottas, J. (1979). *People-processing: The street-level bureaucrat in public service bureaucracies.* Lexington, MA: Lexington Publishers.

Prottas, J. (1981). The cost of free services. *Public Administration Review, 41,* 526–534.

Provan, K., & Milward, H. B. (2001). Do networks really work? A framework for evaluating public-sector organizational networks. *Public Administration Review, 61*(4), 414–423.

Puffer, S., & Meindl, J. (1995). Volunteers from corporations: Work cultures reflect values similar to the voluntary organizations. *Nonprofit Leadership and Management, 5,* 359–375.

Putnam, R. (2000). *Bowling alone.* New York: Touchtone Book.

Pynes, J. E. (1997). *Human resources management for public and nonprofit organizations.* San Francisco: Jossey-Bass.

Ragins, B. R., Townsend, B., & Mattis, M. (1998). Gender gap in the executive suite: CEOs and female executives report on breaking the glass ceiling. *Academy of Management Executive, 12*(1), 28–43.

Rago, W. (1996). Struggles in transformation: A study of TQM, leadership, and organizational culture in a government agency. *Public Administration Review, 56,* 227–234.

Rapp, C., & Poertner, J. (1992). *Social administration: A client-centered approach.* New York: Longman.

Rapp, C., Shera, W., & Kisthardt, W. (1993). Research strategies for consumer empowerment of people with severe mental illness. *Social Work, 38*(6), 727–736.

Rawls, J. (1971). *A theory of justice.* Cambridge, MA: Harvard University Press.

Reamer, F. (1998). *Ethical standards in social work: A critical review of the NASW code of ethics.* Washington, DC: National Association of Social Workers.

Reamer, F. (2000). Administrative ethics. In R. Patti (Ed.), *The handbook of social welfare management* (pp. 69–86). Thousand Oaks, CA: Sage.

Reese, D., & Sontag, M. (2001). Successful interprofessional collaboration on the hospice team. *Health and Social Work, 26,* 167–175.

Reeser, L. C., & Epstien, I. (1990). *Professionalization and activism in social work.* New York: Columbia University Press.

Reid, W. (2002). Knowledge for direct social work practice: An analysis of trends. *Social Service Review, 76,* 6–33.

Rein, M. (1983). *From policy to practice.* Armonk, NY: M. E. Sharpe.

Reisch, M. (1990). Organizational structure and client advocacy: Lessons from the 1980's. *Social Work, 35*(1), 73–74.

Reisch, M., & Lowe, J. I. (2000). "Of means and ends" revisited: Teaching ethical community organizing in an unethical society. *Journal of Community Practice,* 7(1), 19–38.

Reisch, M., & Rivera, F. (1999). Ethical and racial conflicts in urban-based action research. *Journal of Community Practice, 6*(2), 49–62.

Reisch, M., Wenocur, S., & Sherman, W. (1981). Empowerment, conscientization and animation as core social work skills. *Social Development Issues, 5,* 108–120.

Rimer, E. (1987). Social administration education: Reconceptualizing the conflict between MPA, MBA, and MPH programs. *Administration in Social Work, 11*(2), 45–55.

Rivera, F., & Erlich, J. (1999). *Community organizing in a diverse society* (3rd ed.). Boston: Allyn & Bacon.

Robert's rules of order. (1982). New York: Bantam Books.

Rodwell, M. (1998). *Social work constructivist research.* New York: Garland.

Rose, S. (1972). *The betrayal of the poor.* Cambridge, MA: Schenkman.

Rose, S. (2000). Reflections on empowerment-based practice. *Social Work, 45,* 403–420.

Rose, S., & Black, B. (1985). *Advocacy and empowerment.* Boston: Routledge & Kegan Paul.

Rosenthal, M. (2003). Faith-based social services and the role of the state. Retrieved March 5, 2005, from http://www.religionandsocialpolicy.org/docs/events/2003_spring_research_conference/rosenthal.pdf.

Rossi, P., & Freeman, H. (1982). *Evaluation: A systematic approach.* Beverly Hills, CA: Sage.

Rossiter, A. (1996). A perspective on critical social work. *Journal of Progressive Human Services, 7*(2), 23–41.

Rothman, J. (1995). Approaches to community intervention. In F. Cox, J. Erlich, J. Rothman, & J. Tropman (Eds.), *Strategies of community organization* (5th ed., pp. 26–63). Itasca, IL: F. E. Peacock.

Rothman, J. (1996). The interweaving of community intervention approaches. *Journal of Community Practice, 3*(3/4), 69–99.

Royse, D. (2004). *Research methods for social work* (4th ed.). Pacific Grove, CA: Thomson/Brooks Cole.

Royse, D., & Thyer, B. (1996). *Program evaluation: An introduction.* Chicago: Nelson-Hall.

Rubin, A., & Babbie, E. (2001). *Research methods for social work* (4th ed.). Belmont, CA: Wadsworth.

Rundall, T., Celetano, D., Marconi, K., Bender-Kitz, S., Kwait, J., & Gentry, D. (1994, November). *The impact of the Ryan White CARE Act on the organization and availability of HIV-related services in Baltimore and Oakland.* Paper presented at the Annual Meeting of the Association for Research on Nonprofit Organizations and Voluntary Action, Berkeley, CA.

Sagie, A., & Koslowsky, M. (2000). *Participation and empowerment in organizations: Modeling, effectiveness and application.* Thousand Oaks, CA: Sage.

Salahu-Din, S. (2003). *Social work research: An applied approach.* Boston: Pearson Education.

Salamon, L. (1995). *Partners in public service: Government-nonprofit relations in the modern welfare state.* Baltimore: Johns Hopkins University Press.

Saleeby, D. (1997). *The strengths perspective in social work practice* (2nd ed.). New York: Longman.

Sandfort, J., Kalil, A., & Gottschalk, J. (1999). The mirror has two faces: Welfare clients and front-line workers view policy reforms. *Journal of Poverty, 3*(3), 71–91.

Schein, E. H. (1992). *Organization culture and leadership.* San Francisco: Jossey-Bass.

Schmid, H. (1992). Executive leadership in human service organizations. In Y. Hasenfeld (Ed.), *Human services as complex organizations* (pp. 98–117). Thousand Oaks, CA: Sage.

Schmid, H. (2000). Agency-environment relations: Understanding task environments. In R. Patti (Ed.), *The handbook of social welfare management* (pp. 133–154). Thousand Oaks, CA: Sage Publications.

Schmid, H. (2004). The role of nonprofit human service organizations in providing social services: A prefatory essay. *Administration in Social Work, 28*, 1–21.

Schmuck, R. (1997). *Practical action research for change.* Arlington Heights, IL: SkyLight Professional Development.

Schneider, R., and Lester, L. (2001). *Social work advocacy: A framework for action.* Belmont, CA: Wadsworth.

Schopler, J. (1994). Inter-organizational groups in the human services. *Journal of Community Practice, 1*(3), 7–27.

Schriver, J. (2003). *Human behavior and the social environment: Shifting paradigms in essential knowledge for social work practice* (4th ed.). Boston: Allyn & Bacon.

Scott, W. R. (1987). *Organizations: Rational, natural, and open systems.* Englewood Cliffs, NJ: Prentice-Hall.

Scott, W. R. (1995). *Institutions and organizations.* Thousand Oaks, CA: Sage.

Secret, M., Jordan, A., & Ford, J. (1999). Empowerment evaluation as a social work strategy. *Health & Social Work, 24*(2), 120–127.

Segal, S., & Silverman, C. (1993). Empowerment and self-help agency practice for people with mental disabilities. *Social Work, 38*, 705–713.

Sendjaya, S., & Sarros, J. (2002). Servant leadership: Its origin, development, and application in organizations. *Journal of Leadership and Organizational Studies, 9*, 57–64.

Shank, B. (1994). Sexual harassment: Definitions, policy frameworks, and legal issues. In M. Weil, M. Hughes, & N. Hooyman (Eds.), *Sexual harassment and schools of social work* (pp. 12–24). Alexandria, VA: Council on Social Work Education.

Shera, W. (1996). Market mechanisms and consumer involvement in the delivery of mental health services. *Journal of Sociology and Social Welfare, 23*, 13–22.

Shera, W., & Page, J. (1995). Creating more effective human service organizations through strategies of empowerment. *Administration in Social Work, 19*(4), 1–15.

Sider, R., & Unruh, H. R. (2004). Typology of religious characteristics of social service and educational organizations and programs. *Nonprofit and Voluntary Sector Quarterly, 33*, 109–134.

Silverman, R. (2003). *Citizens' district councils in Detroit: The promise and limits of using planning advisory boards to promote citizen participation.* Retrieved July 7, 2004, from http://comm-org.utoledo.edu/papers2003/silverman.htm.

Silvestre, A., Faber, J., Shankle, M., & Kopelman, J. (2002). A model for involving youth in health planning: HIV prevention in Pennsylvania. *Perspectives on Sexual and Reproductive Health, 34*(2), 91–98.

Simpson, R. (1990). *Conflict styles and social network relations as predictors of marital relations: A comparison of black and white spouses.* Unpublished doctoral dissertation, University of Michigan.

Simpson, R. (2003, January). *The practice of cultural competence: An ethnoconscious approach.* Paper presented at the Central California Public Health Partnership 2nd Annual Multicultural Public Health Conference, Fresno, CA.

Skidmore, R. (1995). *Social work administration: Dynamic management and human relationships* (3rd ed.). Needham Heights, MA: Allyn & Bacon.

Skinner, B. F. (1969). *Contingencies of reinforcement.* New York: Appleton-Century-Crofts.

Smith, B., Montagno, R., & Kuzmenko, T. (2004). Transformational and servant leadership: content and contextual comparisons. *Journal of Leadership and Organizational Studies, 10,* 80–91.

Smith, D. H., & Shen, C. (1996). Factors characterizing the most effective nonprofits managed by volunteers. *Nonprofit Management & Leadership, 6,* 271–289.

Smith, S. (1997). Deepening participatory action research. In S. Smith, D. Wilms, & N. Johnson (Eds.), *Nurtured by knowledge* (pp. 173–257). New York: Apex Press.

Smith, S. R., & Lipsky, M. (1993). *Nonprofits for hire.* Cambridge, MA: Harvard University Press.

Sohng, S. (1998). Research as an empowerment strategy. In L. Gutierrez, R. Parsons, & E. O. Cox (Eds.), *Empowerment in social work practice: A source book* (pp. 187–201). Pacific Grove, CA: Brooks/Cole.

Solomon, B. (1976). *Black empowerment.* New York: Columbia University Press.

Sommer, R. (1990). Family advocacy and the mental health system: The recent rise of the Alliance for the Mentally Ill. *Psychiatric Quarterly, 61,* 205–221.

Spreitzer, G. (1995). Psychological empowerment in the workplace: Dimensions, measurement, and validation. *Academy of Management Journal, 38,* 1442–1465.

Spreitzer, G. (1996). Social structural characteristics of psychological empowerment. *Academy of Management Journal, 39,* 483–504.

Stack, C. (1974). *All our kin.* New York: Harper.

Staples, L. (1999). Consumer empowerment in a mental health system: Stakeholder roles and responsibilities. In W. Shera & L. Wells (Eds.), *Empowerment practice in social work* (pp. 119–141). Toronto, Canada: Canadian Scholars' Press.

Stevens, M., & Yarish, M. (1999). *Training for team effectiveness.* In E. Sundstrom (Ed.), *Supporting work effectiveness* (pp. 24–62). San Francisco: Jossey-Bass.

Stevenson, K. M., Cheung, K. M., & Leung, P. (1992) A new approach to training child protective services workers for ethnically sensitive practice. *Child Welfare, 71,* 291–305.

Strachan, J. (1998). Understanding nonprofit financial management. In R. L. Edwards, J. A. Yankey, & M. A. Altpeter (Eds.), *Skills for effective management of nonprofit organizations* (pp. 78–97). Washington, DC: National Association of Social Workers.

Stringer, E. (1999). *Action research* (2nd ed.). Thousand Oaks: Sage.

Stromwall, L. (2002). Mental health barriers to employment for TANF recipients. *Journal of Poverty,* 6(3), 109–120.

Sundstrom, E., & Associates. (1999). *Supporting work team effectiveness.* San Francisco: Jossey-Bass.

Sunstein, C. (1990). *Feminism and political theory.* Chicago: University of Chicago Press.

Swank, E., & Clapp, J. (1999). Some methodological concerns when estimating the size of organizing activities. *Journal of Community Practice,* 6(3), 49–69.

Taggar, S., Hackett, R., & Saha, S. (1999). Leadership emergence in autonomous work teams: Antecedents and outcomes. *Personnel Psychology, 52,* 899–917.

Tambor, M. (1995). Employment-at-will or just cause: The right choice. *Administration in Social Work, 19*(3), 45–57.

Tauxe, C. (1995). Marginalizing public participation in local planning: An ethnographic account. *Journal of the American Planning Association, 61*(4), 471–482.

Telfair, J., & Mulvihill, B. (2000). Bridging science and practice: The integrated model of community-based evaluation (IMCBE). *Journal of Community Practice,* 7(3), 37–65.

The Constitution of the United States with the Declaration of Independence. (1973). Boston: Pathfinder Publication.

Thomsett.com. (2004). *Managing large projects.* Retrieved August 29, 2004, from http://www.thomsett.com.au/main/articles/largeprojects/large_pt3.htm.

Tourginy, A., & Miller, J. (1981). Community-based organizations: Theory and practice. *Administration in Social Work, 8,* 13–23.

Tropman, J. (1997). *Successful community leadership.* Washington, DC: National Association of Social Workers Press.

Tucker, D., Baum, J., & Singh, J. (1992). The institutional ecology of human service organizations. In Y. Hasenfeld (Ed.), *Human services as complex organizations* (pp. 47–72). Newbury Park, CA: Sage.

Ungar, M., Manuel, S., Mealy, S., Thomas, G., & Campbell, C. (2004). A study of community guides: Lessons for professionals practicing with and in communities. *Social Work, 49,* 550–561.

U.S. Commission on Civil Rights. (2002). *Voting rights in Florida, 2002: Briefing summary.* Retrieved November 29, 2002, from http://www.usccr.gov/pub/vote2000/sum0802.htm.

U.S. General Accounting Office. (1998). *Voters with disabilities: Access to polling places and alternative voting methods.* Retrieved March 27, 2005, from http://www.gao.new.items/do2107.pdf.

Van Den Bergh, N., & Crisp, C. (2004). Defining culturally competent practice with sexual minorities: Implications for social work education and practice. *Journal of Social Work Education, 40,* 221–238.

Van der Vegt, G., Emans, B., Van de Vliert, E. (2001). Patterns of interdependence in work teams. *Personnel Psychology, 54,* 51–69.

Vaughn, M., & Stamp, G. (2003). The empowerment dilemma: The dialectic of emancipation and control in staff/client interactions at shelters for battered women. *Communication Studies, 54,* 154–168.

Venkatesh, S. (1997). The three-tiered model: How helping occurs in urban, poor communities. *Social Service Review, 71,* 574–606.

Verba, S., Schlozman, K., & Brady, H. (1997). The big tilt: Participatory inequality in America. *The American Prospect, 32,* 74–80.

Vinokur-Kaplan, D. (1995). Treatment teams that work (and those that don't): An application of Hackman's group effectiveness model to interdisciplinary teams in psychiatric hospitals. *Journal of Applied Behavioral Science, 31,* 303–327.

Voss, R., White Hat, A., Bates, J., Lunderman, M., & Lunderman, A. (2005). Social work education in the homeland. *Journal of Social Work Education, 41,* 209–227.

Vroom, V. (1965). *Work and motivation.* New York: Wiley.

Walker, R., & Staton, M. (2000). Multiculturalism in social work ethics. *Journal of Social Work Education, 36,* 449–462.

Wamsley, G., & Zald, M. (1973). *The political economy of public organizations.* Lexington, MA: Lexington Books.

Weinbach, R. (1998). *The social worker as manager* (3rd ed.). Boston: Allyn & Bacon.

Weir, K., & Robertson, J. (1998). Teaching geographic information systems for social work applications. *Journal of Social Work Education, 34*(1), 81–97.

Weisner, C., & Schmidt, L. (1992). Gender disparities in treatment for alcohol problems. *Journal of the American Medical Association, 268*(14), 1872–1876.

Wellman, B., & Wortly, S. (1990). Different strokes from different folks: Community ties and social support. *American Journal of Sociology, 96*(3), 558–588.

Wheelan, S. (1999). *Creating effective teams: A guide for members and leaders.* Thousand Oaks, CA: Sage.

Widmer, C. (1987). Minority participation on boards of directors of human service agencies: Some evidence and suggestions. *Journal of Voluntary Action Research, 16*(4), 33–44.

Williams, M., Unrau, Y., & Grinnell, R. (1998). *Introduction to social work research.* Itasca, IL: F. E. Peacock.

Wilson, W. (1996). *When work disappears.* New York: Vintage Books.

Wimpfheimer, S. (2004). Leadership and management competencies defined by practicing social work managers. An overview of standards developed by the National Network for Social Work Managers. *Administration in Social Work, 28*(1), 45–56.

Winkle, C. (1991). Inequity and power in the nonprofit sector. *Nonprofit and Voluntary Sector Quarterly, 20,* 312–328.

Wolfson, M. (1995). The legislative impact of social movement organizations: The anti-driving movement and the 21-year-old drinking age. *Social Science Quarterly, 76*(2), 311–325.

Wright, B. (2001). Public-sector work motivation: A review of the current literature and a revised conceptual model. *Journal of Public Administration Research and Theory, 11*, 559–587.

Yamashiro, G., & Matsuoka, J. (1997). Help-seeking among Asian and Pacific Americans: A multiperspective analysis. *Social Work, 42*, 176–186.

Yamatani, H., Soska, T., & Baltimore, T. (1999, January 10). *A study of community collaboratives.* Paper presented at the conference of the Council on Social Work Education, New York, NY.

Yoshihama, M., & Carr, E. (2002). Community participation reconsidered: Feminist participatory action research with Hmong women. *Journal of Community Practice, 10*(4), 85–103.

Zachary, E. (2000). Grassroots leadership training. *Journal of Community Practice, 7*(1), 71–93.

Zhou, F., Euler, G., McPhee, S., Nguygen, T., Lam, T., Wong, C., & Mock, J. (2003). Economic analysis of promotion of hepatitis B vaccinations among Vietnamese-American children and adolescents in Houston and Dallas. *Pediatrics, 111*(6), 1289–1787.

Zimmerman, L., & Broughton, A. (1998). Assessing, planning, and managing information technology. In R. Edwards, J. Yankey, & M. Altpeter (Eds.), *Skills for effective management of nonprofit organizations* (pp. 325–342). Washington, DC: National Association of Social Workers.

Zimmerman, M. (1995). Psychological empowerment: Issues and illustrations. *American Journal of Community Psychology, 23*, 581–599.

Zimmerman, M., Israel, B., Schulz, A., & Checkoway, B. (1992). Further explorations in empowerment theory: An empirical analysis of psychological empowerment. *American Journal of Community Psychology, 20*, 707–728.

Zimmerman, M., & Rappaport, J. (1988). Citizen participation, perceived control, and psychological empowerment. *American Journal of Community Psychology, 16*(5), 725–750.

Index

A

B

C

D

E

N

O

P

SPRINGER PUBLISHING COMPANY

Critical Thinking for Addiction Professionals

Michael J. Taleff, PhD, CSAC, MAC

"Dr. Taleff has provided an insightful analysis of the kinds of thinking errors often made by counselors. The text should be required reading in all areas of health and human services. The concepts and discussion are as valuable to experienced helpers as they are to novices."

—**Gregory Blevins,** PhD, Professor
Governors State University

In this easy-to-read guide—the first to bring together critical thinking and addiction work—critical thinking expert and addiction professional, Dr. Michael Taleff, offers readers the tools they need to think critically and make better decisions.

Contents

- The World of Critical Thinking
- Critical Thinking: An Overview of Key Elements
- Poor Thinking: From the Individual to the Field
- Time For A Little Test
- Critical Thinking: The Basics
- What Drives Bad Thinking?
- A Crash Course in Fallacies
- Fallacies That Appeal to Authority and Irrelevant Fallacies
- Causal Fallacies and Weak Inductions
- Fallacies That Presume A Conclusion Before it is
- Proven and Classification Fallacies
- Fallacies Caused by Perception Problems and
- Fallacies of Manner and Style
- The Ethics of Using Critical Thinking
- What Price Critical Thinking?

2006 · 174pp · 0-8261-1824-0 · softcover

11 West 42nd Street, New York, NY 10036-8002 • Fax: 212-941-7842
Order Toll-Free: 877-687-7476 • Order On-line: www.springerpub.com

SPRINGER PUBLISHING COMPANY

Social Structures, Aging, and Self-Regulation in the Elderly

K. Warner Schaie, PhD
Laura L. Carstensen, PhD, Editors

In this intriguing new book, experts K. Warner Schaie and Laura L. Carstensen present the interplay and influence of self-regulation and social structures on the physical and economic outcomes of old age.

Providing a thorough review of current research, the editors and contributors examine the effects, considerations, and consequences of the following important factors related to the aging population:

- Age distribution, immigration, longevity, and family change
- Cognitive function, social resilience, and self-regulation
- The aging population and the decreasing population that supports it

For researchers involved in the study of social and behavioral influences on the aging population, this critical new volume provides valuable commentary and insight on the impact of self-regulation on adult development.

Contents:

- Societal Influences that Affect Cognitive Functioning in Old Age
- Wisdom in Social Context
- Social Influences on Adult Personality, Self-Regulation and Health
- Social Norms, Rules of Thumb, and Retirement: Evidence for Rationality in Retirement Planning
- Race and Self-Regulatory Health Behaviors: The Role of the Stress Response and the HPA Axis in Physical and Mental Health Disparities

2006 · 260pp · 0-8261-2406-2· hardcover

11 West 42nd Street, New York, NY 10036-8002 • Fax: 212-941-7842
Order Toll-Free: 877-687-7476 • Order On-line: www.springerpub.com